Making the Gods Speak

HARVARD-YENCHING INSTITUTE MONOGRAPH SERIES 131

Making the Gods Speak

The Ritual Production of Revelation in Chinese Religious History

Vincent Goossaert

Published by the Harvard University Asia Center
Distributed by Harvard University Press
Cambridge (Massachusetts) and London 2022

Printed in the United States of America

The Harvard University Asia Center publishes a monograph series and, in coordination with the Fairbank Center for Chinese Studies, the Korea Institute, the Reischauer Institute of Japanese Studies, and other faculties and institutes, administers research projects designed to further scholarly understanding of China, Japan, Vietnam, Korea, and other Asian countries. The Center also sponsors projects addressing multidisciplinary and regional issues in Asia.

The Harvard-Yenching Institute, founded in 1928, is an independent foundation dedicated to the advancement of higher education in the humanities and social sciences in Asia. Headquartered on the campus of Harvard University, the Institute provides fellowships for advanced research, training, and graduate studies at Harvard by competitively selected faculty and graduate students from Asia. The Institute also supports a range of academic activities at its fifty partner universities and research institutes across Asia. At Harvard, the Institute promotes East Asian studies through annual contributions to the Harvard-Yenching Library and publication of the *Harvard Journal of Asiatic Studies* and the Harvard-Yenching Institute Monograph Series.

Library of Congress Cataloging-in-Publication Data
Names: Goossaert, Vincent, author.
Title: Making the gods speak : the ritual production of revelation in Chinese religious history / Vincent Goossaert.
Other titles: Harvard-Yenching Institute monograph series ; 131.
Description: Cambridge, Massachusetts : Harvard University Asia Center, 2022. | Series: Harvard-Yenching Institute monograph series ; 131 | Includes bibliographical references and index. |
Identifiers: LCCN 2021062646 | ISBN 9780674270947 (hardcover)
Subjects: LCSH: Revelation--History of doctrines. | Spirit writings--China--History. | Divination--China--History. | Ritual--China--History. | China--Religion--History.
Classification: LCC BL475.5 .G66 2022 | DDC 202/.1170951--dc23/eng20220218
LC record available at https://lccn.loc.gov/2021062646

Index by the author
♾ Printed on acid-free paper
Last figure below indicates year of this printing
30 29 28 27 26 25 24 23 22

The largest part of this book was written during the Covid-19 pandemic, part of it spent in lockdown at home with my family and my books. A staggering number of people suffered during these events, which did not strike equally across gender, class, and country; I dedicate it to the memory of those who died and to the brighter future of those who did not have the good luck to be able to stay home and do something rewarding, such as writing about Chinese gods.

Contents

Contents

Acknowledgments

Dominic Steavu, Hu Jiechen, and John Lagerwey have taken the time to read a complete draft of the present book and have offered many corrections and comments; I am extremely grateful to them. The two reviewers for the Asia Center have also engaged with the manuscript in depth and helped improve it in many ways.

A condensed version of chapter 4 (with a few passages from chapters 3 and 5) will be published as part of a conference volume on the history of spirit-writing edited by Elena Valussi and Matthias Schumann; I am very grateful to them for their close reading of that chapter, which also helped me refine this book manuscript.

Chapter 7 is a revised version of my article "Spirit-Writing, Canonization and the Rise of Divine Saviors: Wenchang, Lüzu, and Guandi, 1700–1858," *Late Imperial China*, 36.2, 2015, 82–125.

Chapter 8 is partly based on my "Competing Eschatological Scenarios during the Taiping War, 1851–1864," in Hans-Christian Lehner, ed., *The End(s) of Time(s). Apocalypticism, Messianism, and Utopianism*. Leiden: Brill, 2021, 269–306.

Note to the Reader

Translations

I have sought to make this book accessible by translating Chinese terms, but a few key concepts are kept in *pinyin* transliteration:

daofa 道法: the exorcistic and therapeutic Daoist ritual traditions that emerge during the early modern period

fashi 法師: the priests performing the *daofa*

jitan 乩壇: spirit-writing altar

Periodization

medieval: third–sixth centuries

Tang: seventh–ninth centuries

early modern: tenth–fifteenth centuries

modern: sixteenth–early twentieth centuries

Introduction

> In the *jiashen* year of the Jiading reign (1224), our patriarch the Transcendent Lord Xu manifested himself in Jinling (present-day Nanjing), exposed the teaching of loyalty and filial piety, and converted crowds of people who all joined the correct way.
>
> 嘉定甲申之歲, 祖師許真君降于金陵, 示陳忠孝之教, 溥化眾生, 咸歸正道。[1]

This sort of record is found in overwhelming numbers throughout Chinese religious history, particularly as here, in a Daoist context, but by no means exclusively so. Gods, ancestors, Buddhas, and immortals keep manifesting themselves in the world, events that are described with terms such as *jiang* 降 (literally, descend or make descend), *lin* 臨 (approach), *xia* 下 (come down), and many others.[2]

What happens when gods manifest themselves? How are we to understand statements such as the one translated above? Did Transcen-

1. *Xishan Xu zhenjun bashiwu hua lu*, preface 跋. All translations are the author's own unless otherwise noted.

2. For a good discussion of the term *jiang*, see Pan Junliang, "A la recherche de l'unité," 12–17.

dent Lord Xu 許真君 appear in the flesh (for some, or for everyone present)? Or did a medium channel him, or a statue move? How did he expose his teachings? Did he speak, write, or hand out some sort of document? The text does not say, although we will see that in this particular case we can find out this information from other sources—what happened was spirit-writing. But entirely similar language is used to describe other ways of making gods instruct humanity. The present book explores these various ways and attempts to sketch out their deployment throughout history.

The Question

My starting point is the sheer mass of religious texts of all kinds of genres and content that circulated in the early modern (tenth to fourteenth centuries), late imperial (fifteenth to early twentieth centuries), and contemporary Chinese societies, among which a large part present themselves as divine revelations. The mapping of this massive religious literature is now being developed, among other endeavors, by a collective project named CRTA (Chinese Religious Texts Authority).[3] During this whole millennium, teachings ascribed to a large assortment of divine beings continued to be reprinted and read, while new ones appeared unceasingly. China was and still is characterized by continuous revelation, and this has been a driving force behind religious, cultural, and social change. My initial interest, and the main focus of the present book, remains on spirit-writing, but it must be understood in the larger framework of the multifaceted production of divine texts. My question then is, how did this production evolve throughout history?

Revelation is a well-established theme in the field of the comparative history of religions. Many approaches have been explored. My anal-

3 For more information about the project, see their website https://crta.info/index.php?title=Main_Page (accessed July 27, 2021).

ysis here deliberately puts aside several of them. I will not attempt a positivist history, trying to reveal, as it were, what "really" happened when people claimed to have received divine instructions, who were the human authors, and what were their intentions. Neither will I engage with phenomenology or psychology, trying to understand what kind of religious experiences underlined and made possible the written texts that present themselves as revealed. These might be fruitful approaches, no doubt, but my sources do not easily invite them. I am not primarily engaging here in a history of the contents of revelation either; I will of course discuss new religious ideas brought about by revealed texts, but always in connection with the process of production itself. Instead, I aim to bring together the extraordinarily rich history of revelations in the Chinese world and to make sense of its development through the question of the ritual production of divine discourse.

From a religious perspective, revelations simply appear by divine will, but from a scholarly one, they are produced. Over time, China developed different techniques for producing revelations; even as new techniques emerged, earlier ones continued to be practiced. Thus, they coexisted in what I aim to analyze as a revelatory ecology. These different techniques served different purposes and allowed for different types of content. In this ecology, the various types of revelation thrived in niches where they made specific contributions to religious discourse and practice, complementing more often than competing with each other.

Sources

Three types of written sources shed light on revelations: narrative accounts, revealed texts, and ritual documents that prescribe the acts of making gods speak or write—in other words, context, content, and technique. There also exist visual sources that both represent revelatory events and are themselves revealed, and I will discuss and use them (too sparingly, without doubt) along with narratives and revealed texts.[4]

Narratives of the events are crucial, not only for our understanding of what happens during a revelation but also of how Chinese people, not necessarily party or even sympathetic to the revelation, received it. Some narratives are part of, or attached to, the revelations in the form of prefaces, glosses, or commentaries, but we also have large numbers of stories about revelatory events of which nothing else survives. The rich Chinese hagiographical tradition can be endlessly mined for stories of revelations. At a more critical distance, we also have the equally rich genre of stories and anecdotes about saints and gods, such as is contained in the vast collections of medieval "records of the strange," *zhiguai* 志怪, stories and early modern anecdotes, *biji* 筆記.

Second, the revealed texts themselves and their contents offer a very different perspective, focused less on social dynamics and more on the contents of the divine message: theology, cosmology, salvation, ritual, self-cultivation, morality, and more. In ideal circumstances, historians have both revealed content and narratives of the revelation, but this is far from being the case for many if not most of them. Third, and so far largely neglected by scholars (especially in the case of spirit-writing), are the liturgical prescriptions: how, precisely, does one produce a revelation by controlling the process of making gods speak or write?

Focusing on one or the other of these types of sources results in markedly different understandings. A focus on narratives is usually articulated in the scholarly literature through miracles, ideas about gods and spirits, and more generally a cultural history of religion. A focus on the revealed scriptures brings us into the realm of the doctrinal history of specific religions, notably Buddhism, Daoism, and the sectarian tradition.[5] Attention to liturgical manuals needs to be embedded in the larger

4. For a fine study of visual material for the history of spirit-writing see Hu Jiechen, "Zailun fuji de fangfa yu leixing."

5. By sectarian tradition, discussed in chapter 8, I refer to the devotional, messianic traditions emerging during the Ming period and worshipping the Eternal Mother, Wusheng laomu 無生老母.

history of ritual, even though so far this field has not treated revelation as a major issue. I aim to combine these three approaches and hope that the special attention paid to the last—ritual techniques—will account for a large part of this book's unique contribution.

The corpus of relevant sources briefly outlined above is simply overwhelming and beyond the grasp of a dedicated research team, let alone a single scholar. I thus anticipate critiques to the effect that this project tries to embrace too much. A low estimate of the number of revealed Chinese texts (from small tracts to long scriptures) through history would be in the several tens of thousands. I readily accept that the vast majority of them will not be present in this monograph and that a serious study of them would—hopefully will—imply serious revisions to my historical outline. I do not claim that all the revelations I discuss in some detail are either representative or especially important. I simply use them to build a general analytical framework that hopefully will prove useful as we continue to progress in our understanding of how the Chinese make their gods speak and write.

A fourth kind of source is, of course, ethnography. We are blessed to be able to study Chinese religions as living traditions. In the case of spirit-writing, which is a central concern of this monograph, the practice can be observed in many different places; indeed, some of the most exciting work on spirit-writing is based on in-depth field observation. I have observed spirit-writing in a number of locations, most often in Hong Kong; and I have conducted fieldwork to study the modern historical development of one particular network of spirit-writing groups in Jiangnan.[6] These experiences have to an important extent shaped my approach to the topic and helped me ask many questions about the historical sources that I would probably not have thought of otherwise. I have, however, decided to write the present book as a resolutely historical and text-based endeavor, as I realized that scholars often tend to read contemporary practice back onto

6. Goossaert, "The Jin'gaishan Network."

earlier documents and minimize evolutions as a result. For this reason, ethnography remains mostly in the background here, an important but discreet presence.

Definitions

Because revelation is an important concept in the field of the comparative history of religions, I need to define the terms I use precisely to avoid confusion and make this book accessible to nonspecialists. I will return to the comparative question briefly in the conclusion, but I think that the time for full-fledged, comprehensive comparisons may have not come yet, because we need to first establish a robust framework for the Chinese evidence and practices; there is still so much that scholars of Chinese religions disagree about or simply do not know. For this reason, my definitions of key terms are anchored in the Chinese evidence and sometime deviate from standard usage in the larger field.

I study revelations and the various modes of their production within the larger context of ritual techniques for creating divine presence, as revelations are one of the effects—but not the most frequent—of such presence. By divine presence I mean an experience as anticipated or narrated by persons who have felt a divine being close to them and in a situation where an interaction was possible, such as seeing, hearing, or otherwise feeling the god, or being affected (enlightened, cured, or struck) by it. The most common term to describe this presence is *ling* 靈; although this is not standard usage, I translate *ling* as "divine presence." This keyword within Chinese religions can mean different things in different contexts, including the soul of the dead, efficacy, or spirituality.[7] I am particularly interested in the extremely numerous cases where it refers to the fact that at a given time (not before and, just as importantly, not after) divine presence is experienced and recorded with awe.

7. Meyer, *Concept of Ling*.

In its many usages, *ling* appears in connection with a wide variety of other terms; sometimes *ling* is the qualifier (such as *lingtan* 靈壇, an altar where gods are present), and sometimes it is the object of an action: verb+*ling*. Two verbs are particularly common: *jiang* and *xian* 顯 (to appear). Both of them can be either declarative or causative: *jiangling* 降靈 can mean "the god manifests itself" or "the priest causes the god to manifest itself." The distinction is crucial because it locates the agency either with the human or with the divine party. Yet, this distinction is frequently blurred, especially when the text is not explicit and the phrase can be translated either way, depending on how we interpret it. Expressions such as *jiangshen* 降神 or *jiangfu* 降福 (to manifest blessings) also exist, in a more or less identical sense, but *ling* refers more directly to the sensory experience of divine presence.[8]

The types of divine presence in general, and revelations in particular, discussed in the present book involve the whole array of Chinese nonhuman entities: gods (deceased humans with a title in the divine bureaucracy), *shen* 神; Buddhas, *fo* 佛, and bodhisattvas, *pusa* 菩薩; immortals, *xian* 仙, and transcendents, *zhenren* 真人; sages, *sheng* 聖; ancestors, *zu* 祖; and the dead, *gui* 鬼. I will pay attention to how specific ritual techniques, modes of divine presence, and revelations relate to these theological categories, but I use the term **spirit** (and occasionally "divine entity" to avoid repetition) in the most encompassing sense of nonhuman entities. This is an etic strategy for the sake of simplicity, but it is also emically valid because of the considerable overlaps and crossovers between the different categories that are included.

For the purposes of the present book, I define **revelation** as discursive content that is presented as given by a spirit to one or several living humans and is of general interest, as opposed to answering a specific issue raised by one person—this is a more restrictive definition than is often seen in religious studies. Revelations often provide

8. A locus classicus is the *Shuowen jiezi*'s 說文解字 definition of the *wu* 巫 as someone who can cause gods to manifest their presence through her/his physical performance 以舞降神者也.

explanations about the origins and functioning of the cosmos, the identity, history, and roles of the gods, the laws that govern human destiny, and the ways humans may obtain salvation. Whereas the standard modern Chinese term for revelation is *qishi* 啟示, both revelation and *qishi* are etic categories that encompass many different emic concepts used throughout Chinese history that I will explore here.[9]

One of the difficulties we will have to cope with is the moot distinction between spirits and masters; the latter are in some cases already considered as divine before their death, or are said to have transmitted teachings at a moment when it is unclear to us latter-day historians whether they were still alive or already apotheosized. Indeed, the vocabulary for master-to-disciple transmission and revelation overlap to a considerable extent. And of course, for many spiritual leaders, we have texts they wrote in person and others they revealed after their apotheosis, and separating the two is a delicate exercise, which for the devotees themselves seems pointless and misguided.[10] The list of ambiguous terms runs long, including phrases such as "instructions handed down," *chuixun* 垂訓, quite typical of spirit-written tracts in late imperial times but commonly used to describe masters teaching disciples in other contexts.

Because it distinguishes between content of general interest, as opposed to answers to specific issues, this definition of revelation is intimately linked to that of **divination** and, more precisely, inspired divination (as opposed to deductive divination where gods do not intervene), which I define here as an exchange between a human asking a question and a spirit providing an answer.[11] For my present purposes, I consider

9. One of the best critical discussions of the category of revelation in the Chinese context is Espesset, "La religiosité de l'Autre." On p. 51, Espesset provides a list of fifteen Chinese terms that fit his definition. This definition is based on four criteria: experience, contact, divulgation, and rupture (a decisive break with the past); my own definition is more inclusive, as it does not include the fourth criterion (rupture).

10. See for instance Burton-Rose, "A Prolific Spirit."

11. The scope of the notion of divination in the Chinese context varies widely between authors, some focusing on *Yijing*-based mantic techniques and excluding spirit-

certain divinatory exchanges to qualify as revelations (e.g., a person asking how to obtain salvation and a god detailing a program of self-cultivation) whereas others do not (e.g., a patient asking for the outcome of an illness and a god saying it will be favorable). The former tend to be destined for publication and dissemination, and the latter are not. Yet, I readily admit the boundary can be quite blurry. In other words: some revelations are the result of divination (many revelations are prompted by a question from a human), some are not; conversely, divination can lead to revelation, but not necessarily (and usually it does not).

The same qualification (content of general interest) explains why not all pronouncements by supernatural entities are revelations. The spirit of a dead human or a nature god can manifest itself through a medium or other means, typically to request sacrifices or help from the living (to have a proper grave built, to redress injustice inflicted on it, etc.). This is not a revelation. By contrast, when higher gods express themselves, their words typically carry weight and qualify as revelations.

One further category that lies at the core of the comparative study of religions and revelation is **prophecy**. I use this term in the Chinese context as a subcategory of revelations—all prophecies are revelations but not all revelations are prophecies. A prophecy predicts future events of concern to the whole empire (including the births, deaths, and successions of emperors, as well as changes of dynasties) or the whole of humanity (major disasters and eschatological events). Typically, prophecies are spontaneous divine pronouncements rather than answers to human questions.

Revelation is a broad category that can be analyzed in many ways; I would like to briefly point out two particularly salient issues that will be present throughout this book. First, as already mentioned, some revelations are particular (answering a question) and others are universal, that is, they they provide a discourse of absolute truth without any contextualization. Particular revelations can include spontaneous instructions

writing and other techniques for conversing with the gods. For a comprehensive overview of this question, see Lackner and Lu, eds., *Handbook of Prognostication*.

given by a god to a human as well as dialogues, that is, humans asking questions to the gods, notably divination, advice on practice, and confirmation in the course of ritual procedures.

The second distinction is between secret (the revelation is for one favored individual only and her/his privileged disciples and friends, who will be punished by the gods if they share it with the uninitiated) and open, when the receiver is chosen by the gods as a transmitter who should disseminate the revelation for the benefit of all humanity.

Finally, because this is the type of revelation that is my primary focus, I will define **spirit-writing.**[12] It is a Western etic term that encompasses a broad range of Chinese techniques and is meant to invite comparison with Western techniques, such as the planchette and the Ouija board. Such a comparison was prominent in the earliest descriptions of the Chinese technique by Western observers in the late nineteenth century, but it is not part of our concern here. As the term is etic, scholars have used various definitions; the broadest ones naturally span a longer time period and include early cases of divinely inspired writing (notably through visualization) that stricter definitions exclude.[13]

Here I define spirit-writing as any technique where spirits (from high gods to recently deceased humans) are invited through prescribed ritual means (typically involving incantations, *zhou* 咒, and/or talismans, *fu* 符) to manifest themselves (*jiang*) either in a writing implement (a brush or a piece of wood) and/or in the person(s) wielding this implement in order to write characters, often in response to questions. An important aspect of the practice is that it is usually collective, with people observing the process and thus serving as witnesses to its reliability.

Defined in this way, spirit-writing seems to appear in the eleventh and twelfth centuries and thus constitutes one aspect of the religious transformations of early modern China. From there, the practice diffused

12. This definition derives from Clart and Goossaert, "Spirit Writing."

13. See notably in chapter 2 the discussion on Shangqing visionary revelations and their relation to spirit-writing.

to other parts of the Sinophone world (notably Vietnam, Korea, and Japan) where it interacted with local traditions of spirit possession and revelation. As I will argue, spirit-writing evolved through the second millennium from being one ritual niche within the repertoire of techniques for producing divine presence to being the most common means of producing revelations in the modern period.

Structure of the Book

A red thread running through the present book is that the various ritual techniques used to produce revelations were all commonly used for other purposes, notably performing rituals to secure divine blessings; revelation was most of the time an extra development of such rituals. This is why I attempt to start, in chapter 1, with a very wide and encompassing panorama of techniques for producing divine presence in Chinese cultures. This will allow us to define criteria to distinguish, at least at the ideal-typical level, between different ritual techniques and modes of divine presence, and to situate revelations among them. I will notably propose a dichotomy between divine-agency-driven and human-agency-driven modes of presence that apply to all events of divine presence and revelations in particular.

Chapter 2 builds on this model to look at the origins and developments of revelation through the first millennium, between the Han dynasty and the tenth century, and the emergence then of what we may call modern Chinese religion. By surveying the various types of revelations produced during this period, we will be able to develop a typology of revelation consisting of five main types—sutra, possession, encounter, visualization, and presence—based on how revealed texts present themselves and the conditions of their revelation.

Four of these ideal types of revelation were common in medieval times (third–sixth centuries), whereas the fifth, the presence type, emerged in early modern times. Chapter 3 is devoted to this type: it sketches the ritual traditions (the so-called *daofa* 道法) that developed it and how their priests needed the controlled, perceptible presence of certain gods to successfully perform their rituals, leading in some cases to oral, dreamed, or written revelations.

Chapter 4 explores the early history of spirit-writing, the most successful presence-type ritual, between the eleventh and the fourteenth centuries by mapping the variety of terms and techniques that this category encompasses, surveying the various performers and gods involved, and showing their intimate relation with exorcistic rites before attempting to reconstruct a history of its development.

Chapter 5 covers the same historical ground as chapter 4 but focuses on the revealed texts and their different genres. It argues that spirit-written revelations occupied a specific niche in the ecology of revelations, usually as personal instructions and commentaries that complement sutra-type scriptures.

Chapter 6 defines a new stage in the historical development of spirit-writing, from the late sixteenth century to the early Qing, when new spirit-writing techniques and more open groups of practitioners (called the *jitan* 乩壇) brought the practice to an unprecedented visibility, and there was a new focus on producing, printing, and disseminating divine instructions, notably morality books. This ushered in a golden age of spirit-writing, which became the most common way to produce new religious knowledge and discourse.

Chapter 7 continues with this chronological development by documenting a movement in the eighteenth and early nineteenth centuries to bring order to the massive production of new revelations through processes of canonization, both textual (with published canons authenticating the major revelations) and individual (with the spirit-writing gods being promoted by the state).

Chapter 8 identifies the last major turning point in the history of spirit-writing, the mid-nineteenth century, especially in the context of the Taiping War (1851–64), when sectarian traditions, in particular the Xiantiandao 先天道, which had hitherto mostly relied on other techniques for producing revelations, adopted spirit-writing in their turn. Consequently, this technique was now enthusiastically practiced across the board in the Chinese religious landscape, and as a result, the religious innovations of the various groups cross-hybridized in various innovative ways.

The conclusion envelops us in a landscape of revealed texts and revelation-producing groups and institutions in early twentieth-century China, the result of a long process of adding new ritual techniques to an ever-expanding repertoire to make gods present and address humans.

CHAPTER ONE

Modes of Divine Presence

I start my analysis with as encompassing a framework as possible in order to identify the various modes of divine presence that were known and experienced in Chinese cultures. This first chapter leaves aside chronology, which is taken up in the next chapter onward; it provides a (hopefully) comprehensive panorama of the various modes when divine presence is produced, including for the purposes of revelation. These various modes appeared at different points in history, but none were ever discarded or forgotten, so they gradually added to the array of possibilities, and this panorama is the modern cumulative result of a long process of inventions. Some of these inventions will be explored in more detail in subsequent chapters.

1.1. Two Paradigms

At the most general level, two modes of divine presence seem to exist in opposition to each other: presence as planned, organized, and controlled by humans, and presence where gods seem to come of their own accord without any forewarning. These are ideal-typical categories; as we will see throughout this book, a mode that may seem spontaneous, especially in hagiographical narratives, was in fact ritually engineered. Keywords used to describe the advent of divine presence, such as *jiang* (manifest oneself, make manifest) can refer to either mode. However, the fact that such events of divine presence were presented and understood as produced or as spontaneous is itself significant for the historian. Therefore, our paradigmatic tension between divine presence in (unexpected) encounters and ritualized invitation will prove very useful throughout our historical explorations, and I will systematically use this vocabulary.

1.1.1. Spontaneous Presence

In spontaneous types of presence, the transaction is decided by the gods and often comes as a surprise. Certain terms, such as "suddenly," *hu* 忽, denote this feeling of being unexpectedly confronted with divine presence. Cases abound where gods speak in the first person and say, "I manifest my divine presence" 吾降靈. Gods can decide to be present through various means.

Possession is certainly the earliest and most common mode of divine presence in Chinese culture. It can be either spontaneous or ritually invited, but even in the latter case the focus is always on the divine agency, hence my discussion of possession in this section on spontaneous presence. The vocabulary for possession is voluminous.[1] Like many other scholars, I observe an analytical difference between spirit possession and **shamanism**—these are not emic categories.[2] In a shamanic séance, the performer enters a state where he or she can travel in other worlds and meet spirits but retains his or her personality and voice; the shaman can make spirits speak, but he or she converses with

1. Pan Junliang, "A la recherche de l'unité," provides the best detailed study of the vocabulary and phenomenology of spirit possession that is focused on medieval China.

2. Some scholars observe a tripartite typology: involuntary possession, voluntary mediumism, and shamanism.

them and maintains agency. The audience thus gets to hear the voices of both the shaman and the spirits. By contrast, the medium, when possessed by a spirit, is emptied of his or her personality, voice, and agency. Mediums routinely claim they cannot remember anything that happened during a performance; it is the spirit alone who speaks (possibly in dialogue with people in the audience), writes, and moves. In contemporary times, both exist in the Chinese world, but possession is much more common.

Some anthropologists reject this opposition, considering possession and shamanism as variations based on the same performance skills and services to the patrons.[3] Their argument makes the best sense when one can work with the performers and focus on what they do and why they do it. But the difference remains significant, because what the sources tell us about the perceived agency of the medium (the spirit speaks) or shaman (the shaman talks) is crucial to how the divine presence (and the revelation, if that is the case) is perceived by both the audience and later people who hear or write about the event.[4] From a historical perspective, the evidence often does not allow us to decide which was being performed. Indeed, the term *wu* 巫 is often translated as either shaman or medium but in some cases also clearly means priest. Some accounts, however, are clearly of the possession type, whereas I have found extremely few accounts of revelations that we could ascribe to a shamanic séance. For the purpose of analyzing how the Chinese produced and thought about the production of divine presence, it is best to maintain a distinction between mediums and shamans. I add that I am not interested in the notions of trance and an altered state of consciousness to analyze these two; I do not deny this might be a fruitful line of enquiry, but it is not an approach that my sources warrant, nor does it allow us to understand the cultural construction of revelation.

3. Baptandier, "Façonner la divinité en soi."

4. My reasoning largely echoes that of Barend ter Haar, "Shamans, Mediums, and Chinese Buddhism."

A second type of spontaneous presence is **dreams,** *meng* 夢. Records of gods appearing in dreams go all the way back to antiquity.[5] They often only mention signs or visions that require interpretation, but sometimes dreamers hear spirits proffer advice or warnings. A third type, in many ways akin to the case of dreams, is that of experiences of visiting and **returning from the underworld,** typically of people who apparently died and were a few days later sent back among the living, either because they were mistaken for someone else by the minions of hell or because they were purposefully summoned to be lectured. In both cases, when they are resurrected, they tell the story of what they have seen, heard, and sometimes read. Such events are documented in an important number of narratives usually described as miracle tales. These stories were a major source of theological knowledge, as the returnees told about what they learned in the underworld, especially in terms of the process of divine punishments, and which rituals work and why; the stories were copied and disseminated as valid information.[6] These narratives of journeys to hell seem to be spontaneous events from the medieval and early modern sources, but here again, like with possession, we would benefit from caution; in the modern and contemporary period, ritual specialists could induce such experiences (termed *youming* 游冥) in their clients, who tell of their encounters, and several influential books were published based on such oral information.[7]

A fourth type is **encounters,** *yu* 遇, with divine beings. Narratives of such encounters not only constitute a very large part of the early and medieval stories of experiencing divine presence, but they also account for many revelations, with texts and oral instructions being conferred as part of these encounters. In an encounter, the human usually meets the god in the flesh, but without any witness. One of the most famous collections of stories of divine encounters is Du Guangting's 杜光庭 (850–933) *Shenxian ganyuzhuan* 神仙感遇傳 (Lives of those who have

5. Campany, *Chinese Dreamscape.*
6. Campany, "Return-from-death Narratives."
7. Zhu Mingchuan, "Gengzi Chuandong shenjiao chu," 61–65.

moved divine immortals to meet them). In his study of this text, Franciscus Verellen highlights how the human agent may have caused the encounter by "moving," *gan* 感, the god through his merits, *gong* 功, yet does not willfully create it and is usually surprised, if not altogether confused, by the encounter event. Advanced practitioners may strive to obtain one by secluding themselves in mountains and engaging in self-cultivation; yet they never know when or if the gods will appear to them.[8] In this category we should add the apparition of divine objects (including texts, images, and drugs) that appear as a response to the merits or exceptional qualities of a person.

Finally, gods may decide to take human form and interact with the living—not just in one secret apparition to an adept, as in an encounter, but for a long time. Such a stable presence can be called **transformation**, *hua* 化, but this term also has a larger, more encompassing meaning of divine manifestation. Buddhist texts brought the notion of *nirmāṇakāya*, "transformation body," *huashen* 化身, meaning a material form emanating from a Buddha to convey teachings. Medieval Daoists adopted the notion, presenting gods as emanations of Yuanshi tianzun 元始天尊 or Taishang laojun.

From there the notion developed in two different directions, which have distinct consequences for revelation practices. On the one hand, there are humans who claim to be emanations (transformation bodies) of Buddhas or other entities and preach as such. A famous early case was Fu Dashi 傅大士 (497–569), who claimed to be Maitreya embodied and contributed to shaping the Maitreya cult (but apparently did not reveal scriptures). Naturally, their messianic potential caused officials to take a dim view of self-proclaimed Buddhas at the same time as countless emperors made similar claims for themselves, but it was a major element in the modern sectarian traditions, where patriarchs claimed to be such transformation bodies and wrote revelations as such. On the other hand, exceptional humans were often described, when

8. Verellen, "Encounter as Revelation."

alive or later, as incarnations of bodhisattvas and other entities, but they themselves made no such claims (several thaumaturgic monks were thus described in hagiographies as incarnations of Guanyin). Incarnation must be clearly distinguished from emanation; the reincarnated being has forgotten his or her earlier or true identity, at least until he or she reaches enlightenment—this is for instance the case with Guanyin's most famous incarnation, Miaoshan 妙善. This idea fed into conceptions of the gods. From the Song period onward, several gods have been given illustrated hagiographies that are organized around the successive forms in which they intervened in the world through transformations. In several cases, this means incarnations; gods who decide (or are sent, sometimes as a punishment decided by the highest gods) to come on Earth and instruct humans are said to "manifest their presence by transforming (into a human)," *jianghua* 降生. They are at first not aware of their divine nature and must undergo self-cultivation before they can teach humans. In late imperial times, it became frequent to describe the sages of antiquity as incarnations of gods (and thus their teachings as revelations), an idea that did not exist in early times.

Beside these types, gods can also manifest their presence and will in nondiscursive ways. Since early medieval times stories of temple foundations often imply a statue or other icon settling in a place in uncanny ways, such as floating upriver or becoming extremely heavy when humans want to move it; in this way, gods express their will to stay put.

1.1.2. Ritualized Presence

In contrast to spontaneous presence, the ritualized modes are predicated on human agency; humans decide to create divine presence and have the specialized knowledge of how to make it happen. The vocabulary here is that of invitation, *qing* 請, or summoning, zhao 召—the nuance between the two, depending on contextual hierarchical asymmetry between ritual specialist and spirit, being quite variable. In Daoist sources, mentions of divine presence (*ling*) are frequently embedded in a ritual context, and therefore humans (typically priests) have performed in such a way as to make *ling* happen. The phrase "Come, appear!" (*jiangling*!) as a command is found within the Daoist canon in hundreds of instances of formulas and hymns declaimed by priests.

The simplest mode of interacting with the gods is through inspired **divination**, that is, asking them a question that they can answer through objects: this covers a large range of techniques, from throwing the blocks, *jiao* 珓 or 筊, to drawing an oracle, *qian* 籤. These techniques allow for obtaining an answer from the gods, but these answers are preformatted and therefore cannot constitute revelation.

The most pervasive, almost default, mode of interaction with gods is **sacrifice**. Rituals inviting divine entities to partake of offerings so as to ask them for blessings are extremely varied, but they all rest upon a basic tripartite structure: 1) inviting the spirits, *qingshen* 請神 (with music and oral formulas); 2) hosting the gods (entertaining them, feasting them, presenting them with documents, notably prayers); and 3) sending off the spirits, *songshen* 送神. Thus, presence is first created, then experienced, and then dispelled. In this schema, gods are supposed to be present, hence the canonical expression "sacrifice as if the gods were present," *rushenzai* 如神在, but this is not necessarily obvious, and the response to the prayer can intervene at a later time.[9]

In divination and sacrifice, the gods are asked to be present, but their presence is not necessarily sensed or experienced. For this to happen, a ritual specialist must intervene to compel a god to become present in a perceptible form, either visible, audible, or through other senses. This can happen either mentally or physically. Making gods present mentally is what I call **visualization**, defined here as spiritual exercises based on training oneself in meditation and learning through texts and images what the gods look like, so as to be able to represent them mentally or recognize them should they appear spontaneously. This concerns the inner part of the ritual that unfolds within the practitioner and is not part of a collective sensory experience. Many if not most of

9. The locus classicus of *rushenzai* is in the *Analects* 3.12 ("Bayi 八佾").

the records of gods manifesting their presence to practitioners in medieval times are linked to precisely scripted solo-visualization practices (most elaborate in the Shangqing 上清 tradition), and this has continued into early modern times and beyond. Daoist rituals are entirely predicated on the priest being able to summon gods through visualization.

If the ritual specialist is to compel the god to become present in a form perceptible to others, then he or she has to use objects. **Talismans,** *fu* 符, are the quickest way ritual specialists can create divine presence. Talismans are usually ephemeral (they are burned, ingested, and consumed—they are highly sensory objects) even though some may be carried on oneself or hung in the house for a period of time. The liturgies concerned with creating talismans are replete with the vocabulary of causing divine presence (*ling*) to happen. To give just one example, taken from an early Song incantation to draw talismans: "empower this divine brush, quickly manifest your powerful presence!" 敕下神筆, 速降威靈.[10] The talisman may be a presence in and of itself; it is a sort of "true form" or "transcendent body," *zhenxing* 真形, of the god. Talismans are also widely used to summon gods to be present in other material media as well, and we will see that they are crucial to spirit-writing, controlled possession, and other means of producing revelation. We find in at least three different early modern liturgical manuals a "talisman to compel the manifestation of divine presence" 降靈(真)符. In commands to the gods, we read sentences such as "Obey my talismanic command and manifest the traces of your presence!" 隨吾符命降靈蹤 (an alternative sentence replaces the talisman with the priest's original *qi* as the means to create divine presence: 隨吾真炁降靈蹤).[11]

Finally, divine presence can be created by providing a body for the gods to use. We have already mentioned possession in this regard; it can

10. The expression *jiang weiling*, where *wei* (awesome) reinforces the sensory, overwhelming effect of *ling*, is very common (over sixty occurrences) in the *Daozang*, mostly found in ritual commands or invitations to the gods.

11. *Daofa huiyuan*, 223.6b–7a.

be described and understood (in emic terms) as spontaneous, but it can also be arranged, with invitations for the god to take hold of the medium's body. A related technique, documented in Han-period ritual codifications and likely already practiced much earlier, is to invite the ancestors to use the body of a descendant, called the "corpse," *shi* 尸, to partake of the offerings. Since their emergence starting from around the eleventh century, the various **spirit-writing** techniques control possession by channeling it into texts rather than through sensory experience. In séances, however, there is a strong feeling of divine presence among participants, and gods address them personally, calling them by their names and sometimes using vehement language, thus creating affect.

Different from possession, but only by degree rather than nature, is **theater.** Actors playing gods (a very common situation) are in some contexts going through a ritual of divine presence, and through them gods are made visible on stage. Such presence enables the ritual, especially the exorcistic functions of certain plays; the expected effects of performing such plays make it plain that when acted the gods are actually present.[12]

If we leave aside simple divination with blocks or oracle sticks and sacrifices that do not produce revelations, we are left with three broad sorts of ritual techniques that produce a divine presence that may result in revelation: possession (and not shamanism), that is, making the spirit use one's body; summoning, that is, using objects and sounds (talismans, invocations) to create a physical presence of the spirit; and visualization, that is, creating a mental presence. They are often combined, but they each have their own logic. One may describe possession, summoning, and visualization as spiritual techniques, especially if one wants to emphasize how they constitute tools for an individual in the quest for self-perfection. I choose, however, to qualify them as ritual techniques in order to better keep in mind that they are commonly used not just for the self but also in the course of ritual performances that aim to benefit

12. Van der Loon, "Les origines rituelles du théâtre chinois"; ter Haar, *Guan Yu*, 129–39.

the larger community; this hopefully will help us pay attention to the collective production of revelation.

Divine presence created by ritual means is perforce ephemeral and clearly bounded by a beginning and an end; as Daoists say, inviting the gods is easy, successfully sending them off less so. There is a considerable body of narratives dealing with this problem of gods creating trouble because they were improperly made present or not successfully sent off.[13] In this regard, the modes of manifesting/creating divine presence in a ritual are distinct from more permanent ways, first and foremost in consecrated icons, notably statues, as well as other objects (books, swords, relics, etc.). The vocabulary of *ling*, so present in spontaneous and ritually invited manifestations of divine presence, is also widely used to discuss statues and their powers, showing that *ling* is not necessarily thought of as ephemeral (though some statues do stop being *ling* at some point). However, I have not yet seen a case of the consecration ritual of a statue (creating a **durable** divine presence) using the term *jiangling* or *xianling* (manifesting divine presence); I would therefore hypothesize that the Chinese emic traditions distinguish between the modes of presence created for the brief ritual time (including revelation) and those aimed at permanent presence.

An icon, be it a statue or a tablet, is, like the medium or the "corpse," a body of the god. Many local gods had and still have highly realistic wooden bodies built for them, with articulated joints and entrails.[14] These bodies are made divine by consecration rituals (the most common term being *kaiguang* 開光).[15] Mummies of saints play a similar role as durable physical presences. In all of these cases, the durable presence brings benefits (protection, blessings), but I am not aware of any revelation that was made through an icon, mummy, or relic. This is therefore a type of divine presence that I will not further discuss in the present book.

13. See, e.g., Goossaert, "Scorched Head Daoists" and *Vies des saints exorcistes*, 205–25.

14. Tao Jin, "The City God's New Clothes."

15. Strickmann, *Mantras et mandarins*, chap. 3.

1.2. Effects of Divine Presence

The above array of modes of divine presence covers very different types of physicality and sensory experience. The most common description in narrative sources of experiences of divine presence is in terms of perceptions by one or several senses without any durable traces left afterward other than the memory of it. I call epiphanies such events of perceptible presence. They include auspicious signs and omens, *rui* 瑞, often understood as divine response to human prayers or spontaneous divine interventions to express threat or promise. The archetype is rain: gods make rain, *jiangyu* 降雨, as either a response to prayers in times of drought or to manifest their pleasure. Epiphanies include a vast array of atmospheric phenomena, strange lights, and other sensory experiences.

A specific type of epiphany is visions of the gods, often in the sky. Visions were considered highly auspicious, based on the idea that only a person with a high level of moral quality or advanced cultivation could benefit from one; they were sought after, especially at pilgrimage sites. One can think, for instance, of bodhisattva Mañjuśrī 文殊, who would sometimes appear to pilgrims on his holy mountain, Wutaishan 五臺山; pilgrims routinely recorded their awe at having a vision, or their disappointment at having failed to have one.[16]

Less common than epiphanies are cases when divine presence allows for objects to be transmitted from the gods to humans. The narrative records contain a good many such cases, with ritual instruments (swords, seals, and bells) given to advanced practitioners, either directly or through divine instructions about where to find them. Maybe the most common case is drugs (often called cinnabar, *dan* 丹), which are given by a god to heal a human. Records of such events may mention that the drug was given in a dream, but just as often, we are told of encounters in the flesh.

16. Birnbaum, "The Manifestation of a Monastery."

Finally, divine presence may also result in discursive content being exchanged, the communications going both ways, as humans often question the gods when the latter are present. This is precisely what I call revelation; contrary to some larger scholarly definitions, I do not include epiphanies in this category.

An obvious distinction opposes oral (words, *yan* 言) to written (texts, *wen* 文), and we will repeatedly explore this distinction between written presence, *lingwen* 靈文, and audible presence, *lingyan* 靈言, throughout this book. This is crucial in some cases: techniques for making gods speak are different from those for making them write, but it is important to state at the onset that this is merely a heuristic tool; many revelations have both oral and written elements. Uttered words are in many cases immediately written down and sometimes checked for accuracy by the revealing god; conversely, many revealed written texts are made for ritual recitation. Furthermore, gods may both speak and write during the same revelatory event. For these reasons, I will not overemphasize the elite, written nature of spirit-writing as opposed to the popular, vernacular, and oral nature of possession and other oral forms of revelation: there is heuristic value in the dichotomy, with the condition that we do not essentialize it.

One more typological dichotomy will be useful throughout our inquiry: revealed text as object versus discourse. In some instances, the revealed text is a numinous object that is, to some extent, legible. The prototypes of numinous documents are the *Luoshu* 洛書 and *Hetu* 河圖, both charts that were understood as describing the structure of the universe and were used by the sage rulers of high antiquity to order the world; narratives of their miraculous apparition (without the explicit direct intervention of gods) date from the Han period.[17] Later on, other documents such as talismans, characters in seal script, *zhuan* 篆, or "transcendent writs," *zhenwen* 真文, also appeared in medieval Daoism: here, the medium is the message. By contrast, oral, but also some writ-

17. Pregadio, "Man-Bird Mountain."

ten, revelations are plain discourses, sometimes entirely vernacular. The gods can speak high, esoteric language, or even a divine tongue (such as the Great Brahma's hidden language, *dafan yinyu* 大梵隱語, of the medieval Lingbao revelations), which requires translation, or they can swear with abandon. Again, as for the opposition between oral and written, this dichotomy between numinous document and discourse is often blurred, as when a revealed discourse becomes a sacred scripture that can subsequently work miracles as an object.

These various modes and effects do not strictly map different types of divine entities; most gods can and have been known to use (or be used) in various modes and create different effects, sometimes appearing in full attire to bestow a vision, sometimes giving objects, and sometimes dictating texts. There are logical connections, however, between theological status and mode of presence. The highest gods tend not to possess mediums and speak; local gods by contrast do not write elaborate texts. By the time revelations appeared, around the beginning of the first millennium, as we will now see, the Chinese religious field was already equipped with a large repertoire of modes of divine presence, with different types of gods manifesting themselves or being conjured in all sorts of ways.

CHAPTER TWO

The Invention of Revelation

Revelation as we have defined it—a type of divine presence that produces discursive content—is not documented in Chinese antiquity and seems to appear during the Han period. Possibly a bit earlier, we find stories of humans receiving documents of a divine nature or origin, such as charts that describe the structure of the universe (the *Luoshu* and *Hetu*), or messages, such as omens and portents delivered by birds.[1] Also, Heaven and other gods sent omens and other signs to be interpreted, but this is fundamentally different from texts. There does not seem to be discursive content ascribed to gods in circulation before the late Han period.

The appearance of revelation seems linked to the rise of eschatological thinking; in times of pressing urgency, gods help humanity by giving them instructions so that they can be saved.[2] This new complex of

1. Pregadio, "Man-Bird Mountain." Csikszentmihalyi, "Traditional Taxonomies and Revealed Texts in the Han," describes the apparition during the third century BCE and the Han of both "natural" revelations (sages reading signs in nature offered by Heaven, such as the *Luoshu* and *Hetu*) and stories of gods directly instructing sages of high antiquity (notably the Yellow Emperor); I prefer to use the term revelation for the second kind only.

2. Puett, "Becoming Laozi"; Hsieh Ts'ung-hui, *Xin tiandi zhi ming*, 80–82.

ideas—eschatological urgency, divine instructions to humans offering the only way to salvation—was very successful and led to the appearance from the second century onward of tens, and soon hundreds, of revealed scriptures. It was not universally accepted, however. Michael J. Puett has shown that the idea of religious knowledge resulting from accumulated writings of living sages rather than any divine gift remained dominant in authors such as Ge Hong 葛洪 (283–343).[3] Even the *Taipingjing* 太平經 (Scripture of great peace; presented as a revelation) writes, in a passage that I cannot date, "Heaven and Earth do not speak to humans, and thus they allow sages to be born every few generations" 天地不與人語也，故時時生聖人.[4] This preference for sagely classics over revelations remains present throughout Chinese history.

One of the most famous and disputed cases of early revelation is indeed the *Taipingjing*.[5] This text promises millenarian bliss if humanity could reject its immoral ways and truly practice the Dao. It (or different scriptures) certainly circulated during the Han period; the texts we now have, however, were later modified and expanded, and the accounts of the revelation have changed and multiplied in different directions over time. The earliest mention of a *Taipingjing* (not necessarily the same one we now have) has a story where the historiographer, writing in the *Hanshu* 漢書 (History of the Han; completed 112 CE), dismisses a claim of revelation:

> At the time of Emperor Cheng (r. 33–7 BCE), Gan Zhongke, a man from Qi, fabricated a Calendar of Heavenly Officials and a *Baoyuan Taipingjing* in twelve scrolls. It said: the house of Han is now meeting a great termination

3. Puett, "Humans, Spirits, and Sages." Puett notes cases in Ge's writings of transcendents who impart alchemical books to living adepts (we will discuss them below) but still categorizes them as human rather than divine; I would not follow him on this point since the same techniques for producing revelations can address transcendents as well as high gods.

4. *Taipingjing hejiao*, 651 (j. 116).

5. Espesset, "Latter Han Religious Mass Movements"; and Espesset, "Cosmologie et tri fonctionnalité"; Hendrischke, *Scripture on Great Peace*; Seidel, "Imperial Treasures and Taoist Sacraments."

> of the world; it must renew its mandate from Heaven. Tiandi has sent the transcendent Chijingzi who has taught me this way.
>
> 成帝時，齊人甘忠可詐造天官曆、包元太平經十二卷，以言「漢家逢天地之大終，當更受命於天，天帝使真人赤精子，下教我此道。」[6]

During the third and fourth centuries, other accounts appeared, ascribing the revelation to a ritual specialist named Gan Ji 干吉 or Yu Ji 于吉, who lived during the late Han and Three Kingdoms period. This version was adopted by Daoists as well as official historiographers and found its way into official histories:

> The "Forest of Treatises" says: at the beginning of Emperor Shun's reign (r. 126–44), Gong Chong from Langye came in audience to present the divine book that his master Yu Ji had found in the waters of Quyang Spring. It was written on white silk with red borders, and was titled *Book of Great Peace with Blue Instructions* in over a hundred scrolls.
>
> 志林曰：初順帝時，琅邪宮崇詣闕上師于吉所得神書於曲陽泉水上，白素朱界，號太平青領道，凡百餘卷。[7]

This may be the earliest occurrence of the term "divine book," *shenshu* 神書.[8] So, by the early second century CE when the *Hanshu* was written, the twofold idea that transcendents could teach humans for the salvation of all humanity and that such teachings could result in books was already circulating. Whether the books were supposed to be written by the transcendents or by the human receiver of the revelation based on oral or mental instructions remains unknown. The *Taipingjing* myth continued to develop, and soon the revelation was ascribed to the highest Daoist god.

6. *Hanshu*, 75.3192.

7. *Sanguo zhi*, 1110, see also *Houhanshu*, 30B.1080, based on earlier historiographical works.

8. Rols, "Les interdits de destruction," chap. 4.

2.1. Daoist Revelations

The majority of texts revealed in China during the Han and medieval period were produced in a very clear and explicit Daoist context (by which I mean related to the cult of the divinized Laozi); even if the eschatological ideas that underpin them are not exclusively Daoist, they were systematically developed there.[9]

2.1.1. TAISHANG LAOJUN

One of the first Daoist gods to produce revelations was Laozi, or Taishang laojun 太上老君 as he was known by the late Han by his transcendent identity, and he remained an essential divine author of Daoist textual production through the ages. During the Han the idea emerged that the mythical figure of Laozi, who wrote the *Daodejing* at Yin Xi's 尹喜 request, was a divine being who once was incarnated as Laozi but manifested himself many other times, both before and after his incarnation as Laozi, to confer teachings on humans, especially emperors. This is detailed in a famous inscription, the 165 CE *Laozi ming* 老子銘 (Stele inscription honoring Laozi), erected to celebrate the imperial cult of Laozi.[10] In this inscription, no revealed text is mentioned, but this soon changed.

The idea that Laozi regularly intervenes to guide humans led to two outcomes. First, texts attributed to Laozi started to appear probably in the late Han. One of the earliest is the *Laozi zhongjing* 老子中經 (The middle scripture of Laozi), a meditation and visualization treatise that clearly presents itself as a revelation in an apocalyptic context. In it he speaks in the first person and addresses his living interlocutors:

9. On the role of Daoist ideas in the development of Buddhist eschatology, see Zürcher, "Prince Moonlight."

10. Seidel, *La divinisation de Lao tseu*. For an overview of the historical development of Laozi's myth in later periods, see Kohn, *God of the Dao*.

> I have repeatedly composed and disseminated these three texts: the Upper and Lower scriptures [the *Daodejing*] and (the present) Middle scripture. I regularly charge the Lord of Destiny to teach the dead and to protect you; you must not wantonly change my words! If one word is incorrect (in your copies), I will know it. Beware of it!
>
> 吾時時自案行此三篇。三篇，上下中經也。吾常使司命教鬼守汝，勿妄增減吾文。一字不具，吾即知之，兆汝慎之！[11]

Another candidate for the earliest Laojun revelation is the *Laozi bianhuajing* 老子變化經 (Scripture of the transformations of Laozi), discovered as a manuscript in Dunhuang and dated by most scholars to ca. 185 CE. As the earliest document to list his incarnations through the ages (ending with the apparitions in Sichuan between 132 and 155), it expresses vibrant millenarian expectations. It has exhortations spoken by Laozi (老子曰吾. . .) during one of his apparitions in the world, where he enjoins adepts to visualize him constantly.[12]

Other texts from the third century onward have him speak in the first person, often simply introduced as "the Dao says," 道曰 or 道言 (we also find "the scripture says" 經曰 and "Laojun says" 老君曰). An important example is the *Nüqing guilü* 女青鬼律 (Demon code of Lady Blue), an eschatological and demonological treatise likely dated to the second or third century and linked to the Tianshidao 天師道, Church of the Heavenly Master—note that this code strongly condemns "vulgar" possession. Yet another is the old ("external" 外) version of the *Huangtingjing* 黄庭經 (Scripture of the yellow court), another visualization manual also spoken by Laojun, likely dating to the late Han or the third century, which was later rewritten into a "new" version by Shangqing adepts.

Second, religious leaders claimed to have received instructions from Laozi and established communities on this account. An early and decisive account of a Laojun revelation concerns the creation of the Church

11. *Laozi zhongjing*, in *Yunji qiqian*, 19.21a.
12. Seidel, *La divinisation de Lao tseu*.

of the Heavenly Master. According to many medieval texts in the Tianshidao tradition, in 142 CE, Zhang Daoling 張道陵 was visited by Taishang laojun, who appeared to him in full glory and named him his vicar on Earth with the title of Heavenly Master, *tianshi* 天師. The dispensation articulated an eschatological vision of saving the initiates—the pure, destined to become immortals, separated from the doomed—through enforcing a strict moral code and rejecting the blood sacrifices to dead humans that were common in the society around them.

One of the earliest sources from within the Church of the Heavenly Master, a short text entitled *Yangpingzhi* 陽平治 (Yangping parish), describes the founding moment of the church:

> On the first day of the fifth month of the Han'an reign period [June 11, 142], I [Zhang Daoling] received the Dao from the divine pneuma of the August Thearch-King of the beginning of the Han. Taking five pecks of rice as a pledge of faith, I want to allow all worthy people capable of transcendence to ascend to salvation.
>
> 吾以漢安元年五月一日，從漢始皇帝王神氣受道，以五斗米為信，欲令可仙之士皆得升度。[13]

Another early text, the *Da daojia lingjie* 大道家令戒 (Precepts and commands of the great Dao), specifies:

> On the first day of the fifth month of the Han'an reign period, at Redstone Castle in Qu District of Linqiong County of Sichuan, the Dao created the Way of the Correct and Unitary Covenant with the powers in order to seal a contract with Heaven and Earth, establish the twenty-four parishes, and distribute the Mysterious, Primordial, and Inaugurating pneumas to govern the citizens.

13. In *Zhengyi fawen tianshi jiao jieke jing*, 20b; translation from Kleeman, *Celestial Masters*, 68. Kleeman dates this text between 220 and 231. Other scholars argue for a later date; see, e.g., Liu Yi, "Myth and History," who claims that the whole myth of the 142 revelation (and thus the role of Zhang Daoling as the founder of the Tianshidao) was a product of the politico-messianic atmosphere of the 410s (with the upcoming Liu Song dynasty claiming to inherit the mandate of the Han dynasty and Daoists portraying Zhang Daoling as the restorer of the Han); I do not find the argument compelling.

道以漢安元年五月一日，於蜀郡臨邛縣渠停赤石城造出正一盟威之道，與天地券要，立二十四治，分布玄元始氣治民。[14]

The *Da daojia lingjie* is a crucial document because it is the earliest chronology of Laojun's interventions in human history that includes revelations, including the *Taipingjing* (that the author describes as having occurred much earlier than the Han), the *Daodejing*, and lastly in the 142 revelation to Zhang Daoling.

Many later Daoist sources would provide details about this crucial moment and make it clear that the deity who had come down from Heaven to enter into a covenant with Zhang Daoling was the Newly Appeared Supreme Old Lord, Xinchu taishang laojun 新出太上老君. The exact place where this event reputedly took place has been the subject of debate, and several sites now vie for the honor, but they are all located near Chengdu. What we have here is not strictly speaking texts but instructions on how to set up the church. The ordination registers, *lu* 籙, may have been part of them, but the registers we have in later versions do not present themselves as revealed. The short Zhang Pu 張普 stele, dated 173, possibly the earliest extant Tianshidao document, also refers to a deceased member of the church, on behalf of Laojun, "giving scriptures" to living priests 詣受微經.[15]

Later narratives tell of many subsequent revelations between 142 and Zhang Daoling's ascension to Heaven (which later hagiographies date to 157). The contents of the revelations also tend to become more specific and abundant when we read later accounts: it thus fully qualifies as a myth. Zhang Daoling's historicity is a debated question, but this does not affect the importance of his divine persona.[16] Yet, by the fourth century at the latest, the idea that a revelation had happened in 142 was widely disseminated. This inspired other aspiring leaders who also had

14. In *Zhengyi fawen tianshi jiao jieke jing*, 14a–b; translation from Kleeman, *Celestial Masters*, 69. Kleeman dates this text from around 255; other scholars argue for a later date.

15. Kleeman, *Celestial Masters*, 76–78.

16. Goossaert, *Heavenly Masters*, chap. 1.

their own visitations from Laojun. One of the best known is Kou Qianzhi 寇謙之 (365?–448). At the end of Kou's retreat on Mount Songshan 嵩山 in 415, Laojun revealed to him the so-called "New Code," *xinke* 新科, which is partly preserved in the canon as *Laojun yinsong jiejing* 老君音誦誡經 (Scripture of admonitions to be chanted and psalmodied, revealed by Laojun), consisting of a series of pronouncements beginning with "Laojun says" 老君曰. Then, in 423, the god's messenger Li Puwen 李譜文 bestowed upon Kou the *Lutu zhenjing* 籙圖真經 (Authentic scripture of registers and charts; now lost) together with a divine appointment as the new Heavenly Master.

In one of his pronouncements, Laojun recounts the 415 revelation:

> That is why I traveled to the East and came down to observe you in the flesh; surely, you were aware of that? The time has not come for me yet and I should not make my body appear in this world. Qianzhi, you must now take the position of Heavenly Master . . . Laojun summoned Qianzhi; who approached and said: "I have not responded properly to what you have given me; I am stupid and have not made progress. I have not received the divine drugs of long life and I am unable to put gods and spirits at my service. How could I transform evil people into good ones, dispel disasters and submit strange appearances?"
>
> 吾是以東遊，臨觀子身，汝知之不乎？吾數未至，不應見身於世。謙之，汝就係天師正位。. . . 老君召謙之，臨言：臣以蒙覆，愚而不進，有不賜長生神藥，不能役使鬼神，何能化惡為善，消災伏異？[17]

Here we have a spoken dialogue between Kou and Laojun; presumably the revelation of the New Code was also uttered by Laojun and then written down by Kou. There was no witness. As an indication of how frequent such events were, Kou dismisses similar revelations received by libationers of the church who "pretend they have seen the Old Lord and elicited a response, and then report the god's instructions" 詐見老君，兼復感悟，如是神教語.[18]

17. *Laojun yinsong jiejing*, 2b–3a. This is also narrated in official histories, see *Weishu*, 114.3051; and *Suishu*, 35.1093; see also Kleeman, *Celestial Masters*, 194–209.

18. *Laojun yinsong jiejing*, 9b.

Because Laojun continued to intervene in human affairs in subsequent centuries, through epiphanies or, in some cases, revelations, Daoists were motivated to compile ever-larger updated records of his manifestations. The longest and latest of those in the Daoist canon, Xie Shouhao's 謝守灝 (1134–1212) *Hunyuan shengji* 混元聖紀 (Saintly annals of the [Lord of] Chaotic Origin), is dated 1191. The first chapter of this vast compendium offers a chronology, starting with the creation of the world and ending in 1112, and lists the various types of manifestations:

> In the second year of the Zhenghe reign, a *renchen* year (1112), Laojun riding a white horse atop auspicious clouds made himself manifest at the Yuchen monastery on Maoshan and gave the *Heavenly Lads Scripture* with punctuation to Liang Guangying. As for the other traces of his visible manifestations, if the historical sources do not provide a date, I do not record them. But, as for his emitting light, manifesting auspicious signs, appearing in dreams, transmitting words, and causing miracles, even when this did not involve him making himself manifest in this world through transforming himself into a human body, I also include them in the present chronology.
>
> 政和二年壬辰，老君乘白馬駕祥雲，降于茅山玉晨觀，授梁光映加句《天童經》。其餘降現事迹，　紀傳不繫時代者不述。與夫放光、見瑞、示夢、傳言、靈驗等事，非化身下降者，亦復載于譜也。[19]

The early modern historiographer thus saw the revelation of oral instructions, *chuanyan* 傳言, as a part of Laozi's guidance of humanity and recorded the early scriptures (such as the *Laozi zhongjing*) and revelations to Zhang Daoling, Kou Qianzhi, and others as milestones in a continuous history. Different as they are in content and historical context, these revelations share several characteristics. First, Laojun is a personal god speaking in the first person; adepts can talk with him and see him, sometimes in grandiose visions of carriages pulled by dragons.

19. *Hunyuan shengji*, 1.40b–41a. I will come back later to a more detailed description of the 1112 revelation.

Second, because of his transcendent identity as Taishang laojun, emanation of the Dao, he is seen as the source of all knowledge and revelations—Xie Shouhao qualifies him in the first sentence of his opus magnum as "the font of all teachings" 萬教之宗元.[20] This implies that Buddhism and Confucianism also originated with Laojun, including the infamous "conversion of the Barbarians," *huahu* 化胡, theory. Because the *huahu* story was so contentious and caused the whole Daoist canon to be destroyed on imperial orders in 1281, it was usually muted in modern Daoist sources but remained very present in internal sources (texts circulating among Daoists) that were intimately connected to the theme of the continuing revelation of new texts by Laozi.[21]

2.1.2. Immortals and Alchemical Revelations

Laojun occupies center stage in the history of revelations, but from early on, he was not alone. An important body of texts that circulated from the late Han and during the whole medieval period was that of laboratory alchemy, notably the Taiqing 太清 tradition that the famed author Ge Hong considered as the foremost method for obtaining transcendence. Ge recounts that the Taiqing texts he was studying had been revealed by an anonymous "divine man": "A long time ago, while Zuo Yuanfang (Zuo Ci 左慈) was devoting himself to meditation practices on Mount Tianzhu (present-day Anhui), a divine being transmitted to him the scriptures of the immortals on the golden elixir" 昔左元放於天柱山中精思, 而神人授之以金丹仙經.[22]

In his hagiography of his spiritual ancestor, the half-mythical Zuo Ci who supposedly lived during the last decades of the Han, Ge adds that Zuo, while in meditation, found these texts in a cave—a theme we will come back to.[23] The Taiqing texts themselves have been partially

20. *Hunyuan shengji*, 1.1a.

21. Goossaert, "*Daojiao yuanliu*."

22. *Baopuzi neipian*, j. 4; translation from Pregadio, *Great Clarity*, 3.

23. *Shenxianzhuan* 神仙傳, discussed in Pregadio, *Great Clarity*, 3; and Campany, *To Live as Long as Heaven and Earth*, 279–86.

transmitted and are found in the Daoist canon; the oldest strata may date from the late Han to the early third century. They use a similar language of revelation, notably a primordial scene when the Mysterious Woman, Xuannü 玄女, gave these texts to the Yellow Emperor (before the latter became a god in his turn), a scene reenacted during the ordination of the new adept in the Taiqing tradition. Such narratives of immortals transmitting self-cultivation texts to advanced adepts remained a major strand of revelation down to the contemporary period.

2.1.3. Yuanshi tianzun and Transcendent Texts

During the fourth century, new types of Daoist revelations emerged that did not originate with Laojun or the immortals. During the 360s, the Shangqing revelations were produced through oral instructions during solo séances of visualizations by virtuoso practitioners; we will return to this technique shortly. A few decades later, a new set of revelations, the Lingbao 靈寶 texts, introduced two theological innovations: the primordial god Heavenly Worthy of Primordial Beginning, Yuanshi tianzun 元始天尊, the first emanation of the Dao before even Taishang laojun; and the idea that the scriptures themselves are transcendent entities that emerged from primordial chaos. They are stored in Heaven and eventually passed on to humans, but being in primordial writing, they are unintelligible to us and must therefore be translated into ordinary human writing.[24]

The Lingbao scriptures recount their own history as originating in the first eons of the universe and being transmitted among high gods for incalculably long periods of time before being eventually given to our world, *chushi* 出世. The most important Lingbao scripture, which continues to be a core Daoist text, is the *Durenjing* 度人經 (Scripture of the salvation of humanity): it recounts its first chanting in Heaven as performed by Yuanshi tianzun and enjoins human readers to reenact

24. Hsieh Shu-wei, "Writing from Heaven."

this primordial chanting, which will produce the same salvific effects.[25] Yuanshi tianzun is the first person to preach the scripture, to other gods, who then eventually transmit it to humans; he does not teach humans directly, nor even speak with them. He is not a personal god the way Taishang laojun is, at least in some of his revelations.

2.2. Sutras

Daoist contributions to the Chinese history of revelations were crucial, and Buddhists also played a key role. When Buddhist texts started to enter China during the first and second centuries CE, they carried with them entirely new and powerful ideas about divine discourse. The most ancient Buddhist texts were presented as the writing down (at some later stage) of the oral teachings of the historical Buddha—this is not revelation. The other two types of canonical texts, discipline and treatises, were human productions as well.

Around the turn of the common era, however, a new type of text emerged, the Mahayana sutras, which presented themselves as teachings delivered by the Buddha in Heaven to bodhisattvas and other nonhuman entities, often claiming to be superior teachings encompassing those contained in the older sutras. How these sutras were composed in various settings (between the Indian world and central Asia) remains an open question, but apparently inspired preachers played a key role, which has no direct equivalent in early and medieval China.[26] Whatever the case, the sutras brought Indian ideas about revelation that resonated

25. Bokenkamp, *Early Daoist Scriptures*, 373–438.

26. Gummer, "Listening to the Dharmabhāṇaka," and Drewes, "Dharmabhāṇakas in Early Mahāyāna," bring attention to the role of the sutra preacher in Indian Mahayana Buddhism, who plays the role of the Buddha and by his performance is bound to become one. Drewes moreover points to sutras containing predictions of their future revelation from a bodhisattva to a preacher. This all seems to suggest that the sutras were actually composed during performances by such inspired preachers. I am grateful to Vincent Eltschinger for bringing this to my attention.

with Chinese tropes; for instance, the Prajnāpāramitā-sūtras are presented as sermons by the Buddha that were hidden in the suboceanic palaces of the Nagas, which is where Nāgārjuna 龍樹 (second–third century) was given them. They brought to China a legitimate format for presenting revelations as something that occurred in a distant past or outside of lived temporality, as well as in an altogether alien place, and were eventually made available to humans through undisclosed circumstances. Together with this idea came a florid imaginaire, with grandiose scenes in Heaven and cosmic-sized miracles and signs accompanying the Buddhas' deliveries of their teachings. This imaginaire captured the attention of the Chinese and retains it to this day; it was widely adopted by all sorts of native revelations, the Lingbao scriptures being the earliest and having become, in turn, a model for subsequent revelations.

Very soon, however, new Buddhist scriptures were composed in China using modes of revelation that combined imported and indigenous ritual techniques to various degrees. Robert F. Campany has explored these medieval Buddhist revelations and shown how they created all kinds of reactions, from enthusiastic adoption to rejection.[27] Indeed, the proliferation of new revelations around the late fourth century forced clerical authorities to devise criteria for orthodoxy and to draw catalogs of authentic, spurious, and false, *weijing* 偽經, texts. The latter two categories, known in scholarship as the apocrypha, account for hundreds of texts, some of which have become central in modern Buddhism.[28] Much research has been done on how Buddhist bibliographers deployed sophisticated tools to separate bona fide scriptures from

27. Campany, "Buddhist Revelation and Taoist Translation." I am very grateful to Sylvie Hureau for helping me navigate this topic. Ter Haar, "Shamans, Mediums, and Chinese Buddhism," has discussed how medieval Buddhists had no qualms in employing mediums or shamans to negotiate with spirits and learn about postmortem destinies, but this was different from producing revelations. He, however, hypothesizes that visits to the netherworld, shamanistic séances, dreams, and visions of the Pure Land shared a narrative structure and may have been based on cognate techniques.

28. Hureau, "Translations, Apocrypha, and the Emergence." It is regrettable that much of the scholarship on apocrypha, even when highlighting their importance and intrinsic interest, qualify them as forgeries rather than looking at indigenous processes of revelation.

apocrypha. Even more important to our topic, however, are records of people having revelations of such apocrypha.

In one case, the young daughter (nicknamed Small Nun 尼子) of a high official in the southern court started to utter unknown scriptures (which others noted down) between 499 and 505; "sometimes, she would close her eyes and sit in meditation, and chant these (new) scriptures. In some cases, she claimed that she had been up in Heaven or had received them from gods" 有時閉目靜坐, 誦出此經。或說上天, 或稱神授.[29] This created a conundrum for Buddhist authorities, with some accepting the revelations, others rejecting them, and others still accepting the scriptures but claiming they were not "received from the gods" but actually remembered from an earlier life, *suxi* 宿習, when the nun had heard them preached—a more acceptable mode of textual production in their view. And yet, several sutras, such as the *Avatamsaka sutra* 華嚴經, offer justification for such revelations, with phrases such as "gods said" 天神言. Other medieval stories, found in either miracle tales or hagiographies, relate how Buddhist scriptures were produced either orally or in writing, in some cases apparently through possession and in others, such as with Small Nun, during visionary exercises.[30] Dreams were also an important venue for Buddhist revelation; such was the case of the sixth-century *Gaowang Guanshiyin jing* 高王觀世音經 (Scripture of Guanyin [revealed] during the reign of King Gao), which is a staple of late imperial devotional literature; monks circulated stories to explain that in a dream, Guanyin gave this scripture to a layman facing death who then incanted it and was saved. We also have stories of Daoist scriptures revealed in dreams.[31] Finally, some of those who died and came

29. *Chu Sanzang jiji*, T. 55.40b; Liu Shufen, "The Return of the State," 337–38; Pan Junliang, "A la recherche de l'unité," 253.

30. There are several such accounts in Wang Yan's 王琰 *Mingxiangji* 冥祥記 (Records of signs from the otherworld; between 485 and 501), including young girls who travel in the air, meet Buddhas, and bring back scriptures; see the translation and commentary in Campany, *Signs from the Unseen Realm*.

31. See for instance a story told by Du Guangting, also involving a young girl visited in dream by Laojun, being first dictated a scripture (that was in fact already in circulation

back to life also remembered sermons and other teachings given to them in the underworld by bodhisattvas.

The grandiose and visually over-charged scenes of revelations in Heaven, which opened the Mahayana sutras and also inspired murals, painted scrolls, and other representations, certainly fueled many visionary practices. Robert F. Campany has gathered evidence that techniques for visualizing the future Buddha Maitreya and asking him questions concerning one own's future destiny and salvation, as well as gaining insights into the scriptures or even full-fledged commentaries and other teachings, circulated in medieval times.[32]

Maybe the most fascinating case is that of the hugely influential monk Daoxuan 道宣 (596–667), a hagiographer, bibliographer, and ultimate authority on disciplinary texts. Daoxuan has left a text, *Daoxuan lüshi gantonglu* 道宣律師感通錄 (Record of communications [with spirits] moved by Vinaya Master Daoxuan), that is a lengthy record of his conversations with deceased Buddhists and divine generals, *jiangjun* 將軍, the protectors of the dharma, an event that took place not long before his death. The text, or a related record of Daoxuan's revelations, is also quoted at some length in a canonical anthology (the *Fayuan zhulin* 法苑珠林), so there is little doubt that, at the very least, seventh-century Buddhist monks approved and circulated a record of oral revelations made to one of their most prestigious masters.[33] This is, to my knowledge, the earliest record of questions and answers about doctrinal and ritual matters between a human and the gods, a genre that flourishes in later periods; interestingly, the questions work both ways, as the gods also ask Daoxuan about doctrinal points. The reputation of Daoxuan as

---

at the time) and a prediction concerning his father, "Yao Yuanchong nü *Jiutian shengshen zhangjing* yan" 姚元崇女九天生神章經驗, *Daojiao lingyanji*, 10.3a–6b.

32. Campany, "Buddhist Revelation and Taoist Translation," 13–15. See also Greene, "Meditation, Repentance, and Visionary Experience," chap. 3; and Greene, *Chan Before Chan*.

33. Campany, "Buddhist Revelation and Taoist Translation"; Shinohara, "Story of the Buddha's Begging Bowl."

a source of revelations endured, with the legend of Miaoshan 妙善, the most famous incarnation of Guanyin, appearing around 1100, as the narrative is said to have been told by the gods to Daoxuan.[34]

2.3. Medieval Scenarios of Revelation

Most of the revelations we have briefly surveyed provide precious little description of how the revelatory event took place. In many cases, we are merely told that a god or a group of gods manifested their presence and conferred (the most common term is *shou* 授) instructions on a given human. In some cases, we do not even know whether they were spoken or written. When circumstances are provided, they fall into two categories: texts hidden and found in grottoes, and instructions conferred during a divine encounter created through visualization. These two configurations thus reflect two different techniques for creating divine presence, external and internal, and fall into the two main paradigms for divine presence discussed in the previous chapter: encounter and invitation.

The most systematic typology of Daoist revelations I have seen was written by Hsieh Ts'ung-hui, who contrasts medieval revelations to spirit-writing ones. I was inspired by his argument and will add to its complexity, nuancing it in several ways.[35] Hsieh argues that before the emergence of spirit-writing in the Song, Daoist revelations were secret and made in a secluded place because of the elect individual's exceptional merits and self-cultivation. The person who receives the revelation goes on to become a founder of a new line, which transmits the revelation very selectively. Hsieh identifies two types of revelatory scenarios: one where the god takes the active role, uttering the revelation when realizing the extent of human misery, and the other with

34. Li Yongping, "Shenshou tianshu."
35. Hsieh Ts'ung-hui, *Xin tiandi zhi ming*, chap. 3.

more human agency, where Daoists pray to the gods on behalf of suffering humanity and the gods respond with the salvific revelation. Within the second type, he identifies three subtypes, whereby exceptional Daoists may "move," *gantong* 感通, the gods to procure the revelation: first, through ascetic retreat, meditation, and self-cultivation; second, the self-cultivator finds the revealed text in a cave; and third, through visualizations. I adapt his typology here by first looking at the narratives of revelation (the scenarios), then at the techniques deployed to produce them, and finally combining the two into a broader typology of revelations that focuses on the resulting revealed text and the manner in which it presents itself.

2.3.1. Visions

Stories of gods and immortals appearing and occasionally saying things are extremely frequent. The cult of the immortals that begins to be well documented during the Han provides good examples. For instance, Wangzi Qiao 王子喬, one of the earliest-documented and most prominent immortals is described in a late Han stele inscription as appearing as an old man and telling locals to respect his ancestor's grave; a temple is built on the site of the miracle.[36]

What is more germane to our purpose here is a vision that results not in a simple request or order but in substantive teaching, even though they should be seen as a continuum rather than as exclusive categories.

The narrative of the Lingbao revelations stages gods descending onto Tiantaishan 天台山 and conferring texts on Ge Xuan 葛玄, a semi-mythical figure and grand uncle of Ge Hong. The latter wrote his biography (in the *Shenxianzhuan* 神仙傳 [Lives of divine transcendents]), which relates how he practiced Daoist cultivation at Tiantaishan, causing Taishang laojun and Taiji zhenren 太極真人 to manifest themselves and bestow the Lingbao scriptures upon him.[37] Another version, *Lingbao lüeji* 靈寶略記, reads as follows:

36. Bujard, "Le culte de Wangzi Qiao."

37. Campany, *To Live as Long as Heaven and Earth*, 152–59.

> (Ge Xuan's practice) moved the Highest Lord, who sent three sagely Transcendents down to manifest themselves and transmit the Lingbao scriptures to him . . . Before the three Transcendents manifested themselves, the Supreme Lord had also ordered Xu Laile, the Primordial Transcendent, to become Ge Xuan's teacher in the methods of the Three Caverns. From him Xuan received the sacred writings in twenty-three scrolls, together with instructions and questions in ten scrolls. Altogether he was honored with thirty-three scrolls.
>
> 感通太上, 遣三聖真人下降, 以《靈寶經》授之。. . . 三真未降之前, 太上又命太極真人徐來勒, 為孝先作三洞法師。孝先凡所受經二十三卷, 並語稟、請問十卷, 合三十三卷。[38]

One key shared characteristic of these various visions is that even though they are well situated in time and space, they occurred without any witnesses.

2.3.2. Hidden Texts

Producing revelations by finding texts hidden in grottoes is a well-known phenomenon in religions around the world; the Chinese cases in particular evoke the Tibetan tradition of the treasure texts, *ter-ma*, with which they most certainly have direct connections.[39] This practice is part of a larger repertoire of techniques of entering sacred sites and tapping their resources (such as finding minerals and plants). Some of the most important early Daoist texts have been produced through these means. One of them is the *Sanhuangwen* 三皇文 (Writ of the three sovereigns), about talismans and other instructions that allow one to control the gods and therefore one's fate.[40] There are several narratives of their invention. Ge Hong recounts:

> All the famous mountains and the Five Peaks have this text [the *Sanhuangwen*], but it is concealed in a cave [lit. stone chamber] in the

38. *Yunji qiqian*, 3.11b.

39. Mayer, "Rethinking Treasure." Yü Chün-fang, *Kuan-yin*, 144, discusses works that evoke the mutual influence of medieval Chinese and Tibetan revelatory techniques.

40. Steavu, *Writ of the Three Sovereigns.*

> most impenetrable place. Those who are fated to obtain the Dao must enter the mountain and meditate on (these hidden texts) with concentration and sincerity, and then the mountain gods will open the doors (of the cave) and they will let them see (the book). As for Bo Zhongli, he obtained it in a mountain and immediately set up an altar to offer silk, drew a copy (of the talismans), and departed.
>
> 諸名山五嶽，皆有此書，但藏之於石室幽隱之地，應得道者，入山精誠思之，則山神自開山，令人見之。如帛仲理者，於山中得之，自立壇委絹，常畫一本而去也。[41]

Other versions of the story explain that Bo had to gaze at the stone wall for three years before seeing the talismans, and he needed oral instructions from his master before he could understand and use them. There was another line of transmission (and story of revelation) of the *Sanhuangwen* involving Bao Jing 鮑靚 and not Bo Zhongli (better known as Bo He 帛和), but it also involved reading its characters on the wall of a cave on the Central Peak, Songshan. Elsewhere, Ge Hong provides more details on the ritual methods to "open the mountain" and find sacred texts.[42]

Another major medieval document found in a cave is the *Lingbao wufuxu* 靈寶五符序 (The five talismans of Lingbao, with a preface). This complex, multilayered book, which contains late Han or third-century material but was later revised, starts with a lengthy account of its revelation. In high antiquity, gods seeing the decline of humanity gave three texts to the mythical Emperor Ku 帝嚳, who could not understand them and hid them in a mythical mountain. They were later found by Yu the Great, who used them to save the world and become an immortal; before rising to Heaven he hid two copies, including one in a sacred island on Taihu Lake 太湖 that was protected by two divine guardians. The latter was found in the third century CE by a hermit who gave it to the king of Wu and related his journey in the underground paradise—an account that served as a template for numerous subsequent stories of travels and initiations in grotto-paradises.[43]

41. *Baopuzi neipian*, 19:337; Steavu, *Writ of the Three Sovereigns*, 9.
42. *Baopuzi neipian*, 17:300–301.
43. Bokenkamp, "Peach Flower Font."

Texts hidden by gods for later discovery are especially important in the medieval period but continue to play a significant role in the revelatory toolbox in later periods; consider for instance the case of the Tang-period short mystical text *Yinfujing* 陰符經 (Scripture of the hidden tally), said to have been revealed to the Yellow Emperor, then hidden in a cave on Songshan by Kou Qianzhi and later found there by Li Quan 李筌 (fl. 713–41),[44] or the secret alchemical instructions hidden in a jade box, *Yuxiaji* 玉匣記, by Transcendent Lord Xu 許真君 and discovered in the twelfth century.[45]

One common characteristic of these different revelation narratives, whether of visions or texts in caves (and in partial contrast to the visualizations discussed below), is the importance of place. We have seen how Laojun's manifestations were all located in sacred mountains, or since we know extremely little about the status of these places before the revelations, they subsequently became sacred sites, such as Hemingshan 鶴鳴山 (one of the mountains that claims to have hosted the 142 revelation to Zhang Daoling), Tiantaishan (Ge Xuan), and Songshan (Kou Qianzhi).[46] Similarly, the discovery of sacred texts in caves happened in sacred mountains.

2.4. Medieval Techniques of Revelation

Separately from these narratives of advanced adepts obtaining revelations, there are also accounts of what techniques were used and how. As I have shown in chapter 1, from medieval times onward, and down to the present, three major sorts of technique are described in narrative and

44. The story is told in the preface to *Huangdi Yinfujing shu*. There is another version of the *Yinfujing*'s revelation, which is due to Li Quan's encounter with a mysterious old lady. In some narratives the two are combined: Li Quan discovers the text in the cave, then the old lady explains its meaning.

45. *Yuxiaji*.

46. Hsieh Ts'ung-hui, *Xin tiandi zhi ming*, 83.

normative sources that together, in their limitless variety and combinations, form the range of possibilities for producing divine presence in general and revelation in particular: possession, that is, making the god use one's body; summoning, that is, using objects and sounds (talismans, invocations) to create the perceptible presence of a god; and visualizations, that is, creating a mental presence. The three sorts of techniques were known and practiced early on in China (possession and summoning as far back as we have records; visualization by the Han period), even if new variations kept appearing throughout history; the combination of the three sorts of techniques allowed for innovations.

2.4.1. Possession

Spirit possession allowing gods to speak has existed as long as we have historical records.[47] During the medieval period, we start to have records of pronouncements from the gods, which are sometimes termed "teachings of the gods," *shenjiao* 神教. One such case is related in the *Shuyiji* 述異記 (Records of uncanny events), a fifth-century collection of stories, which relates an episode where a general seeks help during an expedition:

> There was a female *wu*, Ms. Qin from Fenggao, who was the widow of Mr. Suo from the same county. She was able to make spirits manifest themselves to expound their teachings, and their words were never empty talk. A local official arranged for prayers and asked (the god) when military victory could be obtained. Ms. Qin then uttered the teaching of the god saying: "Heaven has entrusted this affair to a valiant minister, and events are being planned by gods and spirits. There will be an expedition but no battle. Concerning these petty war prisoners, you should not bother to control them. Victory will be obtained on the fifth day of the second month of next year."
>
> 有女巫秦氏、奉高人, 同縣索氏之寡妻也, 能降靈宣教, 言無虛唱。使者設禱, 因訪克捷之期。秦氏乃稱神教曰: 「天授英輔, 神魔所擬, 有征無戰; 蕞爾小虜, 不足制也。到來年二月五日當克。」[48]

47. Lin Fu-shih, "Shamans and Politics."
48. *Shuyiji*, in *Taiping guangji*, 283.2254; Pan Junliang, "A la recherche de l'unité," 15.

In this and many other cases, we are made textual witnesses to divination (asking the gods a question of immediate concern), which sits at the border of our definition of prophecy and thus revelation, since the medium tells about Heaven's decisions and the fate of the empire. But, more importantly, it shows this technique was available to make gods speak and was used by some members of the elite. Scholarly common sense tends to assume mediums, shamans, and their gods were low class and conveyed no articulate teachings. The unrelenting polemics (and sometimes actual attacks) waged by medieval Daoists against "vulgar" mediums and their demonic spirits certainly convey this impression. But this is a risky assumption. In his numerous miracle stories, Du Guangting mentions many cases of mediums conveying divine instructions, some of them of significant doctrinal import, and does not express doubt or criticism.

Within the Church of the Heavenly Master corpus, there are texts where Zhang Daoling seems to be speaking in the first person after his divine apotheosis, including the *Da daojia lingjie* introduced above. According to Terry F. Kleeman, he speaks through a medium, and the office of a supervisor of mediums, identifying and certifying the manifestations of immortals, was actually institutionalized in the early church.[49] The *Da daojia lingjie* says: "the Dao has again and again saved your lives, sometimes speaking to you through the Determiner of pneumas" 道乃往往救汝曹之命。或決氣相語.[50] The idea seems to be that there were desirable and undesirable revelations through possession, hence the need for a supervisor. These teachings from above could and did inspire scissions and new leaders. Spirit possession also played a role in promotions in the church, argues Kleeman. Oral revelations from their apotheosized patriarchs were an openly accepted practice in the early Church of the Heavenly Master. A major leader of the church, Du Jiong 杜炅 (fl. 365), was visited at night by Zhang Lu 張魯 (?–215 or 216), putatively the third Heavenly Master, who "manifested himself and said:

49. Kleeman, *Celestial Masters*, 344–47.

50. *Zhengyi fawen tianshi jiao jieke jing*, 14b; Kleeman, *Celestial Masters*, 345.

'I am Zhang Zhennan, you must transmit my ritual method'" 降云:我張鎮南也。汝應傳吾道法.[51]

Another revealed scripture that may also be a product of possession is the famous eschatological *Dongyuan shenzhou jing* 洞淵神咒經 (Scripture of the divine spells of the cavernous abyss). This early fifth-century revelation, which describes the teachings and rituals of a Church of the Heavenly Master group, is made up of a succession of short pronouncements that begin with "the Dao says." Scholars have considered this style, as well as the unstructured and rather confused contents, to point to the oral pronouncements of a medium; we should note, however, that no hint of possession is found in the text.[52]

2.4.2. Summoning

In contrast to the methods used by mediums and shamans to make gods speak, literate, initiated practitioners could resort to more elaborate techniques. In a certain continuity with age-old sacrifice, but also in overt rupture with it (most medieval Daoists rejected sacrifice), practitioners could summon gods who have an office in the heavenly bureaucracy and ask them questions.

The best-known case is that of the Eight Archivists, Bashi 八史, the personalized gods of the eight trigrams (used in classical deductive divination).[53] As early as the fourth century, Ge Hong described in the *Baopuzi* 抱朴子 (The master who embraces simplicity) the methods, based on talismans and incantations, for summoning these gods, to whom one may then ask questions, notably about the future. The gods

51. *Yunji qiqian*, 111.7a–b, quoting a medieval hagiography. Zhennan is Zhang Lu's civil name. Kleeman, *Celestial Masters*, 212–13, discusses Du Jiong but not the revelation.

52. Mollier, *Une apocalypse taoïste*. In his preface to the scripture, Du Guangting (850–933) describes the revelation as the result of the ritual prayers and visualizations of a Daoist priest, Wang Zuan 王纂. This probably does not shed light on the original revelation but suggests that for an elite late medieval priest like Du, this is how a revelation should occur.

53. Andersen, "Talking to the Gods"; Steavu, *Writ of the Three Sovereigns*, chap. 5.

responded orally or through direct intuition. The technique was apparently aimed at furthering one's own self-cultivation and not at providing services to ordinary people. Several manuals exist in the Daoist canon, one of them apparently predating the Shangqing and Lingbao revelations, and various traditions, notably Lingbao, incorporated them in their own practice. These rituals are time consuming and demanding; many are preceded by a hundred-day fast. I am not aware of any text revealed through this means, and producing teachings was not an aim of the practice; yet it seems important to bear in mind that Daoists had at their disposal ritual techniques that allowed them to reliably ask questions and obtain answers from high gods.

Similar techniques based on talismans to summon gods and ask them questions were at the core of the whole Sanhuang tradition, which formed the third part (Dongshen 洞神) of the medieval Daoist canon, the other two being devoted to self-transcendence and collective rituals of salvation. This tradition was described by Ge Hong as the art of "summoning heavenly gods (and other gods) . . . and making them appear in human form" 召天神 . . . 皆見形如人.[54] As Dominic Steavu has clearly shown, for the codifiers of the medieval canon, after the visualizations of the Dongzhen 洞真 part and the transcendent texts of the Dongxuan 洞玄 part, the Dongshen part was primarily devoted to techniques for summoning gods with talismans, invocations, and other techniques to ask them questions: this was often categorized as "minor rites," *xiaofa* 小法, not as prestigious as visualization or performing Lingbao texts but nonetheless accepted early on as one of the Daoist modes of creating divine presence.[55] It continued during the early modern period. Furthermore, summoning is not antithetic to possession and visualizations; some of the latter techniques included summoning rites.

54. *Baopuzi neipian*, 19:336–37; Steavu, *Writ of the Three Sovereigns*, 9. Elsewhere, Ge explains that once one has summoned the gods, one can ask them questions 對問以諸事, and this is an alternative to possession 入神: *Baopuzi neipian*, 15:272–73; Steavu, *Writ of the Three Sovereigns*, 18.

55. Steavu, *Writ of the Three Sovereigns*, chap. 5.

2.4.3. Visualizations

In agreement with Pan Junliang, I propose to observe a distinction between mediums, who talk to others with the voice of the gods (they perform for an audience), and visualization experts, who see and hear the gods in solitude, engage in dialogue with them, and then transmit their teachings to others in their own voice or writings. Early medieval Daoists seem to have practiced both, but visualization benefited from higher prestige.[56]

Visualizations also follow a different logic from summoning because they are entirely internalized: everything happens within the body of the practitioner—however, the two are not exclusive: some manuals of the Eight Archivists rites require visualizing the gods after having summoned them. Following purification, the adept can invite gods, or externalize deities residing in his or her body (the two procedures often overlap), to come and create an encounter.[57] As the term visualization suggests, particular attention is paid to visions, and adepts have to learn very detailed descriptions of the gods so that they can recognize them when they appear, but other senses are affected too, and many accounts refer to hearing sounds. Visualization texts seem to have first emerged in the late Han period; Michael J. Puett (who has notably studied the *Laozi zhongjing* and the old version of the *Huangtingjing*) has shown how their appearance is strongly linked to divine revelation and apocalyptic expectations. In the *Laozi zhongjing*, the adept is taught to visualize the gods in his own body, including Laozi himself, and to ask them questions.[58]

Obviously, the boundary between visualization and shamanic séance can be blurry (and there certainly was a circulation of techniques

56. Pan Junliang, "A la recherche de l'unité." I complicate Pan's model, however, by introducing into the analysis the third sort of ritual technique, which focuses on summoning gods and seeing them as a continuum rather than a radical dichotomy (Pan presents possession as oral and practical and revelation through visualization as written and doctrinal).

57. On visualization, see the large bibliography gathered in Puett, "Becoming Laozi."

58. Puett, "Becoming Laozi."

and skills between Daoist adepts and shamans), since both involve a trained expert seeing and hearing things that other people cannot and narrating these things to them. I distinguish them for the purpose of the present exercise in typology based on the aim of the practice; the shaman engages in sensing things (including asking questions to the spirits) on behalf of others, whereas visualization is part of self-cultivation regimens. Visualization may in some cases produce a revelation that is then forwarded to some other persons, but this is not its primary goal. John Lagerwey has rightly insisted on the dimension of the interiorization of medieval Daoist revelation as a subjective experience of the Dao, although this is not equally true for all types of revelation during that period.[59]

Visualizations are particularly prominent in the Shangqing tradition, where they are termed *cun* 存 (and various more precise terms based on *cun*); the techniques existed well before the Shangqing revelations in the 360s but thereafter came to be associated with them.[60] These revelations began when specialists, notably Yang Xi 楊羲 (330–86), were hired by an aristocratic family, the Xus 許, living near Maoshan 茅山 to obtain information from the otherworld about the posthumous destinies of their ancestors and their own prospects. Yang not only provided a wealth of such information but told them about his encounters with female transcendents, notably Wei Huacun 魏華存, who offered him a vast amount of instructions, poems, and scriptures, a large part of which has been transmitted in the Daoist canon. Not only did the revelations themselves contain detailed instructions for performing visualizations, but this is also how the Shangqing revelations were produced, notably as documented by the systematic record of the revelatory events compiled

59. Lagerwey, "Introduction," 49. He defines revelation as *gantong* 感通, based on *ganche* 感徹, *ganwu* 感悟, and *ganying* 感應 (three terms used by Kou Qianzhi), which we may translate as "elicited penetration, awakening, or response." This is a much larger definition than the one I use here.

60. Edward Schafer translated the term as "to make sensibly present," which fits my definition of type 5 (Schafer, "Jade Woman," 387). I am grateful to Olivier Boutonnet for pointing this out to me.

by Tao Hongjing 陶弘景 (456–536) in his *Zhengao* 真誥 (Declarations of the transcendents). This text, which has fascinated scholars for fifteen centuries, relates in fine detail how various transcendents manifested (*jiang*) themselves in the oratory of the main producer of early Shangqing texts, Yang Xi, and talked to him. Yang and others had ongoing conversations with the transcendents that they combined into scriptures and hagiographies, which were constantly updated and expanded.

Visualization was the core Shangqing practice but not the only form of communication between transcendents and humans. Yang Xi and others also had dreams, which seemed to often function as "first contact" events before visualization séances allowed Yang and other adepts more sustained exchanges.[61] Similar processes are also described in other sources from the medieval period—a dream set in motion a chain of events that ended with revelation. There were also debates in Shangqing texts about the respective value of visualization techniques within an oratory and occurring in the open where one could welcome descending transcendents.[62]

Some scholars have claimed that the revelatory techniques used by Yang Xi were an early form of spirit-writing; however, as both Terry F. Kleeman and Hsieh Ts'ung-hui note, this is unconvincing.[63] Contrary to spirit-writing, the Shangqing visionary revelations had no witness (a single person received texts alone in his meditation room, which he then showed to his patrons) and there is no mention of specific writing implements. The *Zhengao* does not provide detailed descriptions, but several passages seem to describe scenes where Yang hears the transcendents reveal discursive content to him orally, which he then notes down.[64] We

61. Pan Junliang, "A la recherche de l'unité," 183.

62. Pettit and Wells, "Revelation in Early Daoist Hagiography."

63. The most recent discussion is Bokenkamp, *A Fourth-Century Daoist Family*, 11–17. Bokenkamp uses the term medium (which I prefer not to) and suggests comparative overtures into religious psychology.

64. Kleeman, *God's Own Tale*, 8; Hsieh Ts'ung-hui, *Xin tiandi zhi ming*, 88–92; *Zhengao*, 19.9b. Tao Hongjing's preface is also very clear about this. Isabelle Robinet, *La révélation du Shangqing*, has already shown that the technique described in the *Zhengao* was gods speaking and Yang Xi writing their words down.

even have a (much later) picture of this scene in an illustrated Tang-period hagiography, showing Yang Xi with paper and brush in his hand welcoming one of the transcendents.[65]

One deity says that that it is impossible for her and Yang Xi to communicate by writing, but she can still speak to him.[66] Some talismans were also transmitted, and Yang provides visual descriptions of his encounters, so his visualizations led to both visual and oral communications; in all cases, however, it was Yang's task to translate these communications into human language. This idea that divine knowledge has to be translated into the human language found in the Shangqing texts was later further developed in the Lingbao and other revelations. In some cases in the *Zhengao* narratives, when someone else was present, it is specified that she or he could not see or hear what Yang Xi was experiencing. In one case, a goddess told Yang to take paper and brush and dictated a poem to him.

> After a long while, the Transcendent Consort made herself visible and announced to me: "I want to compose a text to give to you; would it be agreeable for you to take a brush and note down as I (speak) my foolish mind?" I accepted her command, folded a sheet of paper, dipped my brush (in ink), and received her words as she spoke them. The poem was as follows.
>
> 又良久，真妃見告曰：欲作一紙文相贈，便因君以筆運我鄙意，當可爾乎？某答奉命。即襞紙染筆，登口見授，作詩如左。[67]

But, what was most often conveyed were injunctions where the Shangqing gods spoke in the first person. Ambiguous as they often are, these narratives are the earliest detailed descriptions of techniques used to produce revelations that exist in the Chinese world. The Shangqing tradition continued into the early modern period, but few revelations were produced after the time of Tao Hongjing. Also, the scriptures and

65. *Shangqing shi dichen Tongbo zhenren zhen tuzan*, 18a–19a.
66. *Zhengao*, 1.8a–9b.
67. Hsieh Ts'ung-hui, *Xin tiandi zhi ming*, 90–91; *Zhengao*, 1.13b.

other texts revealed to Yang Xi and other Shangqing visionaries were, like the vast majority of medieval revelations in general, secretly transmitted to adepts during ordination. The *Zhengao*, as a narrative of events that includes revelations (poems and explanations but not the most sacred scriptures and instructions), was an exception and soon became widely disseminated, hence its highly peculiar place in the documentation on medieval revelations. It shares this particular status with another equally fascinating account of revelations, also written by Tao Hongjing, the *Zhoushi mingtongji* 周氏冥通記 (Records of Mr. Zhou's communications with the otherworld). This text, based on the autograph manuscripts by Tao's disciple Zhou Ziliang 周子良 (497–516), describes the visions, ever more mystical revelations, and final death by poisoning (some may say suicide) of the young visionary.

Traditions of visualization were more varied and widespread than the elitist Shangqing tradition. I am inclined, for instance, to consider the case of Small Nun, who uttered scriptures that she "received from the gods" while in meditation, as resorting to the vast array of visualization techniques, even though in her case we do not have any description of the techniques she used.

Sensory experiences of divine presence through visualizations continued to be practiced by Daoists through the ages and down to the present, even though, as we will shortly see, they also developed other techniques. As a ritual manual dated ca. 1200 says:

> The gods and spirits that you summon will immediately manifest their presence in your practice room. You will see the heavenly transcendents with your own eyes and listen to their divine music with your own ears.
>
> 所召真靈，立降子室。可以目睹天真，耳聽靈音。[68]

The primary purpose of visualization techniques is to transform oneself; the divine presence experienced allows one to gain transcendence. The case of Yang Xi summoning the transcendents to ask them

68. *Lingbao wuliang duren shangqing dafa*, 10.1a.

questions and produce scriptures is, for the whole medieval period, an exception rather than a rule.

2.4.4. Comparing the Ritual Techniques

As we progress toward a typology, it will be useful to observe the main differences between these three sorts of techniques. As already said, I am interested in them as elements in a repertoire of ritual techniques that are variously accessible and produce different effects, and from this perspective, identifying differences is crucial. This does not preclude the relevance another approach, such as cognitive science, may offer, which would be to see them as just various ways of staging one single phenomenon. It is certainly true that what the revelation techniques all have in common is relying on gifted and trained individuals who have heard and/or read and memorized a huge amount of religious lore and can recycle them in new formulations—revelations are as a rule based on earlier texts. I leave this avenue to scholars better equipped to follow it.

Possession is not codified; we may, with utmost caution, use ethnographical evidence to get a sense of how it was performed in ancient times and how it was a technique mastered through long and intense training, but there are no prescriptive texts and the training is not foregrounded in the narrative accounts. In contrast, summoning and visualizations are the object of manuals that prescribe them in great detail, with the aim of ensuring that the practitioner remains in full control throughout the process. The two share another crucial common trait: in both cases, revelations were produced without any witness (a third party to the god and the recipient) and therefore without any evidence or proof. This is an issue that new ritual techniques of the early modern period will directly address. They were also explicitly based on drugs that allowed one to enhance his or her visions; both Shangqing and Eight Archivist manuals, as well as other medieval Daoist texts, mention the use of hemp seeds (cannabis sativa, *mapo* 麻勃) that were put in the incense burner, filling the meditation room with ecstatic smoke.[69]

69. Andersen, "Talking to the Gods," 12.

But there is another factor that opposes summoning and visualizations: one can visualize the highest gods, including Taishang laojun, but one cannot summon them. Summoning gods implies a certain degree of control over the god being summoned; the Eight Archivists, for instance, are bona fide pure gods with a respectable place in the heavenly order of things, but they are not ultimate authorities who can preach and teach.

How do we match the three sorts of techniques for creating divine presence with the revelation scenarios discussed before? Of course, one can never exclude the possibility that in some cases, someone simply wrote a text with the intention of forging a revelation, then created a story of a vision or encounter with a god who revealed it to him, and told that story persuasively enough that it was accepted. Yet I doubt that can be systematically the case because at least some revelations had to be the product of a widely recognized and trusted ritual technique for the very idea of revelation to have currency. Which techniques, then, were at work when the medieval revelations were written?

As we have said, summoning, although widely known, is nowhere explicitly associated with revealed texts—which of course does not exclude the fact that some were produced this way. Possession is a good candidate for some narratives and texts that focus on orality ("the Dao says"), including Tianshidao tracts and scriptures. Visualization is explicitly mentioned or was likely involved (or was in the mind of the authors of narratives of revelation) in the largest number of cases, where the visual dimension (such as seeing Laojun and his entourage on dragon chariots or the magnificent sight of the Shangqing transcendents) is paramount. A compelling case is the story of Wang Zuan 王纂, a priest (likely of the Church of the Heavenly Master) said to have been active in northern China shortly before 316, who was tasked to pray for the people dying in a famine. He retreated to his meditation room and submitted a memorial to Heaven (a ritual requiring visualizing oneself in audience with the gods), crying for pity for three days before Taishang laojun appeared and gave him a ritual technique to save the people (the *Dongyuan shenzhou jing* is claimed to be the result of this revelation). Whatever the historical truth of the story, some of the accounts of this event are brief, saying Laojun was just "moved" to appear and talk to him, whereas others describe exuberant scenes of visions with gods, dragons, chariots, and the like.[70] This shows how complex visions and revelations were understood to be the result of routine visualizations in the course of performing a ritual.

Many descriptions of revelations, however, cannot easily be assigned to visualization, or summoning, or spirit possession. More importantly, if it is not made explicit, I do not think there is much to be gained by guessing which narrative is underpinned by which technique; rather, we should take full account of the fact that even though the techniques existed (and were certainly employed), the medieval narratives and the revelations themselves chose to ignore exactly which techniques were employed—we will see that this changed in early modern times.

Furthermore, the three techniques were not exclusive. Dominic Steavu has argued that the Sanhuang summoning techniques were simpler than complex visualizations and allowed one to summon gods with just talismans, but the gods manifested themselves in the adept's body or mind, creating mental events that resemble visualizations. Indeed, stories of the discovery of the Sanhuang texts in caves evoke visualizations, especially the one with the adept gazing at the wall of a cave for years.[71] Similarly, as Pan Junliang has argued, Daoists practicing communications with the gods through visualizations and "self-possession" argued with so much vehemence against the mediums precisely because the dividing line could be so fine. In fact, summoning (notably with talismans), possession, and visualization were three major elements of the Daoist ritual tool kit, combined in various ways to perform various kinds of rituals. Daoists routinely employed them (with the partial exception of possession in medieval times), usually not with the aim of producing revelation, but simply as effective means of producing divine presence for themselves and for their constituencies.

70. An example of the exuberant version of Wang Zuan's revelation is in the opening passage of Du Guangting's preface to *Dongyuan shenzhou jing*.

71. Steavu, *Writ of the Three Sovereigns*, chapter 3 on meditation and visualization.

2.5. Five Types of Revelation

Based on the above discussion, I define five broad ideal-typical categories of revelation that will serve as my typology throughout this book. My aim is to identify ways revelations present themselves based on 1) the ritual technique used (if and only if it is mentioned explicitly); 2) the scenario of the event of revelation; and 3) the form and contents of the revealed texts. Three criteria in particular serve to assign any given revelation to one of these types: 1) the circumstances of the revelatory event; 2) the presence of witnesses; and 3) the existence and use of a ritual technique to reliably produce the revelation. This last criterion is particularly important and directly reflects the distinction we have observed in the previous chapter between spontaneous and ritually produced divine presence, that is, a focus on divine or human agency. Either the revelation is decided by the gods depending (mostly) on the merits and spiritual achievements of the recipient, who may seek and aspire for revelation but must wait until the gods have decided the time has come, and ritual methods that give humans control over the event and more or less guarantee the revelation will happen. Naturally, in the second case, gods may refuse to manifest themselves if the practitioner is impure or another precondition is not met; however, the conditions here are the observance of known rules rather than exceptional merit.

My five ideal types serve to understand the significant differences between separate cases, but assigning any given revelation to one type is only contextual. An event that we understand to have happened according to one type may very well be narrated alongside the template of another type. My aim is to typologize how revelations are presented to their intended audiences, not how they were actually produced. The latter is in many cases entirely beyond our reach, or at best conjectural. By contrast, texts or traditions of texts always tell us the nature of the revelation and this is highly relevant to both the content of the revelation and the way it was read (or listened to).

1. The sutra type. A sutra-type text typically describes its own revelation in heaven but does not mention how from there it reached humanity.[72] It is ahistorical, that is, the this-worldly human revelatory event is not narrated, and it is our only type to not be. Its relation to time and space is what sets this type of revelation apart from the others most clearly: sutra-type revelations are timeless; they were preached in cosmic time unrelated to human experience, they tell eternal truths, and they address humanity in general. For this reason, and also because their language can be quite formulaic, some are very difficult to date, and estimates can vary by centuries. They can be oral (dictated by gods) or written (the text itself being a sacred artifact). Examples include Mahayana sutras but also some Lingbao scriptures. The sutra-type texts are geared entirely toward psalmody: the scripture stages its initial performance that must be repeated.[73] Within this type, we can identify a subtype, consisting of texts where Taishang laojun or the Dao preaches directly to humans (there is no scene of predication in Heaven), addressing them as "you" and sometimes alluding to historical contexts (which allows us to date them, at least tentatively). This presence of a human audience marks this subtype apart from the standard sutras; however, what they have in common is that the historical context of the revelation (who? where? when?) is not provided.

2. The encounter type. An encounter-type text is revealed on this planet by a deity (often an immortal) in an encounter with one or a few humans, and we are told how, where, and when (and sometimes why) this encounter took place. We are, however, not informed of any ritual technique used by the receiver to make it happen—we may conjecture that possession or visualization (as in types 3 and 4 below) was in fact involved, but what defines this type is that no such recourse to ritual

72. In the present book, I clearly distinguish "sutra," as a Buddhist scripture preached by the Buddha, and "sutra type," my own etic category defined here that is not limited to Buddhist texts.

73. I translate *song* 誦 as psalmody, a more exact term than the commonly used chanting or recitation.

techniques is mentioned, because what counts is the moral merit or exceptional circumstances of the receiver.

This type has three subtypes. First is the incarnation: the producer of the revelation claims to be an incarnated god having taken on human form in order to transmit the revelation to predestined adepts (this is prevalent in the modern sectarian traditions).[74] Second is the "secret encounter": the revelation is made to one person, who is charged with strictly controlling the subsequent transmission of the revelation to other humans, who are subject to initiation. Third is the "open encounter": this concerns cases where one human is chosen to receive the revelation and spread it. The open encounter subtype became common during the modern period (this will be discussed again in chapter 5) but existed already in medieval times through, notably, stories of visits to the netherworld, where the person brought back to life revealed to others what was told him by underworld gods.

A secret encounter-type revelation is typically produced by virtuosi who seek the revelation by living as recluses in mountains and looking for texts in caves, or obtaining them in dreams. Examples include the Lingbao texts as conferred on Ge Xuan, or instructions given by immortals to adepts. The case of texts found in caves is borderline; it can be an encounter with the text itself rather than with a visible god, but some cases discussed above suggest the texts were actually produced by visualization in a cave, thus resorting to type 4.

3. The possession type. In contrast to the previous type, divine pronouncements through possessed mediums typically have witnesses, who make it a collective experience, remembered as such. As discussed in chapter 1, from an anthropological perspective, possession can be analyzed as a ritual technique where the medium maintains control, but

74. It would be possible to build incarnation as a separate sixth type, because it is stable and durable, but like other encounter-type revelations, incarnation focuses on the merits of those who benefit from it. Naturally, this excludes the writings as being human if an author is subsequently divinized; here, I only consider revealed texts that present themselves as the discourse of an incarnated god.

in emic terms, it is not so, and many cases are described as the uncontrolled, spontaneous interventions of the gods, like encounters. This directly affects how such revelations were received, and I therefore make it a separate type. We have seen above that the medieval literature offers a few cases of divine pronouncements resorting to that type, but not before early modern times do we see the appearance of full-fledged texts presented as the result of this type of revelation. Some early revelations were possibly the result of possession, such as the Church of the Heavenly Master sermons, but they are not presented as such, and the present typology is (even though not fully emic) based on how revelations present themselves, not on how we assume they were produced. I therefore categorize them as type 1, sutra type.[75]

4. The visualization type. In contrast to possession, visualizations are described in the abundant literature as a set of elaborate, precise techniques. It is thus ritually codified; yet, the success of the visualizations also strongly depends (to a much greater extent than in type 5) on the merits and spiritual accomplishment of the adepts, so that whereas technical mastery is necessary, it is not sufficient to guarantee a revelation. Narratives of revelations as a result of visualization often state that the god was "moved," *gan* 感, to offer revelations, thus using a term that is also omnipresent in encounter-type narratives. The concept of *gan* leaves room for agency on both sides, and it is a matter of context and interpretation whether the emphasis is on human agency (the adept does things in such a way that gods come as a natural response) or divine agency (the gods, seeing that a person has merit or potential, react by deciding to appear).

Also, visualizations are strongly internalized; there is no witness, in contrast with the performance of possession by mediums.[76] In such reve-

75. I concede that it is entirely possible that medieval Chinese immediately understood such revelations beginning with "the Dao says" as the product of possession and did not need more explicit statements to that effect; but again, in the absence of better evidence, this is just a possibility.

76. This is the reason why I disagree with the common use of the term "medium" to qualify Yang Xi and other Shangqing adepts.

lations, the adepts can exchange dialogue with the gods and thus produce both universal scriptures (very similar in content to the sutra type) or personal instructions.[77] We know of the existence of the latter (e.g., dialogues mentioned in the *Zhengao* and instructions for interrogating the Eight Archivists), but in medieval and Tang times they were very rarely published. Examples include the Shangqing scriptures and other texts; however, all Daoist traditions routinely practice visualization in the course of ritual, even if usually not with the aim of producing a revelation.

5. The presence type. A presence-type text is produced during an event of divine presence made perceptible by ritual means to an audience (or at least to clients), which can put questions to the spirits; notably, this type includes spirit-writing. It is typically precisely situated in space and time, often with the names of the humans who created the event (such as the ritual specialists and hosts). Therefore, presence-type revelations not only allow scholars to place the revelation in its social context but to understand how and why such texts were written. The reason is that they tend to address particular individuals and questions and to mention specific historical events and situations, even if they also propose forms of eternal truth.

Presence-type revelation most often involves possession brought under firm control by ordained priests or other qualified persons and members of the group producing the revelation.[78] Gods also maintain their agency alongside that of priests and are described as taking the initiative; yet, it remains true that priests can be relied on to make a presence-type revelation happen because they use techniques for summoning the gods,

77. Admittedly, the Shangqing scriptures would qualify as the sutra type if we did not have other material that tells us how they were produced through visualization.

78. I am aware that anthropologists have pointed out the crucial role of assistants to mediums and shamans, who can be said to control and coproduce the event. But, again, I focus on the cultural understanding of revelation, and the role of such assistants is hardly ever discussed in Chinese sources; furthermore, the end product (the revealed texts) of mediums with or without foregrounded, explicit priestly control is very different.

notably talismans and incantations. This type is thus the convergence of the two techniques of summoning and possession.

I would like to caution against the blanket use of the term "mediumistic" to qualify revelations sometimes found in the scholarly literature. In the present typology, the term fully applies only to type 3; type 5 often uses mediums but under control, so for the purposes of the present book, it is not termed "mediumistic" or "mediumism." The case of what Kleeman identifies as the office of the supervisor of mediums in the early Tianshidao may be such a control procedure—but the evidence is far from detailed and explicit enough. Otherwise, this type is characteristic of the modern period and is the subject of the next two chapters.

The first three types emphasize divine agency in the revelation; the last two emphasize human agency. This is a question of degree, as nearly all human-divine interaction presupposes some agency on both sides, and it is more a continuum than a dichotomy. The difference of emphasis, however, is significant as it relates to the prestige and the acceptability of the revelations, which themselves vary according to the context and evolve over time. One cannot fail to discern that over two millennia of revelations, human-agency revelations tend to become more common, but never exclusive. Naturally, the level of acceptability of the techniques of revelation (that is, how much human agency is culturally accepted when manipulating the gods) conditions what the revelation discloses about how it was produced.

Because I will use these types throughout this book, it will be useful to summarize their key characteristics in table 1 below.

TABLE 1 KEY CHARACTERISTICS OF THE FIVE IDEAL-TYPICAL CATEGORIES OF REVELATION

	Circumstances described	*Presence of witnesses*	*Ritual method known and codified*
1. Sutra			
2. Encounter	x		
3. Possession	x	x	
4. Visualization	x		x
5. Presence	x	x	x

Our five types can also be understood as different modes of relating with the gods, from the most distant and impersonal to the most intimate and personalized. They therefore also correspond to different types of divine personas; certain gods cannot be involved in certain types of revelation; to take obvious examples, the Buddha and Yuanshi tianzun do not engage in possession; local gods do not write sutra-type scriptures.[79] This is relative, however, as some gods can engage in revelations in different types, sometimes adopting a modified persona in the process; we will see examples of such modifications in chapters 4 and 6.

As a consequence, the different types of divine persona imply different types of relation with the living recipient of revelations. A revelation creates a bond between the giver and the taker—the bond may preexist the revelation, such as with gods residing in the body or received as one's spirit servants during ordination. In some cases of the encounter type, the bond does not have continued effect (when the god or immortal, after giving instructions, leaves, never to appear again); by contrast, in types 4 and 5, it is supposed to be maintained. The creation of a durable bond determines the duties of both parties (primarily of the human recipient) and establishes a framework for continued interaction, such as asking questions and obtaining gradually higher-level texts and instructions.

The bond that makes continued revelation possible can take different forms. One type of bond was spiritual marriage between the Shangqing adepts and their female transcendent instructors. In the early modern period, another appeared in the form of the oath of alliance, *shi* 誓, where both parties had similar duties (by contrast to medieval oaths that were unidirectional). The most common form is master-disciple. The vocabulary used for transmission of texts is the same whether the giver is a living human or a god. Therefore, it is logical that the connection between the human receiving a revelation and the god granting it is also described in terms of master and disciple. As a result, the terms

79. On the ritual production of divine personas, see also Goossaert, "Ritual Techniques for Creating a Divine Persona."

xianshi 仙師, "immortal master," and *shenshi* 神師, "divine master," have been very common since medieval times in both didactic and narrative records; they allude, all too often without any detail, to bonds based on revelation. In some cases, the living master, after his apotheosis, becomes a divine master who continues to provide guidance and instructions. This was in fact planned and prescribed in Daoist texts: since early medieval times all Daoists have to visualize their three masters, *sanshi* 三師 (one's ordination master, the latter's own master, and again at the third generation), at the beginning of a ritual performance. Like for all kinds of divine presence, this is not done for the purpose of revelation, but the possibility is always present.

CHAPTER THREE

The Arts of Creating Perceptible Presence and Public Revelation

At the end of first millennium, the repertoire of modes of creating divine presence, including revelations, was already very large. Du Guangting's stories, for instance, provide examples of scriptures and other divine instructions obtained through encounters with immortals, found in caves, heard in dreams, given during visualizations, and spoken by mediums. All these techniques continued to be widely practiced during the early modern period and down to the present. New techniques emerged around the tenth century that enlarged the array of possibilities and opened up the way for new types of revelations: the presence type (type 5) with controlled possession, which I do not see in pre-Song sources (with the possible exception of the early Tianshidao).[1] These techniques, called *fa* 法, or *daofa* 道法, are essentially exorcistic and apotropaic and in some cases involve spirit possession and the cult of carnivorous, violent, and impure deities, such as the thunder gods, *leishen* 雷神

1. Hsieh Ts'ung-hui, *Xin tiandi zhi ming*, 81, identifies the key moment of religious change (characterized notably by the emergence of spirit-writing) with the Southern Song, but I argue for pushing this back to the tenth century.

(some of them local gods of demonic origin) who, once they had submitted to Daoist or Buddhist law, could act as powerful enforcers of this law against malevolent spirits.

Some of these traditions developed at the margins of Daoist institutions, in a zone shared with some vernacular Buddhist specialists who brought the rich Tantric repertoire of ritual techniques for creating divine presence. Their practitioners were called *fashi* 法師 (or *faguan* 法官), and at least some *fashi* were not ordained *daoshi* 道士 and were considered as ranking below them.[2] The most important element in the practice of a *daofa* was the knowledge and mastery of talismans, *fu* 符, used to summon martial gods who exorcise, heal, and generally do the work of the *fashi*. The manipulation of violent martial spirits was already part of the early Church of the Heavenly Master liturgy (where such spirits were listed in the registers and at the service of the priest), but the *daofa* developed an intense personal bond between the priest and his allied divine warrior. The strong, unique personality of these martial gods led them to speak or write in the first person in a most assertive voice and to create distinctive discursive styles.

In this chapter, I will first briefly introduce what was the relationship between the *daofa* exorcistic priests and their gods—a relationship that both underlined and was staged in the presence rituals. I will show that *daofa* practitioners employed encounter-type narratives to explain how they first came into contact and created a bond with their divine allies. Once the bond was created, however, the priests needed to actualize the presence of their god in a perceptible way, primarily for the purpose of expediting ritual process, and I will document early liturgical descriptions of how to produce such presence in that context. I will then explore the various forms that this ritually produced presence could take for revelations, in oral, written, and mental (dream) forms, while keeping in mind that these three forms are more often found in conjunction than separately.

2. Davis, *Society and the Supernatural*; Meulenbeld, *Demonic Warfare*; Sakai Norifumi, "Sōdai dōkyō ni okeru dōhō no kenkyū."

3.1. *Daofa* Rituals, Priests, and Gods

By explicit contrast to the art of mediums, early modern *fashi* priests developed a whole array of techniques to produce perceptible divine presence within a bureaucratic framework and using methods that guaranteed authenticity. This they did by several means, the most important of which was triangulation: instead of a dual relationship between god and medium (type 3, possession) or god and priest (type 4, visualization), these techniques introduce a triangle: priest 法師-medium 童子-god 神. The priest validates the revelation (he is qualified to summon gods in the heavenly bureaucracy, to confirm the identity of the god made present, and to confirm the validity of his revelations), and the medium makes it objective, that is, perceptible to others.

These techniques of summoning gods to ask them questions through a priest controlling a medium are to a very significant extent of a Tantric, that is, Indian and Central Asian, origin. Tantric rites were introduced into China during the Tang and proved highly successful; among them was the ritual manipulation of mediums, skt. *āveśa, aweishe* 阿尾奢. Several Tang-period manuals (from around 700 onward) provide detailed instructions and claim one could thereby enquire about the future or enlist the gods' assistance; these techniques were still practiced by Buddhist *fashi* traditions during the Song and were similar to and in competition with their Daoist equivalents. The *āveśa* techniques obviously inspired the *daofa*, which developed them further; Tantric rites seem to be entirely oral or visual, whereas *daofa* rites entailed mediums writing as well as speaking.[3] Techniques to divine using a bowl of water or a mirror, found in Tang Tantric texts, are also later closely associated with spirit-writing in *daofa* texts; there are also early mentions of the karma mirror used to divine one's spiritual status. Both have in common

3. Davis, *Society and the Supernatural*, 123–25; Strickmann, *Chinese Magical Medicine*; Orzech, Sørensen, and Payne, eds., *Esoteric Buddhism and the Tantras in East Asia*; Meinert, "Embodying the Divine in Tantric Ritual Practice."

extreme attention to strict priestly control over the medium (this accounts for the vast majority of the liturgical instructions), notably through talismans and incantations; these two ritual techniques for summoning spirits were constantly elaborated on in the traffic between Buddhist and Daoist specialists.[4] Yet, I am unaware of any revelation produced by such Buddhist ritual specialists based on these techniques (by contrast to what many *daofa* did), maybe simply because the topic has never been researched. For this reason, I will not discuss Tantric techniques for producing divine presence any further here.

The Daoists have, for two millennia, criticized (and, in some cases, struggled against) the mediums, developed cooperative relationships with them, and appropriated and reformulated their techniques. In early modern and contemporary times, Daoist priests often train and assist mediums. The new *daofa* ritual techniques of the early modern period explicitly employ mediums (*tongzi* 童子) in controlled possession for exorcistic and therapeutic purposes, as well as for making the dead speak during funerary rituals. These spectacular manifestations of divine presence contributed to the success of the new Daoist ritual traditions.[5] The huge early-Ming compendium of *daofa* liturgy, *Daofa huiyuan* 道法會元 (Daoist rites joined in their common origin), has methods for inducing spirit possession; in one of them the priest commands: "quickly come and manifest your presence in the body of the medium!" 如是童子, 速來降靈.[6]

These techniques revolve around the key term *jiang*, here in a causative sense: to make gods manifest their perceptible presence. I call it a "perceptible presence" because it affects the senses (hearing, sight, and other bodily sensations) rather than only the mind; these techniques are not merely geared at producing epiphanies (even if some priests were

4. On the use of talismans in Buddhist rites, see Robson, "Signs of Power."

5. When discussing how *daofa* Daoists were apt at creating spectacular effects of manifesting divine presence, one cannot avoid thinking of Judith Boltz's hypothesis concerning their knowledge of gunpowder so as to produce thunder in the course of summoning thunder gods; see "Not by the Seal of Office Alone."

6. *Daofa huiyuan*, 137.15a.

credited with such events), but the god made present should interact with humans. Being able to create a divine presence that people can witness and benefit from defines a priest. Indeed, a Yuan-period commentator on the extremely widespread Big Dipper scripture, *Beidoujing* 北斗經, revealed in the early Song, says: "when you have grasped this teaching, you become a master of creating divine presence, and all the spirits will fear you" 得此道後, 乃為降靈之師, 萬鬼自怖也.[7] The techniques are codified and written down, even though they form priestly knowledge subject to initiation and were thus not readily available to laypersons the way manuals in the canon are now accessible to us.

Last but not least, *daofa* rituals of perceptible presence are entirely open, and indeed they are geared toward witnesses. *Fashi* priests, and modern Daoists in general, regularly practiced visualizations and were perfectly able to produce revelations through this means; if they engaged in presence-type revelations, it was to create something that visualizations could not: an experience for others. Through presence-type performances, the alliance between the priest and the god is made visible to third parties. This is just as true of spirit-writing, which is a group experience, as it is of other forms of presence-type rituals. The cases of solitary spirit-writing, such as the practice of "brush register," *bilu* 筆錄, used by late imperial literati, including during examinations, are marginal (although certainly not inconsequential). Because they were performers of divine presence, ritual innovation was permanent, with new twists or elaborations on the already codified techniques appearing with each new lineage, hence the staggering numbers of different *daofa* presence-type rites in the Daoist canon. Successful *fashi* were sought after for how impressively they could make gods present.

Let us briefly consider the case of Lin Lingsu 林靈素 (1076–1120), who produced the Shenxiao 神霄 revelations, one of the most important *daofa*, which were adopted by Emperor Huizong 徽宗 (r. 1100–1126)

7. *Taishang xuanling beidou benming changsheng miaojing*, 3.13b.

and integrated into the Daoist canon he had compiled in 1116–20. The late Song hagiography of Lin, a document that should be taken with a pinch of salt for factual history but is a reliable mirror of Song conceptions of religious charisma, is largely built around episodes when Huizong asks Lin to make various gods appear and Lin obliges in spectacular ways. Some stories seem to suggest the inducement of hallucinations (smokescreens and drugs), but Lin also teaches the emperor to practice visualizations.[8]

Contrary to encounter-type revelations, where an immortal bestows instructions on a chosen human disciple, techniques for creating perceptible presence are based on a more reciprocal bond. *Fashi* priests contract an alliance with martial gods to work together; they swear an oath of alliance, *shizhang* 誓章, which spells out their respective duties.[9] Besides formal memorials sent to heavenly gods, priests also express their intimate bond by sending "personal letters," *jiashu* 家書, to their divine allies.[10] In many spirit-writing traditions, the human practitioners become the disciples, *dizi* 弟子, of the god through a formal initiation procedure, but with an equally strong personal and emotional bond. In some later cases of spirit-writing, we may even talk of friendship.[11] These are different types of bonds, but they all have in common familiarity and trust rather than hierarchical chains of command.

Indeed, during this period, we see an increase in the use of the rather informal genre of a letter for communications both ways, between living humans and gods, as well as their public nature, including comments by third parties on the calligraphic style. Not all mentions of letters between the living and spirits can be clearly placed in a spirit-writing context, but they certainly belong to the same larger evolution of modes of communication between humans and gods. A fascinating case

8. *Lishi zhenxian tidao tongjian*, 53.1a–16a.

9. Mozina, "Oaths and Curses in Divine Empyrean Practice."

10. Chao Shin-yi, *Daoist Ritual, State Religion, and Popular Practices*, 67–69.

11. Russell, "Chen Tuan at Mount Huangbo," 126–28, even discusses relations between equals.

is that of Zhu Ziying 朱自英 (976–1029), the twenty-third patriarch of the newly invented Shangqing patriarchal line.[12] In several Song and Yuan accounts, Zhu is described as having first encountered an immortal called Wu Baoyi 武抱一, surnamed *xiantong* 仙童, immortal lad (or "medium for immortals"?). In one hagiography, Wu is described as a former novice who was in charge of playing the temple bells at Maoshan and who eventually became an immortal. Then, Zhu was invited to court, and he "received" (in some versions of the story it was delivered by someone who then disappeared) a letter from his immortal friend telling him not to divulge heavenly secrets and to retire and practice in solitude. The letter was later engraved on a stele in 1118, copying the unusual calligraphy.[13] This inscription attests to how, in the new religious atmosphere of the Song, letters received from one's immortal friends and allies were prized yet readily publicized documents.

3.1.1 Revealing the *Daofa*

The various *daofa* traditions were all based on revelations, which consisted of a combination of talismans (necessary to summon the gods), incantations, and short scriptures. We will see in the next chapter that some of these revelations were produced by the very means these ritual traditions created for producing divine presence, notably spirit-writing, but most were produced through means already common in medieval times, mostly our (type 2) encounter, especially hidden texts, and (type 4) visualization types.

Concerning hidden texts, the Tianxin zhengfa 天心正法 (Correct rites of Heaven's heart; one of the earliest and hugely influential *daofa*) is based on several discoveries; the initial one took place when a medium named Chen Shouyuan 陳守元 found talismans that had been hidden by Zhang Daoling. He could not make sense of them, but a Daoist named Tan Zixiao 譚紫霄, active at the Min 閩 (909–45) court in Fuzhou 福州,

12. On the invention of the Shangqing patriarchal line, in imitation of that of the Heavenly Master, see Goossaert, *Heavenly Masters*, 133.

13. *Wu xiantong bei* 武仙童碑, *Maoshanzhi*, 376–77.

deciphered and used them.[14] A second discovery happened when Rao Dongtian 饒洞天 (fl. 994) saw light emitting from Mount Huagai 華蓋山 in central Jiangxi and found a box with further documents. He could not understand them either but was directed to Tan Zixiao (who had by then moved to Lushan 廬山 in northern Jiangxi), who instructed him.[15]

Examples of encounters in the flesh also abound. One example is the case of the Tiantong incantatory scripture, *Taishang taiqing huanglao dijun yunlei tiantong yinfan xianjing* 太上泰清皇老帝君運雷天童隱梵仙經 (Life-protecting scripture of the heavenly lads of utmost purity, revealed by the Supreme [Lord]), a major reference in thunder ritual traditions. The text already existed in the tenth century, but a new version was revealed by Taishang laojun, in 1009 or 1012 according to the various accounts. In the most developed narrative of this revelation, a leper named Liang Guangying 梁光映 gives himself as a serf to a monastery at Maoshan to serve the Daoists. This lowly servant, presumably as a reward for his selfless service, is graced with an impressive encounter:

> One day, as he was bringing water (to the Daoists), he suddenly (saw) a white-haired man wearing plain clothes, riding a white horse with a crimson mane. He was covered by purple smoke and his body emanated light that illuminated all mountains and rivers around. Two men were walking ahead, holding the reins, and they shouted to Liang: "Taishang laojun is coming!" Liang prostrated and kowtowed. Laojun told him: "I have (made) the *Marvelous Scripture on Protecting Life by the Heavenly Lads* circulate in the world long ago, have you heard about it?" Liang said: "I have not." Laojun said: "I now give it to you; you can note it down. When you will psalmody it, you can incant over water and purify yourself, and your illnesses will be healed. You can also help (heal) people this way." He then chanted the scripture.
>
> 一日給水之際，忽一人皓首素衣，乘白馬而朱鬃，紫煙彌覆其上，身放光明，照映山川。前有二人持節，叱梁曰：太上老君來。梁再拜叩頭，老君曰：吾有《天童護命妙經》流傳於世久矣，汝聞之乎。

14. Andersen, "Tan Zixiao," 963–64; Davis, *Society and the Supernatural*, 21–24; Li Zhihong, *Daojiao Tianxin zhengfa yanjiu*.

15. *Huagaishan Fuqiu Wang Guo san zhenjun shishi*, 5.4b–5b; see the translation in Goossaert, *Vies des saints exorcistes*, 101–5.

曰：不識。老君曰：吾今授汝，汝可記之，誦以呪水沐浴，則汝疾當愈，亦可以濟人也。乃誦經。[16]

Here, it seems that Laojun dictates the text orally, and Liang is asked to write it down. Orality indeed dominates in early modern narratives of revelations of scriptures and ritual instructions, but it can also be combined with the discovery of written texts. Most hagiographies of famed early modern exorcists feature such textual encounters; let me just mention a few important cases here. Wang Wenqing 王文卿 (1093–1153), arguably the most important *daofa* codifier along with Bai Yuchan 白玉蟾 (1194–1229?), told how he met his divine mentor, Wang Fire Master 汪火師. He first encountered him on a boat, and Fire Master gave him a ritual technique. Later, when lost at night in a desolate land, he found refuge in an empty inn (that turned out to have been magically conjured), where he found books on thunder rituals, which he learned. He later met Fire Master again, who taught him how to practice the thunder rituals he had been given in the inn. We thus have a series of encounters both with gods in the flesh and with books.[17] Bai Yuchan for his part told the story of how his master Chen Nan 陳楠 (?–1213) met Thunder Lord Xin 辛天君 in person, who took him to a cave where he opened a stone box containing texts.[18]

Another well-known story (a myth that is first attested in the late thirteenth century) is that of the mythical figure of Sa Shoujian 薩守堅 who was lost on his way to Longhushan 龍虎山 (the seat of the Heavenly Master administration) where he wanted to become a *fashi* priest. In a moment of despair, he came across three immortals—who later turned out to be the apotheosized thirtieth Heavenly Master Zhang Jixian 張繼先 (1092–1126), Wang Wenqing, and Lin Lingsu. They each orally taught him a ritual technique and sent him on a path that would

16. *Hunyuan shengji*, 9.45b–46a.

17. *Chongxu tongmiao shichen Wang xiansheng jiahua*, 1a–2a.

18. *Daofa huiyuan*, 108.15b–16b; see the translation in Goossaert, *Vies des saints exorcistes*, 171–78.

eventually lead him to become a world-famous exorcist.[19] All these revelation stories concern the new *daofa* traditions in southern China, but similar events happened in the north. Xiao Baozhen 蕭抱珍 (?–1166) established the Taiyi 太一 teachings under Jurchen Jin's rule (1115–1234); he was merely said to have established this very successful healing and exorcistic tradition after "immortals and saints had given him secret registers" 以仙聖所授秘籙, of which unfortunately nothing has been transmitted.[20]

An atypical but hugely influential case is that of the Shenxiao tradition, whose scriptures (the most important of which is the first text in the modern Daoist canon) were revealed in 1116. According to the most detailed account, the Shenxiao texts had been composed and stored in Heaven in high antiquity under the supervision of a high god, who became incarnated as Emperor Song Huizong. When he met with another incarnated god (Lin Lingsu), they realized the time was ripe for revelation; Huizong went up to Heaven to fetch the texts and entrusted Lin and others to edit and disseminate them. Here we have a case of revelation dispensed through manipulation at the hands of an exceptionally skilled *fashi* by a living incarnated god, This mode of revelation would later flourish in the modern sectarian traditions.[21]

3.2. The Need for Divine Response, *baoying*

We have seen how *fashi* priests used the language of encounter to explain how they first came in contact with their divine allies and forged a bond with them. Once the bond was established, however, the communication between the two became regular, intense, and predictable; it was

19. *Lishi zhenxian tidao tongjian xubian*, 4.1a–3a; Goossaert, *Vies des saints exorcistes*, 149–62.

20. Wang Yun 王惲, *Dadu Wanpingxian Jingxixiang chuangjian Taiyi jixianguan ji* 大都宛平縣京西鄉創建太一集仙觀記 (1297), in *Daojia jinshilüe*, 856–57.

21. *Gaoshang Shenxiao zongshi shoujing shi*, 1a–2a.

not based on the anguished expectations and divine agency of the encounter type anymore, but rather on the routine process of summoning. This, I contend, is first and foremost because the priests effectively needed to have their allied gods present each time they performed a ritual.

Because rituals consist of inviting the gods to be present, there has to be a way to verify, prove, and sense that the gods are present. At a minimum, divine presence is verified by divination: priests routinely throwing blocks (if the result is negative, then the invitation is performed anew).[22] People expect signs of presence, typically, it should rain after a Daoist offering ritual. In some cases, however, people expect more obvious proofs, more immediate experience. In this context, the miracles (*lingyan* 靈驗, *lingying* 靈應, or *lingyi* 靈異) are actually expected proofs that the invitation of the gods was properly and effectively performed. One of the forms this often takes, in both narratives and liturgy, is "manifesting divine presence through light," *jiang lingguang* 降靈光, but smells and sounds are important as well. In some contemporary traditions, such as the Yuanhuang 元皇 lineages of central Hunan, the core of a new priest's ordination ritual is the "knotting of the banner," *jiefan* 結旛, rite, where the priest has to prove he can compel a thunder god to come and knot the strings of a huge banner—thereby proving its presence.[23]

Divine presence must in some cases be more specific than signs. Daoist rituals hinge on written communication between priests and gods, and no communication can work only one way; indeed, Daoists ceaselessly write "I have received an edict from the Jade Emperor," 吾奉帝敕, or similar phrases in their documents. What does this mean exactly?

The documents priests write, present, and send (by burning them) to the gods, the models for which fill thousands of pages of the Daoist canon, are of various kinds. In some (type 1), the priest simply addresses

22. Andersen, "Talking to the Gods," 6–10, has shown that the early Tianshidao ban on divination did not hold for long in the face of the needs of Daoists, especially for expediting rituals.

23. Mozina, *Knotting the Banner*.

a request to the gods, normally on behalf of an individual or community. In others (type 2), he also promulgates (*ban* 頒 and *gao* 告) divine orders, such as the act of absolving a dead person's sins, *sheshu* 赦書. In this case, he writes that he "proclaims (the document) having received an order (from the gods mandating him to do so)" 承誥奉行. Here we have a divine document that is physically written and issued by an authorized living person, that is, a Daoist priest. These are not revelations; they always follow a standard form (nothing new is ever said), yet they show how Daoist priests are authorized to make the gods write.

The third type of ritual document issued by Daoist priests comes closest to our category of revelation: the decisions and orders directly issued by the gods. When priests submit their petitions to the gods, they often explicitly request a formal response from them; it is based on this formal response that the Daoist may continue with the ritual, including issuing documents in the name of the gods. This act of requesting a formal divine response is expressed by different terms, the most frequent of which are "obtaining a response," *qu baoying* 取報應 (in medieval texts, the term *ganying* 感應 also had the same technical sense), and "obtaining a (divine) edict," *quzhi* 取旨. The former, as we will see, can take different forms (written, oral, and mental), and the latter strongly hints at the production of a written document. I have so far been able to find only one description of how "obtaining a (divine) edict" happens in practice, where it is entirely based on visualization techniques. The manual (concerning a salvation rite for the dead) describes how the priest visualizes his audience in Heaven: he sees the god approving his request and dispatching golden lads and maids carrying the boxes with the documents (for ordaining the dead) down to the priest's table. Then, the priest visualizes how these divine documents merge with his own this-worldly copy of the same documents, which he empowers by writing talismans after having made divine *qi* present in his brush.[24] In other words, through visualization, the priest transforms an ordinary paper document into a divine one.

24. *Shangqing Lingbao dafa*, 44.1a–2b.

The term *quzhi*, "obtaining a (divine) edict," is found in the canon in over fifty occurrences in the context of *daofa* rituals, and often in cases of the ordination of a new priest or of a dead person, so as to save them. A spirit code (probably dated to the Yuan period), which dictates the conduct of priests, plans for harsh punishment if they perform a rite even though they had required an edict and failed to obtain it.[25] A late Song ordination manual shows that this process is not routine and that the response can be negative: "the priest chooses an auspicious date, visualizes himself flying up to the Golden Portal and presenting in person his memorial asking to obtain an edict. If he does not obtain a positive edict, he has to present in person again his memorial after a few days, making a most sincere plea" 法師擇日，飛神金闕，面奏取旨。如未得俞旨，越數日又面奏，懇切控告.[26] If the request has failed three times, then he has to forgo the ordination of his disciple. Because a formal nomination to a position in the divine bureaucracy constitutes the core of any Daoist ordination or salvation rite and is therefore crucial, the whole process of securing a heavenly edict is sacralized. In another document for requesting a nomination edict during an ordination, the priest writes that he and his disciple have already received an initial positive response in a dream and now request a formal document.[27]

The cases just discussed show that ever since the medieval period, and through early modern times up to the present, visualization was a major mode of producing written divine ritual documents, and heavenly edicts in particular. But in the *daofa* traditions, it was supplemented by new presence-type techniques. Some *daofa* traditions needed some form of divine response to the priestly request, including written instructions, that were more compelling than visualizations. Techniques for creating perceptible presence are prominent in this context. A fascinating case is

25. *Daofa huiyuan*, 251.19a.

26. *Lingbao lingjiao jidu jinshu*, 2.2b.

27. "Zou quzhi baoying 奏取旨報應," *Gaoshang shenxiao yuqing zhenwang zishu dafa*, 12.9b–10a.

the ash-plate, *huitan* 灰壇, techniques, which are mentioned in a number of *daofa* manuals belonging to different traditions, showing that they were rather widespread. We have one explicit description of the procedure, entitled *Huitan xianji baoying mifa* 灰壇現跡報應祕法 (Secret liturgy for obtaining a response through manifested traces on the ash table).[28] The text is undated but included in a late Yuan compendium. It describes how the priest sets a table covered with ash in front of the stove, with a seat for the Big Dipper, then goes outside and invites the stars of the Big Dipper, as well as Yisheng 翊聖 (aka Black Killer, whom we will meet shortly). The priest visualizes them as they descend (*jiang*), chants incantations, utters his questions, and goes on examine the traces left in the ash. These traces follow various patterns, which the manual provides and deciphers. There are also cases of exorcistic rituals that use ashes: the priest spreads ashes on the altar and convokes the spirit, who leaves traces when he arrives.[29] What we have here, then, is a method for creating presence that is used not only for guilty spirits but also for high gods.

One tantalizing aspect of this method is that it uses an ash table, which also later became (along with the sand table) an essential implement of modern spirit-writing. An early mention of a spirit-writing séance, which explicitly says the writing is done in ashes, is dated from the thirteenth century;[30] another description is dated to around 1300.[31] However, the practice must be much older; one of the earliest mentions of divining by writing with a sieve, found in a story by Xu Xuan 徐鉉 (916–91), tells of "writing in powder" 畫盤粉以卜.[32] Of course, the two

28. *Fahai yizhu*, 42.18a–23a.

29. *Taishang zhuguo jiumin zongzhen biyao*, 7.22b (this is an early mention, but it does not say that the spirits leave traces in the ash); *Lingbao wuliang duren shangqing dafa*, 36.11a.

30. *Youhuan jiwen*, 3.2b; also "Bingjia xiaohong 餅家小紅," in *Yijianzhi, bingzhi* 丙志, j. 19, 522–23. However, some other accounts of sieve spirit-writing explicitly mention writing on paper. "Shen Chengwu Zigu 沈承務紫姑," in *Yijianzhi*, sanzhi 三志, ren 壬, j. 3, 1486–87, surveys various spirit-writing techniques, some with a sieve that is wielded by two persons onto sand and others writing on paper.

31. *Xianjulu*, 4a. In this story, the spirit-writing performer 扶箕者 performs 降仙 and writes in ashes 灰書.

32. *Jishenlu*, 6.14b.

methods are different, since the *Huitan xianji baoying mifa* does not use a writing implement, and what is read is not legible words but shapes that can be interpreted with the aid of the liturgical manual.[33] Nonetheless, it constitutes a technique for obtaining divine responses to the priest's questions, which the god writes on an ash table.

In the same context, there also existed a ritual technique that falls within our definition of spirit-writing, for obtaining divine answers to ritual petitions, called "obtaining a god-written response on a document submitted to him," *pijiang* 批降, or its synonyms *pibao* 批報 and *pishi* 批示. These terms appear frequently in Song, Yuan, and Ming ritual texts, as well as narrative sources, and we also have a full-fledged liturgy for its performance, found in the same late Yuan compendium of exorcistic liturgies that provided the ash-table rites.[34] In this description, a medium (*tongzi*) is manipulated by the priest, who summons a divine general to descend into the medium's hand and write. The term *pi* is also found in narrative sources to qualify the action of the god answering a question through spirit-writing.[35] In the hagiography of a female *fashi*, Wu Yuanzhao 武元照 (?–1141), we are told how she submitted a memorial to Heaven on behalf of an official and obtained his "written answer," *pida* 批答, predicting the official's future honors.[36]

Yet another case is "consecrating (or borrowing, or possessing) the arm (of a medium)," *fengbi* 封臂 or *jiebi* 借臂 or *fubi* 附臂: the *fashi* priest causes the arm of the medium to be possessed by a god, who can then write down his orders and responses.[37] Mentions of such practices are common in Daoist texts from the twelfth century onward.

33. The ancient myth of writing originating in the traces left by birds (Pregadio, "Man-Bird Mountain") reminds us that the premodern Chinese did not think of the two as entirely different.

34. *Fahai yizhu*, 37.4b–5a.

35. See for example a twelfth-century story from northern China, "Huang zhenren 黃真人," in *Xu Yijianzhi*, 34.

36. "Wu Yuanzhao," *Lishi zhenxian tidao tongjian houji*, 6.13a–15b.

37. Notably, see descriptions in *Daofa huiyuan*, 151.6a and 255.12b–13a; and *Fahai yizhu*, 37.8b–9a.

Another similar ritual method is simply called *jiangbi* (the most common term for spirit-writing) or "moving the brush," *yunbi* 運筆; it allows for obtaining the response of a thunder general in the process of healing people through inducing possession.[38] When the medium's hand grows hot, then the god is present and can write. The term *yunbi* is very telling; in Daoist canonical sources, it usually refers to writing talismans. This is not the only term that, in different contexts, can mean either "writing a talisman" or spirit-writing: this is also the case for "transformed brush," *huabi* 化筆, or "divine brush," *shenbi* 神筆. Indeed, these two ritual techniques share important aspects: the consecration of the writing implement and the descent of the god into it.[39] It is likely that the experience of writing talismans inspired the Daoists who developed spirit-writing techniques.

As a result, priests in need of a divine response to their queries had a large array of techniques at hand that, in addition to visualization, covered most of the gamut of presence-type (type 5) techniques. Daoists who codified the liturgies of the *daofa* saw them as complementary rather than exclusive. Consider for instance the following passage from the same manual that describes the ash-table technique:

> If you want to practice that ritual, you have three ways of obtaining a divine response: obtaining a god-written response on a document submitted to him (*pibao*), obtaining a response in a dream, and obtaining a response on the ash table.
>
> 凡行持此法,報應有三,批報、附夢報、灰壇報。[40]

The intimate connection between spirit-writing, obtaining divine responses during the ritual (*baoying*), and *daofa* exorcistic traditions is further documented by yet another liturgical manual in the canon, the

38. "Taiyi huoxi leifu Zhu jiangjun kaofu dafa 太一火犀雷府朱將軍考附大法," in *Daofa huiyuan*, 227.25b–26a.

39. *Lingbao yujian*, 16.19a, describes how the priest causes the divine *qi* to descend into the brush 降筆中.

40. *Fahai yizhu*, 42.14b.

Deng tianjun xuanling bamen baoying neizhi 鄧天君玄靈八門報應內旨 (Inner instructions on obtaining a divine response through the eight gates of dark spirits, [revealed by] Heavenly Lord Deng). The lord is Deng Bowen 鄧伯溫, one of the most venerated thunder gods who is frequently seen in spirit-written revelations from the Yuan down to the modern period. This undated document was probably composed during the late Song or Yuan—it discusses the divinatory techniques of the celebrated *daofa* priest Xu Shouxin 徐守信 (1033–1108). It describes itself in the first sentence as having been revealed by the Heavenly Lord through spirit-writing (*jiangbi*) before detailing a rather complex set of divinatory methods for priests that includes visualizations and computations of times and directions.[41] The priest actualizes Deng and ascends to Heaven with him to question the gods and obtain a response, in the context of curing patients; the responses take the form of various signs and visions to be interpreted.

3.3. Modes of Perceptible Presence

We have seen that *fashi* priests routinely used presence-type ritual techniques, often with a medium, to communicate with their allied gods during rituals. In some cases, this communication could evolve into revelations when the priest or his clients asked a question of general import and the gods provided a substantial response. The generic terms referring to the priestly production of a perceptible divine presence for such a public revelation are *jiangshen* 降神 and *jiangling* 降靈, often functioning as synonyms. They are usually rather allusive, without making the precise mode of presence explicit, but in some cases they are more forthcoming. When authors want to be explicit, they typically use

41. *Deng tianjun xuanling bamen baoying neizhi*, 1a; Steavu, *Writ of the Three Sovereigns*, 196–97, shows how these techniques are part of the early modern resurgence of the medieval Sanhuang tradition with their combination of summoning gods and divination.

expressions that combine the word *jiang* with the mode of perceptible presence: sound, readable text, or vision.

3.3.1. Divine Speak

Two key terms describe the production of oral discourse from the gods in early modern times: *jiangyu* 降語 and *jiangyan* 降言. They can be interchangeable in certain contexts, but they tend to refer to different situations: *jiangyu* usually describes the dead talking through mediums, whereas *jiangyan* is usually reserved for pronouncements from higher gods. This suggests that the techniques were basically similar, but writers felt the need to distinguish them. The term *jiangyan* first appears systematically within a particularly important text in the history of Chinese revelations, the *Yisheng baode zhuan* 翊聖保德傳 (Hagiography of [the Transcendent Lord] who assists the Saint and protects virtue), dated 1016.[42]

This hagiography is devoted to the career of a god, here referred to by the title conferred on him by the Song court but better known elsewhere by the less flattering name of Black Killer, Heisha 黑殺 (or 煞). He is found all over exorcistic liturgical manuals as early as the tenth century. Black Killer is, together with Zhenwu 真武 (canonized as Yousheng 佑聖) and two gods with a strongly Tantric persona (Tianpeng 天蓬 and Tianyou 天猷), a member of the group of Four Saints, *sisheng* 四聖, under the authority of the Northern Emperor, Beidi 北帝.[43] The Four Saints form the core of the rituals of the Tianxin zhengfa. This tradition is not explicitly invoked in our text, but both can be considered as expressions of a larger milieu of exorcistic priests.

42. This work exists in two versions that differ only in details; one is an independent work in the Daoist canon, the other is j. 103 of the great encyclopedia *Yunji qiqian*, compiled a few years later by Zhang Junfang 張君房 (fl. 1008–25). I find the former more reliable than the latter. It was largely circulated and is frequently quoted in Song and later sources. For an introduction and full annotated translation, see Goossaert, *Vies des saints exorcistes*, 3–55.

43. On the medieval exorcistic tradition centered on Beidi, see Mollier, "La méthode de l'empereur du nord du mont Fengdu."

The author, Wang Qinruo 王欽若 (962–1025), was one of the most prominent ministers of Emperor Zhenzong 真宗 (r. 997–1022); the *Yisheng baode zhuan* is the only complete book from him that was transmitted. Wang left his imprint on many aspects of early Song politics when he was in power (997–1019 and again 1022–25) but is most famous for ritual reforms.[44] As a religious (notably Daoist, but not exclusively so) advisor to Emperor Zhenzong, Wang Qinruo compiled this hagiography on his demand, as the emperor had just canonized the god as the Transcendent Lord who assists the Saint and protects virtue in 1014. There he documents and rewrites the story of the interactions between the Daoist cult and the reign of Zhenzong's father and predecessor, Emperor Taizong 太宗 (r. 976–97). The same year, Wang was put in charge of compiling a new Daoist canon, which is now lost.

The hagiography relates how a certain Zhang Shouzhen 張守真 (930–96) began in 960 (the very year of the foundation of the Song dynasty) to receive revelations from a god—Black Killer—who first talked to him out of thin air. Zhang was scared and tried to escape, but the voice followed him and eventually said: "I have been ordered (by the Jade Emperor) to manifest myself in this world, why are you so obdurate and don't listen to my words?" 吾受命降靈, 汝何為頑梗如此, 不聽吾言.[45] Zhang expressed his unwillingness to become a vulgar medium, and the god explained this would not be the case, as he would instead become a respected official. Zhang then became a Daoist at the local monastery, built a small temple for his god, and started performing revelations, asking him questions and causing patrons to hear the divine answers. As a result, Black Killer not only healed people and proffered various teachings but also predicted the death of the founding emperor in 976 and the enthronement of his brother Taizong as the second emperor. The latter immediately built a magnificent temple, Shangqing

44. Unlike the majority of the Song court, composed of northern military men, Wang Qinruo was a southerner, and he may have met Tianxin zhengfa practitioners before going to the Song court.

45. *Yisheng baode zhuan*, 1.1a.

taipinggong 上清太平宮 for the god and his interpreter Zhang Shouzhen, and it was completed in 980 at the foot of the Zhongnan Mountains 終南山, west of today's Xi'an; this well-documented temple remained prominent until at least the Mongol Yuan period, and it was recently rebuilt.

The larger part of the hagiography relates various miracles and revelations from Black Killer to Zhang Shouzhen and other people, dated between 960 and 994. Many of the revelations have theological and liturgical contents. At the outset of his training, Zhang Shouzhen learns from Black Killer two sets of ritual techniques: exorcistic rites—called "sword rites," *jianfa* 劍法—and a codification of *jiao* offerings with the lists of gods to invite. This codification was subsequently adopted in the official Daoist liturgy for state rituals and Wang Qinruo himself presented a liturgy for the *luotian dajiao* 羅天大醮 (Great Offering of All Heaven), together with the hagiography, to the throne. These parallel liturgies clearly express the double identity of Zhang Shouzhen as exorcistic priest, *fashi*, and Daoist, *daoshi*. Other revelations, often in poetic form, concern political prophecies and private predictions, as well as moral exhortations. Revelations and injunctions delivered by Black Killer are brutal; the god never shies away from physical threat and a language of violence that fits the martial character of the rites that deploy him.[46]

The *Yisheng baode zhuan* has mostly attracted historians' attention for the light it sheds on the (possibly murderous) imperial succession in 976. It relates how the future Taizong, still a prince, received prophecies from Black Killer, which must have caused alarm at Taizu's court. The latter summoned Zhang Shouzhen, who produced new prophecies announcing Taizong's imperial destiny; the emperor died the next day, his brother Taizong had himself immediately enthroned and showered Zhang and his god with honors.[47] This context is crucial to understanding

46. On legitimate violence in Chinese religion, see Ter Haar, *Religious Culture and Violence*.

47. Wei Bing, " 'Zhang Shouzhen shenjiang' kaoyi," is the finest study of the various accounts of these events. He shows that the *Yisheng baode zhuan* is a much rewritten

the rise of the cult, the abundance of sources about Zhang Shouzhen, and the writing of a hagiography by one of the most eminent officials of the time; yet, most of the book is not about politics but about Zhang's life and his ritual services in the context of local society.[48] We have other sources on Zhang Shouzhen, and the most remarkable is a biography carved on a stele erected by his own son, Zhang Yuanji 張元濟, in 999. It coheres well with Wang Qinruo's work but adds some information, such as the fact that people called him Zhang Black Killer, showing to what extent the identities of the priest and his allied god were intertwined.[49]

The structure of the hagiography is threefold: the first *juan* is a linear chronology following Zhang Shouzhen from his first encounter with Black Killer until his death; the second relates various miracles, mostly exorcisms, that the god performed for individuals, either officials or simple subjects; and the third, again taking up the whole chronology, provides a verbatim account of the main revelations proffered by Black Killer, most of them as poems. These revelations were immediately and largely circulated; many are quoted in extenso in an official history of the dynasty's first reigns,[50] as well as in later works.

The content of the revelations is very diverse: to his ally Zhang Shouzhen, Black Killer teaches the fundamentals of theology and liturgy. They notably introduce the most important theological innovation of that period, that is, the status of the Jade Emperor as the head of the pantheon of the gods of creation (i.e., all local gods) and the Daoist

account compared to earlier sources. Wei also suggests that the last events in the hagiography, where Black Killer announces the end of his revelations shortly before Zhang Shouzhen's death, is also a political machination; Taizong, who died just after Zhang, did not want the latter's prophecies to interfere in his own succession and had him silenced, maybe by poisoning.

48. The best study from a religious history perspective is Davis, *Society and the Supernatural*, chap. 4; see also Andersen, *Paradox of Being*, 141–43; Soymié, "Histoire et philologie de la Chine médiévale et moderne."

49. *Song Zhuanying dafashi xingzhuang* 宋傳應大法師行狀, *Jinshi cuibian*, 134.2b–4a.

50. *Songchao shishi*, 7.115–21.

name for the Heaven of imperial sacrifices.[51] To officials and commoners, Black Killer provides more practical teachings: he answers their questions about their destinies and repeatedly dispenses moral exhortations.

What was the precise modus operandi of Black Killer's revelations, systematically qualified as *jiangyan* 降言? As said above, Zhang Shouzhen is portrayed saying he did not want to be a medium, because the latter are socially despised. Indeed, what is described is not (or at least not always) possession because he remains conscious and exerts agency. Sometimes, he talks with Black Killer in private; early sources (documents from the Song court and collections of anecdotes) claim that the god manifested himself in Zhang's room with the voice of a small child, which only he could understand.[52] In several cases in the hagiography, however, there are witnesses who can hear, which implies that Zhang resorts to a ritual technique, nowhere described in the hagiography, that allows him to make the god heard by other persons. He seems to learn this technique gradually as the first manifestations take him by surprise, in an uncontrolled manner, *hu* 忽, a term for the not-fully controlled manifestation of divine presence used throughout history. We might conjecture that he was a shaman who dialogued with his god; but this does not fit well with the fact that sometimes the god talked with Zhang and other times with a devotee (without Zhang being part of the discussion). Edward Davis has proposed that, like countless other exorcists in the Song and Yuan periods, Zhang Shouzhen induces and controls the possession of a medium in his service rather than being possessed himself. I find the hypothesis very convincing. Admittedly, neither the *Yisheng baode zhuan* nor any other source mentions such a medium, but such is the case of almost all narratives of *daofa* exorcism, which would be hard to understand if we did not have the liturgical manuals (in the Daoist canon) that detail the role of the medium.[53]

51. Hsieh Ts'ung-hui, *Xin tiandi zhi ming*, chap. 2.
52. *Songchao shishi*, 7.115.
53. Davis, *Society and the Supernatural in Song China*, 79–80.

The alliance promised by the god to his disciples is a key theme running through the hagiography; it first concerns Zhang Shouzhen but is then extended to a whole host of other individuals, from high officials to a humble, illiterate soldier. To Li Zhu 李鑄, the civil official sent by the Song court to manage the temple, Black Killer repeatedly says that they will work together, not in view of ascetic self-cultivation but to govern the population and save people ("With me, you will . . ." 與吾), acquire merits, and obtain long life and a posthumous destiny as a god. With all his interlocutors, including Emperor Taizong, Black Killer goes back and forth, in a direct style devoid of any rhetorical flourish, between the promise of divine blessings and divinization on the one hand and the threat of bloody execution in case of amoral behavior on the other. Such language will be carried over in a large number of tracts revealed by spirit-writing from the Song period down to the present.[54]

With the *Yisheng baode zhuan* we thus have a record of questions and answers between ordinary people and a god under the control of a Daoist priest. These revelations were, in some of the cases, given in public, with an audience, and were noted, disseminated, and printed. We have earlier records of discussions between the living and gods (notably the medieval *Zhengao* and Daoxuan's record), but this is the earliest (as far as I am aware) systematic record of the public oral revelations of a god, a genre that would later become very popular in the form of the "recorded sayings," *yulu* 語錄—the same term used for the records of exchanges between living Chan, Neo-Confucian, or Daoist masters with their disciples.

The revelations of Black Killer have been compiled in the context of another set of revelations in which Wang Qinruo played a role, the so-called "heavenly letters," *tianshu* 天書, affair of 1008. These were auspicious documents that led the emperor to perform the *feng* 封 and *shan* 禪 sacrifices atop Taishan 泰山 the same year, thus claiming the

54. One may for instance compare the poem Black Killer gives to Taizong in *Yisheng baode zhuan*, 1.5b–6a, to the *Wudangshan Xuantian shangdi chuixunwen*, discussed in chapter 5.

status of an accomplished emperor having brought universal peace. Both revelations partake of the same logic of the Daoist legitimation for the dynasty and are well known by historians for this reason, but I would like to mention the "heavenly letters" here from the perspective of revelatory techniques.[55]

The producer of the revelations was a certain Wang Jie 王捷, who first met a Daoist who gave him an elixir and a sword (the encounter trope, type 2) and then learned this Daoist was in fact a high god, Siming zhenjun 司命真君, Transcendent Lord Director of Destinies. Then the lord made himself present on his bed curtain in a visible form and also spoke to him.[56] A court minister, Liu Chenggui 劉承珪, was witness to this and relayed the revelations to the emperor, who soon invited Wang and Liu to perform the manifestation of the god's presence in the palace. Wang's home was turned into a Daoist temple, and Liu was divinized (a statue of him was set up in that temple). The emperor dreamed of him as well, and then a major manifestation took place: the emperor saw the god coming down to his room with his divine retinue. The god revealed himself to be the ancestor of the Zhao imperial family and protector of the dynasty; his cult henceforth became a major part of official rituals. In this story, we thus have a combination of various techniques deployed by a local ritual specialist promoted to the status of officially sanctioned Daoist priest, who could make gods appear and speak for his patrons, on a cloth, as sounds, and in dreams.[57]

Another early case of Daoists publicizing oral communications from their gods is offered by an inscription from the Chengdu area (Sichuan). This document is not well dated (the possible dates range from 1012 to 1252), but I favor an early date.[58] In it we read how a Daoist wanted to create a grotto shrine to a local saint and interrogated the transcendent

55. Lamouroux, "Rites, espaces et finances"; Cahill, "Taoism at the Sung Court."

56. Barend ter Haar shrewdly suggested to me that the curtain appearance may be the result of skillful shadow puppetry.

57. *Songchao shishi*, 7.110–12.

58. *Zhengfayuan Zhu zhenren dong ji* 正法院朱真人洞記, *Daojia jinshilüe*, 424–25. I will develop a full-fledged analysis of this remarkable document in a separate study.

officials 真官, who repeatedly gave him (*jiangyan*) detailed instructions. The author, a disciple of this Daoist, signs with a Tianxin zhengfa ordination title. Here again, we have Daoists of the new exorcistic traditions who publicly make their divine associates speak and publicize their revelations; this is a new phenomenon, as I do not find equivalents before the Song.

We will see more cases where oral and written revelations are part of the same event, but I would like to draw attention here to the fact that the opposition between "popular" revelations from low-ranking spirits as oral utterances of mediums on the one hand, and "elite" spirit-written revelations from high gods on the other—which is often claimed by scholars as a structural feature of Chinese religions—may be true (in many cases at least) in contemporary times, but it should not be read back onto early modern sources.

3.3.2. Divinely Inspired Dreams

Dreams are a very significant vector of religious innovation in early modern times. For instance, Liu Deren 劉德仁 (1122–80) experienced a dreamlike revelation on the meaning of the *Daodejing*, on which basis he founded his school, the Zhendadao 真大道, an important presence in northern China for at least two centuries.[59] Unfortunately, we have neither detailed accounts of the revelation (it is only tersely mentioned in a stele inscription) nor any transmitted Zhendadao teachings.

Dreams would seem at first sight to lie outside the field of ritually induced modes of divine presence, and I have included dreams among type 2 (encounter) in my typology. However, we have just seen that in ritual procedures Daoists could ask questions of the gods and expect a response in a dream, which shows that this was considered as a procedure under some sort of control. A tenth-century story relates how a Daoist priest put a theological question (why is spirit money necessary?)

59. Bussio, "Neither Dust nor Gold," 43–44; Chen Yuan, *Nan Song chu Hebei xin daojiao kao*, 81–89.

to a god and obtained a response in a dream.[60] Dreams were thus brought into the realm of presence-type revelations, that is, controlled by priests—of course, most dreams continued to be experienced by people as encounters, that is, divine-agency events. Ritually induced dreams, unlike other modes of the presence type, do not involve a medium but work along the same ritual logic.

Such techniques were also made available as a service to ordinary people: they are not public (Daoists have not found ritual means to produce collective dreams) but are open to all, and the contents of the revelation can be later shared and printed. Dreaming temples have been active since the early modern period, where the vision of gods in dreams is arranged through ritual preparations.[61] Such dreams also frequently happen (in the narrative evidence) during multiday rituals, when the gods are around. In Song- and Yuan-period liturgies we find instructions on how to induce such dreams. A Zhenwu scripture contains this very explicit incantation: "We pray you to manifest your divine presence in response and to enter our dream, so as to show us what is permissible or not" 乞降靈應入夢，示人可否.[62] Dreaming and spirit-writing are very often closely associated.

One important early moral guide for *fashi* priests, the *Taiwei xianjun gongguoge* 太微仙君功過格 (Ledger of merits and demerits of the Stellar Lord Taiwei; probably linked to the Jingmingfa 淨明法, one of the most important *daofa*), which later spurred the development of spirit-written morality books, was revealed in 1171 through a dream.[63] Its preface recounts:

60. "Nanyue zhenjun 南嶽真君," *Taiping guangji*, 40.256, quoting Sun Guangxian's 孫光憲 (?–968) *Beimeng suoyan* 北夢瑣言.

61. Baptandier, "Entrer en montagne pour y rêver."

62. *Taishang yuanshi tianzun shuo Beidi fumo shenzhou miaojing*, 9.11b.

63. On this text, see Brokaw, *Ledgers*, chap. 1; and Goossaert, "Divine Codes." Barend ter Haar, "Book Review," shows that the connection with Jingmingfa is uncertain, but I find sufficient overall coherence between the Ledger and the Jingming corpus to maintain it.

> The second day of the second month of spring in the *xingmao* year of the Dading reign (1171), at the *zi* hour, I found myself in dream in audience in the Purple Palace of the Immortal Lord of Great Tenuity. I received from him the "Ledger of Merits and Demerits" so that I could transmit it to the faithful. I suddenly woke up from this dream and could clearly remember each item of merit and demerit; then I dressed up and sat, thinking silently about this experience, and realized that a high dignitary among the immortals had manifested his divine presence to me, and I could not allow any negligence on my part. I adjusted my robe and crown, prepared ink and paper, and swiftly noted down (this revelation), without thinking about it and allowing my own ideas to interfere.
>
> 余於大定辛卯之歲，仲春二日子正之時，夢遊紫府，朝禮太微仙君，得受功過之格，令傳信心之士。忽然夢覺，遂思功過，條目歷歷明了，尋乃披衣正坐，默而思之，知是高仙降靈，不敢疏慢，遂整衣戴冠，滌硯揮牋，走筆書之，不時而就，皆出乎無思，非干於用意。[64]

3.3.3. Divine Writing

Spirit-writing, for which the most common term in early modern times is *jiangbi* 降筆, is one among an array of techniques of perceptible presence. It has often been compared to the visualization practices of the Shangqing revelations, but because it relies on talismans to summon the gods, it is actually just as comparable to the summoning techniques, such as those of the Eight Archivists. The latter were used in early medieval times for divination, as was early modern spirit-writing, but the practice was also applied to the production of revelations. In its lexicon (*jiangbi* as parallel to *jiangyan*), the context in which it was codified (to obtain divine responses in the process of expediting ritual paperwork), and the style of the public revelations it produced, spirit-writing is clearly part of the larger category that also included controlled talking mediums and dreams.

The *fashi* priests and the mediums under their control often produced oral utterances, written words and other documents, and movements at the same time. A story of such a priest, Zhao Zujian 趙祖

64. *Taiwei xianjun gongguoge*, preface.

堅, told in Hong Mai's 洪邁 (1123–1202) *Yijianzhi* 夷堅志 (Records of the listener) shows this clearly. Zhao was a practitioner of the Tianxin zhengfa who had to resign from his heavenly appointment because one of the spirits under his command had become corrupted. He then wanted to learn thunder rites and prayed to one of his divinized patriarchs. During a ritual, the patriarch possessed the medium under Zhao's control and told him he would teach him the rites and give him the relevant talismans; a dialogue ensued and the patriarch told him to prepare paper. After a while, the patriarch told him (through the medium) to take the sheets of paper, and they were indeed covered with the required talismans.[65] This is not conventional spirit-writing (although it is akin to automatic writing techniques of which we will see more cases), but it shows how *daofa* rituals with controlled possession implied the revelation of written content from gods to humans, among other effects of divine presence. As we will now see in the next chapter, spirit-writing rose to become the most successful and influential of all presence-type ritual techniques.

65. "Tan zhenren 譚真人," *Yijianzhi*, zhiyi 支乙, j. 5, 830–31. This story is discussed in Davis, *Society and the Supernatural*, 80–83; and Goossaert, *Bureaucratie et salut*, 101–3.

CHAPTER FOUR

The Development of Spirit-Writing, 1000–1400

I have defined spirit-writing as any technique where spirits (from high gods to recently deceased humans) are invited through prescribed ritual means (typically involving incantations and talismans) to possess either a writing implement (a brush or piece of wood) and/or the person(s) wielding this implement in order to write messages, often in response to questions.

In this chapter we look through the evidence on the various forms of spirit-writing dating from the early modern period in order to determine its contours and logic; some of these sources are not well dated, so I will proceed analytically before attempting to sketch a historical development in the conclusion. This chapter will look at the practice of spirit-writing (who, where, why, and how?), and the next one will focus on the revelations themselves and their contents.

4.1. Technical Terms

Terms that can be translated as spirit-writing according to our definition include: "making a god present in a brush," *jiangbi* 降筆; "wielding the sieve," *fuji* 扶箕; "sieve brush," *jibi* 箕筆; "wielding the phoenix," *fuluan* 扶鸞; "making the phoenix fly," *feiluan* 飛鸞; "phoenix sieve," *luanji* 鸞箕; "phoenix brush," *luanbi* 鸞筆; "summoning immortals," *zhaoxian* 召仙; "inviting immortals," *qingxian* 請仙; "welcoming the Purple Maiden," *ying Zigu* 迎紫姑; "making immortals manifest themselves," *jiangxian* 降仙; "consecrating an arm," *fengbi* 封臂; "obtaining a god-written response on a document submitted to him," *pijiang* 批降; "brush register," *bilu* 筆錄; and further combinations of these terms. The most common word in modern usage, *fuji* 扶乩, only appears in the late Ming, and I will discuss it in chapter 6.

The abundant vocabulary describing spirit-writing clearly shows that it was not a monolithic tradition but something that was constantly adopted, adapted, and elaborated by various parties toward various aims. Some of these terms refer to the specific implement being used: the sieve or winnowing basket (*ji*); and the phoenix (*luan*), a wooden iconic instrument. Others refer to the divine entities being made present. Yet others refer to the human action being performed. Many of these terms refer to specific traditions of spirit-writing but are often not strictly distinguished; in many instances, different terms are used in a single story and appear to be interchangeable. *Jiangbi* seems to be the most general, encompassing term, as well as the most common, until the Ming.

To what extent these various spirit-writing practices interacted or were independent traditions is unclear in the present state of research. They seem to have served different primary functions, even though important overlaps may have existed. The flying phoenix produced scriptures, whereas the Daoist priestly techniques (such as *pijiang* or *fengbi*, discussed in chapter 3) largely served the need for judicial paperwork in the course of conducting exorcistic judgments and ordinations, and the sieve technique was apparently closely associated with divination, that is, asking the gods specific questions about one's life. Another major function of spirit-writing, healing, is not well documented in the early records, but by the Qing dynasty it had become prominent.

Hsieh Ts'ung-hui has argued for a strict distinction between the *feiluan* and the *fuji* (wielding the sieve) traditions. He proposes that the latter is popular and essentially aimed at divination, whereas the former is elite and entirely integrated into the cult of the Jade Emperor; *feiluan* practitioners saw themselves as ministers of the heavenly bureaucracy and as transmitters, through *feiluan* revelations, of the edicts and orders of the Jade Emperor.[1] His analysis has radically renewed our understanding of spirit-writing, and I wish to refine and nuance it further. High gods other than Wenchang also revealed scriptures under the authority of the Jade Emperor, yet without using the *luan* vocabulary. Terms were often recombined by authors; a late Yuan account discusses "suspended sieve, wielding the phoenix, and summoning immortals" 懸箕扶鸞召仙 apparently not as different practices but as a single one.[2]

My own approach is to view spirit-writing as codified and in most cases practiced as part of the *fashi* priests' techniques to make gods intervene in human affairs; these priests are all by definition heavenly officials and evince a strong bureaucratic ethos. From this perspective, *feiluan* is merely one of the forms of a larger phenomenon in continuity with *fuji*. This is a heuristic advantage of working with spirit-writing as an etic term rather than with emic terms only.

4.2. Contexts and Purposes

4.2.1. The Purple Maiden Cult

Most scholars who have discussed the origins of spirit-writing trace it to the cult of the Purple Maiden, Zigu 紫姑, or the Goddess of the Privy.[3]

1. Hsieh Ts'ung-hui, *Xin tiandi zhi ming*, 105–12. Wang Chien-ch'uan ("Song-Ming shiqi") has criticized this interpretation, suggesting that *feiluan* is first and foremost a technical term for a spirit-writing technique without a human medium holding the writing instrument.

2. "Jixian yongshi 箕仙詠史," *Nancun chuogenglu*, 20:245–46; this provides the full text of a long spirit-written poem recounting the whole history of China.

3. Xu Dishan, *Fuji mixin de yanjiu*; Chao Wei-pang, "Origin and Growth of the Fu

The Purple Maiden was a concubine who died at the hands of her husband's cruel wife and became a protective deity, especially for women. The cult is attested since early medieval times, but records from the tenth century show that by then, summoning this deity involved writing messages: a sieve or winnowing basket would be dressed like her, with a chopstick inserted into it, and the object was manipulated in order to write.[4] This practice was called "wielding the sieve," *fuji* 扶箕. Originally practiced once a year on the maiden's death day by women, who asked questions about their lives—such a practice was still alive in the modern period—it was eventually adopted by literate men. We do not have extant texts revealed by this means other than short poems, some of them revealed not only by Zigu but also by deceased humans. It thus seems that the practice of writing with a sieve that originated in the Purple Maiden cult was soon adopted in different contexts, where the term Zigu may or may not be used and if used would refer to the technique rather than the deity.

An important and oft-quoted source is a discussion by the celebrated polymath Shen Kua 沈括 (1031–95). Shen calls the practice "welcoming Zigu," 迎紫姑. He mentions that he used to do it playfully as a child but was once scared and stopped doing it. He also mentions other instances among literati. He recounts:

> During the Jingyou era (1034–38), the Erudite in Ritual Wang Lun had "welcoming Zigu" performed at his home and a goddess made herself present in the body of a young girl. She claimed to be among the women of the harem of Shangdi (God of Heaven) and was very good at writing prose; her texts were clear and elegant. They circulate today under the title of *Anthology of the Female Immortal.*
>
> 景祐中，太常博士王綸家因迎紫姑，有神降其閨女，自稱上帝後宮諸女，能文章，頗清麗，今謂之《女仙集》，行于世。[5]

Chi"; Boltz, "On the Legacy of Zigu"; Wang Chien-ch'uan, "Song-Ming shiqi"; He Lei, "Songdai 'jixian' shi kaolun."

4. The earliest description is found in Xu Xuan's 徐鉉 (917–92) *Jishenlu*, 6.14b; see Kleeman, *God's Own Tale*, 8–9.

5. *Mengxi bitan*, 21.5a–b.

Shen, who had seen the originals, admired the calligraphy. Here is a clear case of spirit-writing combined with other forms of producing divine presence (including possession), since the female immortals are visible and audible; Shen comments on their beauty and their music. Only the upper half of the immortals' bodies was visible, and one once took young girls on her cloud for a tour with her. Shen also notes that the immortals knew medicine, which suggests their revelations could be used for cures. That Purple Maiden spirit-writing was seen as continuous with other techniques for producing divine presence is also documented by other southern stories. Hong Mai related the case of a young man having a romantic affair with a young woman who manifested herself in his room. To his predictably alarmed father, the young man explained that she was what people call the Purple Maiden, but he was able to have physical contact, whereas ordinary people could only have exchanges with her in writing (in other words, he flaunted his superior skills or merits); indeed, his brother tried to negotiate with the otherworldly girl through spirit-writing and asked why he could not see her when his brother could.[6]

The term "welcoming Zigu," however, is rare in the extant documentation; we have only a few other mentions from the poets Su Shi 蘇軾 (Dongpo 東坡, 1037–1101) and Lu You 陸游 (1125–1210). Su recounts how a puppet manipulated by children (*tongzi*, which here probably means real children rather than mediums) wrote with a chopstick; the goddess thereby recounted her life and wrote poems. He also informs us that in most cases the goddess only wrote a few words, but in one house, she would answer questions and sometimes use a beautiful but illegible archaic script.[7] Su Dongpo relates another séance with the sieve that took place in 1094 in the room of a Daoist master with a lofty title—

6. "Zheng Mingzhi 鄭明之," *Yijianzhi*, bu 補, j. 13, 1667–68. In the end, the divine girl made some accurate predictions and caused no harm; the story was told to Hong Mai by the brother's son.

7. "Zigushen ji 紫姑神記," "Tianzhuan ji 天篆記," *Dongpo quanji*, 38.14a–15b and 15b–16b.

suggesting this was a technique used by Daoists: "a divine being made itself present in his room, saying she was a female transcendent" 有神仙降於其室，自言女仙也; she wrote high-brow mystical poetry, which Su judged to be incomparable with Zigu's vulgar utterances.[8]

There are some more mentions of spirit-writing that are connected to the Purple Maiden during the Southern Song, in essays and poems by literati as well as anecdotes.[9] Scholars, starting from Xu Dishan, have relied on the few records of this particular practice to argue that spirit-writing was, from its origins, largely a lay practice that people usually engaged in playfully to exchange poetry with the deceased or imaginary friends, such as young, talented female ghosts. Such a practice concerns only a very small proportion of the evidence about early modern spirit-writing, which is largely about communal rituals, divining serious business, or instructing humans in religious techniques. Indeed, many records about spirit-writing, and producing divine presence in general, make a point of cautioning against playfulness lest it be interpreted as disrespect for the gods, as well as the dangers of inviting gods and spirits in unclean spaces or futile circumstances.[10] The Daoist literature is replete with cautionary stories about how easy it is to summon gods (including for spirit-writing) but that doing so without good reason may anger them, and an angry thunder god is a very scary prospect.[11]

It seems that the Purple Maiden cult was originally a divination technique implying possession. By the eleventh century, some people

8. *Dongpo zhilin*, 3.96.

9. Wang Chien-ch'uan, "Song-Ming shiqi." Bikir, "Divination et destinée sous la dynastie Song," 191–97, provides a comprehensive list of twenty anecdotes concerning the Zigu spirit-writing cult in the *Yijianzhi* as well as a preliminary analysis (but does not discuss the other cases of spirit-writing not mentioning Zigu that I discuss in the present book).

10. "Xi'an Zigu 西安紫姑," *Yijianzhi*, zhijing 支景, j. 6, 928–29, where a participant in a spirit-writing session is punished by the god for having brought in a prostitute.

11. Goossaert, "Scorched Head Daoists" and *Vies des saints exorcistes*, 205–25. Already in medieval times, manuals for summoning the gods warned of the awful consequences of summoning them for no good reason and keeping the gods present for too long; see Andersen, "Talking to the Gods," 15.

developed it into a way of writing more developed texts. These are among the earliest mentions of spirit-written texts, but they only account for a tiny minority of texts produced. Yet, the practice was soon adopted by Daoists, who integrated it into their repertoire of presence rites.

4.2.2. Divination

Most of the records mentioning the Purple Maiden (either the deity herself or the practice of "inviting Zigu") concern divination, and we have many more instances (not mentioning her) of spirit-writing using either a sieve or other implements to ask questions of spirits about future events and the fate of the dead. In some of the anecdotal stories, the Purple Maiden cult is a regular, long-term, domestic-based worship where the god advises a family through business.[12] Anecdotal records document how spirit-writing also was, early on, used as an ad hoc technique by literati in anguish about their personal fate or examination results (gods routinely decline to disclose the examination topics in advance), generals and officers seeking to divine the outcome of battles, or even magistrates trying to solve criminal cases (in which case spirit-writing becomes one of the ritual means to enact divine as well as this-worldly justice).[13] In such cases they resorted to spirit-writing experts—apparently some well-staffed officials even had a resident expert.

A telling example is provided by a story included in a late Song compilation of the cult of the god of Lushan (northern Jiangxi). The story tells about a revolt staged in 1206 by a military officer in Sichuan. The Song general fighting him had in his retinue a man who was "good at

12. "Bilantang 碧瀾堂," *Yijianzhi, jiazhi* 甲志, j. 16, 140.

13. There are several such cases in the *Yijianzhi*. "Xinchengxian zei 新城縣賊," *Yijianzhi, bu* 補, j. 13, 1668, is especially interesting because the magistrate insists he has never asked a favor or put a question to the gods for his personal interest (for fear of being disrespectful, *dushen* 瀆神) but now addresses the gods through a spirit-writing specialist (in a Daoist monastery) only because this is a matter of life-and-death for the people under his charge, thus showing the very opposite of the playful attitude sometimes attributed to literati.

making all sorts of gods manifest their presence" 善降諸神; he performed spirit-writing, *jibi* 箕筆, and received a message (the god is not identified here, but another passage confirms it was the god of Lushan[14]) stating that Shangdi would execute the rebel but that this divine decision should be kept secret for three months. The general "became terrified that he may leak the (secret) divine words and thereby provoke misfortune, so he sealed the spirit-written document" 懼泄神語召禍, 緘封甚密.[15] The secret nature of divine revelations concerning state affairs echoes similar remarks found in the oral revelations of Black Killer, as well as stories about Zhenwu, such as the one concerning a traveling official who first sees Zhenwu appear and then hears him speak (*jiangyan*); Zhenwu enjoins him to keep the information he gives secret and for the emperor's ear only.[16] This sets us in a very different world from the playful poetry exchanged between literati and their dead friends.

Spirit-writing also developed into more permanent, institutionalized ways of questioning the gods. We have seen how priests deployed spirit-writing, along with other presence-type techniques, as a way to routinely communicate with the gods during rituals. They also devised ways to provide such access to laypeople. This service met with massive demand in the context of the temple-centric and god-centric society of early modern China, where personal gods became very important in people's lives.[17]

One of the ways in which people, from the Song onward, could question their favorite personal god was through oracles, *lingqian* 靈籤, numbered sets of cryptic poems that constitute the answer to the question of a devotee who selects a stick in a box (the number on the stick

14. *Lushan Taiping xingguogong Caifang zhenjun shishi*, 3.15a.

15. "Kaixi zhu ni Xi shi 開禧誅逆曦事," *Lushan Taiping xingguogong Caifang zhenjun shishi*, 7.12b–14a.

16. "Zhenhe xingfu 鎮河興福," *Xuantian shangdi qishenglu*, 6.6b–7b.

17. There is an abundant literature on the rise of temples cults during the Song period and its connections to the making of modern Chinese society; a recent and comprehensive overview is Lagerwey, "Introduction: Special Issue on the Emergence."

points to the appropriate poem, which often needs to be interpreted to fit the question).[18] The connection between oracles and spirit-writing is extremely intimate. Of the eight sets of oracles in the *Daozang*, all dating from the Southern Song, Yuan, or early Ming periods, almost all are from deities known to practice spirit-writing: Zhenwu, Wenchang, and the Xu 徐 brothers (discussed in chapter 5). Furthermore, as is frequently the case in later times, at least one set presents itself explicitly as having been revealed through spirit-writing: the undated *Sisheng zhenjun lingqian* 四聖真君靈籤 (Oracles of the Four Saints Transcendent Lords) begins with "sagely words to admonish the world (revealed by) manifested divine presence" 降靈勸世格言, an obviously spirit-written moral tract that provides a framework for the contents of the forty-nine oracles. Another case is Wenchang's oracles, which are preceded by a preface spirit-written by himself, where he explains that he used to answer questions from his devotees through dreams, but because of the demand in his temples, he has composed this set of oracles.[19] A Southern Song scholar also discusses approvingly another set of oracles revealed through *jibi* 箕筆.[20]

Spirit-writing divination services for individual, ordinary purposes may have been as common and frequent in early modern times as they are in the twenty-first century, but as such, divination is not often mentioned in early modern sources. Not surprisingly, more portentous questions about collective destinies have attracted more attention in the transmitted sources. This is a dimension of spirit-writing that certainly contributed both to its popularity and its being banned by successive imperial regimes: prophecies about disasters and regime change, often in an apocalyptic setting, sometimes went hand-in-hand with spirit-writing, as we shall see in chapter 5.

18. Kalinowski, "La littérature divinatoire dans le Daozang"; Strickmann, *Chinese Poetry and Prophecy*.

19. *Xuanzhen lingying baoqian*.

20. Liu Kezhuang 劉克莊 (1187–1269), "Ba Cijiqian 跋慈濟籤," *Quan Songwen*, 330.61.

4.2.3. Ritual Contexts

Like all ritual services, spirit-writing could be offered in temples, in the homes of patrons who requested the service from a specialist for a private or family ritual, or during communal rituals in public spaces; we have early modern narrative accounts for all three contexts. The third case is important because it shows how spirit-writing was articulated with other ritual techniques for producing divine presence. We have already seen in the previous chapter that spirit-writing techniques were largely employed, among other ways of creating divine presence, by priests in the course of their communications with the gods. Such communications were not necessarily public or performed for audiences. There were, however, other occasions, notably toward the end of a communal celebration, especially *jiao* 醮 offerings when all the gods were invited, which created an appropriate venue for members of the community to question the gods. Let me mention a later source, a Ming anecdote, to show how this practice continued after the Song. The leader of a militia in Huizhou, after fighting bandits, sponsored a large Daoist ritual at the main local Daoist temple for the salvation of the dead militiamen. Then, during the ritual, Lord Deng, the fierce thunder god we have already met, spirit-wrote (*jiangbi*) that the leader had also committed crimes and would be punished, which of course happened.[21] Here, we have a commonly seen context for spirit-writing: communal ritual, thunder gods, and moral judgment.

Revelations during a *jiao* are not limited to explicit spirit-writing cases; it was already the case in the *Yisheng baode zhuan*, where Black Killer gave several pronouncements during a *jiao*. There is also the fascinating case of a short scripture revealed in northern China in 1143, the *Taishang yuhua dongzhang bawang dushi shengxian miaojing* 太上玉華洞章拔亡度世昇仙妙經 (Marvelous scripture of the cavern stanzas of the jade flower of the Supreme [Lord] for rescuing souls from hell, saving the world, and ascension to Heaven), a sutra-type scenario for saving

21. "Deng tianjun jiangbi 鄧天君降筆," *Kezuo xinwen*, 10.400.

humans through morality and alchemy. Appended to the scripture is a detailed narrative of the revelations: a young shepherd boy after having encountered an immortal started to divine and heal people; the Daoists of the local dilapidated monastery invited him and built him a hermitage so that he could heal people there and generate donations for the monastery. The boy told them he had a scripture not yet revealed to the world 余有太上真經一卷，未行於世; the Daoists organized three successive *jiao* during which they received 傳授 the scripture written on silk, which they then had printed and disseminated. Here we have a presence-type revelation, and it is likely the Daoists acted as *fashi* controlling the young medium, even though it remains unclear whether the medium boy was writing or speaking.[22]

One late Yuan description of a ritual performed in a Hangzhou temple in 1356, praying for rain, relates how the god, once present, started to spirit-write (*jiangbi*) about himself.[23] Another Mongol-period story relates how a man who had struck it rich during the early years of the Yuan period met the Zhang Heavenly Master in Nanjing, and asked him to perform a *jiao* offering and to practice spirit-writing 召神降筆 during the ritual so as to learn about his destiny. The pontiff obliged and set up a suspended phoenix 縣鸞筆, which then wrote a message predicting imminent disaster for the patron.[24]

A related context is funerals. It is still common for priests or mediums to have the dead for whom the salvation ritual is being performed to be made present toward the end of the process and ensure she or he is now safe and happy. Although this is most often done by oral possession, there are also cases of spirit-writing.[25]

22. "Xu chuanshou jing shi 敘傳授經事," appendix to *Taishang yuhua dongzhang bawang dushi shengxian miaojing*.

23. "Lidi 厲狄," *Nancun chuogenglu*, 27:342.

24. *Yinju tongyi*, 30.13a. *Xian* 縣 is a common substitute for *xuan* 懸, "suspended."

25. *Shanfang suibi*, 1.14a, provides a Yuan-period example (using the term *jiangbi*). For a discussion of modern and contemporary practices, see Wang Chien-ch'uan, "Jindai fuji tuanti zhong de youming yu wangling duihua."

4.2.4. Divinization and Self-Divinization

Revelation techniques have been used to process divinization and for the promotion of living and deceased adepts since medieval times: we have seen that the Church of the Heavenly Master may have used mediums to that end, and dialogues between Yang Xi or other Shangqing practitioners and the transcendents during visualization séances often dealt with such issues. As seen in the previous chapter, in the early modern period, both visualizations and presence-type techniques were used to produce divine appointments, often with a formal nomination edict issued by heavenly authorities. Buddhists also resorted to revelatory techniques to ascertain whether someone had been reborn in the Pure Land, but whereas mediums had been used previously, dreams had by early modern times become the favored Buddhist means for confirming apotheosis.[26] In contrast, the Daoist presence-type techniques allowed for more detailed information and dialogue.

A story found in the *Xuantian shangdi qishenglu* 玄天上帝啟聖錄 (Record of the saintly manifestations of the Supreme Emperor of Dark Heaven), the great anthology of Zhenwu's miracles that contains many presence-type revelations, tells us the case of one of his devotees, a certain Fu Hong 傅鴻. Fu becomes a celibate Daoist at the Shangqing taipinggong and a disciple of Zhang Shouzhen, the priest who famously made Black Killer speak. Fu announces his imminent death, prepares himself, and starts to address the community from the teaching hall. He is then possessed by Zhenwu 託身降言 and utters a political prophecy (concerning the birth of the future Renzong emperor as an incarnation of a god); after that he disappears entirely. When the prophecy is realized, the emperor has a shrine built for Fu in the temple and the title of transcendent awarded to him, 立傅鴻祠堂，贈號勝因真人.[27] Thus, Fu, like his master Zhang Shouzhen, is a priest who, thanks to his alliance with martial gods that he makes present, becomes a god himself.

26. Ter Haar, "Shamans, Mediums, and Chinese Buddhism." Some Qing spirit-writing groups asked about the rebirth in the Pure Land of their deceased members.

27. "Baoyun chongxin 寶運重新," *Xuantian shangdi qishenglu*, 3.5b–6b.

Confirming the divine status of their deceased masters and predecessors was a key concern of all the *daofa* traditions. Self-divinization was also a central goal of all the spirit-writing groups and continues to be so to the present day.[28] Naturally, *fashi* and *daoshi* were already living gods, having through ordination obtained a rank in the divine bureaucracy. The leaders of the spirit-writing altars, often being *fashi*, were referred to in texts by such divine titles: for instance Liu Ansheng 劉安勝 (late twelfth century), who produced many early Wenchang revelations and whose title was Transcendent Assistant of the Immortals in the Phoenix Bureau 鸞府侍仙真人.[29]

Through spirit-writing, high gods could confirm the canonization of apotheosized *fashi* in the thunder ministries, and the latter could also communicate directly with their disciples and continuators. An early example of such a phenomenon is provided by the figure of Ning Benli 寧本立 (1101–81), a major codifier of the Lingbao dafa 靈寶大法 tradition, one of the most important *daofa*; at one point punished by the gods for having disrespected ritual procedures (he goes blind), he nonetheless undergoes posthumous apotheosis, which is confirmed by spirit-writing (*pijiang*).[30]

Another case is Lei Shizhong 雷時中 (Moan 默庵, 1221–95), a central figure in a *daofa* ritual tradition known as the Hunyuan teachings 混元教, well documented in the Daoist canon,[31] that focuses on the ritual use of the *Durenjing* for the salvation of the dead. Lei's personal thunder deity was Lord Xin.[32] His hagiography concludes:

> After his death, Thunderclap God (Xin) produced several spirit-written revelations, saying "Shangdi (Heaven) has promoted Transcendent (Lei) to

28. On self-divinization, see Goossaert, *Bureaucratie et salut*, where I argue for the vast expansion and popularity of ritual techniques for obtaining a status in the divine bureaucracy beginning in the Song period, spirit-writing being one of them.

29. *Gaoshang dadong Wenchang silu ziyang baolu*, 1.2b.

30. "Zanhua xiansheng Ning zhenren shishi" 贊化先生寧真人事實, in *Daofa huiyuan*, 244.3a–8a; similar text in *Lingbao lingjiao jidu jinshu*, sijiaolu 嗣教錄, 1a–6a.

31. *Daofa huiyuan*, j. 154–55.

32. On Lei Moan's hagiography, see Goossaert, *Vies des saints exorcistes*, 189–95.

> the function of Minister of the Arcane Capital and to the title of Transcendent Lord saving the whole of humanity, from the Hunyuan mystical tradition, and Heavenly Worthy spreading the teaching of Noisy Thunder."
>
> 後雷霆累降筆云：上帝已陞真人為玄都上相、混元妙道普濟真君、雷聲演教天尊。[33]

The spirit-written teachings from Lord Xin are documented. Lei's commentary on the *Durenjing* includes a spirit-written exhortation, dated 1290, in which Xin admonishes the priests under his authority to be morally upright and to serve humanity, while promising them a career in the divine bureaucracy.[34] This revelation shows how a discourse on morality and divinization formed part of the spirit-written exhortations from the thunder gods to their priests, as well as other devotees: Xin's exhortation first addresses his descendants in the *daofa* (lineage), *fazi* 法子, then the ordinary adepts, *xinshi* 信士.[35] It is characterized by the god speaking in the first person ("I adjure you. . .") and directly addressing his adepts, telling of his own divine career as an example to follow and promising help and eventual divinization. This text ends with a question raised by a priest (regarding ordination ranks) and Lord Xin's response, *pi* 批.

Note that this revelation from Lord Xin was published as part of a commentary on the *Durenjing*, that is, a book for open circulation. A shorter, similar text where Lord Xin also speaks in the first person was declaimed by priests in the course of the rituals as an oath, *shizhang*.[36]

33. *Lishi zhenxian tidao tongjian xubian*, 5.11b–14a.

34. On the revelations of Xin tianjun and his various *daofa* traditions, see Xu Wei, "Xin tianjun fa yu Hunyuan daofa de gouzao."

35. *Duren shangpin miaojing tongyi*, 4.28a–30b. We know little about the level of initiation and knowledge of these *xinshi*; in this book I have refrained from using the term "lay" (except when discussing scholars who use it) that suggests an opposition to clergy, which often proves to be misleading in ethnography and well-documented historical cases.

36. "Fufeng mengli Xin tianjun dafa 負風猛吏辛天君大法," *Daofa huiyuan*, 81.2a–3a; Xu Wei, "Xin tianjun fa yu Hunyuan daofa de gouzao," 155. These oaths that horizontally bound priest and gods were fundamentally different from the oaths sworn to the gods that had been practiced since the Han period at the latest, which were vertical.

In the ritual manual authored by Lei Moan, we have Lord Xin's postface to the *Durenjing*, presumably (but not explicitly) spirit written; Lei comments on this revelation by explaining how to visualize Lord Xin.[37] We thus have a complex ritual tradition that combines spirit-writing, visualizations, and other modes of divine presence.

One of Lei's disciples, Xue Jizhao 薛季昭 (fl. 1303) relates in his own commentary on the *Durenjing* how he received revelations from both Lord Xin and the divinized Lei Moan, some through spirit-writing and some in dreams, also confirming their divine apotheosis.[38] Another member of Lei's lineage and ritual tradition, named Zhang Tianquan 張天全, is described in a late Yuan anecdote as extraordinarily adept at causing gods to manifest themselves in this world, either through spoken words or phrases written in ink, 託諸言語筆墨以顯於世. He caused a Heavenly Lord (a thunder marshal) to write in the house of a Mongol official, in such sublime calligraphy that they had it printed.[39]

Besides confirming the divine apotheosis of priests as well as their parents, spirit-writing from its earliest stages also played an important role in the invention and identification of new local gods; indeed, one cannot dissociate the rise of the temple-centric society and that of spirit-writing.[40] This link became even more important in modern times when divine titles granted to local gods through spirit-writing became a major means of legitimizing cults. Indeed, when one looks at local gazetteers and inscriptions, the most common context for spirit-writing is the legitimation of local cults with autohagiographies and canonization. The latter has three main forms: state canonization, *guofeng* 國封; Daoist canonization, *daofeng* 道封, through a heavenly decree promul-

They were a theological innovation of the *daofa*, and especially the Shenxiao tradition, see Mozina, "Oaths and Curses in Divine Empyrean Practice."

37. "Tianjun ba jing yu 天君跋經語," *Daofa huiyuan*, 154.6a–7b.

38. *Yuanshi wuliang duren shangpin miaojing zhujie*, "houxu 後序."

39. "Ti Zhang Tianquan suoke tianjun jiangbi hou 題張天全所刻天君降筆後," *Yunyangji*, 10.5a–b.

40. Xu Wei, "Wenben liuchuan yu keyi pinjie," 154, discusses twelfth-century spirit-written procedures for the divinization of the priest's parents.

gated by the Heavenly Master; and through a similar heavenly decree granted by the Jade Emperor, *yufeng* 玉封, revealed through spirit-writing. The last of the three was obviously the simplest and cheapest method, and unsurprisingly was criticized by both state and Daoist authorities. We will see it criticized by Lü Yuansu 呂元素 (fl. 1188–1207). The Heavenly Master institution did not disclose the precise process through which they produced their heavenly edicts, but it was very likely through visualization.[41]

Spirit-written revelations frequently involve the god introducing him or herself and providing an autobiography—the *Zitong dijun huashu* 梓潼帝君化書 (Book of transformations of the Imperial Lord of Zitong), dated 1181, (discussed below) is the most exalted form of this type of revelation, which was already proliferating in more modest forms throughout the Song empire. In his great geographical encyclopedia, Wang Xiangzhi 王象之 (*jinshi* 1196) provides a telling example when discussing a local cult (a hero who had lived in the tenth century) in what is now Sichuan. Wang found a stele inscription where the god told of his own life through *jiangbi*; he comments: "In general, vernacular specialists in Sichuan often make up stories through spirit-writing or dreams so as to give divine authority to their inventions" 大抵蜀之巫師多假降筆及夢想以神其事耳.[42] Spirit-written confirmations of gods' integration within the divine bureaucracy were particularly useful and welcome when these gods had contentious identities: for instance, in the story of the Wuxian 五顯 (the orthodox title of the notorious Wutong 五通 spirit-possession cult) related in a Ming local gazetteer and followed by the note, "spirit written" 降筆之文也.[43] Other such stories have historical figures protesting through spirit-writing against the

41. Goossaert, "Heavenly Master, Canonization, and the Daoist Construction"; see also Gao Zhenhong, "Chaofeng, daofeng yu minfeng."

42. *Yudi jisheng*, 175.9b. Here, as is often the case in early modern and modern literati's writings, *wushi* 巫師 is as likely to refer to *fashi* priests as to mediums, hence my translation as "vernacular specialists."

43. *Shuzhong guangji*, 79.11b. On the history of the Wutong cult, including its more or less sanitized forms, see von Glahn, *Sinister Way*, chaps. 4–5.

biased treatment they get in historical writings, insisting they achieved great merit as well as ultimate success in self-cultivation, became immortals, and are therefore worthy of a cult.[44]

One story in the *Yijianzhi* nicely encapsulates these different facets of spirit-writing: the role of Daoist priests, communal rituals, and the identification of local gods. It relates how Chen Wenshu 陳文叔, a young scholar who was studying for the examinations, learned the spirit-writing technique 迎致箕神 from someone in his home county (the one date given in the story is 1178).[45] He proved extraordinarily gifted, producing remarkable poems. The god who was writing through him revealed his identity as a transcendent, Penglai zixia zhenren 蓬萊紫霞真人, and performed miracles, so that people started to organize *jiao* offerings in his honor. He excelled at exorcisms and cures and invented his own ritual procedures, writing his petitions to the higher gods on special paper. Then one day he possessed, *ping* 憑, someone who said (thus through oral possession, not spirit-writing) that he had manifested himself among humans as an exiled immortal but had now completed his time, was returning to Heaven, and would no longer manifest himself. So here we have a spirit-writing performer who started providing divination services; as the cult expanded, the god was integrated into Daoist pantheons, and the performer came to serve as an exorcist. There are other stories where an exorcistic ritual is conducted through spirit-writing in a way entirely similar to the (more frequent) cases of the induced possession of a speaking medium controlled by a priest.[46]

4.3. The Performers

Contrary to the idea sometimes found in the secondary literature that spirit-writing was a "popular" practice engaged in, more or less playfully,

44. "Liu Cha sihou wen 劉叉死後文," *Yijianzhi, yizhi* 乙志, j. 6, 233–34.
45. "Penglai zixia zhenren 蓬萊紫霞真人," *Yijianzhi, sanzhi* 三志, xin 辛, j. 10, 1463.
46. "Bingjia xiaohong," *Yijianzhi*, 522–23.

by pretty much anyone who cared to, the vast majority of narrative accounts mention that it was done by an expert (*fangshi* 方士, *shushi* 術士, or just *shan* [verb] *zhe* 善 [. . .] 者). Even Xu Dishan, who ignored the Daoist material in his survey of spirit-writing, noticed the role of ritual specialists.[47]

In many narrative accounts, the performer is not mentioned, only the host, typically the family where the performance is taking place. This does not necessarily mean that there was no specialized performer involved—indeed, anecdotal (*biji*) accounts of divine presence (the majority being cases of possession), for reasons of narrative efficacy, often do not mention ritual roles and foreground the god and the human hero of the story (who may be a passive participant in the ritual or performance). Narratives of possession rarely mention that the spirit is speaking through a medium, but this is obvious to the readers. Some spirit-writing narratives explicitly state that the hand doing the writing belonged to someone who was not prepared for this (suggesting this was unusual)—and even then, we do not know whether there was a priest staging the performance or not. Some stories about literati engaging in the practice to request poems or divine examination results suggest they were wielding the sieve themselves; Zhou Mi 周密 (1232–1308) collected several such accounts, which he introduced by saying that people think those who wield the sieve are just frauds or merely remember poems, but he insists the technique is real.[48] That certain scholars could perform it, however, does not necessarily mean anyone could and that it was not a ritual technique one had to be trained in. One young scholar in the Southern Song is described as "having obtained the incantations and ritual formulas to invite the Purple Maiden" 傳得召紫姑呪訣.[49] The same Zhou Mi elsewhere tells us about a specialist (*shushi*) who performed spirit-writing for patrons, and his performance style included

47. Xu Dishan, *Fuji mixin de yanjiu*, 29.

48. "Jiangxian 降仙," *Qidong yeyu*, 16.14b–17a. Zhou describes relatives and other scholars wielding the sieve, *pengji* 捧箕.

49. "Deng shi Zigu shi 鄧氏紫姑詩," *Yijianzhi, sanzhi* 三志, ren 壬, j. 5, 1505.

heavy drinking—a trait typical of *fashi*.[50] There is also mention of illiterate youths, most certainly mediums, wielding the sieve.[51]

Other stories reveal that both Daoist priests and mediums were involved. In the hagiographical collection devoted to the Three immortal saints of Mount Huagai (Jiangxi), which we have already seen as a sacred site of the Tianxin ritual tradition, is a story set in 1157. A court official who had received high-level Daoist ordination (with Shangqing registers) came to the mountain to pray to the immortals. The temple's medium was suddenly possessed by one of the immortals; he first spoke strangely, then requested paper and ink and wrote a poem and a postface saying the immortal would come and visit him. The official proposed to build a Yuanguangting 圓光亭, that is, a pavilion to practice "perfect light" mediumistic divination.[52] He had a Daoist priest from the temple ask the immortal whether he agreed and requested a response (*baoying*); they obtained a "decree from the immortals," *xianzhi* 仙旨, which is a spirit-written answer (we will see later other occurrences of this term), asking him to also build a pavilion for talismanic healing. When the two buildings were completed, the medium was again possessed to provide the immortal's answer (*baoying*).[53]

Tao Zongyi has a story about the great poet and Daoist (and occasionally Buddhist) practitioner Yu Ji 虞集 (1272–1348) wanting to engage in spirit-writing for divination together with friends: they sought out a Daoist to summon spirits and immortals, *zhao guixian* 召鬼仙, for them.[54] The priest duly performed the spirit-writing rite (*fa*), which I

50. "Li zui jiangxian 李醉降仙," *Guixin zashi xuji*, 1.11b–12a.

51. "Zigu lanzhoushi 紫姑藍粥詩," *Yijianzhi, dingzhi* 丁志, j. 18, 687.

52. This divination method is well-documented already in medieval times: it involves a mirror or water basin on which the priest makes incantations and a boy medium who then looks at it and sees things.

53. "Zhenxian jiangfu tongzi 真仙降附童子," *Huagaishan Fuqiu Wang Guo san zhenjun shishi*, 5.13a–14a. On this source, see Hymes, *Way and Byway*.

54. "Jixian youyan 箕仙有驗," *Nancun chuogenglu*, 26.328. In the event, the local god who made himself present asked for the scholars' help in obtaining his promotion to city god, and they obliged—this puts an interesting spin on the role of spirit-writing in divinization.

will return to below. Other stories focus on these priests. One Yuan account tells of a Hangzhou priest, Ying Zhongfu 應中甫, who had mastered the spirit-writing ritual 請仙降筆法. He could not afford to buy sacrificial offerings to his divine generals but managed to borrow money from the immortals, who made themselves present to him through spirit-writing (*jiangbi* and *jiangxian* 降仙).[55] In a stele inscription from the Yuan period, we are told that a Daoist official, faced with the takeover of the main local Daoist temple by Buddhists in the wake of the Mongol conquest, seeks the gods' help through *jiangbi*, and the gods advise him on how to build a new temple; here, not only is spirit-writing a tool for Daoist institutional development, but it is also publicly presented as such in a quasi-official document.[56]

I disagree on this point with Hsieh Ts'ung-hui's otherwise remarkable study of the Wenchang spirit-writing cults when he claims that most mediums were not (identified as) Daoists.[57] Hsieh means that these mediums were identified as scholars, not as *daoshi*, and were not affiliated with a Daoist monastery. I prefer to use a wider definition of "Daoist" as anyone who has a rank in the divine bureaucracy. The spirit-writing performer need not be a professional, full-time priest, but he certainly needs an initiation and most often, as a result, a Daoist title. Spirit-writing is a form of summoning gods, and all such rites, when codified, require the performer to have a title in the heavenly bureaucracy. This is a norm, and obviously many people chose to ignore it, summoning gods as they pleased; but the narrative evidence shows this norm was widely known and accepted. The initiation is necessary to master the summoning techniques; moreover, regular intimate copresence with gods requires one to become a god oneself.

This is clearly explained in an anecdote told by Hong Mai. The story, set in 1135, concerns a local official and his friend, who "knows how to

55. *Shanju xinhua*, 1.8a.

56. *Jiaxinglu chongchuang Yuanmiaoguan ji* 嘉興路重創元妙觀記, in (*Wanli*) *Xiushui xianzhi*, 9.38a–39a.

57. Hsieh Ts'ung-hui, *Xin tiandi zhi ming*, 124–32.

psalmody and perform the instructions to invite the great immortals" 能誦訣邀大仙 using a sieve. The official engages in an intense relationship with the spirit (a recently deceased literatus) through his friend. The spirit then tells the official that the latter has Daoist bones 道骨 and will become an immortal; he instructs him to set up a clean, sealed-off room for practicing and to create a sieve with a brush that should be suspended from the rafter, promising that he will come and write answers to all the questions. The official does as instructed, but once he is ready, his friend has gone, he has not memorized the ritual instructions for inviting the spirits, *qingjue* 請訣, and the spirit never returns.[58] What we read about here is an official who invites an initiated specialist to perform spirit-writing for his family and friends and becomes engrossed in the experience, fancies himself a Daoist, and wishes to practice himself but fails because of insufficient training.

Therefore, the most common situation in narratives of spirit-writing in Song and Yuan China was for an initiated ritual specialist (often explicitly Daoist) to take charge of the process; in some cases, the priest caused the possession of a medium who wrote (or spoke, or both), and in others he wrote himself. In all cases, I call this controlled possession (and it falls within my type 5, presence, not type 3, possession): the control is made possible by the status of the priest and the very detailed ritual procedures he follows.[59] I add that this, in terms of ideal types, is different from cases of possession when the speaking medium also writes things; in contemporary times, mediums would routinely write simple talismans to give to patients, but extremely rarely anything discursive. As we will see in chapter 6, the modalities of control evolved in later times, but the principle remained. This shows that interpretations of spirit-writing as a secularized way of communicating directly

58. "Xu Nanling qing daxian 徐南陵請大仙," *Yijianzhi*, zhiyi 支乙, j. 8, 855–56.

59. A medium performing possession for a cult is also subjected to control, both by himself and helpers; otherwise it would demonic possession. My point, however, is that this control is not made apparent, and what is visible is the agency of the god. By contrast, in what I term "controlled possession," the controlling priest makes his own agency obvious.

with the gods and dispensing with clerical mediation are quite off the mark.

The focus of the existing scholarship is on literati as opposed to clerics and temples; authors such as Terry F. Kleeman and Hsieh Ts'ung-hui present *feiluan* as a lay religious tradition, bent on unmediated connections with the gods (i.e., without clerics). This is in direct continuity with the interpretation of other scholars working on later periods; Lai Chi Tim, in particular, insists that spirit-writing is a lay form of Daoism that is very distinct from clerical, temple-based Daoism.[60] These analyses may hold at two conditions: 1) that we do not generalize them; the gentry's practice of venerating high gods and producing scriptures may be but one particular form of spirit-writing, which does not exist in isolation from other forms; and 2) even more importantly, that we do not reify the opposition between lay literati and Daoist priests, as the two have never been exclusive categories.

4.4. The Gods

Spirits invited through spirit-writing can be broadly divided into two categories: the dead and the high gods. The former are questioned about the fate of deceased family members or future events, and they write poetry. No substantial text of this type has been preserved. The latter, properly speaking, account for revelations. Let us now examine these high gods who communicated on a regular basis with living humans and instructed them.

4.4.1. Zhenwu and Other Exorcists

We cannot but remark how a large part of the gods associated with spirit-writing during the early modern period are those of the *daofa* traditions,

60. Lai Chi Tim, "Cult of Spirit-Writing in the Qing"; see also Shiga Ichiko, *Chūgoku no kokkurisan.*

notably their fierce thunder generals. We have already encountered two of them, Lords Deng and Xin, and will meet the Transcendent Lord Xu below. Tianyou, the Tantric deity closely associated with Black Killer and Zhenwu, is also present in the spirit-written revelations.[61] These martial gods also engage in possession, and their written revelations are just one aspect of their powerful presence when Daoist priests are near. The central role of thunder generals remained obvious throughout the various stages of the development of spirit-writing in the Ming and Qing. To take just one example from the Ming, in a Buddhist collection of miracle tales there is the story of an official who was engaged in a campaign of destroying illicit temples during the Zhengde reign (1506–21); arriving at a shrine of a martial god (within a Buddhist monastery), an illiterate servant of his was possessed by the god, who yelled at the official, requested brush and paper, and wrote (*jiangbi*) a powerful poem telling of his life as a murdered human officer, then demon, then divine general in the service of the heavenly bureaucracy—typical *daofa* lore. The official, as could be expected, recanted and sponsored the temple.[62]

Probably the most frequently mentioned and most prominent of these martial gods bent on manifesting their divine presence in words is Zhenwu (aka Xuantian Shangdi 玄天上帝), one of the highest-ranking deities of the *daofa* traditions beginning with Tianxin zhengfa.[63] The corpus of texts related to Zhenwu in the Daoist canon is the largest of all deities; it includes dozens of scriptures, liturgies, and hagiographies. Mentions of the manifestations of his divine presence abound, and they are particularly detailed in two important works: the commentary by

61. Tianyou is the author of prefaces to the spirit-written *Yuhuangjing*, on which see more below: Hsieh Ts'ung-hui, *Xin tiandi zhi ming*, 127.

62. "Huangzhou Anguosi Zhang zhenjun pin xiaozu jiangbi 黃州安國寺張真君憑小卒降筆," *Xianguo suilu*, 3.41a–b. This text was apparently well known and is found in various local gazetteers.

63. On the emergence of the Zhenwu cult, see Chao Shin-yi, *Daoist Ritual, State Religion, and Popular Practices*; De Bruyn, *Le Wudang shan*; and Wang Chien-ch'uan, "Zhenwu xinyang zai jinshi Zhongguo de chuanbo." On Zhenwu revelations, see Wang Chien-ch'uan and Pi Qingsheng, *Zhongguo jinshi minjian xinyang*, 214–24.

Chen Zhong 陳伀 (fl. 1236) of one of his scriptures (*Taishang shuo Xuantian dasheng Zhenwu benzhuan shenzhou miaojing* 太上說玄天大聖真武本傳神呪妙經, Marvelous scripture of the divine incantations and hagiography of Zhenwu, Great Saint of Dark Heavens, preached by the Supreme [Lord]) and the large compendium of his miracles, the *Xuantian shangdi qishenglu*. Furthermore, an important moral tract spirit-written by Zhenwu in 1302 is not included in the canon but was widely disseminated in later periods, and I return to this document in the next chapter.

What is possibly the record of the earliest spirit-writing revelations of texts concerns a group of Zhenwu devotees active in early Song Sichuan, especially the Chengdu region. The dating for this, as happens so often, is rather difficult: the account is found in a large liturgical compendium, the *Daomen kefan daquanji* 道門科範大全集 (Great compendium of the liturgical norms of Daoism), which is partially attributed to the great liturgist Du Guangting and certainly contains material from his hand but was edited, with many additions, in the early fifteenth century. One passage devoted to Zhenwu tells of two people who received his revelations, a certain Ash Li 燂灰李 (a possible reference to writing on an ash table?) and a Du Ming 杜明—neither is documented anywhere else.[64] Zhenwu manifested himself at their home altar on a number of occasions; sometimes he spoke 降語, sometimes he appeared in dreams, and sometimes he transmitted scriptures, presumably through spirit-writing; to Li he is said to have transmitted the Five Dipper scriptures 真君降於其家, 傳以五斗經, 行於世.[65] This is intriguing because these extremely popular scriptures, especially the Northern one (for the Big Dipper) (*Taishang xuanling beidou benming changsheng miaojing* 太上玄靈北斗本命長生妙經, in short *Beidoujing*), present themselves as having been revealed to Zhang Daoling by Taishang laojun in 155 CE (an encounter scenario) but do not appear before the Song; it is entirely possible, then, that

64. *Daomen kefan daquanji*, 63.3a–5b.
65. *Daomen kefan daquanji*, 63.4a.

they were spirit written, which would make them the earliest known spirit-written scriptures. Our text narrates in more detail the career of Du Ming, which resembles that of his near-contemporary Zhang Shouzhen. He begins operating from home during the Xianping era (998–1004); his revelations play a role in quashing a military rebellion, and he becomes successful and settles in a major Daoist temple, where he runs the Zhenwu cult and delivers more oral revelations. Zhenwu also announces through him that he will visually appear to the emperor.

Stories told by Chen Zhong and the *Xuantian shangdi qishenglu* similarly show Zhenwu manifesting himself through a wide variety of means. He occasionally appears visible, especially during battles, when he scares the enemy, or in the presence of the emperor. He can possess mediums and speak.[66] But he is equally bent on spirit-writing. Chen Zhong repeatedly quotes his spirit-written sayings, and even mentions his *Jiangbi shilu* 降筆實錄 (Record of spirit-written words), which is unfortunately lost, ten times; the quotes concern Zhenwu's own history and place in the pantheon.[67] Chen describes the revelation in some detail; it happened in 1184 at a Zixu altar 紫虛壇 in Xiangyang 襄陽 (Hubei), the head of which was a Daoist named Zhang Mingdao 降授道士張明道.[68] The *Jiangbi shilu* was edited and revealed by a thunder deity, named Transcendent Lord Dong 董真君, under the orders of Zhenwu; Wenchang and other deities also wrote prefaces and other revelations, which Chen quotes. Terms used include *jiangbi* and *pijiang* (which as we have seen refer primarily to written communication between the priest and god during a ritual), and there is no mention of the phoenix.

66. In "Fuyu qiqing 附語祈晴," *Xuantian shangdi qishenglu*, 4.17b–19a, the medium is clearly described as unconscious when Zhenwu possesses him (*jiangyu*, *jiangling*).

67. *Taishang shuo Xuantian dasheng zhenwu benzhuan shenzhou miaojing*, 6.5b.

68. *Taishang shuo Xuantian dasheng zhenwu benzhuan shenzhou miaojing*, 1.4b; 6.27b; see also Hsieh T'sung-hui, *Xin tiandi zhi ming*, 119–21.

4.4.2. Wenchang

The best-studied early spirit-writing cult is that of Imperial Lord Wenchang 文昌帝君, certainly because it represents the earliest well-documented stage in the history of the production of spirit-written books (as opposed to short poems): I rely here on the pioneering work of Terry Kleeman and Hsieh Ts'ung-hui.[69] The cult originated in Zitong, northern Sichuan, and the god (originally a snake), who performed miracles to protect this area during wars and other disasters, was eventually elevated to the title of Imperial Lord of Zitong 梓潼帝君. He gradually came to be considered the divine person in charge of the Wenchang office, a constellation in charge of human destinies and official appointments in particular. The Wenchang constellation was an ancient official cult, and not all literati approved of its assimilation to the Zitong cult, but by the thirteenth century, this was nonetheless mainstream opinion; for the sake of simplicity, I call this god Wenchang throughout. The Wenchang cult did not rely solely on spirit-writing, and the god manifested himself in visible human form several times before starting to write. He also conveyed prognostication through the weather (wind and storms) and in dreams; there was a hall for requesting dreams, Yingmengtai 應夢臺, at the god's temple at Zitong from the Song period onward. One of the spirit-written revelations (see below) provides the types of dreams Wenchang gave and how to interpret them.[70]

The Wenchang spirit-written revelations developed in Sichuan in the late twelfth century, when a network of devotees produced various texts in various locations. The earliest, revealed in 1168, was the *Taishang wuji zongzhen Wenchang dadong xianjing* 太上無極總真文昌大洞仙經 (Great cavern immortality scripture, by Wenchang [head of] all transcendents, of the supreme ultimate), a revised version of the fourth-century most-eminent Shangqing scripture. The same group, led by Liu Ansheng 劉安勝 at Baopingshan 寶屏山, revealed between 1168 and

69. Kleeman, *God's Own Tale*; Hsieh Ts'ung-hui, *Xin tiandi zhi ming*.

70. Kleeman, *God's Own Tale*, 13–15; *Gaoshang dadong Wenchang silu ziyang baolu*, 3.11a–14b.

1177 a short divine autobiography titled *Qinghe neizhuan* 清河內傳 (Esoteric biography of Qinghe).[71] Next, in 1181, came an ordination register, *Gaoshang dadong Wenchang silu ziyang baolu* 高上大洞文昌司祿紫陽寶籙 (Precious purple *yang* register of the Wenchang office for official careers, of the most high great cavern).[72] This allowed the members of the spirit-writing group and devotees to become officials, either in the imperial bureaucracy and/or as gods in Wenchang's heavenly administration—thus fulfilling the self-divinization purpose of spirit-writing in a standardized Daoist manner. Indeed, as already said, Liu Ansheng is named with his divine title.

That same year and to the same group, Wenchang revealed the long version of his hagiography, the *Zitong dijun huashu*, in seventy-three "transformations," that is, successive lives—additional lives were revealed in subsequent sessions from 1194 to 1316 by various other groups in Sichuan, Guizhou, and Guangxi.[73] Furthermore, according to Hsieh Ts'ung-hui, a Wenchang altar closely connected to those who had produced the above revelations also revealed in 1218, and again, with corrections, in 1220, the *Gaoshang Yuhuang benxing jijing* 高上玉皇本行集經 (Collected scripture of the fundamental acts of the venerable Jade Emperor; henceforth *Yuhuangjing*). This scripture was to become one of the most commonly chanted texts by modern Daoists; it describes the career and salvific role of the Jade Emperor.[74] Wang Chien-ch'uan for his part argues that the Wenchang revelation consisted in the commentary, preface, and editing of the *Yuhuangjing*, but not the scripture itself, even though the two textual layers are close in terms of theological content.[75]

71. This revelation is found in the first part (1a–3a) of the expanded book by that name in the Daoist canon.

72. Hu Jiechen (personal communication, March 27, 2021) considers that the *Ziyang baolu* was revealed later in the Song period and dated back to 1181.

73. The original seventy-three transformations have been translated in Kleeman, *God's Own Tale*.

74. Hsieh Ts'ung-hui, *Xin tiandi zhi ming*, chap. 4 (also in Hsieh, "*Yuhuang benxing jijing* chushi de beijing"), retraces in great detail all the various altars that contributed to these successive revelations; Wang Chien-ch'uan, "Song-Ming shiqi," provides several further modifications.

75. Wang Chien-ch'uan, "Song-Ming shiqi."

The Wenchang revelations have a lot in common with those of Zhenwu and other deities in terms of their social context and content. One of their most original features is the term *feiluan*, after the name of the wooden writing implement sculpted in the shape of the legendary bird; it was apparently wielded by a single person. Furthermore, there also existed within the Wenchang cult communities a specific technique of revelation (apparently) without a medium: the phoenix, suspended from the rafters by a rope, moved by itself in a locked room called Jiangbiting 降筆亭. When it had finished, a bell rang, and the devotees, led by the local official, opened the door to find sheets of paper covered with the revealed texts, which they took "to read the god's response" 觀報應.[76] This is a special case within the realm of spirit-writing techniques; we are not apprised of any ritual procedures, and the witnesses are made to see the a posteriori results of the divine presence rather than feel the presence itself. However, as we will see, this automatic spirit-writing technique was listed alongside *jiangbi* and other terms among the various *daofa* rites for making gods write. It was not unique to the Wenchang cult and is mentioned in other contexts; we have already seen examples above. In yet another instance, a twelfth-century story in northern China tells of an employee in a local administration who was "good at praying immortals" 好祈仙 and set up a cult for Immortal Huang 黃, with a suspended brush in front of his portrait 懸筆畫前.[77] A more detailed description is offered by Hong Mai, who writes about a Southern Song ritual specialist working from a small shrine filled with the icons of nine Daoist transcendents. His clients wrote their prayer, *xinshu* 心疏, sealed and burned it, and then the clients and priest offer white paper and pray outside the closed shrine; when they hear the sound of the brush put down on the table, they come in and find the paper covered with the response (*bao*) of the gods, sometimes with talismans to protect the client.[78]

76. This description is first found in Wenchang's entry in the late Yuan hagiography *Xinbian lianxiang Soushen guangji*, 33, and again in Ming sources; see Hsieh Ts'ung-hui, *Xin tiandi zhi ming*, 111.

77. "Huang zhenren 黃真人," *Xu Yijianzhi*, 34.

78. "Shen Chengwu Zigu," *Yijianzhi*, 1486–87.

Wenchang's revelations were (with the exception of the ordination register and liturgical manuals) in open circulation and widely distributed. A proclamation in which he speaks in the first person and expounds his mission of transforming (*hua*) the populations of Sichuan was carved on a stele in 1207, one of the earliest spirit-written texts made into a public monument; an even earlier inscription is dated 1177.[79]

The popularity of the Wenchang revelations is also documented by their opponents. Fang Hui 方回 (1227–1307), a high-ranking official, developed a scathing attack on the Wenchang revelations in the context of criticizing late Song political attempts to flatter Emperor Lizong (r. 1225–64) by linking him to Wenchang prophecies:

> Nowadays, the techniques of spirit-writing with a phoenix and a suspended board, from gods such as "Great immortals" or Ziru (certainly Zigu), are all fake.[80] And there is no fake that has met with such a raging success as Zitong's.
>
> 世之扶鸞懸板，如大仙紫如等事，無非作偽，然未有梓潼之作偽盛大昌熾者也。[81]

Fang outright claims that Wenchang does not exist and that the original mediums who produced the *Huashu* have passed away without an able successor, so that the Zitong temple had to make up new prophecies to keep the cult going.

4.4.3. Transcendent Lord Xu

As important as Wenchang is in the larger picture of Chinese religious history, so too are the revelations from Transcendent Lord Xu 許真君

79. *Song Yingxian wulie zhongyou guangji wang xiangbei* 宋英顯武烈忠佑廣濟王像碑, in Hsieh Ts'ung-hui, *Xin tiandi zhi ming*, 116; and "Zifu Feixiadong ji 紫府飛霞洞記," *Ba-Shu daojiao beiwen jicheng*, 154–55.

80. I have not found any other source that uses this term to refer to spirit-writing techniques.

81. "Zheng Qingzhi suojin Shengyu kao 4 鄭清之所進聖語攷四," *Quan Yuanwen*, 7:285–86.

(Xu Xun 許遜) and his ritual tradition, the Pure and Bright, Loyal and Filial Liturgy, Jingming zhongxiao fa 淨明忠孝法 (henceforth Jingmingfa). Xu is a local saint from northern Jiangxi, who reputedly lived in the fourth century and was already adopted during the Tang by Daoists, who wrote his hagiographies, managed his temples, and celebrated *jiao* offerings for him. Xu's core temple, Yulong wanshougong 玉隆萬壽宮 at Xishan 西山 (near Nanchang, Jiangxi) has been for centuries the center of a pilgrimage that has remained vibrant to this day.[82] During the Song, his cult developed its own set of exorcistic and healing *daofa* rituals that are part of the larger family of Lingbao *daofa* liturgy. The well-documented codification, which has continued uninterrupted until the present (unlike many *daofa* traditions), includes moral rules, self-divinization procedures for adepts, and prophecies.[83] Spirit-writing has been closely associated with the Jingmingfa texts from their origin and through the ages, and we will meet them again in the following chapters. As in other traditions, it was not exclusive of other revelatory techniques, as its moral code, a ledger of merits and demerits (discussed in chapter 3), was revealed through a dream in 1171.

The most explicit description of early Jingming spirit-writing is the narrative of events in 1131 that led to a canonical manual, *Lingbao jingming xinxiu Jiulao shenyin fumo mifa* 靈寶淨明新修九老神印伏魔秘法 (Lingbao Jingming secret method to subdue demons with the divine seal newly created by the nine elders). The preface to this work does not use any technical term for spirit-writing but is entirely unambiguous. In that year, "the six transcendents manifested their divine presence in Yushui and revealed the secret liturgy of Lingbao jingming" 六真降神於渝水, 出示靈寶淨明秘法. The following year, Lord Xu (under his title Gaoming dashi 高明大使) suddenly descended 覒欻臨 to his main temple (the Yulong wanshougong). He gathered his adepts in an

82. Schipper, "Taoist Ritual and Local Cults of the T'ang Dynasty"; Akizuki Kan'ei, *Chūgoku kinsei dōkyō no keisei*; Xu Wei, *Duanlie yu jiangou*.

83. Wang Gang, "Mingdai Jingmingdao," has argued that after the Mongol period, the Jingmingfa declined as a ritual tradition even though the cult remained vibrant.

"altar" called Yizhentan 翼真壇, and there, when they had doubts or problems regarding the scriptures, they could always ask the god 凡經典疑難, 悉聽扣問. As a result, the present liturgy was compiled. Once completed, it was presented to the lord for inspection, and he approved it 書成, 以呈真鑒, 賜可.[84] Indeed, three gods are listed as the authors of this book. Even though there is no specific, technical term employed for spirit-writing here, this entirely fits my definition of it because we have a ritual set-up (an altar), which implies ritual procedures for inviting the gods, written questions to the gods, and written answers by them, which were then published as instructions given by the gods in the first person to named disciples.

Two other Jingming texts document the spirit-written exchanges between living adepts and their divine mentors, containing instructions on ritual procedures but also doctrine and inner alchemy, *neidan* 內丹, self-cultivation; these two aspects are closely linked since thunder rites hinged on inner-alchemical procedures. Both texts record the questions asked by a certain Zhou Fangwen 周方文 to his Transcendent Master Xu 真師. Zhou is not known elsewhere but provides a short account of his pursuit of inner alchemy with various (living) masters and mentions he was a local official; however, recent scholars have shown he was the main priest behind the 1131 revelations, and his two texts are part of the same effort.[85] The first text is titled *Lingbao jingming huangsu shu shiyi bijue* 靈寶淨明黃素書釋義秘訣 (Secret formulas and glosses of the *Yellow and White Book* of the Lingbao Jingming lineage); the *Yellow and White Book* is another Jingming text on self-cultivation extant in the canon.[86] For each question, Zhou quotes the passage from the *Yellow and White Book*, then formulates his question, often quoting other sources, notably the famed immortals Zhongli Quan 鍾離權 and Lü

84. *Lingbao jingming xinxiu Jiulao shenyin fumo mifa*, preface.

85. Wang Ya, "Nansong Jingmingdao de fa, zhi, lu," building on the seminal work of Xu Wei.

86. *Gaoshang yuegong taiyin yuanjun xiaodao xianwang Lingbao jingming huangsu shu*.

Dongbin 呂洞賓, and then provides the answer (by Xu). The language used by Zhou is unmistakably that of spirit-writing: "I await your jade edict," 伏望玉旨; "(I ask) for your bestowing clear explanations," 分明垂教; "I humbly beg you to reveal your clear explanations," 伏乞分明指示; "I humbly beg you to secretly grant your teaching," 伏乞密賜垂教; "I wish you will grant me oral instructions," 願賜口訣; "I humbly beg my transcendent master to reveal a transcendent book so as to teach the members of the altar," 伏乞真師頒示真本, 以教在壇之士; and "I beg you to respond to my request (*baoying*) and explain in detail," 乞報應詳示. Although some of the instructions are described by both Zhou and Xu as "oral secrets," Zhou uses the language of submitting written requests, *chengfu* 呈覆, *bingwen* 禀問, and asks for Xu's written response, *pishi* or *pihui* 批誨 (a standard term for responding to a letter from a student). Xu's answers are relatively straightforward; he uses "I" and "you" and recounts his own initiation and training.

The second text, *Lingbao jingmingyuan jiaoshi Zhou zhengong qiqing huayi* 靈寶淨明院教師周真公起請畫一 (Questions for unification by the Instructor from the Jingming Court, Transcendent Master Zhou), follows the same format, without reference to a particular text. Zhou asks his divine master to elucidate; the questions range from technical aspects of ritual practice (the most common theme) to advice on his moral life. They resemble the "recorded sayings" (*yulu*) of living masters, a genre favored particularly by Quanzhen 全真 and southern *daofa* teachers such as Wang Wenqing and Bai Yuchan. They thus constitute the earliest case of a *yulu* between living adepts and divine masters produced by spirit-writing; we have seen that medieval adepts (Yang Xi and Daoxuan) could question their divine master through visualizations and that the early Song *Yisheng baode zhuan* already contained a proto-*yulu* record of oral responses by the god to personal questions on self-cultivation and morality. Here, for the first time, we have books entirely devoted to a spirit-written pedagogical dialogue. Zhou concludes the *Zhou zhengong qiqing huayi* by saying, "Now that I have seen your written answers" 方文伏睹真師批誨, he can instruct the other adepts and resolve their doubts. Some instructions are thus secret, but not all of them are.

One of Zhou's questions concerns the initiation of Jingmingfa Daoists. Zhou, quoting liturgical documents, states that the ordinand must pray to Lord Xu, who will then answer. He asks: how is one to obtain Xu's answer (*baoying*), in a dream, or through a "decree from the immortals" (*xianzhi*), that is, a spirit-written approval? Zhou says that in such cases he does not dare submit a formal memorial 具表申奏 to Xu (that is, in the course of an audience 朝 ritual) but just burns dispatches asking for either a dream or for the officers of merits (who transmit all ritual documents between the various heavenly offices) to send an "immortal edict" *xianzhi* 或乞夢, 或乞四直功曹, 傳仙旨也.[87] These *xianzhi* are mentioned in several other Jingming liturgical manuals in the canon. Thus, this is the earliest systematic description of the use of spirit-writing for initiating adepts, accepted individually by the immortal master, something that continues to be practiced in modern and contemporary times.

Other Jingming texts bear traces of similar activities and events. We have seen in the introduction to the present book how the preface to a Jingming hagiography tells us that Lord Xu revealed his teachings in Nanjing in 1224:

> In the *jiashen* year of the Jiading reign (1224), our patriarch, the Transcendent Lord Xu, manifested himself in Jinling (present-day Nanjing), exposed the teaching of loyalty and filial piety, and converted crowds of people, who all joined the correct way.
>
> 嘉定甲申之歲, 祖師許真君降于金陵, 示陳忠孝之教, 溥化眾生, 咸歸正道。[88]

More importantly, as Hsieh Ts'ung-hui has noted, the 1131 revelation is also discussed in the compendium of Jingmingfa teachings, the *Jing-*

87. *Lingbao jingmingyuan jiaoshi Zhou zhengong qiqing huayi*, 7b.
88. *Xishan Xu zhenjun bashiwu hua lu*, preface 跋, 1a.

ming zhongxiao quanshu 淨明忠孝全書 (Canon of the pure and bright, loyal and filial [lineage]) compiled by Liu Yu 劉玉 (1257–1308) and his disciple Huang Yuanji 黃元吉 (1271–1326) and placed in an eschatological context (the wars between the Song and the Jin).[89] In Liu's hagiography within that compendium, we read that the 1131 revelation was the foundation of this tradition that Liu Yu wished to renew: he had visions of immortals, who predicted that Lord Xu would make himself present in his home 下降予家 in 1297, just as he had done back in 1131. Lord Xu indeed came and bestowed various scriptures, which are included in the same compendium.[90] This rich biography is essentially made up of accounts of successive revelations of different types, showing how virtuosi such as Liu Yu could quite freely use the vast repertoire of revelatory techniques and deploy them at their altar (*tan*) in order to recruit disciples. In some cases, he is explicitly engaging in visualizations and ascending to Heaven to meet gods; in others the latter descend in spectacular encounters, with visions, smells, and divine objects conferred on him, along with other sensory experiences. His disciple Huang Yuanji is also instructed in dreams. Liu is also given texts, mostly by Lord Xu's subordinate gods. These texts are instructions signed by the gods, spoken in the first person, and they address Liu and other initiates as "descendants in my ritual lineage" (*fazi*), exactly like in Lord Xin's 1290 spirit-written revelations. It thus appears that, even if no technical word such as *jiangbi* is used in the Jingmingfa corpus, *jiang* here refers to spirit-writing. This Jingming zhongxiao canon, in large part spirit written, was repeatedly reprinted during the Ming and Qing periods and continued to serve as the scriptural core of a large and influential tradition, centered on the Jiangxi and Jiangnan regions.

The Jingming spirit-writing practices are far better documented in the canon than those associated with Wenchang or Zhenwu. Whereas for Wenchang there are almost only the open-circulation texts (scriptures

89. Hsieh Ts'ung-hui, *Xin tiandi zhi ming*, 124–25; Xu Wei, *Duanlie yu jiangou*, chap. 2; *Jingming zhongxiao quanshu*, 1.35.

90. *Jingming zhongxiao quanshu*, 1.36–39.

and hagiography), for Jingming we have, in addition to these, many internal, restricted-circulation documents, including liturgy and "secret" instructions. This is most certainly due to the fact that Jingming groups existed continuously from the early twelfth century until the Ming (and beyond), whereas the ritual techniques of the Wenchang cult (including its spirit-writing) may have been partly discontinued (likely because of the massive destruction in Sichuan during the late Song and again in the late Ming). Yet, these rituals were important at the time: one of the Wenchang revelations was an ordination register (*Gaoshang dadong Wenchang silu ziyang baolu*) full of exorcistic language. This register empowered adepts to perform certain rites and explicitly mentioned a companion Dadongfa 大洞法 (Liturgy of the great cavern) revealed at the same time; this Dadongfa, being Wenchang's exorcistic rites, is also mentioned elsewhere in canonical texts. Elements of the Dadongfa were transmitted, others possibly reinvented in the Ming and Qing periods, and it was practiced among late imperial spirit-writing altars, for exorcism, healing, and salvation of the dead, among other purposes.[91] In his spirit-written autohagiography, Wenchang recounts how he became an exorcistic priest.[92] The Wenchang texts circulated to be sure, and Wenchang temples were active throughout the Chinese world. An inscription dated 1341 and preserved in the canon suggests that by the late Yuan many officials were involved in his spirit-writing cult.[93] But we have no trace of the transmission of the ritual techniques that provided the framework for the original revelations in Sichuan.

91. The extent Dadongfa liturgies found in the Daoist canon are solely for solo visualizations and performance of the *Dadong xianjing*; it is unclear whether there also existed communal versions. See Kim Jihyun. "The Invention of Traditions." The most detailed liturgy for the Dadongfa is found in an 1840 edition, *Wenchang Dadong xianjing*. I discuss this source and the late imperial Dadongfa rituals in detail in my next book, *Spirit-writing and Elite Religiosity in Modern Jiangnan*.

92. *Zitong dijun huashu*, transformation n°12.

93. "Xingciji 行祠記," *Qinghe neizhuan*, 9a–13a.

4.4.4. The Great Rites of the Jade Hall

The relationship between spirit-writing and *daofa* rituals went beyond the fact that priests used the former to process the rituals; they also sometimes used it to actually create the whole ritual tradition: indeed, some of the *daofa* liturgies were revealed through spirit-writing. We have already encountered an example in the short manual revealed by Lord Deng and, more importantly, in Jingming manuals. The Great Rites of the Jade Hall, Yutang dafa 玉堂大法, provide an even earlier case. This tradition was created by Lu Shizhong 路時中 (fl. 1120–30) in the Maoshan and Nanjing areas. It is based on the earlier Tianxin zhengfa, adding meditation practices and alchemical salvation, *liandu* 煉度, rituals for saving the dead; it is marked by a very explicit recruitment among literati (including officials) and disdain for "vulgar Daoists (i.e., vernacular priests without an elite education)."[94] In fact, most *daofa* traditions had their own version of the *liandu* alchemical salvation of the dead, and it was one of their most prestigious rites: it allowed scholars to practice self-cultivation and gain merits by saving others at the same time.[95] Many of the early modern spirit-written instructions, including the Jingming ones discussed above, concern alchemical salvation. This connection between *daofa*, alchemical salvation, and spirit-writing will continue into the modern period, as we shall see in chapter 6.

The events of the revelations that Lu received are narrated in two colophons within his liturgical compendium. In the first, he recounts how during the night of the Upper Prime day of 1120, he was meditating in his retreat room when he had a vision of Zhao Sheng 趙昇 (the favorite disciple of the first Heavenly Master Zhang Daoling), who told him he had long before concealed a secret text atop Maoshan and instructed Lu to find it. Lu indeed found a light-emitting box with the text that contained the liturgy.[96] The second narrative is as follows:

94. *Wushang xuanyuan santian yutang dafa*, 26.1a–3a.
95. Capitanio, "Ritual and Self-Cultivation."
96. *Wushang xuanyuan santian yutang dafa*, 1.7a–8a.

> All the instructions on the seven levels (of ordination) given above are oral instructions given by secret manifestations of the Heavenly Lord, Master of the Teachings, repeatedly between the fifteenth day of the first month and the seventh day of the seventh month of 1107. After that and until 1119, the book of ordination levels and the book of exorcisms were revealed through spirit-writing (*jiangbi*). The transmission was completed in 1158. When the Heavenly Lord manifested himself in the meditation room, he spoke with a voice like that of a small child; only myself and my disciple Zhai Ruwen were able to hear and record it.
>
> 已上七品格言，並大觀元年正月十五日至七月初七日，累受大教主天君密降口訣。自後至宣和元年，《品書》、《禁書》並降筆。以傳真，在紹興戊寅也。天君降靖中，如嬰兒聲，惟時中與弟子翟汝文親聞筆記也。[97]

Thus, the Jade Hall liturgy is the result of several types of revelatory techniques; the most sacred texts (the talismans) are produced via the time-honored method of cave discovery, but the much more abundant discursive material, which makes them usable, is revealed, first through oral and then written methods using mediums. The note on the god speaking with the voice of a child, very similar to what was noted about Zhang Shouzhen, clearly hints at the presence of a child acting as medium.

4.4.5. Altars as Venues for Spirit-Writing

The 1131 description of Jingming revelations is, to my knowledge, the earliest record of adepts grouped in an altar (*tan*) and taken as disciples (*dizi*) by a god who instructs them through spirit-writing; later Jingming spirit-writing altars include the Yinzhentan 隱真壇. This model was also, a few years later, developed by the Wenchang groups, who established various similarly named *tan*.[98] By 1184 we also have records of Zhenwu spirit-writing at a Zixu altar 紫虛壇. By the modern period, this vocabulary of altars and discipleship became a very common way to

97. *Wushang xuanyuan santian yutang dafa*, 28.7b–8a.
98. A very convenient list in Hsieh Ts'ung-hui, *Xin tiandi zhi ming*, 135–36.

refer to the members of a spirit-writing group, and we begin to have much more detailed descriptions of the operation and rules of such an altar than we have for the Song, Yuan, and Ming periods.

I have not found any evidence of people claiming to be disciples of a god and permanent members of an altar outside a spirit-writing context. Expressions such as "disciples of the altar," *tan dizi* 壇弟子, or the "community of the altar," *tanzhong* 壇眾, refer, in Buddhist and (less commonly) Daoist contexts, to ordinands, but they are only called thus during the ordination ritual, not permanently, and they are the disciples of the living ordination master, not a god. In Song-period liturgical texts, these expressions can also refer to the Daoist troupe, that is, the main priest (*gaogong* 高功, *shi* 師, *fashi* 法師) and his acolytes; the latter are also called *fazi* 法子 (or *fazhong* 法眾). Only in a few modern liturgical manuals for lamp 燈 or penance 懺 rituals (where they are all allowed to stand next to the priest, unlike in the *jiao*) are the ordinary participants called *tanzhong*, but again, only for the duration of the ritual. In these cases, *tan* refers to the ephemeral ritual arena, not an institution.

With the twelfth-century emergence of spirit-writing altars, we thus see the rise of a new idea: through the practice of spirit-writing, ordinary people (not only ascetics engaged in advanced self-cultivation) become the disciples (*dizi*) of a god or an immortal and become permanent members of a divine community.

Why were these spirit-writing communities called altars? The reason is, I think, that they are established by an initiated *fashi* priest; a group of priests working together is called a *tan*, and *daofa* practitioners in particular are organized around their thunder altar, *leitan* 雷壇. Individual *tan*, as durable entities with their own names, are an innovation of the Song-period *daofa* and do not seem to have existed beforehand. Like all *daofa* innovations, this met with some resistance. The great twelfth-century ritual codifier Ning Benli, whom we met as divinized through spirit-writing, has a diatribe against institutions called Xuanling tongzhentan 玄靈通真壇, which apparently produced prophecies; Ning insists that only the three official ordination altars could have the name of a permanent altar.[99] He does not mention spirit-writing explicitly, but it is likely part of what is being criticized.

Spirit-writing was part of the larger repertoire of *daofa* rituals. Indeed, all of the spirit-writing deities we have met have their own ritual tradition (*fa*), even if, in the case of Wenchang, this is less prominent than for Lord Xu, Lord Xin, or Zhenwu. Some *daofa* altars (i.e., troupes) must have practiced spirit-writing particularly well and often as a service, and they attracted aspiring members. Such altars initiated and ordained disciples to perform (or help with) spirit-writing and other rituals and spread the teachings of the exorcistic gods revealed through spirit-writing. The 1290 Lord Xin revelation is addressed to both priests (*fazi*) and ordinary adepts (*xinshi*), suggesting that some of these altars observed two degrees of ordination.

I see no reason to consider the *tan* that produced revelations as essentially different from other Daoist troupes, better known for other ritual services, such as *jiao* offerings, exorcisms, and healings. Several sources show that these altars specializing in spirit-writing also performed other rituals for the laity; the later supplements to the *Huashu* discuss how devotees visited one of the spirit-writing altars in times of disaster to present a memorial prayer to Heaven.[100] Chen Zhong, the Zhenwu devotee writing around 1236, relates a Wenchang spirit-writing (*jiangbi*) revelation in 1197 transmitting an order from the Jade Emperor that all people should collect funds to organize a massive *jiao* offering ritual, during which they should register in order to escape the coming apocalypse 度末劫. The order explains that Wenchang was in charge of written communication between people and the Jade Emperor.[101] Chen Zhong goes on to mention other cases where spirit-writing (*jiangbi* and *pijiang*) is used to process communications between the Jade Emperor,

99. *Shangqing Lingbao dafa*, 27.18b–19a. The three permanent ordination centers, also called the Three Mountains, were Longhushan, Gezaoshan 閤皂山, and Maoshan.

100. *Zitong dijun huashu*, 4.32b–35a; Hsieh Ts'ung-hui, *Xin tiandi zhi ming*, 119.

101. *Taishang shuo Xuantian dasheng zhenwu benzhuan shenzhou miaojing*, 5.11b–12a.

Wenchang, lower-level gods (city gods and Earth gods), and Daoist priests in a ritual context, to administer salvation.

In addition to such community rituals that aimed at universal salvation, the spirit-writing altars also provided more mundane ritual services; these were, and remain today, institutions where people come and request healing, advice, and other forms of divine help. It seems the Wenchang spirit-writing altars were consulted by patrons wishing to know about their future careers; the revelations contain scenes about Daoists consulting Wenchang on behalf of their clients.[102] The revelations likely developed from this regular ritual service as a way to explain to the patrons how the divine administration worked and what were the moral rules they applied. People thereby helped by the gods could ask to be initiated and accepted as members of the altar. Cults like those of Zhenwu, Wenchang, Transcendent Lord Xu, and others are both universal (their texts circulated throughout the empire) and local (with temples serving the everyday needs of their communities).[103]

4.5. The Codification of Spirit-Writing as Part of the *daofa* Exorcistic Liturgy

So far, we have seen that during the early modern period, Daoist priests employed various spirit-writing techniques (using a brush, a sieve, or a wooden phoenix) to expedite formal, written communications with the gods in the course of conducting rituals, especially within the exorcistic liturgy. We also have instructions, either to priests or to a larger audience, revealed by these martial Daoist gods during this period. Spirit-writing contributed significantly to the spread of the *daofa* rites, their textual development, and their moral worldview. Some *fashi* specialized

102. Kleeman, *God's Own Tale*, 45.

103. Wang Chien-ch'uan, "Song-Ming shiqi," shows that the group around Liu Ansheng provided healing services.

(but not exclusively) in it, and their altars attracted disciples from among literati and produced revelations. All this explains why spirit-writing techniques were to an important extent developed by and considered the preserve of the *fashi* priests, and the codification of spirit-writing rites was during this period conducted entirely within the milieu of the *daofa*.

There are several sources documenting claims by Song- and Yuan-period *fashi* priests that spirit-writing was their preserve. First, the *Tianhuang zhidao taiqing yuce* 天皇至道太清玉冊 (Most pure and precious books on the supreme Dao of August Heaven), a comprehensive encyclopedic description of Daoism compiled in 1444 by Prince Zhu Quan 朱權 (1378–1448; one of the first Ming emperor's many sons), lists various techniques of spirit-writing within its enumeration of *daofa* traditions, showing they were considered at the time as knowledge monopolized by the *fashi* priests (all *daofa* put a strong emphasis on not showing liturgical documents and manuals to the uninitiated).[104] The end of this list reads: summoning cranes, *zhaohe* 召鶴;[105] perfect light mediumistic divination (*yuanguang*); spirit possession, *futi* 附體; dancing immortal lads, *wu xiantong* 舞仙童; visiting the world of the dead, *guoyin* 過陰; catching (the spirits), *zhuishe* 追攝; spirit-writing (*jiangbi*); the phoenix of the great ultimate, *taiji luan* 太極鸞; the phoenix with a brush affixed to a frame, *bijia luan* 筆架鸞; the phoenix suspended from a silk thread, *xuansi luan* 懸絲鸞; and the phoenix inside a sealed box, *fengxia luan* 封匣鸞.

This remarkable list combines various spirit-writing techniques with other divination methods, all of which allow the priest or his client to obtain divine answers to their questions, and most of which involve a priest manipulating a medium. I have not found any other mention of

104. *Tianhuang zhidao taiqing yuce*, 3.3.31b. On this encyclopedia and its author, see Schachter, "Nanji Chongxu Miaodao Zhenjun." Schachter comments (516–18) on this list and wonders whether Zhu Quan may have practiced spirit-writing or revealed texts through spirit-writing once divinized.

105. The appearance of cranes is a much-mentioned divine response to prayers. A ritual technique for making them appear is described in *Fahai yizhu*, 14.3b–9b.

the latter four variant phoenix techniques, but their names evoke descriptions seen elsewhere: some Wenchang revelations have been described as occurring in a closed room with the writing implement being suspended and moving without any human intervention. We also have a story that evokes the last name, also a technique for writing without a medium; a Song scholar wrote that "the methods of spirit-writing are very diverse; the one called 'spirit-writing within a closed book' is the most mysterious" 降筆之法甚多，封書降筆者最異 and went on to criticize it as a fraud.[106] Like many *daofa* codified during the early modern period, some of these techniques (especially those without a medium) have been discontinued, whereas others thrived and continued to evolve.

The clearest proof that spirit-writing was an affair of the *fashi* priests is that the only liturgies—actual instructions for performers as opposed to factual descriptions by witnesses—we have for the early modern period are found in the two main compendia of ritual manuals for exorcistic traditions, the *Daofa huiyuan* and the *Fahai yizhu* 法海遺珠 (Pearls from the ocean of *daofa* rites). We have already seen some of them in the preceding chapter in the context of instructions to priests on how to obtain divine responses (*baoying*) during rituals. The most detailed, and the one with the clearest connections to modern practice, is found in the latter collection and is entitled *Zhao Zigu xian fa* 召紫姑仙法 (Liturgy for summoning Zigu immortals). It can be no later than the compendium itself, most likely compiled in the late Yuan.[107]

We owe thanks to Judith Boltz for a translation and analysis of this text, which provides a comprehensive script of the process, including talismans and incantations to conjure the gods. She argues that this liturgy was clearly intended for *fashi* priests and involves visualizations and ritual offerings.[108] Of course, priests never held an effective monopoly

106. "Qing fengshu xian 請封書僊," *Quyi shuo*, 10b–11a; this description comes as a part of a larger set of stories about *daofa* techniques.

107. *Zhao Zigu xian fa*, *Fahai yizhu*, 20.1a–4b.

108. Boltz, "On the Legacy of Zigu."

over spirit-writing at any point in history—the Song-period evidence proves the opposite—but the point is that they felt they should.

4.6. Spirit-Writing's Discontents

As with any practice involving interactions between humans and supernatural entities, spirit-writing generated a fair amount of criticism. There is an uninterrupted string of comments by literati from the Song to the present criticizing or ridiculing it as fraud, although such material is not particularly abundant and there exist no grounds for suggesting that the majority of scholars entirely rejected it—the opposite is considerably more likely. Most informative are two types of critique: those from the very milieu that practiced it, Daoists, and those from the state that attempted to ban it.

4.6.1. Internal Critique: Daoists

Daoists developed critiques of spirit-writing early on; they form part of a larger field of vibrant debates that animated Daoist milieus through the Song, Yuan, and early Ming periods concerning the new ritual techniques introduced by the *daofa*. These critiques were the flip side of the coin in the process of adopting the gods, languages, and techniques of these traditions within the classical liturgy: such adoption went very deep and transformed the whole Daoist practice, but each practitioner and codifier drew his own red lines and identified what was judged unacceptable. Spirit-writing was as contentious as other practices involving possession and direct interventions by gods of questionable origins. An important example is provided by Lü Yuansu in his *Daomen dingzhi* 道門定制 (Fixed institutions for Daoism, preface 1188). When discussing the names of the celestial officers who can be addressed in ritual requests and memorials, Lü warns against adding those not warranted by the classical liturgical sources.

> All the more (you are mistaken if) you trust those earnest (dead people) who communicate through spirit-writing, mistake them for superior transcendents, and worship them. You should know that they are like the manifestations of Guanyin discussed in the *Yishengzhuan*.
>
> 況信自降筆至誠之士，誤為上真而敬事之。不知此即《翊聖傳》中所謂化見觀音之類爾。[109]

Later on, Lü insists that gods known through spirit-writing are not trustworthy 若降筆所傳，皆未可信 and that "spirit-writing is a demonic (perversion) of our teachings, and the Daoist novices who 'sell words' know nothing about Daoist liturgy" 降筆爲教門之魔而鬻字道童不曉科教.[110] This suggests Daoists were doing good business when providing spirit-writing services for clients. An esspecially powerful voice in these debates is the towering figure of Bai Yuchan, one of the most influential authors on the *daofa* traditions and a man who never shied away from polemics. In a dialogue with his disciples, Bai states:

> Some mix the oral techniques of the *wu* with the proper liturgy; others call "secret transmission" the words obtained from spirits and immortals through spirit-writing. When asked, they say that it conforms to the liturgy; when shown that they are wrong, they cling to their revelations saying it is true transmission. Alas! The errors of these perverse masters are not the fault of the masses, but the result is that the blind lead the many and that delusions produce more delusion. What a pity!
>
> 或以師巫之訣而雜正法，或以鬼仙降筆而謂祕傳，問之則答為依科，別之則執為真授，嘻！邪師過謬，非眾生咎，一盲引眾，迷以傳迷。哀哉！[111]

This sort of judgment and the fear of letting spirit-writing practitioners introduce uncontrolled innovations found their way into codifi-

109. *Daomen dingzhi*, 1.12a. This mention of the Guanyin transformations does not appear in the extant versions of the *Yisheng baode zhuan*.

110. *Daomen dingzhi*, 3.49a, 7.36b.

111. *Haiqiong Bai zhenren yulu*, 2.15b.

cations and ritual documents—including the *Tiantan yuge* 天壇玉格 (Jade rules for the heavenly altar), the manual for codifying ordinations compiled and used by the Heavenly Master institution at Longhushan. In this work, probably compiled during the Yuan period, one model memorial to Heaven, sent by a priest who has ordained a novice in a *daofa* tradition, reads: "I certify this novice is not someone who has been trained in perverse rites, who is unfilial and disloyal, who holds to perversity and practices spirit-writing, and whose immoral behavior ruins moral principles" 曾受邪法, 不忠不孝, 挾邪降筆, 淫亂大倫等人.[112]

In his important summary of Daoist history, doctrine, and practice, *Daomen shigui* 道門十規 (Ten principles of Daoism), the forty-third Heavenly Master Zhang Yuchu 張宇初 (1361–1410) very explicitly rejects spirit-writing, along with other divination techniques, in a list quite similar to that of Zhu Quan:

> Perfect light (divination), spirit possession, making divine generals manifest their presence, sieve possession, wielding the phoenix, water contemplation (divination): all of these perverse ideas and practices are not things that practitioners of the correct rituals should mention.
>
> 又等圓光、附體、降將、附箕、扶鸞、照水諸項邪說行持，正法之士所不宜道。[113]

We also have a pronouncement from an unnamed master of the Qingwei 清微 tradition (the most prestigious *daofa* from the Yuan period onward); this master is probably Zhao Yizhen 趙宜真 (?–1382) or his disciple Liu Yuanran 劉淵然 (1351–1432), who restates the same idea in a more nuanced way. This passage discusses how thunder gods can arrive immediately and should not be summoned (made present) lightly:

112. "Baoguan zhuang shi 保官狀式," *Tiantan yuge, Daofa huiyuan*, 249.15a. On this text, see Goossaert, *Heavenly Masters*, 115–27.

113. *Daomen shigui*, 12a.

> Spirit possession, opening the light,[114] making divine generals manifest their presence, obtaining a (divine) response in one's fingers,[115] water contemplation, consecrating the arm (of a medium), seizing the dead, causing the banners to fall:[116] in all cases, the spirits of the dead (thus summoned) are not divine, and the rituals performed for them do not produce (divine) responses. They are mere techniques. One could use them to instruct people based on the teachings of the gods, but people who really know the Dao do not engage in them.
>
> 附體、開光、降將、報指、照水、封臂、攝亡、墜幡。其鬼不神,其事不應,皆術法也。可以神道設教,知道者不為也。[117]

In other words, our codifier recognizes that priests use spirit-writing (here *fengbi*) among other techniques to make spirits present, but this is a lower technique.

One cannot fail to notice that the very same Daoist milieus both use spirit-writing with abandon and criticize it. Indeed, Lü Yuansu has no qualms about quoting approvingly a theological statement from an oral revelation by Zhenwu, even though he rejects spirit-writing.[118] Zhang Yuchu included many spirit-written texts in the Daoist canon whose compilation he oversaw—he even included Lord Xin's 1290 spirit-written revelation in a text he edited. This is not a case of two forms of Daoism ("popular" and "elite," if you will) differing about orthodoxy and heterodoxy. Rather, we see a moment of extremely intense ritual and textual

114. This certainly refers here to a divination technique similar to *yuanguang* rather than the more common meaning of consecrating an icon.

115. This technique, mentioned in a few places in the Daoist canon, is described in a text by a Quanzhen Daoist, Niu Daochun 牛道淳 (fl. 1296): the *fashi* priest causes the patient or medium to place his hand above the incense burner, and from how the heat affects the fingers he divines the response to his question; *Wenshi zhenjing zhu*, 7.12a. This passage also discusses *pijiang* as a method where the gods write on paper and predict future events. It constitutes a rare indication that early Quanzhen Daoists were familiar with spirit-writing.

116. I have found only one other mention of this technique in the Daoist canon, which does not provide any explanation.

117. *Qingwei yuanjiang dafa*, 25.7b. This passage, with some variants, is also included in *Daofa huiyuan*, 1.6a, which adds: "these are not *daofa*" 非道法也.

118. *Daomen dingzhi*, 2.1b.

creativity with a number of persons in authority who use the spirit-written texts and practices they approve of while being wary of what others may be up to if left to their own devices. This tension, already plainly in evidence in the early stages of spirit-writing history, always remains.

4.6.2. External Polemics: Buddhists and Others

We have seen that already in medieval times, Buddhists produced revelations using techniques that were uncannily similar to Daoist ones. Buddhists contributed to the development of presence-type rites through the Sinicization of Tantric techniques; however, they remained wary of producing revelations, and by the early modern period, the flow of indigenous apocrypha of medieval times had largely dried out. We would thus expect elite Buddhist monks (the ones who left writings for us to read) to hold a rather dim view of the essentially Daoist revelatory frenzy going on around them. Yet, not all Buddhist mentions of spirit-writing are negative; apparently, some Buddhist authors found it a legitimate way to learn from the gods, and we find casual references to spirit-writing in the writings of several Yuan- and Ming-period monks, some suggesting the monks themselves practiced it.[119]

However, there were also more hostile Buddhist responses to the rise of spirit-writing. One of them was expressed in the context of the bitter religious conflict that opposed Buddhists and Daoists at the Mongol court between the 1250s and 1280s. Buddhists accused Quanzhen Daoist leaders of appropriating Buddhist monasteries and spreading, in written and pictorial form, defamatory stories concerning the famous *huahu* theory, according to which the Buddha was just a form taken by Laozi to teach barbarians a lesser, cruder form of religion. Buddhists won debates at court in 1255 and 1258, leading to the destruction of a list of books containing the *huahu* stories, and in 1281, in a fit of rage, Emperor Qubilai ordered the destruction of the whole Daoist canon. Then a Buddhist monk, Xiangmai 祥邁, was tasked in 1291 to

119. He Lei, "Songdai 'jixian' shi kaolun," 263.

present the throne with a comprehensive account of these debates from a Buddhist perspective. The resulting text, *Bianweilu* 辯偽錄 (Record of distinguishing the false), is an important but biased source on debates about scriptures and revelations. Xiangmai writes: "Today's Daoists indulge ever more in shallow techniques. Some practice phoenix writing and disorder the religious texts; they only crave for occasions to drink at night" 今之道士更騁淺術。或有扶鸞而亂書，秖貪夜飲.[120] Then follows a long list of ritual and self-cultivation techniques of which the Buddhist monk disapproves.

The line here is that spirit-writing allows ill-intentioned persons to alter scriptures and mix their own inventions with truth; it does not necessarily imply that all spirit-writing is a fraud, but it is unverifiable by nature and therefore to be avoided. This line will remain the mainstream Buddhist attitude toward the practice in the following centuries: better to rely on the orthodox scriptures than to take chances with unreliable texts. Buddhist monastic leaders were consistently trying to discourage their lay (married) adepts from engaging in it, and yet many of them nonetheless did.[121]

An entirely different line of attack is to portray spirit-writing not merely as unreliable, or even a fraud, but as downright dangerous possession. This line is taken in a story, dated 1165, by Hong Mai, where he discusses a young man practicing spirit-writing and becoming haunted by a female spirit pretending to be an immortal. The hapless young man is trapped in a love relationship with the spirit, who manifests herself through writing poems, visiting him in his dreams, and appearing in the flesh—once again showing the continuities between the various types of presence. She has taken such control of him that, says Hong Mai, she writes with his own hand, not needing the sieve anymore. His life can only be saved by the performance of a Daoist judicial ritual.[122]

120. *Bianweilu*, 2.761a. Further, the author accuses Qiu Changchun 丘長春 (1148–1227) of having practiced *xingluan* 行鸞 (*Bianweilu*, 2.761a), a term that indeed appears in one of Qiu's poems, but I have not found any other evidence that this term may refer to spirit-writing.

121. Fan Chun-wu, "Jinxiandai Zhongguo fojiao yu fuji."

122. "Nügui huo Qiu Duo 女鬼惑仇鐸," *Yijianzhi*, yi 乙, j. 17, 328–29; a very similar story in "Pengying zhenren 蓬瀛真人," *Yijianzhi*, zhigeng 支庚, j. 2, 1148–49.

4.6.3. State Interventions

Writing in the early thirteenth century, Yue Ke 岳珂 (1183–1234; a scholar-official and grandson of Yue Fei) denounces two popular religious activities in the capital (Hangzhou) that he finds abhorrent: Buddhists engaging in public shows of self-mutilation and Daoists setting up "shops" along the streets to practice spirit-writing 列肆通衢爲箕筆之妖. He reports that people considered there was nothing the state could do about it but invokes an 1116 imperial edict (which can indeed be found in official records) that successfully wiped out similar practices in the then-capital Kaifeng. He quotes this edict as saying, "(Ruffians) use spirit-writing to build temples and gather crowds, and give (their gods) titles such as Heavenly worthy or Great immortal; the words they write are useless and their spoken words are nonsense" 以箕筆聚衆立堂, 號曰天尊大仙之名。書字無取, 語言不經.[123] This edict points to how the practice was organized, public, and popular, as well as controversial, early on. It also makes the important point that oral and written revelations were practiced in the same place and by the same specialists. This policy was followed by the Yuan regime, who banned spirit-writing (*fuluan*) in 1317.[124] However, we do not have many traces of effective curbs on the practice during the whole Song and Yuan periods. As we will see, the same pattern continued under the Ming and Qing.

4.7. A Chronology

The abundant data discussed above was arranged analytically in order to make sense of the various types of sources and contexts for the practice of spirit-writing; as a conclusion, it will be useful to replace them on a timeline in order to attempt to identify a developmental logic. As previ-

123. "Xianshi yijiao zhi jin 仙釋異教之禁," *Kuitanlu*, 6.15b–16b; for the 1116 edict, see *Song huiyao jigao*, 65.

124. Article "Qisai shenshe" 祈賽神社, *Yuan dianzhang*, Xingbu 刑部, 19.

ously mentioned, several scholars have clearly distinguished between different independent spirit-writing traditions; the Purple Maiden cult using the sieve and channeling the dead and the phoenix techniques channeling high gods and producing scriptures. But I would like to insist on the continuities: the most common term for spirit-writing is *jiangbi*, which is used both in Daoist ritual contexts and for high gods and, in domestic contexts, for interrogating the dead. Rather than two different traditions, then, I propose a scenario of progressive development.

In all likelihood, the earliest forms of spirit-writing were possession-type practices, where mediums wrote instead of or, more likely, in addition to speaking. They caused the dead, known or unknown, to write down brief information, advice, and prognostication. At some point, during the tenth century at the latest, Daoists started to work with such mediums and develop new rites (the *daofa*) to integrate and control these mediums and their gods within a Daoist bureaucratic framework and deploy them for their own purposes. In so doing, they were following the lead of Tang-period Buddhists practicing Tantric rites of interrogating the gods through a medium. As a result, they developed presence-type rites, which make gods perceptible to the audience, who can hear them speak or see them write, within a framework dense with control procedures: liturgies for precisely staging the manifestation of divine presence, procedures for nominating gods and humans to divine positions, and moral codes to ensure no priest or god becomes unruly.[125] Many spirit-writing and other presence-type rites during this period involved a *fashi* controlling a medium, but not all, as *fashi* also practiced controlled self-possession (such as in the Wenchang tradition); in any case, it is the control framework that distinguishes presence-type production of divine presence and revelations from the possession type.

While the presence-type rites (notably spirit-writing) of the *fashi* thrived from the tenth century onwards, the tradition of the mediums naturally continued to exist, but by the Song, Daoist *fashi* were the most

125. Goossaert, "Divine Codes."

respected, most sought after, and possibly most common performers of spirit-writing. They included many educated laypeople, even officials, initiated as *fashi* but not living as professional priests, hence the common but flawed impression that spirit-writing was a lay technique providing ordinary people with unmediated communication with the divine.[126] These *fashi* often used spirit-writing during communal rituals or at the request of patrons; it was part of the Daoist liturgical tool kit and therefore served different purposes in different contexts.

Because manifestations of divine presence as practiced by the *fashi* took place within a moral bureaucratic framework, it could—indeed, should—be used to manifest spirits of a higher level than just the dead. The *fashi* priests first and foremost performed the divine presence of their divine allies to whom they were sworn brothers, disciples, or subordinate officials (all stable, long-term, and emotionally charged relationships), not the unknown dead or distant deities. These divine allies were mainly comprised of the ambiguous and powerful gods of the *daofa*: thunder gods and other martial exorcists, such as Black Killer and Zhenwu, as well as, in a more civilian (but still eschatological and exorcist) mode, Wenchang and Transcendent Lord Xu. The *fashi* made their allied gods write down divine edicts and judgments, notably when nominating humans in the heavenly bureaucracy (the living when ordained, the dead when receiving posthumous salvation). In some cases, they requested advice on ritual and self-cultivation practices, and the advice came as recorded question-and-answers sessions, tracts and exhortations, moral narratives (the gods telling their own lives as a model for living humans to emulate), technical instructions, commentaries and explanations on scriptures, and in a few cases as scriptures themselves: I will explore these genres in the next chapter. All of these constitute spirit-written revelations, a discursive product of the larger use of spirit-writing by *fashi* priests.[127] Not all spirit-writing performers

126. Boltz, "Not by the Seal of Office Alone."

127. I concede that none of the manuals describing the use of spirit-writing to expedite ritual procedures can be safely dated earlier than the twelfth-century revelations,

who made the dead write poetry, as discussed in the collections of anecdotes, were *fashi* priests, but all revelations—the focus here—were produced by them.

The personal bond created between the god and the living disciple through the revelation extends the logic of the bond between priest and his allied god: they have long-term reciprocal duties, and breaching them entails grave consequences—unlike a visitor to a temple asking a question through divination. Black Killer repeats ad nauseam to his devotees that if they do not live by his oral commandments, they will suffer grievously for it. Chen Zhong claims that those who despise Zhenwu's oral revelations and instructions or claim they are nonsense will soon die of nasty diseases.[128]

A few tenth- and eleventh-century cases of such revelations are mentioned in later sources but not firmly confirmed. They become a solid fact from the twelfth century onward, when we see complex texts produced by *fashi* altars dedicated to the worship of savior gods: 1107 for Zhao Sheng, 1131 for Xu Xun, 1168 for Wenchang, and 1184 for Zhenwu. They are regional variations (Zhao Sheng in Jiangnan, Wenchang in Sichuan, Xu in Jiangnan and Jiangxi, and Zhenwu in Hubei) of the same model. The groups that produced these texts are characterized by three elements that would later become constant features of late imperial, modern, and contemporary spirit-writing groups. The first element is the affiliation of adepts to the god producing the revelations as disciples (*dizi*) within an altar (*tan*). Disciples receive from the god an ordination name, and thus are inscribed in heavenly registers. The second element is the representation of the revealing god as both a full-fledged member of the heavenly bureaucracy and a personal savior playing a unique role in the salvation of humanity and caring individually for each of his devotees.

---

suggesting my developmental scheme (first, routine use of spirit-writing by *fashi* for their ritual needs, then some groups expanding the practice into the production of revelation) is not based on a bullet-proof textual chronology.

128. *Taishang shuo Xuantian dasheng zhenwu benzhuan shenzhou miaojing*, 6.20a.

The third element is an eschatological scenario: early Wenchang texts present him as sent by the Jade Emperor to help humans avoid the apocalypse—a basic theme elaborated on by subsequent groups ever since.[129] The preface of the *Huashu* explains that the *feiluan* spirit-writing technique was devised in Heaven precisely to save humans in a time of eschatological urgency:

> I have created the rite of the flying phoenix to civilize and enlighten (people), so that I can manifest myself in spirit-writing among humans: this is based on the principle of complete communication between this world and the otherworld. I have humbly received the (Jade) Emperor's approval (of this procedure) in his humane love of ordinary people.
>
> 作飛鸞闡化之法，筆降人間，為幽明通貫之理，仰蒙帝意，仁愛下民。[130]

The same message is found in the Jingming and Zhenwu revelations; the 1131 Jingming texts are set in the context of the disastrous Jurchen invasions and clearly discuss the salvation of the Chinese; the Zhenwu texts are apocalyptic through and through.

4.8. Conclusion: A Daoist Model?

The analysis deployed in this chapter goes against the grain of most of the existing literature on spirit-writing, which sees little or no role for Daoists, whereas I see the latter as key actors in the story. Mainstream historiography sees spirit-writing as evolving from the Zigu divination practices and being gradually appropriated by literati at large.[131] The

129. Hsieh Ts'ung-hui, *Xin tiandi zhi ming*, 113–15; Goossaert, "Modern Daoist Eschatology."

130. *Zitong dijun huashu*, preface, 4a.

131. Xu Dishan, *Fuji mixin de yanjiu*; Chao Wei-pang, "Origin and Growth of the Fu Chi"; Boltz, "On the Legacy of Zigu"; Wang Chien-ch'uan, "Song-Ming shiqi"; He Lei, "Songdai 'jixian' shi kaolun"; Jordan and Overmyer, *Flying Phoenix*; Hu Jiechen, "Terminology and Typology."

main reason for my different perspective is that as argued in the introduction, in addition to narratives (who, when?) and revealed texts (what?), I also pay attention to liturgical instructions (how?). And all the instructions on spirit-writing performance predating the fifteenth century are found in *daofa* manuals in the Daoist canon; there are about a dozen (all quoted in this and the previous chapter), ranging in length and detail from a few lines to a whole chapter. This is a sizable and significant testimony to the widespread adoption of spirit-writing in Daoist ritual. I also noted that almost all substantial spirit-written texts (as opposed to short occasional poems) we have from this period are linked to *daofa* gods and are found in the Daoist canon.

I do not mean my analysis to refute mainstream historiography but to expand our vision. The early modern period certainly was a time of effervescent ritual innovations, and many people across the social hierarchies experimented at manipulating spirits to gain knowledge or power. Daoists were never alone in the game, and literati playing at "inviting Zigu" on their own are also part of the story. If this book was about writing poetry, it might be possible to adopt a less "Daoist-centric" perspective; but I work here on revelations, and the evidence is overwhelmingly linked to Daoist ritual traditions.

To further clarify my analytical framework, I must also restate a key point: by "Daoist" I mean a person who has obtained an initiation (the standard form being receiving an ordination register giving one a rank in the divine administration). Throughout history, from early medieval times to the present, many of these people were not clerics living in a temple (and being recognized by the state as clerics) or running a professional ritual business, but they were scholars, merchants, or housewives. Thinking of scholars and Daoists as opposed to one another uses an excessively narrow definition of "Daoist" that opens many pitfalls. Many of the ritual codifications and revelations discussed in this chapter and the rest of the book were produced by people who were both scholars (sometimes officials) and Daoists—this is true of the Wenchang adepts, who had their own ordination register and performed Lingbao rituals, of the Yutang dafa codifier Lu Shizhong, and of many others.

My analytical model, which focuses on ritual techniques and therefore foregrounds the role of Daoists, attempts to explain the development of early spirit-writing from the perspective of internal logic, focusing on evolving modes of the production of divine presence to meet various religious needs. Hsieh Ts'ung-hui in his own analysis also lists external causes, such as the twelfth-century Jurchen invasions and subsequent eschatological anxiety; the merchant economy and print culture, as well as the growing education and examination system that boosted literacy and the demand for texts; the rise of temple cults and their gods, who were eager to communicate with their patrons and to amass legitimacy; and the "Three Teachings" discourse favoring new religious syntheses outside of clerical institutions.[132] These are all important factors in the rise of spirit-writing—and similar arguments can be made about the second phase of spirit-writing development in the late Ming, as we will see in chapter 6. In this book, however, I hope to show that the same demand for revelations from gods could be met with different modes of production and that spirit-writing had a specific ritual logic.

What innovations did spirit-writing bring to the repertoire of techniques to make the gods speak and write? It combined the advantages of two preexisting types of revelation. Like type 3 (possession), it was public and could offer the sensory experience of divine presence to audiences and therefore convince and involve them in the works of the gods; yet, like type 4 (visualization), it allowed the advanced adepts to secure divinization and advancement in the divine bureaucracy. Its personal instructions, even though they were tied to specific humans, were deemed of general use and value and disseminated, either within groups of initiates or in some cases (scriptures and hagiographies) to a general audience. To better explore this issue, we must now turn to the contents of the early spirit-written revelations.

132. Hsieh Ts'ung-hui, *Xin tiandi zhi ming*, 132–35.

CHAPTER FIVE

Revealed Texts, 1000–1400

In the previous chapter, I examined the records detailing the practice of spirit-writing in the early modern period, including narratives as well as manuals prescribing how to perform it. In this chapter, I will focus on the revealed texts themselves and look at their genres and content in the context of other revelations during the same period.

5.1. The Early Modern Revelatory Landscape

The flurry of revealed texts during the early modern period created new religious knowledge, even though we must remain wary of taking the beautiful trees of elaborate revealed scriptures for the forest of religious discourse. Reading through the literature of this period, especially anecdotes and morality tales, one gets the distinct impression that knowledge about the otherworld—Who are the gods? What happens after death? How to protect oneself from demons and illness?—is still largely derived from dreams, visits to the netherworld, and other encounters, rather than revealed texts.

Earlier, I defined five broad, ideal-typical categories of revelation: 1) sutra, 2) encounter, 3) possession, 4) visualization, and 5) presence—all of which are represented in the textual productions of the early modern period (1000–1400). Among them we can identify two key innovations, the emergence and rapid development of type 5, presence, and new developments in type 2, encounter, which I call "open encounter." The former has been extensively discussed in chapters 3 and 4. Let me now introduce the latter so as to complete our panorama of the revelatory landscape up to 1400 before discussing the dynamics of that landscape.

The open-encounter type is intimately linked to the rise of inner alchemy, which constitutes one of the most important turning points in the history of Daoism.[1] It inherited from the tradition of operative alchemy, with its secret revealed texts, but it established new paradigms of textual production. Although the master-disciple bond remained sacred and paramount, the transmission of secret scriptures became largely irrelevant; most of the key texts in inner alchemy were poems or essays written by living masters and were freely available on the book market, such as Zhang Boduan's 張伯端 (eleventh century) *Wuzhenpian* 悟真篇 (Verses on the awakening to transcendence). What were not openly accessible were the oral instructions from the master. Does this mean there is no revelation in inner alchemy? This is far from being the case.

First, there are some earlier revealed sutra-type scriptures (such as the Tang-period *Yinfujing* 陰符經, "Scripture of the hidden tally") that served as foundational texts for inner-alchemical commentaries. Then there are, in the early stages of the development of inner alchemy, revelations of a classical secret-encounter type. In the preface to the *Lingbao bifa* 靈寶畢法 (Definitive method of the Lingbao; eleventh or early twelfth century), the legendary Zhongli Quan tells how he found a *Lingbaojing* 靈寶經 (Scripture of Lingbao) in a cave in the Zhongnan Mountains; this text was in three parts, authored by Yuanshi tianzun,

1. For a thorough recent introduction to inner alchemy, see Pregadio, *Way of the Golden Elixir*.

Yuanhuang 元皇, and Taishang laojun respectively.[2] He then rewrote the material into the *Lingbao bifa* for circulation in the world. Then, there are also cases of presence-type revelations; we have seen how a Jingming Daoïst recorded his dialogues with Transcendent Lord Xu about inner alchemy as well as exorcistic rituals.

But the bulk of the inner-alchemical texts ascribed to immortals and other divine entities were not scriptures; they were oral instructions and poems. An important example is the many poems on self-cultivation authored by the legendary Lü Dongbin—or, to use his common epithet in modern times, Patriarch Lü 呂祖. From the late Ming onward, Patriarch Lü became an extraordinarily prolific author of spirit-written texts. His corpus before 1550, however, is quite sizable but without any mention of spirit-writing. Lai Chi Tim makes the crucial point that around 1570 we see the first spirit-writing texts from Patriarch Lü at the same time as a shift in his soteriological discourse, from saving individuals (whom he encounters and instructs) to saving the world, *dushi* 度世.[3] This corresponds to a shift in his persona: Patriarch Lü who teaches through encounters is often whimsical, difficult to approach, and enigmatic in his teachings; this stands in contrast to spirit-written instructions from Wenchang or Lord Xu, which are straightforward, serious, and dependable. Patriarch Lü, when later teaching through spirit-writing, will in his turn become more predictable and dependable.

How were Patriarch Lü's and the other immortals' poems that were circulating between the early Song and Ming produced? Isabelle Ang has argued that a mediumistic cult of Lü Dongbin developed under the Southern Song, as did spirit-written instructions.[4] This is possible, but the evidence is very scant: we have a Song-period autobiography by him, *zizhuan* 自傳, but we do not know how it was revealed.[5] Ang also

2. *Bichuan Zhengyang zhenren lingbao bifa*, preface.

3. Lai Chi Tim, "Ming Qing daojiao Lüzu jiangji xinyang de fazhan," 141–43.

4. Ang, "Le culte de Lü Dongbin sous les Song du Sud," 484–85.

5. Lai Chi Tim, "Ming Qing daojiao Lüzu jiangji xinyang de fazhan," 141. The autobiography is found in *Nenggaizhai manlu*, 18.2a–b.

mentions two anecdotes in the *Yijianzhi.* The first concerns a female ghost writing through a young man, who says that she was instructed in self-cultivation by Patriarch Lü—this does not imply that Patriarch Lü instructed living adepts in this way.[6] The second relates the case of a son of an elite family in Suzhou who becomes mad and lives as an antinomian ascetic, nicknamed Master Grass Robe, Suoyi xiansheng 蓑衣先生, and rejects all social contact. He acquires divinatory powers and answers the questions of those who beseech him by appearing in their dreams. He instructs people to worship Patriarch Lü; on several occasions, he leaves instructions for them written on walls, and his poems circulated widely. In other words, we have a person who behaves like Patriarch Lü, but I see no clear indication that he is a medium of Patriarch Lü.[7]

The mention of Master Grass Robe writing on walls is crucial to his imitation of Patriarch Lü. This is indeed a frequent form of Patriarch Lü's writing. The amount of poetry produced by Patriarch Lü during the Song and Yuan periods is considerable and has been collected in several anthologies. Nowhere are we told how they were produced, with the exception of poems written on walls. What actually happened before a poem was found on a wall? Different scenarios are plausible and may have played out in different cases: first, an ascetic identifies so much with Patriarch Lü or another immortal that he writes on walls, signing Patriarch Lü. Second, people may have encountered Patriarch Lü in dreams or visualizations and been instructed to go and write on walls on his behalf. Whatever the case, this act of writing on walls creates a new subtype in our typology of revelation: it is the result of an encounter, but the very act of writing in a public place means that this revelation is for the whole of humanity, not one privileged ascetic. Noga Ganany has shown how poems on walls constitute a genre that is linked to the immortals' traveling, where leaving plainly visible traces of their encounters with humans, which are sometimes infructuous, served as a warning

6. "Nügui huo Qiu Duo," *Yijianzhi,* 328–29.
7. "Suoyi xiansheng 蓑衣先生," *Yijianzhi,* bu 補, j. 12, 1657–60.

to others.[8] It is thus markedly different from secret encounters that are mostly talked about by people who have no access to them. But it is equally different from spirit-writing, because there is no known way to control it ritually; indeed, there is no ritual method (*daofa*) associated with Patriarch Lü that gave humans any control whatsoever over him. No early modern Daoist claimed to be able to make Patriarch Lü present.

Other documents show that, during the early modern period, communication with Patriarch Lü and the other immortals was played out in the encounter mode, with the immortal appearing in flesh, or in dreams, or as a voice. In the largest Yuan-period collection of stories about him, the *Chunyang dijun shenhua miaotongji* 純陽帝君神化妙通紀 (Annals of the marvelous communications through divine transformations of the Imperial Lord Pure Yang), Patriarch Lü takes disciples and engages in dialogues with them; he instructs them but does not provide full-fledged essays or scriptures, rather he guides them in the practice.[9] The same structure characterizes the development of inner alchemy in general. When immortals (later identified as Zhongli Quan and Lü Dongbin) encounter Wang Chongyang 王重陽 (1113–70), the future first patriarch of the Quanzhen order, they instruct him orally and give him the *Wupian miyu* 五篇祕語 (Five secret instructions), basically an injunction for him to practice self-cultivation. But the Quanzhen order did not keep this text secret, for it is published in a widely circulated hagiography and even carved onto two stele inscriptions.[10] And, just as significant, it was never considered a particularly important text for Quanzhen Daoists.

A similar pattern of an encounter with an immortal who instructs the adept orally, and whose instructions the adept writes down in his own manual, is found in the highly influential case of Zhang Boduan. In his preface to his masterwork, Zhang writes that in 1069, while working

8. Ganany, "Origin Narratives," 255–64.

9. On this source, see Ang, "Le culte de Lü Dongbin des origines"; and Katz, *Images of the Immortal.*

10. Marsone, *Wang Chongyang*, 46.

as a clerk, "I moved a transcendent to give me the instructions for the golden elixir, the medicine, and the fire phasing; his words were very accessible" 感真人授金丹、藥物、火候之訣，其言甚簡. On this basis, Zhang later wrote the *Wuzhenpian*.[11] It was only in the writings of later-generation disciples that this anonymous transcendent would be identified as Liu Haichan 劉海蟾, another legendary immortal who was as prominent as Patriarch Lü and Zhongli Quan in twelfth-century lore before his relative importance diminished.

What kind of relationship did early modern inner alchemists maintain with their immortal predecessors? They obviously worshiped them and sometimes were graced with successive encounters. But they do not seem to have maintained regular, sustained communication, as was the case in the *daofa*. To take one example, Bai Yuchan wrote a letter to Zhang Boduan, whom he considered the patriarch of his lineage, but it is not clear what he expected in response.[12] I hasten to add that this contrast between *daofa* and *neidan* is not between two separate sects but between textual traditions; some (most eminently Bai Yuchan) combined them.

With a few exceptions, then, the whole *neidan* tradition depended greatly on revelations, but these were encounter-type, personal, oral instructions, which usually did not result in a substantial revealed text; instead, the beneficiaries of the revelations "translated" them in their own words. This follows a logic entirely different from spirit-writing. It is to some extent counterintuitive that in a highly literate and erudite tradition such as inner alchemy, revelations remain elusive words. Indeed, alchemical self-cultivators are bent on hearing voices. To take one example, the Daoist canon has a remarkable hagiographical record of the otherwise unknown Dong Shouzhi 董守志 (1160–1227), who lived at the same time and was part of the same religious milieu as the early Quanzhen leaders. The *Ningyang Dong zhenren yuxian ji* 凝陽董真人

11. Skar, "Golden Elixir Alchemy," chap. 4.

12. "Xie Zhang Ziyang shu 謝張紫陽書," *Xiuzhen shishu*, 6.1a–4b; according to Skar, "Golden Elixir Alchemy," 185, it was written in 1215 or 1216.

遇仙記 (Record of the Transcendent Dong Congealed Yang's encounters with immortals) tells how Dong, a Jurchen soldier living in the region of present-day Shaanxi and Gansu, first had a vision of an immortal enjoining him to become a Daoist; he then repeatedly heard voices coming from out of the blue—just like Black Killer first making himself manifest to Zhang Shouzhen—and met in the flesh with three immortals, Zhongli Quan, Lü Dongbin, and Liu Haichan. The latter gave him a seal and talismans so that he could become a successful healer, as well as instructions and poems, which are noted down in the hagiography.

5.2. The Ecology of Revelations

The dynamics of the different types of revelations are not fruitfully analyzed as a competition between different religious groups that stuck to their own established ways of making their gods speak and write—indeed, we have seen several cases of traditions that made simultaneous use of different types. Rather, it allows for the production of different sorts of revealed texts from different categories of gods. The type 5, presence-type texts are revealed by gods who answer summons from the ritual specialists and are therefore not the highest gods—even though Zhenwu and Wenchang were credited with exalted positions in the heavenly bureaucracy. (In their revelations, they are presented not as the local gods they originally were but as primordial stellar gods who became incarnated to undergo exemplary self-perfection and eventually regain their divine status.) The heavenly worthies and the Buddhas, who preach sutra-type scriptures, were not subjected to spirit-writing or other presence-type (summoning) procedures.

Seen in this light, the five types seem to be complementary more than they seem to be opposed to each other. There is a clear connection between the mode of revelation and the discursive content: for expounding general principles, type 1, sutra-type revelations are the most appropriate; to intervene in the course of human affairs, type 5, presence-type ones are more proper. For this reason, the two types have, since the emergence of presence-type revelations, coexisted in a sort of textual ecology. Indeed, even though ritual techniques for producing presence-type texts were available, sutra-type texts continued to be produced in large numbers during the Song and Yuan and ever since. Even in the *daofa* milieu that developed spirit-writing, key texts produced during the Song and Yuan and later still present themselves as preached in Heaven without giving any indication whatsoever regarding how they reached humans.

This becomes particularly clear when we examine the textual legacy of the most important revealing gods of the early modern period: Zhenwu, Wenchang, and Transcendent Lord Xu. In all three cases, we see from the twelfth century onward the formation of corpora of texts by and about these deities that comprise both sutra-type, *jing* 經, without any indication of time and space, and spirit-written (as well as, in the case of Zhenwu, oral) revelations that do not carry the word *jing* in their title but rather provide hagiographic accounts, tracts, and records of pronouncements, *lu* 錄. Consider Zhenwu, from whom we have five different scriptures. One of them, *Taishang shuo Xuantian dasheng zhenwu benzhuan shenzhou miaojing*, has a commentary by Chen Zhong, who abundantly quotes spirit-written content, but the scripture itself is a sutra-type scripture preached in Heaven and simply ends with the indication that "these words were secretly recorded in a jade box, waiting for a later time when an exiled immortal would transmit it to humans" 祕籙琅函, 後有謫仙, 傳於人世 (commenting on this, Chen Zhong relates the history of Zhang Daoling and his successors).[13] Similarly, Wenchang spirit-wrote his autobiography; but the scripture that explains his divine mission, including the Jade Emperor enjoining Wenchang to use spirit-writing to reform humans, the *Yuanshi tianzun shuo Zitong dijun benyuanjing* 元始天尊說梓潼帝君本願經 (Scripture of the original vow of the Imperial Lord of Zitong, preached by the

13. *Taishang shuo Xuantian dasheng zhenwu benzhuan shenzhou miaojing*, 6.23b–24a.

Heavenly Worthy of Primordial Beginning), does not hint at being revealed by spirit-writing. It may very well have been, but it is not presented as such.

Indeed, during the early modern period, spirit-writing is more often associated with oral instructions as well as commentaries on the scriptures than with the scriptures themselves. By the Song period, we begin to see full-fledged commentaries on scriptures revealed by spirit-writing. An early collection of commentaries on the *Daodejing* that lists its sources includes two revealed by gods 鸞筆. One is dated 1253, and the other, undated, was revealed by Wenchang.[14] Both seem to have been lost as independent books but are quoted in this collection.

Even more crucially, we have spirit-written commentaries on modern sutra-type scriptures. Let us take two examples that feature among the most popular and most often chanted scriptures of modern Daoists: the *Yushujing* 玉樞經 (Jade pivot scripture), devoted to the supreme thunder god Puhua tianzun 普化天尊, and the Big Dipper scripture, *Beidoujing*, which we have already encountered. Both appear during the Song period, without any hint at the revelatory method (even though we have seen a story that suggests spirit-writing in the case of the *Beidoujing*). A Daoist named Xu Daoling 徐道齡, active during the 1330s, composed commentaries for both scriptures.[15] His commentary on the "Jade pivot scripture" was "found" by Xu Daoling and is comprised of glosses by Bai Yuchan, Zhang Daoling, a thunder god called Heavenly Lord Zhang 張天君, and Patriarch Lü. How these glosses were produced is not said, but the identity of the gods suggests spirit-writing.[16] Things are more explicit in the Big Dipper scripture. Remaining vague, Xu writes, "it felt as if I had divine inspiration" 似有神助 when writing it.[17] Even more tellingly,

14. *Daode zhenjing jiyi dazhi*, 1.11b.

15. *Jiutian yingyuan leisheng puhua tianzun yushu baojing jizhu*; and *Taishang xuanling beidou benming yansheng zhenjing zhu*.

16. That would be an exception to my claim that there is no spirit-written text by Patriarch Lü before the late Ming period.

17. *Taishang xuanling beidou benming yansheng zhenjing zhu*, "houxu 後序."

Wenchang wrote a preface stating that he read the commentary and approved it.

Yet another scripture, also completely embedded in thunder rituals, shows a comparable pattern: the *Taishang shuo Chaotian xielei zhenjing* 太上說朝天謝雷真經 (True scripture spoken by the Supreme Lord on audience to Heaven and asking forgiveness of the thunder gods). The scripture explains how thunder gods apply the divine code and punish human sins. It does not explain how it was transmitted to humans, but it has two appendices that are clearly spirit-written: first, several talismans and poems "composed in person" 親製 or 親書, by Wenchang and various thunder gods, and then a short exhortation by Heavenly Lord Qingdi 青帝天君 that says "I wrote this eulogy on the scripture through manifesting myself in the brush at the Chengzhen altar" 吾讚經附於誠真靖筆.[18] Here again, the scripture in sutra-type language is explained in more direct human language, in the first person, by exorcistic gods through spirit-writing.

One cannot exclude the possibility that these scriptures were actually produced by spirit-writing, but I have not seen any explicit claim to that effect. There are two exceptions: the *Taishang xiuzhen tiyuan miaodaojing* 太上修真體元妙道經 (Scripture on the marvelous Dao of embodying the origin and cultivating transcendence, by the Supreme Lord) was revealed through spirit-writing in 1261; and, more importantly, *Taishang wuji zongzhen Wenchang dadong xianjing* was spirit-written in 1168. Such cases of explicitly spirit-written scriptures would become very numerous in the next phase of the history of spirit-writing, from the late Ming onwards. For the early modern period, however, the general rule remains that whoever composed *jing* scriptures felt that they should not mention themselves, possibly because the predominant concept was that *jing* are given by the high gods to exceptional humans (such as Zhang Daoling), not to present-day people.

18. *Taishang shuo Chaotian xielei zhenjing*, 18a. The term *jing* 靖 refers to a priest's oratory and can be used as a synonym of altar (*tan*). *Fu* 附 is a standard term for possession.

There is a further case, the *Gaoshang Yuhuang benxing jijing* (in short, *Yuhuangjing*). The two editions (one with commentaries revealed by Zhang Liang) in the Daoist canon do not carry any indication of the mode of revelation. However, as Hsieh Ts'ung-hui has shown, a 1423 edition that retains the original prefaces (removed from the canonical versions), very clearly suggests how the whole scripture was revealed through spirit-writing, *tuoluan* 託鸞.[19] This is an interesting case where sutra-type scenarios are embedded into a spirit-written (i.e., presence-type) revelation. And this was apparently a cause for discomfort for some people, who chose to remove the spirit-writing indications in the canonical edition. The obfuscation of the actual-world origins of sutra-type revelations was seemingly considered necessary for such scriptures to work their purpose.

We also have a detailed revelation narrative of a shortened version of the same scripture, the *Gaoshang Yuhuang benxing jingsui* 高上玉皇本行經髓 (The marrow of the biographical scripture of venerable Jade Emperor). Appended to the scripture itself, this narrative relates how a Qingwei priest, Liu Chuyuan 劉處源, during a moonlit solitary night in 1344 met an immortal sitting in meditation atop a large stone (a trope of encounter narratives). Based on his astrological signs, the immortal predicted upcoming disasters for him but gave him the scripture as a way to ensure protection through psalmody. He gave him the book wrapped in yellow silk.[20] What we have here is the book as an object, transmitted during an encounter, different from the book as a text, written or spoken word by word during a ritualized session. Yet the two types of production coexisted in the same traditions.

19. Hsieh Ts'ung-hui, *Xin tiandi zhi ming*, chaps. 5–6; Hsieh Ts'ung-hui, "*Yuhuang benxing jijing* chushi." I have already mentioned that Wang Chien-ch'uan, "Song-Ming shiqi," reads the evidence differently.

20. "Chuanjing yuanliu 傳經源流," *Gaoshang Yuhuang benxing jingsui*.

5.3. Secrecy and Divulgation

One of the most salient distinctions between our five types of revelation is their specific attitudes to divulgation. Sutra-type texts are by nature universal and open: they are given to humanity as a whole without any anchor in space and time that would limit their relevance to particular categories of humans. In seemingly perfect contrast, encounter-type revelations are given to one particular, deserving human, and thus are logically not to be divulged to other undeserving individuals. This is repeated ad nauseam in medieval revelations, with countless dire warnings to recipients that they will suffer grievously should they divulge it to unqualified persons 非人. Early modern open-encounter revelations, in particular those associated with inner alchemy, stray from that posture to some extent; the poems left on walls by Patriarch Lü could be openly published—but the idea was often that they were not self-sufficient instructions if not illuminated by oral instructions, themselves subjected to restricted transmission.

A Mongol-period hagiographic account of a female immortal, Zhao 趙仙姑, recounts how she met with an immortal when going to the mountains to pick tea, started to practice self-cultivation, and set up her own pure chamber where she was visited at night by that immortal; people could hear them talk. Her kin, justifiably anxious, spied on their conversation, whereupon the immortal declared that "your parents are now eavesdropping on my mystical instructions; this amounts to divulging Heaven's secrets: I must now leave" 汝父母竊聽玄言, 恐泄天機, 吾今去矣.[21] This account stages a dialogue between a human practitioner and an immortal, with the former asking questions and the latter providing teaching, and there is no hint of such teaching taking written form. This theme of "divulging Heaven's secrets" remains very common in the self-cultivation literature down to the present day.

21. "Zhao xiangu 趙仙姑," *Lishi zhenxian tidao tongjian houji*, 6.3b–6b, the quote is on 4a–b.

Presence-type revelations are found in the middle ground between open revelation and secrecy. They sometimes include portions that should not be openly publicized (typically concerning political prophecies as well as liturgy), but such portions are edited out of the published revelation (usually explicitly so), showing them to be special cases in a body of revelations that, although explicitly given to particular people at a particular moment, are meant for the benefit and instruction of the whole of humanity—thus elevating these people to an exalted role as disseminators of divine knowledge. On the other hand, moral instructions and hagiography were for public dissemination; some of the Wenchang revelations were even carved on stele inscriptions.

5.4. Presence-Type Revelations: Content and Innovations

Now that we have placed presence-type texts (mostly produced by spirit-writing) in the larger field of early modern revelations, let us look at their content so as to understand how they brought about innovations in terms of genres and ideas. Because the spirit-writing techniques were varied, we cannot associate this type of revelation with a specific textual style that would be easily recognizable; the level of language, the length of revelations, and the intertextual connections with earlier material all vary considerably. However, the corpus of early modern spirit-written texts coheres around certain genres.

5.4.1. Prophecy and Eschatology

Revelations are an effective way of conveying a message that would be very dangerous to utter in one's own voice, in particular political comments. The prophetic nature of presence-type revelations was already obvious in the *Yisheng baode zhuan*; not only did the revelations of Black Killer play a decisive role in the succession of the suspiciously deceased Taizu, but his divine messages are informed through and through by messianic prophecies of an imminent age of Great Peace, Taiping; the god admonishes the emperor and officials to make this happen and promises them eternal life. The most famous spirit-written political prophecies, however, were the words of Zhenwu.

During the wars between the Jin and the Song, and later during the Mongol invasion of southern China, Zhenwu revealed various texts about the events, which have been thoroughly gathered and analyzed by Pierre-Henry De Bruyn.[22] The earliest one occurred in 1217, when Zhenwu admonished, through spirit-writing (*jiangbi*), the Song general Zhao Fang 趙方 (?–1222), who was holding the region around Wudangshan 武當山 (Zhenwu's sacred mountain) against the Jurchen armies.[23] A few years later, the Mongol armies took the region; the previous year (1233) Zhenwu had revealed through *jiangbi* that "the Black Killer from the north is coming, I too must avoid him." 至聖降筆曰北方黑煞來，吾當避之, and then the god made himself visible atop a tree for three days.[24] The Black Killer here is not his associate Yisheng but rather the fearful Tantric deity Mahakala, who was to become one of the martial protectors of the Yuan Mongol regime, along with Zhenwu, whom the Mongols co-opted. This amounts to an announcement of a regime change. Again, in the area of the Wudangshan, which remained on the frontline for decades, a Buddhist source informs us that in 1273 people prayed to Zhenwu for help, and he answered through spirit-writing (*jiangbi*) that "there is a great black god leading armies from the northeast, I cannot but avoid him" 降筆云：有大黑神，領兵西北方來。吾亦當避. Hearing this, the locals surrendered peacefully and avoided a massacre.[25] De Bruyn has discussed the complex relationship between Zhenwu and

22. De Bruyn, *Le Wudang shan*, 121–33.

23. *Qiantang yishi*, 3.8b. This message is a more personal admonition, treating Zhao as a demon-soldier (under his command), than a prophecy.

24. *Guierji*, 3.25a.

25. *Fozu lidai tongzai*, 22:726.

Mahakala, who clearly had much in common in terms of divine persona but were also enemies.

Even more importantly, a late Yuan source spells out the anti-Mongol nature of the Zhenwu prophecies:

> In 1276, when Jiangnan had just been submitted (to Yuan rule), a poem to the tune of "Moon over East River" spirit-written by Zhenwu at Wudangshan widely circulated among the people. It was carved on wood blocks, printed on yellow paper, and pasted onto walls. It went:
>
> The nine and nine of Heaven and earth have been fixed,
> Flowers blossom after the Qingming festival.
> Mi and Tian (*Fan* 番, barbarians) have turned the world into chaos like (scattered grains of) hemp,
> We are waiting for the dragon and snake (Chinese) to follow after the horses (Mongols).
> Then, like of old, China will (again) be a blessed land,
> And Gu-Yue (*Hu* 胡, barbarians) will return home.
> But for now, if you are hoping for a good life,
> You will die under the moon at East River.
>
> 至元十三年, 江南初内附, 民間盛傳武當山真武降筆書長短句曰西江月者, 鋟刻于梓, 黄紙模印, 貼壁間。其詞云:九九乾坤已定, 清明節候開花。米田天下亂如麻, 直待龍蛇繼馬。依舊中華福地, 古月一陣還家。當初指望作生涯, 死在西江月下。[26]

This text had a considerable fortune in later times. It has been constantly reprinted and transmitted in the sectarian traditions of the Ming and Qing periods, whose apocalyptic eschatology was deeply informed by the ethnic conflicts between the Han Chinese and the northern steppe people.[27]

The same source contains another spirit-written prophecy, this time with the term "wielding the sieve" (*fuji*), and without any identified divine author:

26. "Wudangshan jiangbi 武當山降筆," *Nancun chuogenglu*, 26:328.

27. Cao Xinyu, oral information, September 2019; see also Wang Chien-ch'uan and Pi Qingsheng, *Zhongguo jinshi minjian xinyang*, 220–24 and 224–28, on Zhenwu spirit-written prophecies of the end of the Ming dynasty.

Heaven sends an army of demons to kill inequality,
Unequal people kill unequal people,
Unequal people kill unequal ones,
Only when inequality is exhausted will there be Great Peace.
These spirit-written words have now proven true.

天遣魔軍殺不平，不平人殺不平人，不平者，殺盡不平方太平。此扶箕語，驗之今日，果然。[28]

The Transcendent Lord Xu's cult and its Jingming ritual tradition, so deeply rooted in spirit-writing practices, also had their own prophecy, the so-called Dragon Sand prophecy 龍沙讖, less political but nonetheless highly motivating for adepts. The prophecy itself dates from late medieval times, when hagiographies of Transcendent Lord Xu have him predict that 1,240 years after his apotheosis, a sand islet will form near his temple and 800 of his adepts will become immortals. Lai Chi Tim has brought attention to how this prophecy excited the eschatological imagination of first the Song-Yuan and then late Ming literati, who engaged in spirit-writing communication with Xu and other saints while claiming or hoping they were part of the elect.[29]

Spirit-written prophecies became extremely frequent in the nineteenth century. But during the early modern period, they were still a minority among all prophecies; we have many more examples of children's songs, *tongyao* 童謠, or other such anonymous revelations, one of the most famous being the *Wugongjing* 五公經 (Scripture of the Five Lords), a sutra-type collection that seems to have long circulated in oral form with many variants.[30] If spirit-writing was just one means among others for revealing prophecies, it was the primary vehicle for a whole new eschatological theory that provided a framework for prophecies. This theory, which I call "modern elite eschatology," was (before the modern era) unique to spirit-written revelations and their closely related

28. "Fuji shi 扶箕詩," *Nancun chuogenglu*, 27:343. I follow the translation in ter Haar, "Rumours and Prophecies," 391.

29. Lai Chi Tim, "Ming Qing daojiao Lüzu jiangji xinyang de fazhan," 151–52.

30. Ter Haar, "Sutra of the Five Lords."

scriptures. It is based on the threat of an imminent apocalypse decided by the Jade Emperor and negotiations for postponing it on the basis of humanity's moral reform under the guidance of spirit-writing gods, as opposed to the predictions of fixed, unavoidable dates for the final reckoning. It is an eschatology that emphasizes human agency.[31]

This eschatological message is most developed in the Wenchang revelations. All of the texts spirit-written by Wenchang during the Southern Song, as well as the two early scriptures of the Wenchang cult expounding his mission and cosmic role, *Yuanshi tianzun shuo Zitong dijun benyuanjing* and *Yuanshi tianzun shuo Zitong dijun yingyanjing* 元始天尊說梓潼帝君應驗經 (Scripture of the miraculous responses of the Imperial Lord of Zitong, preached by the Heavenly Worthy of Primordial Beginning), develop a discourse in which the gods are about to unleash apocalyptic disasters onto humanity, and Wenchang is sent on a mission, using spirit-writing, to save as many as possible. To take just one passage:

> I entrust him (Wenchang) to engage in spirit-writing to enlighten and convert humans and to manifest himself throughout the world. Thus, even though the end of the kalpa cannot be called off yet, if one hopes to dispel it, then it should be thanks to this god (Wenchang). I will now summon him for your benefit, and charge him with saving humanity on the brink of the end of the kalpa, so that the human race is not entirely annihilated.
>
> 委行飛鸞, 開化人間, 顯跡天下, 蓋此末劫實未可除, 若欲消之, 此神其可, 吾當為汝等召之, 俾救度末世, 勿使類絕。[32]

Similarly, the preface to the *Huashu* goes: "I have previously received an edict from the Jade Emperor, giving me the right to using the flying phoenix of my own accord; since then, my ink traces have covered the world, so as to save humanity from the apocalypse." 吾先奉玉帝敕, 授以如意飛鸞, 墨跡于天地之間也, 救末劫.[33] This narrative was accepted beyond the circles of the Wenchang cult in Sichuan. In his

31. Goossaert, "Modern Daoist Eschatology."
32. *Yuanshi tianzun shuo Zitong dijun benyuanjing*, 2b.
33. *Zitong dijun huashu*, preface.

commentary on a Zhenwu scripture, Chen Zhong also offers a long, detailed account of the process through which the Jade Emperor announced the end of the kalpa in 1197 and the brutal punishment of sinful humanity, tasked Wenchang to practice spirit-writing in order to warn people, and himself spirit-wrote an edict.[34]

5.4.2. Liturgy and Alchemy

We have seen above that spirit-writing was central to the codification of several ritual traditions, notably the Jingmingfa and Yutang dafa, and produced other manuals, such as the *Deng tianjun xuanling bamen baoying neizhi*. Liturgy was thus an important aspect of the contents of early spirit-written revelation, more so than self-cultivation. The most elaborate *daofa* traditions paid great attention to self-cultivation, and more specifically to inner alchemy, and there was, therefore, as early as the Song period a role for spirit-writing in the development of inner alchemy. But we have seen that the vast majority of alchemical teachings by immortals during that period cannot be ascribed to spirit-writing, and their revelations seem to resort instead to the encounter type. The only piece identified as being spirit-written in the late Yuan anthology *Minghe yuyin* 鳴鶴餘音 (Echoes of the cranes' songs), a large collection of Daoist self-cultivation (mostly inner alchemy) poetry with many pieces by immortals and gods, is revealed by the thunder god Lord Xin.[35] This poem is simply entitled "Spirit-written at Wudang(shan)," 武當降筆, which suggests a close connection between Lord Xin and the contemporary revelations from Zhenwu.

5.4.3. Theology and Doctrine

By the Song, we also begin to see purely doctrinal content revealed through spirit-writing. A good example is the *Taishang xiuzhen tiyuan*

34. *Taishang shuo Xuantian dasheng zhenwu benzhuan shenzhou miaojing*, 5.12a–15a.

35. *Minghe yuyin*, 3.11a.

miaodaojing (Scripture on the Marvelous Dao of cultivating transcendence and embodying the origin, by the Lord on High). This rather long scripture on cosmology and self-cultivation theory appears rather similar in language and content to other sutra-type Daoist scriptures, except that it does not offer an initial scene of dispensation in the heavens. A colophon tells us that it was revealed through spirit-writing in 1261 in the house of a certain Liu Yuanrui 劉元瑞, a Daoist devotee otherwise unknown.[36] Liu could not understand the "transcendent book (produced by) the divine presence" 降靈真本 and hid it, but after he died, it was published by another adept. The revealing deity has a title from a thunder ministry and is called Transcendent Lord Yuansu 元素真君, which in other Song texts is a title given to Zhang Daoling.

5.4.4. Moral Tracts

Moral teachings were an important component of presence-type revelations from the start; their gods are committed to moral reform and the enforcement of the divine codes. The *Yisheng baode zhuan* is replete with injunctions to morality, notably for officials to be fair, loyal, and disinterested. Wenchang's autobiography, the *Huashu*, shows him performing all the standard acts of morality—filial piety, loyalty, compassion, and sexual restraint—and his mission as appointed by the Jade Emperor is to "rectify people's hearts," *zheng renxin* 正人心.

Zhenwu's revealed teachings, in both written and oral form, are equally informed by the god's urge to change humans' perverse ways of life. In one story, a merchant decides to become an activist vegetarian who prints and distributes tracts exhorting people not to kill animals; he meets with opponents. Zhenwu then possesses the merchant and delivers a message explaining the retribution for taking life; later, the merchant is found dead, without having been ill (i.e., he has been divinized).[37] Chen Zhong's commentary, one of the best sources on

36. The same name appears as a divinized patriarch of the Qingwei tradition, but it is not certain it is the same person.

37. "Hua shi shayu 華氏殺魚," *Xuantian shangdi qishenglu*, 8.5a–6b.

Zhenwu's revelations, claims that following the teachings of the *Taishang ganyingpian* 太上感應篇 (The Supreme Lord's tract on action and retribution, the most revered morality book, discussed in the next chapter) allows one to avoid demons.[38]

The corpus of Wenchang revelations contains two short tracts that are the direct antecedents of a genre that would strongly flourish from the late Ming onward. The first is *Quan jing zizhi wen* 勸敬字紙文 (Exhortation to respect papers with characters written on them), calling people to respect written characters. The moral injunction not to sully any written character goes back to the early medieval Daoist precepts, *jie* 戒, and would become a major theme in modern morality books.[39] The second is *Jie shizi wen* 戒士子文 (Admonishment to scholars), revealed by Yan Hui 顏回, Confucius's favorite disciple, who by Song times had gone on to a career within Wenchang's divine administration.[40]

Arguably the most influential of all moral tracts revealed through spirit-writing during the early modern period is the *Wudangshan Xuantian shangdi chuixunwen* 武當山玄天上帝垂訓文 (Instructions revealed by Supreme Emperor of Dark Heavens from Wudang Mountains), dated 1302.[41] This text, alternatively titled *Xuantian shangdi jinke yulü* 玄天上帝金科玉律 (Jade code and gold law of the Supreme Lord of Dark Heavens) was largely circulated during the Ming and Qing periods and was frequently included in anthologies as one of the four "classic" morality books.[42] This short, powerful exhortation, deeply tinged

38. *Taishang shuo Xuantian dasheng Zhenwu benzhuan shenzhou miaojing*, 5.15b.

39. On cherishing written characters, see Liang Qizi, *Shishan yu jiaohua*, 172–203; Goossaert, *L'Interdit du boeuf*, 174–76.

40. *Qinghe neizhuan*, 13b–14b and 14b–18b respectively. Yan Hui is also mentioned with the same divine title in Chen Zhong's *Taishang shuo Xuantian dasheng Zhenwu benzhuan shenzhou miaojing*, 5.14a.

41. See Goossaert, *Livres de morale*, 53–67; Wang Chien-ch'uan, "Zhenwu xinyang zai jinshi Zhongguo de chuanbo," 106–10.

42. The "four classics" are *Taishang ganyingpian*, *Wenchang dijun yinzhiwen* 文昌帝君陰騭文, *Guansheng dijun jueshi zhenjing* 關聖帝君覺世真經, and the *Wudangshan Xuantian shangdi chuixunwen*.

with apocalyptic overtones, amplifies eschatological themes already present in the Song-period scripture *Taishang shuo Xuantian dasheng zhenwu benchuan shenzhou miaojing*. It repeatedly evokes the final cataclysm, when hordes of murderous demons will usher in the end of this world, *mojie* 末劫; it calls on humans to follow Zhenwu and his moral teachings so as to be spared:

> I make a precise record of all good and bad actions,
> And I measure exactly the sins and the blessings of everyone;
> when the sins are minor, I spare the life of half (the family)
> But when they are heavy I exterminate the whole family.
> The virtuous will be allowed to continue seeing the light of day,
> But the sinners will never see the advent of the Great Peace.
> Those who trust in me will survive the apocalypse,
> And the others will lose life and soul.
>
> 記錄作善作惡, 較量罪福重輕, 輕則減死一半, 重則死絕滅門。
> 善者得見天日, 惡者不見太平, 信者得度末劫, 不信喪命亡魂。

Like the 1290 revelations of Lord Xin, Zhenwu speaks in the first person, recalls his own divine career, and exhorts his adepts to act morally, quoting the *Taishang ganyingpian*; unlike them, he does not explicitly mention priests as recipients of the revelations, but the text still presents itself as revealed in a major center of *daofa* codification, Wudangshan. One passage articulates divine codes (*tianlü* 天律 or *guilü* 鬼律, core *daofa* liturgical documents), the god's mission as a cosmic moral enforcer, and ledgers of merits and demerits, *gongguoge* 功過格. In this and countless later spirit-written morality books, the existence of divine codes and the role of thunder and other martial deities in their enforcement are repeatedly affirmed, together with the salvific value of practicing moral self-cultivation through ledgers of merits and demerits.:

> I have been nominated by an edict from the Jade Emperor
> To the rank of god granting blessings, governing the world, and
> granting long life.
> Among the Buddhas, I am Amitāyus,

In the Dao, I am an emanation of the Golden Gate (i.e., Jade Emperor).
I command Heavenly gods and generals,
And I make inspections tours up and down the universe.
I adjudicate on the merits and demerits of both gods and humans,
And I submit a report (to the Jade Emperor) once a month.
I note each and every meritorious action,
And I punish each and every demeritorious deed.
My rewards and punishments strictly conform to the Heavenly code,
And I cannot let the slightest personal inclination come into play.
When gods acquire merits, I submit a memorial to recommend their promotion,
And they are elevated to a higher rank according to the Jade Rules.
When humans acquire merits, I enroll them in my service,
And have them enlisted among the immortals.
When gods acquire demerits, I punish them by relegating them among lowly spirits,[43]
And when spirits acquire demerits, I annihilate and dismember them.
When humans acquire demerits, according to the seriousness (of the sin),
I punish them to death by fire, drowning, illness, or torture at the hands of officials.
For the gravest crimes,
Thunder will break out in the sky.
I will not protect a sinner because he has worshiped me,
And I will not get angry at someone because he has not worshiped me.

吾受玉帝敕命,長生治世福神。佛中即無量壽,道乃金闕化身。
統轄天神天將,天上天下遊巡。糾察神人功過,一月一度奏呈。
所作有功必錄,所作有過必懲。賞罰定依天律,分毫不順私情。
神若有功保奏,名依玉格擢陞。人若有功錄用,即與仙籍標名。
神過罰為下鬼,鬼過滅跡分形。人過各依輕重,水火瘟疫官刑。
若有十分重罪,虛空霹靂一聲。不以奉吾私庇,不以不奉生嗔。[44]

43. *Gui* 鬼 here, as often, refers to the spirits of the dead who are still in the netherworld, rather than demons.

44. This passage is from a critical edition of the text (based on a Ming copy reproduced in *Zangwai daoshu*, vol. 22, and several Qing-period morality books), in Goossaert, *Livres de morale*, 64–65.

5.4.5. Poetry

Anecdotal sources have shown that the exchange of poetry between the living and spirits was a significant aspect of early modern spirit-writing. A sizable part of the known revelations, including the moral tract introduced above, is in poetic format. One spirit-writing cult, however, made its mark as a locus for conjoining spirituality, Daoist ritual, and belles lettres: the Transcendent Lords of Vast Grace and Divine Help, Hongen lingji zhenjun 洪恩靈濟真君 cult devoted to the two Xu brothers (Xu Zhizheng 徐知證 and Xu Zhie 徐知諤), historical figures who lived in the tenth century. They were adoptive brothers of the founder of the Southern Tang dynasty (937–76), whose legacy in Song culture and religion is massive, and they quickly became the object of a thriving cult in and around the city of Fuzhou (Fujian).[45] The Daoist canon contains an abundant and varied amount of documents about the cult, including liturgies, historical records, and official proclamations, notably linked to the patronage of the cult at the Ming court.

The spirit-writing activities of the Xu brothers and their devotees are documented in two ways. First, several historical records mention them, although with rather few details, using various terms such as *luanji* or *jibi*. A Ming imperial stele for the Xu brothers' temple in Beijing reads:

> Later, even though the gods had moved far away, their spirit was still active; they manifested their divine presence in this temple and there are many fascinating records of the immortal tablets left with their divine brush; people worshiped them even more devoutly.
>
> 厥後神雖云逝，而精爽不沒，乃降靈是祠，神筆仙簡，具有奇跡，而民事之益謹。[46]

One document claims the practice started in 955: that year, "the princes (their then title) started to use spirit-writing to allocate talismans

45. Schipper and Verellen, eds., *Taoist Canon*, 1210–16; Davis, "Arms and the Tao, 1"; Davis, "Arms and the Tao, 2."

46. "Yuzhi chongxiu Hong'en Jigong bei 御製重修洪恩濟宮碑," *Xuxian zhenlu*, 3.7a.

and drugs to heal people" 後周顯德二年乙卯王始降筆判符藥以濟人.[47] This may be the earliest known record of spirit-writing, but it is not highly reliable. What is certain is that by the late Song and Yuan periods the cult was based on temples offering ritual services from the resident Daoist priests, among which spirit-writing (for healing, divination, and exorcism) was central: this model continued to thrive during the Ming and Qing periods. It was probably rather similar to what the Wenchang, Zhenwu, and other altars practiced, but on a larger and more popular scale.

Second, we have a whole anthology of their spirit-writing production, the *Xuxian hancao* 徐仙翰藻 (Belles lettres of the immortal Xus). This fourteen-*juan* book looks in many ways like a standard literary anthology of a scholar, with all major genres represented: lyrical prose, *fu* 賦; stele inscriptions; essays; and poetry of various genres and meters. The collection was apparently completed in 1305, the date of the colophon, but few of the pieces are dated. This cult also produced, among other texts, one short sutra-type scripture, in which a high-ranking Daoist deity reveals he has sent the Xu brothers to Earth to teach morality and save humanity, which is on the brink of collapse under the weight of its own sins.[48] It further produced many ritual documents (prayers, memorials, and other texts exchanged between humans and gods), including some devoted to the alchemical salvation rituals for the dead, a *daofa* tradition that we have repeatedly seen associated with spirit-writing, as well as detailed records of the canonization processes for the gods, involving the Heavenly Master.[49] Thus, here is a configuration similar to the *daofa* altars but with a particular interest among the literati patrons and members of the cult to produce and publish spirit-written poetry and essays.

47. *Xuxian zhenlu*, 1.13a.

48. *Lingbao tianzun shuo Hong'en lingji zhenjun miaojing*.

49. *Xuxian hancao*, j. 9–10; Gao Zhenhong, "Chaofeng, daofeng yu minfeng," 58–64.

5.5. Presence-Type Texts in the Ecology of Revelation

The various forms of early modern presence-type revelations we have surveyed show that by the early Ming, this type of divine text flourished and became varied and influential. Moreover, in addition to the extant texts, Ming library catalogs provide a few titles of what seem to be lost spirit-written texts, and they appear to be similar to those we have. For instance, the mid-sixteenth-century *Chao shi Baowentang shumu* 晁氏寶文堂書目 (Catalog of the Baowen Library of Mr. Chao), after the *Taiwei xianjun gongguoge* and the 1302 Zhenwu revelation, lists a *Leiting Deng tianjun xunshi* 雷霆鄧天君訓世 (Instruction to the world by Heavenly Lord Deng of the Thunderclap), a *Leifu Xin tianjun chuixun* 雷府辛天君垂訓 (Instruction from Heavenly Lord Xin of the Thunder Bureau), and a *Wei shi yuanjun xunshi* 魏世元君訓世 (Instruction to the world by female Lord Wei Shi).[50] This fits the pattern of moral tracts revealed by thunder gods.

However, in spite of such flourishing, a larger view of the early modern divine texts shows that by that time, presence-type revelations still occupied a specific and rather small niche within the larger ecology of revelation. First, the numbers are still not highly impressive: we have many short tracts, prefaces, and commentaries, but full-fledged book-length revelations only number around twenty. Second, all the revelations we have surveyed were produced in clearly Daoist contexts and are now preserved in the Daoist canon—the 1302 Zhenwu revelation is an exception only in appearance. Other religious groups and traditions adopted the presence-type modes of revelations only very gradually and at later stages. Spirit-writing and oral revelations remained contentious until the last decades of the sixteenth century.

50. *Chao shi Baowentang shumu*, 107.

CHAPTER SIX

The Late Ming Turn

Until the late sixteenth century, the encounter and sutra types remained dominant among revelations. This situation dramatically changed within a few decades, when spirit-written texts appeared in large numbers. It is unclear how this trend relates to the growing prevalence of spirit-writing in general, but its place in the production of religious texts did change in a few decades: our focus here is the production of published revelations, not the prevalence of spirit-writing in everyday life. This chapter attempts to describe and explain such a turn.

The practice of spirit-writing is well attested, and spirit-written texts circulated between the twelfth and sixteenth centuries, but the Wanli reign (1573–1620) ushered in a new era because it was when spirit-writing became a mainstream activity among Chinese with at least some literacy. One of the results of this sea change was a surge in revelations, notably the massive production of revealed morality books, *shanshu* 善書, that became a major venue to express individual and social values. These books still circulate and shape visions of society and the good life in the contemporary period.

Most historical studies of spirit-writing start in the late Ming and pay little attention to what happened before. And indeed, even though we do have a fair amount of spirit-written texts from the Song, Yuan, and early Ming periods, this corpus is dwarfed by the flow that starts in the late sixteenth century. Qing and twentieth-century anthologies on morality include large amounts of spirit-written material that almost entirely post-dates 1600. Similarly, in the canons—*Lüzu quanshu* 呂祖全書 (Canon of Patriarch Lü), *Wendi quanshu* 文帝全書 (Canon of Wendi), and *Daozang jiyao* 道藏輯要 (Essentials of the Daoist canon)—compiled in the 1740s and later, the overwhelming majority of texts date from after 1600.[1] It was indeed the rapid acceleration of revelations in the seventeenth century that created the need for the processes of canonization in the eighteenth century, which will be analyzed in chapter 7.

The number of well-documented spirit-writing altars also increased severalfold around that time. The spirit-writing techniques had been there for a long time, but something happened that made them more commonly used for producing published texts—which, again, does not necessarily mean the practice itself was equally spectacularly expanding.

6.1. The Late Ming Revelatory Landscape

Late imperial Chinese society was characterized by revelations of all sorts; Ming and Qing novels and stories are replete with scenes of gods speaking in dreams, appearing in the flesh, or giving books and objects; spirit-writing is but a rather small part of such representations.[2] The late Ming rise of spirit-written revelations should be placed in the larger context of modern changes in religious organization and text production. Some religious groups, often embodying the religiosities and aspirations

1. Lai Chi Tim, "Ming Qing daojiao Lüzu jiangji xinyang de fazhan."

2. One case of a detailed description of spirit-writing in a major novel is found in the mid-eighteenth century *Rulin waishi* 儒林外史 (Unofficial history of the scholars); see translation and discussion in Hu Jiechen, "Terminology and Typology." Hu also mentions a scene in the *Hongloumeng* 紅樓夢 (Dream of the red pavilion).

of specific social classes and formations, expressed their difference by the way they produced and consumed religious texts. Spirit-writing came to be seen as the way of the gentry. During the same period, the sectarian groups developed new genres of their own, the *baojuan* 寶卷 or precious volumes. *Baojuan*, prosimetric texts (alternating simple classic or vernacular prose with verse) for group recitation, existed before and continued to be written by humans to tell the stories of the gods, morality tales, and other narrative content. There also appeared (in the nineteenth century) spirit-written morality *baojuan*.[3] The *baojuan* format, however, was massively adopted by the sectarian traditions during the mid-Ming period, at the same time as gentry groups adopted spirit-writing; these are the two facets of Chinese religious modernity. Sectarian *baojuan* are the revealed words of the Buddhas and other deities. Some of them unfold a sutra-type scenario without information on the revelatory event, but some are explicitly presented as the words of Maitreya incarnated as a sectarian patriarch: the book is presented as written by a human and is a revelation.[4] In the general typology outlined in chapter 2, I defined this as belonging to the encounter type. It is a type of revelation following a very different logic from spirit-writing, as it is based on the charisma of the leader as a unique living god as opposed to the spirit-writing adepts' aspirations to enter the service of the gods.

During this period, dreams also continued to be the medium for producing major revelations. As discussed in chapter 2, there already existed sutra-type scriptures revealed in dreams in medieval times, but the dream account was not part of the scripture. In the modern period, dream revelations, especially in Buddhist contexts, claimed such a status. An early and significant case is a Buddhist sutra revealed in a dream to a Ming empress, Yongle's consort Renxiao (1362–1407), titled

3. Jordan and Overmyer, *Flying Phoenix*, 46–49, present the *Yulü baojuan* 玉律寶卷 (a morality book) as the earliest spirit-written book they know, a claim based on a 1622 preface, but this seems spurious (as, alas, is often the case in prefaces to revealed books) since Patriarch Lü's title in that book was given in the nineteenth century.

4. Overmyer, *Precious Volumes*, esp. 136, 185–88, 254–55. On the use of scriptures in the sectarian traditions, see ter Haar, *Practicing Scriptures*.

Da Ming Renxiao huanghou menggan Fo shuo diyi xiyou dagongde jing 大明仁孝皇后夢感佛說第一希有大功德經 (The greatly meritorious sutra, of foremost rarity, spoken by the Buddha in a dream to Empress Renxiao of the great Ming). It starts with a preface explaining how in 1398, on the eve of the Hongwu emperor's death, she was reading scriptures and meditating when she had a vision of Guanyin, who took her to Heaven in a dreamlike state. They visited heavenly palaces before Guanyin gave her the prophecy of the future Yongle emperor's enthronement (thus justifying the soon-to-begin civil war and murder of the Jianwen emperor) and a scroll (The greatly meritorious sutra) to chant. She chanted it and memorized it so she could write it down when returning to a normal state.[5] There were precedents to Chinese rulers manipulating scriptures to legitimize their usurpations, but to my knowledge this is the first full-fledged scripture explicitly revealed to and for the benefit of the ruler in question.[6]

This model—a dream revelation providing legitimacy to an empress and her husband, in that order—would be repeated with the famed mother of the Wanli emperor (Empress Dowager Xiaoding 孝定, née Li 李, 1544–1614) and her dream revelations from the hitherto unknown Nine Lotus Bodhisattva 九蓮菩薩, who taught the empress she was her incarnation. The resulting scripture, *Foshuo daci zhisheng jiulian pusa huashen dushi zunjing* 佛說大慈至聖九蓮菩薩化身度世尊經 (The venerable sutra spoken by the Buddha on the Nine Lotus bodhisattva of great compassion and ultimate saintliness incarnating to save the world), was printed in 1616 by the Wanli emperor.[7] Beyond the rather

5. Yü Chün-fang, *Kuan-yin*, 141–44, who wonders whether the Tibetan *ter-ma* tradition may have influenced this mode of revelation; however, we have seen Chinese non-Buddhist precedents, such as the *Taiwei xianjun gongguoge*.

6. The best-known precedent is Empress Wu Zetian 武則天 (r. 690–705), but she did not produce her own explicit revelation, rather she had clerics at her service insert an apocryphal prophecy (of her being a bodhisattva and a legitimate ruler) within an existing scripture as well as write a commentary (thus, not a revelation) to the same effect; see Hughes, "Re-examining the *Zhengming Jing*." The message is similar, but the technique of textual production is very different.

7. Li and Naquin, "Baoming Temple," 160–61; Yü Chün-fang, *Kuan-yin*, 144–48.

obvious aura of political fabrication and manipulation, this shows how presence-type modes of revelation of Daoist origins had by the Ming become acceptable as a method for creating Buddhist scriptures.

Empresses had no monopoly over dream revelations. A major figure in the rise of the genre of morality books, Yuan Huang 袁黃 (1533–1606) popularized the earliest ledger of merits and demerits, the *Taiwei xianjun gongguoge*, revealed in a dream in 1171, and himself had dreams of gods giving him advice on his practice.[8] A devout lay Buddhist—a disciple of Lianchi Zhuhong 蓮池袾宏 (1535–1615), who himself promoted the use of the ledgers—Yuan is not known to have engaged in spirit-writing. Another major religious figure of this period, a young female mystic known as Tanyangzi 曇陽子 (1557–80) who had several of the highest-ranking officials as disciples, is known through a detailed account of her encounters with gods, in dreams and then in presence; she received scriptures, but spirit-writing is not mentioned.[9] But dreams could also complement spirit-writing revelations: different revelatory techniques can be applied to the same texts. In 1677 and again in 1692, Yan Zhangjing 顏章敬 (*zi* Shengyu 生愉) added sentences revealed in dreams to Wenchang's *Yinzhiwen* 陰隲文 (Tract of hidden retribution; discussed below), thus creating the text as it circulated from then on. More popular tracts were revealed in dreams, such as the *Fumo baojuan* 伏魔寶卷 (Precious volume on subduing demons) telling of Guandi's 關帝 (i.e., Guan Yu 關羽) divine powers in a sectarian framework, dictated by Guandi himself at some point in the seventeenth century.[10]

One of the most popular Chinese religious texts during the nineteenth century and ever since is the *Yuli baochao* 玉歷寶鈔 (Precious manuscript of the jade calendar), a description of the netherworld and how its administration deals with the dead and metes out divine justice in cruel ways. It presents itself as revealed in a dream to a monk during the Song, but as it appears in the late eighteenth century, we do not

8. Brokaw, *Ledgers*, 88.
9. Waltner, "T'an-yang-tzu and Wang Shih-chen."
10. Overmyer, *Precious Volumes*, 350.

know how it was composed.[11] In any case, it attests to the legitimacy of dreams as a revelatory technique and to how, even in an age of massive spirit-written morality book production, other means were still used to great success. In brief, then, the late Ming rise of spirit-written texts is not an effect of the decline in other types of revelations.

One more example of a modern Buddhist revelation shows how encounters along with dreams continued to be a powerful resource: the *Xiangshan baojuan* 香山寶卷 (Precious volume of Xiangshan), the story of the pious and filial girl who becomes Guanyin, one of the most popular religious narratives for group recitation in modern times, appears in a 1773 edition (where it is not titled a *baojuan* but a sutra) with a preface explaining how a mysterious monk (who of course eventually turns out to have been Guanyin herself) comes to see Puming 普明, a Buddhist cleric, and dictates the story to him, which Puming writes down and edits. Interestingly, the same text (known in many editions), had a new edition published by the sectarian Xiantiandao tradition in the late nineteenth century, with an added preface narrating the discovery in a cave.[12] In other words, for these texts that present themselves as being revealed to a Buddhist monk, all revelation techniques are mentioned, except spirit-writing.

6.2. The Emergence of the *jitan* Spirit-Writing Altar

The practice of spirit-writing in private contexts, that is, families or small groups inviting an expert to use spirit-writing to communicate with the dead, continued to be common during the Ming period, as attested by

11. Wang Chien-ch'uan, introduction to *Ming Qing minjian zongjiao jingjuan wenxian*, 19–12.

12. Li Yongping, "Shenshou tianshu." This article gathers the relevant evidence but is analytically flawed and fails to see spurious dates. For a full translation, see Idema, *Personal Salvation and Filial Piety*.

numerous mentions in collections of anecdotes and notes written by scholars, and in spite of the ban on *fuluan* enacted in 1370, which continued a Yuan ban. The ban may have simply caused the term *fuluan* to be rarely used and replaced henceforth by synonyms. The Yongle emperor and his successors enthusiastically promoted and officialized the Hongji spirit-writing cult for the Xu brothers by building a grandiose temple in Beijing. The Jiajing emperor (r. 1522–67) even made political decisions based on spirit-written revelations produced by one of his Daoist advisers, Lan Daoxing 藍道行.[13]

There were also public venues for the practice, where everyone could come and request spirit-writing advice. Local temples served as centers where one could come to question the gods, not only through mediums but also dreams and spirit-writing. The Xu brothers' cult was certainly one such case. We have other examples from the same region, Fujian (a hotbed of *daofa* innovations)—although there is no reason to suppose it was unique to that area. A prominent center for this was Shizhushan 石竹山, near the provincial capital Fuzhou (also the home of the Xu brothers), devoted to the Nine Immortals 九仙, originally spirits of carps in a sacred lake but euhemerized in modern times as nine brothers. It is nowadays particularly famous as a dream temple; people come with a prayer and under the guidance of the temple Daoists sleep in the temple to obtain a divine response.[14] In the sixteenth century, it also operated as a spirit-writing center; a key deity active there was the Daoist Chen Tuan 陳摶 (ca. 920–ca. 989). Around 1600 one of the Nine Immortals also started to use spirit-writing to produce poetry, plaques, and inscriptions for other temples, and even draw portraits. The place was patronized by eminent Buddhist monks during the 1640s and 1650s, who then settled in Japan (where they founded the influential Ōbaku Zen lineage 黄檗宗) and left records of their spirit-writing experienc-

13. Wang Chien-ch'uan, "Song-Ming shiqi"; Xu Dishan, *Fuji mixin de yanjiu*, 101. Lan was a dignitary from the Jingming lineage.

14. Baptandier, "Entrer en montagne pour y rêver."

es.[15] They indicate that the Chen Tuan spirit-writing cult at Shizhushan was successful due to the efforts of the performer who had gone to train in far-away Nanjing and whom they called a Daoist, *yushi* 羽士.

During this period, we see more and more local saints developing their cults through spirit-writing. In one case from southern Zhejiang, a temple was rebuilt after being burned down by pirates in 1552, and henceforth the gods repeatedly produced miracles in times of drought, epidemics, and other disasters and wrote (*jiangbi*) large amounts of poetry for the local gentry.[16] A remarkable example is Wu Ben 吳本 (also later written as Wu Tao 夲), known as the Great Emperor Who Protects Life, Baosheng dadi 保生大帝, a healer who is one of the most popular saints in Fujian and Taiwan.[17] In 1602, he had one of his immortal disciples dictate his hagiography, *Wu zhenren shixiu daoguo bei* 吳真人世修道果碑 (Inscription on the practice and attainments of Transcendent Wu), including his canonization by the Jade Emperor, through spirit-writing (*jibi*) to a student of the Confucian school in Quanzhou who had it carved on a stele.[18] Here we see the continuation of the early Daoist practices of processing divine appointments by spirit-writing. Another inscription for the same cult in the same region and period says that devotees have their questions answered "through dreams, or divination blocks, or spirit-writing, or spirit possession" 迄今禱者或夢、或珓、或乩、或降神附人.[19] The Daoist context is not absent at all; in a related note by a local scholar, Transcendent Wu "manifested himself at the altar to proclaim his decision" 降壇判示 that people should organize a large *jiao* offering ritual to prevent an upcoming epidemic.[20]

15. Russell, "Chen Tuan at Mount Huangbo."

16. (*Wanli*) *Huangyan xianzhi*, 7.9a.

17. On Baosheng dadi, see Dean, *Taoist Ritual*, chap. 2.

18. *Wu zhenren shixiu daoguo bei*, in *Fujian zongjiao beiming huibian. Quanzhoufu fence*, 649–51.

19. Quoted by Wang Chien-ch'uan, "Song-Ming shiqi."

20. *Ji Dadao zhenjun wen bingxu* 祭大道真君文並序, quoted by Wang Chien-ch'uan, "Song-Ming shiqi."

These spirit-writing practices, either private or public, were important for individual and social lives but produced few published revelations. The dramatic increase in such publication was due to the emergence of a new type of group, commonly called *jitan* 乩壇, where *ji* refers to a new spirit-writing technique with a Y- or T-shaped wooden writing implement, discussed below. This term is both emic and etic; it is found in some of the primary sources and has become the standard scholarly term for discussing modern spirit-writing groups (but one should be cautious not to apply it to pre-Wanli cases). The *jitan* were voluntary, open groups of educated people devoted to the double aim of self-cultivation (for their own divinization) and universal salvation through moral reform. They engaged in a variety of practices, at the core of which was the production of revelations and their wide distribution through printing. They shared traits with the temples providing the spirit-writing services introduced above and may have exchanged or cross-trained mediums with them, but the temples did not, as far we know, publish revealed books.

The *jitan* were in continuity with the altars of the Song-Yuan period that composed scriptures, but they also brought innovations. First, the early altars seem to have been comprised of only a few people, either a family or a priest and his disciples. By contrast, the *jitan* seem early on to have been quite open and sometimes counted large numbers of members; people often circulated between different *jitan* or were concurrently affiliated with more than one. Second, early altars received both public revelations (scriptures and hagiographies) and secret, internal documents (for the initiates only); by contrast, I have not seen *jitan* discussing any secret revelations. Third, the early altars proposed a large range of ritual services, including *jiao* offerings and *daofa* exorcism and healing, whereas most later *jitan* had a more limited offering, although it was by no means negligible. Naturally, they form a continuum rather than a dichotomy, and some late imperial *jitan* did practice exorcisms and other complex rituals in continuity with their early modern predecessors.

The new wave of revelation produced by the *jitan* is characterized by the prevalence of gods not previously known for spirit-writing, new types of revealed contents, and a new social role for the spirit-writing groups. We will now discuss these three aspects in turn.

6.3. The Patriarch Lü Cult

The main spirit-writing gods in the early modern phase were *daofa* patriarchs. Some of them (Wenchang and Transcendent Lord Xu) remained prominent in Ming and Qing times. The rise of the *jitan*, however, was characterized by gods who were not associated with an exorcistic ritual lineage. The most prominent among them, by far, is Patriarch Lü. We have seen that the immortal had a long history of producing revelations, but by other means. Patriarch Lü's poems (written on walls and heard by adepts) were repeatedly reprinted during this period, including in the 1607 *Wanli xu Daozang* 萬曆續道藏 (Supplement to the Daoist canon), but also in commercial editions. Ganany has drawn attention to Patriarch Lü's revelations included as an appendix to a novel published in 1573, the *Baxian chuchu dongyou ji* 八仙出處東遊記 (Origin tale of the Eight Immortals and their journey to the East), consisting of short narratives and poems given, *shi* 示, to named humans.[21] These texts cannot be safely ascribed to spirit-writing (but we cannot rule the possibility out either).

One of the earliest documents on Patriarch Lü using spirit-writing to teach inner alchemy is the records of Lu Xixing 陸西星 (1520–1601 or 1606).[22] Lu, a married Daoist adept not known to have been ordained, was a prolific author who left an abundant oeuvre of commentaries on

21. Ganany, "Origin Narratives," 267. Seaman, "Divine Authorship," has argued that the late Ming novel on Zhenwu, *Beiyouji* 北游記, was spirit written, but his argument is unconvincing; it may be that some spirit-written textual elements were incorporated, but likely not the novel as a whole; see also his translation, Seaman, *Journey to the North*.

22. Mozias, "Immortals and Alchemists"; *Literati Path to Immortality*.

classics and essays on inner alchemy. He also wrote a lesser-known record of his interactions with his divine master Patriarch Lü titled *Sanzang zhenquan* 三藏真詮 (Truthful explanation of the three depositories), which long remained a manuscript and was only published in the twentieth century. This text relates the interaction between Lu and two of his companions with Patriarch Lü, as well as other immortals, chronologically over twenty-six years, between 1547 and 1572.

The descriptions in *Sanzang zhenquan* are sometimes couched in the language of actual physical encounters and are marked by a perennial lack of closure: Lu never obtains complete and definitive teachings, only hints and encouragements. Patriarch Lü never gave a scripture, but he gave many short instructions, often using the first person, which Lu finally edited as a volume. He insisted on secrecy, hence the manuscript format and the fact that the record is not included in Lu's published oeuvre. Like in later records of spirit-written instructions, we are given for each entry the question and the date and place where the divine response was delivered. The text usually does not use a specific technical term for spirit-writing, but occasionally mentions the sieve. Patriarch Lü and other immortals are said to manifest their presence (*jiang*) and give instructions 示, 授; sometimes it is very explicit that they write 書 and request paper 索紙. But in other cases they speak, and Lu tries to note down their words, sometimes after the fact, or they appear as a visible presence to give medicine or to show objects. As Lu himself noted, immortals descend either in spirit, using a sieve, or in *qi* (possessing the adept), or in form, becoming visible.[23] We have thus a group of adepts who concurrently use different forms of presence-type techniques, as well as visualizations.

The *Sanzang zhenquan* is part of a tradition of asking personal instructions of one's divine master that was conducted through visualizations in medieval times and later, and from the tenth century onward, through presence-type techniques. We have seen an early case of a

23. Mozias, "Immortals and Alchemists," 94.

Daoist, probably during the Southern Song, who edited his questions and spirit-written responses from Transcendent Lord Xu. Such cases were not considered (or were only partly considered) appropriate for open circulation (the *Yisheng baode zhuan* being largely an exception) and may have been much more common than the examples given here. We will see that soon these instructions would lose their secret nature in the context of the *jitan*.

Lu Xixing's case is certainly not unique. During the same period, a high official, Gu Bingqian 顧秉謙 (1550–?), left, on a stone inscription, an autobiographical account (showing how the practice could be publicly acknowledged) of how he sought guidance from Patriarch Lü from 1579 onward, sometimes through spirit-writing and sometimes through dreams.[24]

Other spiritual leaders and alchemists of that period knew of spirit-writing but favored other techniques of creating Patriarch Lü's and other immortals' divine presence. For instance, the biography of Lin Zhaoen 林兆恩 (1517–98), the charismatic founder of the Three-in-One religion 三一教 in Fujian, relates his numerous visions, dreams, and meetings in the flesh with immortals (one of his disciples met Patriarch Lü in a market and obtained oral instructions from him), including one instance when Maitreya manifested himself in Lin's meditation room and dictated a scripture to him. Spirit-writing (*fuluan*) is only explicitly mentioned once, as practiced by another specialist (called a *fangshi* 方士) who revealed a chart confirming Lin's divine identity.[25]

These cases attest to the emergence of Patriarch Lü as a spirit-writing instructor, but what they describe is different from the most important innovation of that period: the adoption of Patriarch Lü as the main god of the *jitan* and his revelation of full-fledged scriptures. The first such revelation we have is the *Bapinjing* 八品經 (Scripture in eight chapters). The history of the *Bapinjing* is remarkably complex: it is made

24. Schachter, "Printing the Dao," 76.

25. *Linzi benxing shilu*, 40b–41a; Dean, *Lord of the Three in One*, chap. 2, esp. 86. Lin explicitly drew on the Dragon Sand prophecy mentioned in chapter 5.

up of five sections that were revealed to different altars in different parts of the Jiangnan region, apparently following a planned sequence; finally, a 1589 preface tells us that in that year Patriarch Lü requested a certain Li Yingyang 李應陽 to edit them together.[26] In his preface, Li used the term sieve, *ji* 箕, to refer to the spirit-writing technique. He makes the crucial point that Patriarch Lü intervenes among humans to save them by different means: "he would either make revelations in dreams, or proclaim edicts by appearing in person, or teach through spirit-writing with the sieve; the records are more abundant than we can write" 或以夢示, 或以形諭, 或以箕演, 紀載不足以盡之.[27] That this production was made by large *jitan* groups is clear from several passages that mention "the many members of the altars" 在壇眾生.[28]

The innovation here is that Patriarch Lü reveals not only secret instructions for a few disciples but also scriptures to be disseminated for the salvation of all humankind. Lai Chi Tim makes the crucial point that around 1570 we see the first spirit-writing texts from Patriarch Lü at the same time as we see a shift in his soteriological discourse, from saving individuals (whom he encounters and instructs) to saving the world, *dushi* 度世.[29] I have discussed elsewhere the doctrinal parallel between the new Patriarch Lü's spirit-written scriptures and the sectarian *baojuan* that both propound inner alchemy as a vehicle for universal salvation in apocalyptic times and that both flourished in the late sixteenth century but have antecedents in earlier movements.[30]

This innovation proved very successful and was soon imitated by others. The next revelation anthologized in the Patriarch Lü canon of 1744

26. "Heke Bapin xianjing yuanxu 合刻八品仙經原序," *Lüzu quanshu* (33-*juan* edition), j. 9. See Philip Clart's entry in Lai Chi Tim, ed., *Daozang jiyao tiyao*, 893–903.

27. "Heke Bapin xianjing yuanxu," *Lüzu quanshu* (33-*juan* edition), j. 9. The meaning of the expression "proclaim edicts by appearing in person" is unclear. It may refer to possession of a medium or visualization; yet *yu* (edicts) is a common term in spirit-writing revelations. I have found no other source using the term.

28. *Bapinjing*, *Lüzu quanshu* (33-*juan* edition), j. 9, section 1 and 5.

29. Lai Chi Tim, "Ming Qing daojiao Lüzu jiangji xinyang de fazhan," 141–43.

30. Goossaert, "Inner Alchemy and Eschatology."

(see chapter 7) is the *Wupinjing* 五品經 (Scripture in five chapters), revealed in 1679 by a group near present-day Wuhan led by a charismatic physician. But there were even more revelations that eventually were ignored by, or simply not known to, the 1744 canon compilers. One early source is a mammoth anthology of Daoist texts, apparently finished around 1681, the *Lidai shenxian tongji* 歷代神仙通紀 (General annals of divine transcendents through the ages), where the author copied vast amounts of hagiographical and other narrative material, as well as rules and scriptures. It contains several spirit-written revelations from Patriarch Lü, including one scripture (not attested anywhere else) that explains how he is sent to Earth as a universal savior.[31] Adepts were aware of this late Ming innovation in the Patriarch Lü cult but saw it as an evolution rather than a revolution; for instance, the *Haishan qiyu* 海山奇遇 (Uncanny encounters on seas and mountains, ca. 1840s, a long chronicle of his manifestations in the world clearly inspired by similar, earlier chronicles about Laojun, Wenchang, Zhenwu, and other gods) starts mentioning spirit-writing revelations to various *jitan* in the late Ming, while continuing to record other types of presence, such as encounters.

During this period, other gods not previously attested in spirit-writing contexts also begin to reveal tracts and scriptures, although none of them can compare with Patriarch Lü in terms of numbers of mentions and the circulation of their revelations. We will see below how Guan Yu 關羽 (whom I always call Guandi 關帝 here) starts revealing morality tracts; we also have early Qing texts from the Emperor of the Eastern Peak, Dongyue dadi 東嶽大帝, and the Mother of the Dipper, Doumu 斗姆. All of these gods have a clear Daoist identity (including Guandi who, since the Song, was one of the fierce marshals of *daofa* traditions, as well as a popular local cult in northern China and among the military). Indeed, we see very few spirit-written revelations from bodhisattvas or other Buddhist saviors until a later phase in the nineteenth century.

31. *Taiji penglai shanggong Chunyang dijun shuo Dadao zhisui xianjing* 太極蓬萊上宮純陽帝君說大道至髓仙經, in *Lidai shenxian tongji*, chap. 6, 84–96. On this source, see Yin Zhihua, "*Lidai shenxian tongji* chutan."

Linked to the rise of the Patriarch Lü spirit-writing cult, we also witness the emergence of historical Quanzhen patriarchs, especially Qiu Changchun 丘長春 (1148–1227), as revealing gods, a phenomenon that has continued ever since. An important early case is an expansive commentary on the *Yuhuangjing* edited by a court-favored Quanzhen cleric, Zhou Xuanzhen 周玄貞 (1555–1627), who was one of the editors of the 1607 supplement to the Daoist canon.[32] This work, with a preface dated 1585, includes commentaries as well as prefatory material authored not only by Wenchang, who was closely associated with the original revelation of this scripture, and two thunder gods but also Patriarch Lü and Qiu Changchun. This documents how Patriarch Lü and other Quanzhen immortals had entered the group of spirit-writing gods in the context of Quanzhen clerics and court Daoism. Another Quanzhen cleric would produce a whole *yulu*, spirit-written recorded sayings, of Qiu Changchun in the 1660s.[33]

6.4. New Content

6.4.1. Morality Books

Morality books (*shanshu*) form the core genre of modern spirit-written production, and indeed, the rise of this genre and the multiplication of *jitan* openly publishing their revelations are two facets of the same phenomenon. Because the genre has never been a well-defined category in the Chinese bibliographical tradition, its contours and origins are hazy, but by any definition it existed before the late Ming turning point.[34] Yet, early morality books are relatively few, and spirit-writing revelations

32. *Huangjing jizhu*. See Schachter, "Printing the Dao," 73; and Hsieh Ts'ung-hui, *Xin tiandi zhi ming*, 237–46.

33. *Qiuzu yulu*. Lai Chi Tim, "Revisiting *the Jingming Origin*," 60–62.

34. For a solid definition and overview, see Yau Chi-on, *Shan yu ren tong*.

play a very minor role in them; in other words, by 1600, we have very few spirit-written *shanshu*. To understand how modern revealed morality books appeared, we need to first briefly go back in time and look at the productions of their predecessors.

The preeminent morality book classic is the *Taishang ganyingpian* 太上感應篇 (The Supreme Lord's tract on action and retribution). Its title clearly expresses its revealed nature, but it does not disclose the manner of the revelation. In the Daoist canon edition, it comes with a memorial, dated 1233, written when it was presented to the throne, which mentions it was already part of the 1116–19 Daoist canon.[35] The only extant narrative of the *Ganyingpian*'s revelation is found in the great chronicle of Laojun's revelations, *Hunyuan shengji* (dated 1191), where we are told that it was given to Ge Xuan together with the Lingbao scriptures, a late mythical invention, which is hardly informative about the real conditions of the revelation.[36] The *Ganyingpian* was put into its present state around 1164 by Li Shi 李石 (*zi* Changling 昌齡, died ca. 1182) who added a very substantial thirty-*juan* commentary.[37] Li was the author of another morality book, *Leshanlu* 樂善錄 (Records of those who took pleasure in virtue), which also includes the *Ganyingpian*.[38] The *Leshanlu* quotes a number of revelations, including a good number of pronouncements from Black Killer and one from Zhenwu, as well as dreams and revelations obtained by Daoists in visualizations, but it does not record any instances of spirit-writing.

The *Leshanlu* is typical of early morality books: it is a collection of stories about moral retribution (taken either from classical sources or

35. On the origins of this extremely influential text, see Brokaw, *Ledgers*, 36–43; Li Yi, "*Taishang ganyingpian* wenben laiyuan"; and Goossaert, *Livres de morale*, 1–13. Li Yi dates it to the years 1116–18 based on close textual parallels to other texts composed in that period at Huizong's court.

36. *Hunyuan shengji*, 7.30a. The manuscript edition of this text, much closer to the original than the massaged canonical edition, has the same passage but interestingly includes the whole text of the *Ganyingpian*, see *Taishang shilu*, 5.37b–43a.

37. Brokaw, *Ledgers*, 41. The commentary is sometimes erroneously attributed to the homonymous Li Changling 李昌齡 (937–1008). Kleeman, *God's Own Tale*, 65, claims that Li was a devotee of Wenchang, but he provides no evidence and I have not found any.

38. *Leshanlu*, 4.13b–18a.

from the same kind of material that filled the anecdotal *biji* collections), explained with quotations from authoritative sources, such as the classics and essays by major thinkers. Early Ming morality collections, such as the *Da Ming Renxiao huanghou quanshanshu* 大明仁孝皇后勸善書 (Exhortation to morality, compiled by the Renxiao empress of the great Ming), from the Yongle emperor's consort whom we have already met producing revelations, the *Weishan yinzhi* 為善陰隲 (Hidden rewards for virtuous actions), compiled under the orders of the Yongle emperor himself in 1419 and widely distributed through official networks, and the *Mingxin baojian* 明心寶鑑 (Precious mirror for enlightening the mind), compiled before 1441, follow the same pattern.[39] The latter quotes over 250 different sources; among them, only a few are spirit-written. In the edition I perused, I identified one quote from a Wenchang revelation and the *Zixu yuanjun jieyu xinwen* 紫虛元君戒諭心文 (Text to admonish the minds by the female Lord Zixu).[40]

Yet, that does not mean pre-1600 spirit-written revelations did not address issues of moral self-cultivation and retribution; on the contrary, these issues have always been at the core of presence-type revelations and spirit-writing in particular. The divine hagiographies, such as Wenchang's *Huashu*, and the instructions from exorcistic gods to their living disciples all hinge on the idea that moral conduct, which includes performing rituals to help others, is the key to divinization. They build on the concept of quantifying merits that underlines the *Ganyingpian* as well as the *Taiwei xianjun gongguoge*. But these spirit-written moral instructions were often in internal circulation and only a few were widely disseminated—especially the 1302 Zhenwu tract and the Wenchang *Huashu*.

In short, before 1600, we have morality books that are primarily human narratives and spirit-written moral teachings aimed, in the first place, at adepts, and there is relatively little overlap between the two. Two related phenomena bring a radical change to this situation during

39. Hu Jiechen, "*Wenchang dijun yinzhiwen* qiyuan xinyan"; Clart, "*Mingxin baojuan.*"
40. *Mingxin baojian*, 64, 27.

the seventeenth century. First, short spirit-written morality books appear and meet with instant success; second, larger anthologies and collections built around these revelations become a significant part of the print culture.

The first phenomenon seems to begin with a new wave of Wenchang revelations, notably: the *Yinzhiwen*, a text in part modeled after the *Taishang ganyingpian*; the *Jiujie baozhang* 救劫寶章 (Precious stanzas to save humanity from the apocalypse), where Wenchang speaks in the first person, recalling his own human lives and calling for moral reform in the face of imminent apocalypse;[41] and Wenchang's own version of the classic of filial piety, *Xiaojing* 孝經. Hu Jiechen has conducted definitive research on these revelations and their dating, and I will not repeat his detailed analysis here.[42] In short, it seems that during the late sixteenth century, both the *Jiujie baozhang* and a prototype of the *Yinzhiwen* (called *Quanxing yinzhiwen* 勸行) were written and circulated. The latter may have been a human affair entirely, but the former is very explicitly a revelation, and most likely spirit-written; a section from it (the injunction to recite the text daily, together with the *Ganyingpian*, and the evocation of high Daoist gods) is presented as spirit-written (*jiangbi*) in an early Qing work.[43] Then, sometime after these two new Wenchang texts were produced, the *Yinzhiwen* was composed, using material from both. It eventually eclipsed its predecessors in popularity, becoming the most revered and widely distributed Wenchang text in the modern period.

The *Yinzhiwen* was apparently not spirit-written—yet it is included in a collection of scriptures, some newly revealed, titled the *Xinke huiji Wanzhen miaodi jiejing* 新刊彙集完真妙諦捷經 (Newly printed collection of short scriptures on the marvelous truths about completing

41. This text is sometimes titled *Jiujie baojing* 經; I systematically use the generic title *Jiujie baozhang* here for the sake of clarity.

42. Hu Jiechen, "*Wenchang dijun yinzhiwen* qiyuan xinyan."

43. *Danguiji*, 1.31a.

transcendence), printed in the Tianqi era (1621–27). But, around 1689, a Jiangnan scholar, Yan Zhangjing, received dream revelations and further modified the *Yinzhiwen*. Yan published a long commentary, attributed to his father, under the title *Danguiji* 丹桂籍 (Records of the Red Cinnamon [Palace]), which contains numerous records of spirit-writing. From this point on, the Wenchang revelations became a major part of the corpus of morality books, and new spirit-written tracts and essays from Wenchang appeared in rapid succession, culminating in the canonizations discussed in the next chapter. It seems there was no direct continuity between the individuals and groups that produced these new revelations and the earlier, Song-Yuan Wenchang altars, even though the producers of the seventeenth-century revelations knew the earlier Wenchang texts very well and placed their work in that line.

During the same period, Guandi revealed his own morality tracts, *Zhongyijing* 忠義經 (Scripture on loyalty and justice) and *Jueshi zhenjing* 覺世真經 (True scripture to awaken the world). They, too, have a complex textual history, which I will only briefly outline here.[44] The *Zhongyijing* has a preface of uncertain reliability by the high official Yang Bo 楊博, who writes that he obtained the book in 1556; he makes no allusion to spirit-writing, but later generations assumed it was spirit-written. The *Zhongyijing* is a morality book focusing on the law of retribution and moral decadence, without an eschatological framework. Guandi himself is not represented as playing a central role in the working of the divine bureaucracy managing retribution.

Similarly, the *Jueshi zhenjing* does not explain how it was revealed, but later readers assumed spirit-writing. Until the turn of the nineteenth century, the *Jueshi zhenjing* was the most quoted, annotated, and republished text attributed to Guandi.[45] This short text (around 650 characters) is very close in style, themes, and inspiration to the *Taishang ganyingpian* and the *Yinzhiwen*, and it even lifts entire sentences from these two illustrious morality books. Like the *Yinzhiwen*, which likely

44. Goossaert, "Textual Canonization"; ter Haar, *Guan Yu*, chap. 8.

45. For a discussion and translation in French, see Goossaert, *Livres de morale*, 25–31.

served as a template, the *Jueshi zhenjing* starts with parallel prose, then quickly adopts a rigid structure of three- and then four-character sentences that do not rhyme. This suggests it was aimed for reading and recitation but not chanting. The text's narrative structure follows its changes in prosody: it starts with praise of the gentleman whose moral conscience is always vigilant and then evokes the heavenly system of moral monitoring that punishes any wrongdoing. This is followed by a long list of good actions to be performed and bad actions to be shunned. As a conclusion, Guandi promises his blessings to those who will follow the path of virtue. Some themes found in the *Jueshi zhenjing* would come to characterize the whole later corpus of Guandi texts: a focus (albeit not exclusive) on patriarchal family values and a martial identity that pushes him to threaten sinners with violent execution: "If you ignore my instructions, you will taste of my sword!" 若負吾教, 請試吾刀.[46] The revelation of the *Jueshi zhenjing* seems to date from the early Kangxi reign, around 1660–80; some editions carry a claim that the revelation took place in 1668.[47] The earliest reliably dated preface was written in 1691, and the earliest known edition was published during the 1720s.

One more influential example is the moral tracts produced by Peng Dingqiu 彭定求 (1645–1719), the eminent early Qing scholar whose success as the first laureate in the 1676 palace examinations was credited to a divine reward for the merits accumulated by his lineage.[48] Peng Dingqiu was a Wenchang devotee, an enthusiastic spirit-writing practitioner, and a morality book publisher—three practices his powerful Suzhou-based family continued until the nineteenth century. He was deified right after his death, and the divine Peng Dingqiu produced revelations of his own. In 1674, before his rise to fame, Peng Dingqiu produced two short moral tracts that present themselves as a result of "producing divine presence in the stylus," *jiangji* 降乩, one from Wenchang and one

46. Goossaert, *Livres de morale*, 28.

47. On dating the *Jueshi zhenjing*, see Sakai Tadao, *Zōho Chūgoku zensho*, 2:184–85; and Yau Chi-on, "Fuhua yunei," 222–25.

48. Burton-Rose, "A Prolific Spirit."

from Doumu, which he had carved on a stele erected at a local shrine patronized by the city's scholars.[49] These tracts were latter reprinted in many different anthologies and collections.

These new revealed morality books created a hybrid textual status that is characteristic of the post-Wanli phase of revelations. Like the *Ganyingpian*, the *Yinzhiwen* is not titled a scripture (*jing*): they are not staged in Heaven and are written in a simple, straightforward language. Yet, they are treated as scriptures; they are psalmodied; indeed, by the high Qing period, the daily psalmody of the *Ganyingpian* and other morality books had become a very common spiritual exercise for scholars.[50] A different use of these classics produced abundant commentaries on them. After Li Shi's original twelfth-century commentary (which does not quote any spirit-written material), the *Ganyingpian* was circulated and quoted, but new commentaries appear and multiply from the seventeenth century onward, and we have dozens, with illustrations, stories, and other appended revelations. The *Yinzhiwen* and *Jueshi zhenjing* were also published with abundant commentaries from the 1690s onward.

In the same format, short tracts, most often entitled *xunwen* 訓文, or *jiewen* 戒文, or *chuixun* 垂訓, multiplied during the Qing, so that by the eighteenth and nineteenth centuries, the canons of revelations discussed in the next chapter contain hundreds of them. The paratexts of these tracts, when they exist, invariably mention spirit-writing and often refer to specific *jitan*. Many of these tracts are moral admonitions in general, building on the early example, maybe datable to the Yuan, of the Wenchang *Jie shizi wen* 戒士子文.[51] We also find large numbers aimed at a particular audience (women, merchants, peasants, officials, or the youth) or focused on a specific moral problem (animal life, filial piety, respect for written characters, sexuality, or charity). For instance,

49. Burton-Rose, "Establishing a Literati Spirit-Writing Altar."

50. Goossaert, "Late Imperial Chinese Piety Books."

51. These Wenchang tracts, together with the *Ganyingpian* and essays by Yuan and Ming authors, are included in an anthology of moral texts included in the 1607 supplement to the Daoist canon, *Shuijinglu* 水鏡錄.

at the thriving spirit-writing center at Shizhushan during the 1640s, Chen Tuan composed morality tracts focused on animal life that do not seem to have been transmitted.[52]

It is less the moral theology that changes between the early modern spirit-writing revelations and the post-1600 phase than the genres in which revelations are couched. Instructions on moral life in the early period were most often addressed to the initiated members of the spirit-writing altars; they are now addressed to all and sundry. We will see that this new orientation is related to the evolving social profile of the spirit-writing institutions: the *jitan* engaged in moral-reform activism.

The second phenomenon was the compilation of large anthologies that included stories of retribution and quotations from classics and Confucian authors, like the early morality books, but in a secondary position to the spirit-written revelations, which now enjoyed the highest authority. Let us take one example: the *Jingxinlu* 敬信錄 (Records of reverence and commitment). Prefaces suggest that it was compiled by a certain Zhou Dingchen 周鼎臣 and appeared in 1749, but there is no extant copy of this original edition.[53] I have used a 1797 edition, entitled *Zengding Jingxinlu* 增訂, kept at the Bibliothèque nationale in Paris. Its 150 pages open with the *Taishang ganyingpian* and instructions for its psalmody, followed by a series of Wenchang revelations (Wenchang is the dominant god in this collection) and scriptures by other gods (including Guandi, Doumu, and Zhenwu), the earliest extant ledger (the twelfth-century *Taiwei xianjun gongguoge*), some more moral tracts written by humans, and medical prescriptions. The structure of the book, especially in its latter part, is less than clear, but there is an obvious descending order, from the most sacred revelations (mostly spirit-written) to more practical, human-written texts. Some of the revealed content dates back to the Song-Yuan period, such as the twelfth-century *Ganyingpian* and

52. Russell, "Chen Tuan at Mount Huangbo," 135.

53. A study of the *Jingxinlu* is found in Sakai Tadao, *Zōho Chūgoku zensho*, 2:171–202; see also Goossaert, "Late Imperial Piety Books."

Gongguoge, a canonical Wenchang scripture, and the 1302 Zhenwu revelation. The dozen other tracts are undated but are not documented in any source before 1600; they include one produced by Peng Dingqiu in 1674. It thus appears that for a compiler of an anthology of essential morality tracts working in 1749, most of the spirit-written material was composed during the last hundred years. Other similar anthologies include the *Chenzhonglu* 晨鐘錄 (Records [as clear as] as a bell sounding at dawn; 1763), and the *Shengjing huizuan* 聖經會纂 (Compendium of the scriptures revealed by the saints; 1806).

6.4.2. Recorded Sayings (*yulu*)

The *jitan* produced and published morality books and tracts addressed to society at large (or certain social classes), but they also recorded and made public revelations specifically given to their members. We have already seen that there is a tradition of records of personal divine instructions going back to medieval times and running through the eleventh-century *Yisheng baode zhuan*, Jingming texts, and Lu Xixing. The innovation brought by the *jitan* was to dispense with the notion of secrecy and to publish these instructions, even when nominally addressed to one member of the spirit-writing group. In the seventeenth century, more and more altars started publishing records of the instructions given by their divine teachers, often arranged chronologically. This type of revelation is different from scriptures (which are designed for psalmody or ritual use) and morality books and tracts, which are short and highly readable; the recorded sayings by contrast are less reader friendly, because they are not organized thematically, but they nonetheless offer very rich material on interactions between humans and gods. These recorded sayings reflect the questions, interests, aspirations, and anxieties of the members of the *jitan*; as such they are highly informative about their religiosity and practices. They notably provide significant amount of instruction on self-cultivation, including inner alchemy but also meditation, self-healing, hygiene, and other practices.

One example is provided by a *jitan* in Yangzhou (Jiangsu), where in 1677 Patriarch Lü revealed a scripture, the *Shengde zhupinjing* 聖德諸品經 (Scriptures in all chapters on saintly virtue), to which was appended a record of question-and-answer séances between the *jitan* members and the immortal.[54] A better-known case is provided by the spirit-writing altars patronized by the elite society of Suzhou in the early decades of the Qing. Daniel Burton-Rose has shown that several altars were active there during the 1670s; in 1674, three of them (dedicated to Zhenwu, Doumu, and Wenchang respectively) merged into one, the Jade altar, Yutan 玉壇, which continued to exist for at least 120 years.[55] Its ever-accumulating records were compiled in one large collection, titled *Yuquan* 玉詮 (Jade expositions; five *juan*). This is a series of rather short texts by different gods, mostly dealing with cosmology, self-cultivation, and ritual practice. Another volume of similar revelations received by Peng Dingqiu, *Zhishenlu* 質神錄 (Record of soliciting confirmation from the gods; published 1773), was edited chronologically (the first revelations dated 1678) by the eminent lay Buddhist Peng Shaosheng 彭紹升 (1740–96), Peng Dingqiu's great-grandson.

During the eighteenth century, such publications of serialized short instructions appeared ever more frequently. The canon *Daozang jiyao* (edited ca. 1806) even contains a collection of such collections, *Yulu daguan* 語錄大觀 (Great compendium of recorded sayings), which anthologizes the recorded sayings from Patriarch Lü at different altars in different parts of the empire during the seventeenth and eighteenth centuries.

6.4.3. Scriptures

We have seen that in earlier periods, the scriptures were typically of the sutra type, whereas explicitly spirit-written content tended to be commentaries and short instructions about the scriptures. The new

54. They are included in the 1850 edition of the *Lüzu quanshu*; see Lai Chi Tim, "Ming Qing daojiao Lüzu jiangji xinyang de fazhan," 159.

55. Burton-Rose, "Establishing a Literati Spirit-Writing Altar."

phase that began in the late Ming changed that situation, with the multiplication of explicitly spirit-written scriptures and their defining role for spirit-writing groups.[56] The *Bapinjing* introduced above is a very good early example. It has a spirit-written self-preface 自序 by Patriarch Lü; even if the preface was not chanted when the scripture was performed, it was on the printed copy, so no one could ignore how the scripture came to be. The scripture begins with a revelation scene in Heaven, like all sutra-type texts, but immediately after the first two words characteristic of this type's revelation scenario, "In times of yore" 爾時, an interlinear commentary hastens to explain that this means two things: the original preaching in Heaven and the actual revelation on Earth 說經 through spirit-writing. So, the time-honored form of the sutra type was maintained but incorporated into the very different temporality of spirit-written revelations.

Some sutra-type scriptures were actually produced by spirit-writing before the late Ming (we have notably seen the case of the *Yuhuangjing*). However, for the general ecology of revelations, I see a very significant difference between such a scripture that we know (through narratives and records found elsewhere) was produced in such a way but not necessarily everyone knew, on the one hand, and a scripture that presents itself as spirit-written. The emergence of the latter changed the place of spirit-writing within the larger landscape of Chinese religious literature.

The emergence of spirit-written scriptures had two main effects in terms of theological innovations. First, it served to elevate the status of the revealing gods. This is particularly clear in the case of Patriarch Lü; whereas in the previous literature ascribed to him he was "merely" an immortal, the spirit-written scriptures present him as a Buddha, a Heavenly Worthy (pure cosmic deity) *tianzun*, and a universal savior. Moreover, each new revelation seems to attempt to elevate him further, fueling an ever more grandiose array of titles and descriptions of his cosmic role.[57]

56. On ethnographic discussions of the role of scriptures in such groups, see Clart, "Text and Context."

57. Lai Chi Tim, "Ming Qing daojiao Lüzu jiangji xinyang de fazhan."

Second, the spirit-written scriptures articulated and developed the elite eschatological message already present in the Song-period Wenchang scriptures.[58] This message was present in some shorter morality books revealed in the late Ming (notably Wenchang's *Jiujie baozhang*), but it could be expressed in much more detail in the longer scriptures. Indeed, a heightened interest in eschatology (that would itself need to be explained) may have spurred the production of spirit-written instructions on how to prepare for the final reckoning and save oneself and the world. The notion of *jiujie* 救劫 is omnipresent in the modern spirit-written scriptures and is found in many of their titles.

The soteriological scheme of the spirit-written scriptures produced by the *jitan* is deployed under the authority of a revealing god who introduces himself (or herself) as a unique or at least privileged savior and provider of help and blessings. The scripture so defined is an ideal type, and numerous texts actually straddle the categories.[59] Four criteria, however, allow us to point out its characteristics: 1) a sutra-type prologue staging the dispensation of the scripture in Heaven (in direct continuity with the style of the Mahayana and Lingbao scriptures), which precisely places the revealing god and his mission within the cosmic-bureaucratic order; 2) a cosmological vocabulary (which can be used just for its legitimizing value or to support a real cosmological discourse); 3) a focus on the situation of humanity as a whole and its collective fate; and 4) on the level of style, a regular prosody fit for recitation. I label these types of texts as scriptures and qualify them as "doctrinal"—independently of the originality and coherence of their contents—because they aim at integrating morality, liturgy, theology, cosmology, and self-cultivation into one discourse that attempts to account for everything the devotee should know.

58. Goossaert, "Modern Daoist Eschatology."

59. For example, the *Lüzu xingxin zhenjing* presents most characteristics of a revealed scripture, but its contents are basically that of a morality book.

6.4.4. New Liturgies

The *jitan* altars that mushroomed after the Wanli era may have had a somewhat different Daoist identity from their Song-Yuan period predecessors; they nonetheless revealed and practiced Daoist rituals. Liturgical texts provide the group with the means to ensure the well-being and posthumous salvation of its members, and often outsiders as well. The main difference is that the early altars largely produced exorcistic *daofa* rites, which strictly require formal ordination as *fashi*. The *jitan* altars produced little *daofa* liturgy as far as we know, yet, the world of the members of the *jitan* and that of the professional priests performing funerals and exorcisms were not exclusive; Tao Jin has shown how precepts, *jie* 戒, revealed in spirit-writing were integrated in a funerary ritual now performed by Daoists in Suzhou.[60]

What the *jitan* produced was large numbers of litanies of penance, *chan* 懺. Litanies, a genre that originated in medieval Buddhism, are liturgical texts that enumerate comprehensive lists of sins that the community sponsoring the ritual swears to repent from, and they invoke long series of Buddhas or gods called on to absolve the sinners. In many cases, a *chan* litany is included within a *jing* scripture. These litanies, which do not require a full ordination as *daoshi* to be performed (because they do not imply the submission of a written memorial to the gods, only oral recitation, and require no advanced ritual technique), were very popular among educated elites in the modern and contemporary period; they performed it for themselves as well as for families or communities who invited them to perform. Litanies are the ritual of choice of the *jitan*, not only because they are rather easily and collectively performed but also because they are very strongly moralistic; they constitute the ritual enactment of the moral self-examination exposed in the morality books.

The first Patriarch Lü litany seems to be the *Xiuzhen xianchan* 修真仙懺 (Litany of immortals for practicing transcendence), revealed

60. Tao Jin, "Suzhou *Dadong wushang jiuji tianxian chuanjie keyi* chutan."

together with the *Wupinjing* in 1679; the earliest Wenchang litany would seem to be the *Yuju xinchan* 玉局心懺 (Heart litany of the Jade Bureau; revealed to Peng Dingqiu in 1680), the latter being closely associated with the Peng family altars in Suzhou.[61] The earliest Guandi litany is mentioned in a bibliography of the late Qianlong period, yet no independent litany was included in a Guandi canon before 1858. The production of litanies was so plentiful that one of the longest revealed texts in the *Daozang jiyao* is the monumental *Chanfa daguan* 懺法大觀 (Grand compendium of litany rites), which compiles a vast series of revealed litanies devoted to the main gods in the Daoist pantheon. Another similar type of revealed text for regular psalmody is the *Zhongxiaogao* 忠孝誥 (Hymns on loyalty and filial piety), which is to be recited daily, revealed in Hunan in 1633.[62]

I will return in chapter 7 to how these different types of production can be, in some cases, correlated with the developmental phases of the largest and most institutionalized *jitan*.

6.5. Explaining the Turn

So far, we have described the post-Wanli turn in the production of revelations in terms of new gods and new genres. In order to explain how and why this turn happened, we now have to look at the social groups that ushered it in, that is, we have to place the *jitan* and their revelations in their social context.

The fact that many deep-running transformations happened in the late Ming and affected Chinese society, culture, and religions is hardly news, and it is more than likely that these other changes (including demographic growth and rising social mobility, the rise of literacy, opening to the outside world, and the rise of the lineage-centric society) have

61. *Lüzu quanshu* (33-*juan* edition), j. 23; and *Wendi quanshu*, j. 38 respectively.
62. *Lüzu quanshu* (33-*juan* edition), j. 7–8.

something to do with the boom in spirit-written revelations. Specifically, the background to the emergence of the *jitan* is a growing class of highly educated scholars not finding employment, frustrated with politics, and seeking a meaningful social role by actively participating in spirit-writing groups and their charitable activities. These factors, however, are necessary but not sufficient conditions, and they also produced many other religious innovations. We must now look more precisely at the religious dynamics behind the emergence of the *jitan*.

6.5.1. New Techniques

In the milieu of the *jitan*, established terms for naming spirit-writing (*jiangbi*, *fuluan*, and wielding the sieve) continued to be widely used, but a new term soon gained prominence, which gave its name to the *jitan*: *fuji* 扶乩. This term has become the most common one in the modern period and is the best equivalent of "spirit-writing" as an encompassing category. It refers to a Y- or T-shaped wooden implement (which I call a stylus) used to write in ashes or sand and wielded by either one medium (*jishou* 乩手, holding both handles) or two (each holding one handle, in which case there is usually a main and an assistant medium).[63] They usually stand in front of an altar on which the ash or sand plate is arranged; another member of the altar sits next to them and writes down all characters written with the stylus (see fig. 1). This has become the most common form of spirit-writing, but we should beware not to take it as a normative definition: other techniques, including writing with a brush, or without a human medium wielding the instrument, have remained common in modern and contemporary times.

As Wang Chien-ch'uan has shown, this technique and the term *fuji* appear around 1500 and quickly become standard.[64] The origins of the

63. Stylus is commonly used in the scholarly literature on spirit-writing, but sometimes with different meanings. In this book, I use "stylus" exclusively to translate *ji* 乩. Hu Jiechen, "Zailun fuji de fangfa yu leixing," argues that the T shape preceded the Y shape.

64. Wang Chien-ch'uan, "Song-Ming shiqi."

A spirit-writing séance in *Dianshizhai huabao*. ("Feiluan xinyu 飛鸞新語," in *Dianshizhai huabao* 點石齋畫報, vol. Bing, p. 22, 1885).

character *ji* 乩 are unclear; it may be a simplification of both *ji* 箕 and *luan* 鸞.[65] It is tempting to suppose that this new spirit-writing technique contributed to the spread of the practice, because it was simpler and more accessible than the procedures used heretofore. More specifically, some scholars have suggested that *fuji* does not require any participation from a Daoist priest and therefore represents some sort of secularization of the practice. Lai Chi Tim in particular has argued forcefully for a *jitan* tradition that is not related to clerical Daoism and represents an entirely different and new form of lay Daoism accessible to all literati.[66] If we graft this hypothesis onto the history of spirit-writing we have outlined so far, then we must suppose that transformations of the *daofa* ritual traditions and their modes of initiation may have caused the "trade secret" of spirit-writing to be open to a much larger audience and to be simplified, and that it became more legitimate for nonordained persons to engage in it.

Judith Boltz, who has studied the earliest detailed liturgical manual for performing spirit-writing (one of the fourteenth-century texts discussed above), has made the very important point that this liturgy was clearly meant for *fashi* priests; however, later versions of these instructions, albeit in general continuity with the Yuan text, appear in general circulation and do not refer to the role of the priest anymore; in particular, she discusses a 1478 edition of the encyclopedia *Shilin guangji* 事林廣記 (Vast collection of the forest of facts) and later manuals of household ritual techniques that circulated widely during the late Ming and Qing periods, such as *Wanfa guizong* 萬法歸宗 (Return to the origin of the myriad rites) and *Fuzhou quanshu* 符咒全書 (Canon of talismans and incantations).[67] Another late Ming popular encyclopedia that introduces readers to spirit-writing techniques is the 1597 *Wuche*

65. Hu Jiechen, "Terminology and Typology."

66. Lai Chi Tim, "Cult of Spirit-Writing in the Qing."

67. Boltz, "On the Legacy of Zigu." Hu Jiechen, "Zailun fuji de fangfa yu leixing," discusses this liturgy in an earlier edition, dated to between 1330 and 1332, of the *Shilin guangji*.

bajin 五車拔錦 (Brocades taken from the five carts). The detailed liturgy is found under the category "Mysterious teachings" 玄教門 (that is, Daoism).[68] It is indeed structured by numerous incantations, talismans, hand gestures, uses of the wooden block commanding divine soldiers, *lingpai* 令牌, and other ritual elements typical of the *daofa* tradition. The practitioner, who refers to himself as a "disciple" (*dizi*), summons martial gods, notably Zhenwu, Guan Yu, and Zhao Gongming 趙公明, and various *daofa* patriarchs. Hu Jiechen has conducted a thorough study of spirit-writing liturgies in these popular encyclopedias and showed that they are variations of a same model.[69]

In sum, we would seem to have here a development of priestly knowledge gradually entering general circulation. I have shown elsewhere that the same processes applied to other aspects of the *daofa* traditions: the divine codes and the ledgers of merits and demerits, originally both internal documents for initiated members of the *daofa* traditions, had by the late Ming entered general-circulation morality books.[70]

Fuji, then, could be understood as a ritual technique inspired by those of the *fashi* priests but simplified and made accessible to nonpriests; it is certainly the case that we do not see in the *jitan* the complex visualizations and medium-controlling rites that characterized early modern altars. But we need to nuance and complexify this scenario; the Daoists never left the picture entirely. Spirit-writing did not become entirely independent of priestly knowledge, but it was easier to learn it from Daoists, or from a line that ultimately went back to one. Terence C. Russell has translated a rare description of the spirit-writing techniques used at Shizhushan in the 1640s; a Y-stick with a brush was attached to a sieve, again showing how different ritual techniques are endlessly recombined. Immortals were invited through invocations and talismans taught by Daoists: he translates the notes from a participant who wrote

68. "Jiang jibi fa 降箕筆法," *Wuche bajin*, j. 31. This chapter also has other ritual techniques for inducing possession in mediums and divination over a mirror.

69. Hu Jiechen, "Zailun fuji de fangfa yu leixing."

70. Goossaert, "Divine Codes."

"anytime men of letters have idle time they study spells [Russell's term for incantations] and talismans from Daoist priests."[71] Another scholar in the early seventeenth century writes that he learned the talismans for summoning gods for spirit-writing, *zhaoji* 召乩, from a Daoist and discusses in some detail variant ritual techniques.[72] Yet another scholar writing around 1612 states that "Recently, the people who summon the gods and immortals will use peachwood to make a Phoenix-stylus and ask mediums to wield it. The immortals will manifest their presence when (summoned by) the talisman" 近世召神仙者, 以桃木爲鸞乩, 命童子扶之, 隨符而降.[73] Here again, mediums and talismans are required. Again, in the eighteenth-century novel *Rulin waishi* 儒林外史, a ritual expert is invited when the literati need to organize spirit-writing.[74]

Fuji spirit-writing as practiced by the gentry was part of a larger movement of the diffusion of simple ritual techniques among ordinary people. The open-circulation manuals and handbooks discussed by Boltz are full of talismans that they present as Daoist and tell readers they can use so as to produce the divine presence for healing (mostly), divination, or protection. At the same time, no one denied that Daoists remained the best performers of these ritual techniques and the best resource from whom to learn them. More often than learning simple ritual techniques such as talismans and incantations from a book, ordinary adepts were taught by a cleric (Daoist but also Buddhist or a sectarian leader), and then they transmitted their knowledge among themselves.

The fact that one needed talismans and incantations to perform spirit-writing is discussed in an introduction, dated 1707, to a morality book revealed by Patriarch Lü, the *Lüzu xingxin zhenjing* 呂祖醒心真經 (True scripture on awakening the minds, by Patriarch Lü). In this

71. Russell, "Chen Tuan at Mount Huangbo," 134.

72. "Zhaoji 召乩," *Huadangge congtan*, 5.15a–22b.

73. Shen Changqing 沈長卿, *Shenshi yishuo* 沈氏弋說, j. 5, quoted in Hu Jiechen, "Terminology and Typology."

74. Hu Jiechen, "Terminology and Typology."

text, Gu Zhougeng 顧周庚, an otherwise unknown scholar from Taicang (near Suzhou) explains that he is a strict Confucian who has never read Daoist or Buddhist texts 佛老二家言屏不一覽, but who happens to own a talisman to summon deities. A family friend, looking for a cure for his wife, begs him to use the talisman; Gu accepts, fasts so as to be pure, prepares an altar for spirit-writing, and burns the talisman. Immediately, Patriarch Lü possesses the medium (Gu himself?) and responds with perfect precision and superb calligraphy to the requests of the friend, as well as all the neighbors who soon come to put their requests to Patriarch Lü. A few days later, Patriarch Lü declares that on the injunctions of the Jade Emperor, he wishes to reveal a text to save humanity. Thus the *Lüzu xingxin zhenjing* is composed, and Gu's friends have it printed. Gu insists that this text fully accords with Confucius and Mencius and is even superior to the *Taishang ganyingpian* and *Yinzhiwen*; indeed, it is a morality book with an eschatological framework. This narrative suggests how doctrinal texts can be the product of spirit-writing activities that were first motivated by individual demands (notably cures) among educated elites who are nonetheless very attracted to discourses of universal salvation, *jiushi* 救世.[75]

In this account, Gu is neither a Daoist nor has he trained with one, but he has a talisman, which presumably was drawn by a Daoist or another expert. There are cases of people who mentioned performing without the need for incantations and talismans (showing it was considered atypical), and some contemporary traditions likewise dispense with them. Historically, however, control mechanisms through talismans and incantation were central to spirit-writing.

Another early account is even more explicit on the importance of incantations and talismans. Hong Ruogao 洪若皋, a 1655 *jinshi* from Linhai (Taizhou, central Zhejiang), recounts that a neighbor formed a spirit-writing group that enrolled his brother and himself; the neighbor

75. *Lüzu xingxin zhenjing*; Goossaert, *Livres de morale*, 77–98.

had been taught an incantation by Patriarch Lü, which he taught to the other members—remarkably, Hong publishes the incantation as an appendix to his story.[76] When intensively practiced, the incantation allowed the performer to enter a state where he could write the appropriate talismans and cause Patriarch Lü and other gods to be present. This rich account also explains how Patriarch Lü trained the adepts for the civil examinations by correcting their copies and gave them various objects; it also relates in detail a healing session during which the immortal cured the author's father.

Mao Xianglin 毛祥麟 (1812–?), a scholar and painter from Shanghai, wrote around 1870 saying there were two types of spirit-writing groups; the first practiced divination and used talismans, the second produced morality books with a simpler ritual framework.

> Those (among spirit-writers) who transmit talismans and ordination registers gather at night in a quiet place; they burn talismans and chant the incantations, then the gods make themselves present in the *ji*, and they ask about the future; the divine answers are often accurate. Nowadays, most (spirit-writing groups) congregate for the purpose of teaching people the divine ways, and do not use talismans and incantations. They only set up their altar and chant scriptures and then heal people. They do not discuss divine retribution (to individuals). They mostly talk of good deeds, so people contribute money, which they say they will use for such and such a charitable project. This in fact is merely using spirit-writing to collect money, as people are easily credulous of it. As for my own experience of talismans and incantations, I have seen cases where they were efficacious and cases where they were not.
>
> 其有傳符籙者，每至深宵人靜，焚符誦咒，神即降乩，叩休咎，往往有驗。今時則大都以神道設教，不施符咒，惟設壇誦經，為人治病，不言禍福，造語多道善，因而集捐，言作種種善事。然不過假乩以斂財，使人易信耳。即余所聞符咒之術，亦有驗有不驗。[77]

76. "Jixian ji 乩仙記," *Nansha wenji*, 5.48a–52b. The same text is found in *Yuchu xinzhi*, 1.437–440.

77. *Moyulu*, 92–93. Attention to this source was first drawn by Kleeman, *God's Own Tale*, 12.

There is no denying that many people experimented outside of clerical supervision and away from set ritual procedures. It is likely that most experimentations failed, but the few successful ones further enlarged the array of spirit-writing techniques. Some of the bolder experimentations involved solo spirit-writing without supervision. This was the case for young Peng Dingqiu, who in 1674 practiced alone (just worshiping Doumu and Wenchang and wielding the stylus), saying pointedly he did not use talismans and incantations, which was against standard practice. He was driven by mental and physical distress, showing once again how personal motivations underline spirit-writing endeavors. Peng then announced he had received a spirit-written prediction of his success at the next *jinshi* examination, which indeed happened two years later. As Daniel Burton-Rose recounts, his family and friends, who were all spirit-writing adepts, rejected this uncontrolled revelation, which was only validated when the prediction was realized.[78] Yet, the practice of solo spirit-writing, *bilu*, also came to be codified and recognized from the late Ming onward.[79] To this we must add the troubling fact that Peng Dingqiu's and other descriptions of their practice occasionally mention their seeing the god; the illustrated autobiography of You Tong 尤侗 (1618–1704), a friend of Peng Dingqiu and fellow spirit-writer, shows him meeting the gods who invite him to become a member of the Jade Bureau, Wenchang's divine administration.[80] How, we will unfortunately never know, but we have to keep in mind that spirit-writing is not exclusive of other techniques, both presence type and visualizations.

Furthermore, advanced visualization techniques were still combined with spirit-writing among the early Qing gentry—and there is no reason to suppose that this entirely disappeared afterwards. Chen Jisi 陳濟思, one of the leaders of the Yutan, the spirit-writing altar that Peng Shaosheng patronized, described his spirit-writing technique 侍鸞

78. Burton-Rose, "Establishing a Literati Spirit-Writing Altar."

79. Hu Jiechen, " 'Bilu' gouchen."

80. Burton-Rose, "Establishing a Literati Spirit-Writing Altar," who also mentions Peng Dingqiu seeing Wenchang's divine emissary.

之法 as based on a meditative state in which he could also hear the transcendents.[81] This reminds us once again that spirit-writing is not a monolithic tradition but a large array of ritual techniques that are combined in multifarious ways by each practitioner.

With its absence of a *fashi* priest, *fuji* spirit-writing is different from but in continuity with spirit-writing rituals directed by a *fashi* priest controlling a medium, as found in Song- and Yuan-period sources. I have argued in previous chapters that the latter constituted "controlled possession"; this continues to be the case with modern *fuji*. First, members of the *jitan* groups are usually given a divine status, often as disciples of the altar's main god, and many consider themselves Daoists, as seen from the titles that they sign their texts with. As current practices show, some members of certain groups train themselves in Daoist rituals; this is even one of several reasons for people joining a group.[82] So, even though many of the early modern presence-type rituals are not practiced anymore, the idea that divine presence is created within set procedures and a heavenly bureaucratic framework by authorized persons has continued to underpin modern and contemporary spirit-writing. Philip Clart has shown the clear difference, in both emic and etic terms, between the spirit-writing "moral mediums" (i.e., obeying moral rules, under control) and the talking mediums in the temples.[83] Second, control over possession is also carried out by the group that is collectively responsible for the revelations, notably the person who writes down the words written by the one or two members wielding the spirit-writing implement. The stylus technique may be simpler, but it absolutely requires interpretation because the scribbling in sand or ashes is both hard to decipher and ephemeral; by contrast, spirit-writing techniques with a brush can produce legible and durable written documents. For this reason, the *jitan* revelations are

81. *Yixing juji*, 7.3b.

82. See notably the cases of the Jin'gaishan network and the *jitan* in the Cantonese world; Goossaert, "The Jin'gaishan Network"; Shiga Ichiko, *Kindai Chūgoku no shāmanizumu to dōkyō*.

83. Clart, "Moral Mediums."

group productions to a larger extent than earlier spirit-written revelations, and we find in modern times large editorial teams with a precise division of labor behind spirit-written books, something that is not recorded for earlier periods.[84]

This line of reasoning raises an obvious question: if spirit-writing was originally a technique of the *fashi* priests that by the late Ming had morphed into a technique used by literati (who learned it from *fashi* at some point), why did the *fashi* stop using it? The answer is simple: they did not. Spirit-writing was practiced in Daoist institutions in the seventeenth century and later. To take one example, Shi Daoyuan 施道淵 (1616–78), the most famous early Qing Daoist leader in the Jiangnan area and a formidable exorcist (and master of Peng Dingqiu), built a large temple on a hill near Suzhou, Qionglongshan 穹窿山. His gentry disciples (whom he ordained with the abovementioned Wenchang register), as divine officials in the Wenchang administration, compiled a large gazetteer for that mountain, where they praise his demon-chasing feats. The gazetteer contains spirit-written prefaces from Wenchang and Patriarch Lü.[85] We do not know how exactly they were produced. But the gazetteer has abundant evidence of Shi making thunder gods speak through mediums. An important example is Divine official Wang, Wang lingguan 王靈官,[86] who was central in both Shi's exorcisms and in spirit-writing revelations. The ritual, performance-oriented *daofa* techniques of Shi Daoyuan and the book-writing-oriented practice of the *jitan* are not two separate worlds; in this case, they are intimately connected but only differ by their orientation.

It is certainly the case that some of the various spirit-writing techniques described in Song- and Yuan-period *daofa* manuals (introduced in chapter 4) were eventually lost—this is the case in general for many

84. Jordan and Overmyer, *Flying Phoenix*, have remarkable ethnographic stories about group control over the medium.

85. *Qionglongshan zhi*, 1.69–80; on Shi Daoyuan, see Goossaert, "Daoism and Local Cults."

86. Goossaert, ""Ritual Techniques for Creating a Divine Persona."

of the complex rituals found in *Daofa huiyuan* and other such compilations. The use of spirit-writing in exorcistic and healing rituals is well attested during the Ming and Qing (I have mentioned an early Qing example above). It is not well documented in contemporary times, possibly because we simply do not have the documentation and also because spirit-writing is politically problematic in the People's Republic of China (PRC), but *jitan* in Hong Kong and Taiwan perform *jiao* and salvation rituals. Some Daoists continued all the same to use spirit-writing, along with other presence-type rites, during communal rituals, for patrons, or even for themselves; one such person was the eminent Quanzhen monk Gao Rentong 高仁峒 (1841–1908), abbot of the Baiyunguan 白雲觀 monastery in Beijing.[87] In 1912–14, a lineage in Guizhou Province invited two Daoists to perform judicial rituals to settle disputes involving graves and produced a large spirit-written documentation in the process.[88] Their practice was usually not aimed at publishing the revelations, and they maintained notions of secret revelations; by contrast, the *jitan* during our period started to produce massive amounts of revelations because, unlike the Daoist clerics, their aim was publication. From the published record, one easily gets the impression that Daoists had ceased to be part of the spirit-writing world, but that is not the case. The *jitan* had simply found spaces to develop with autonomy.

6.5.2. The *Jitan* as a Social Institution

During the modern period, some people continued to practice spirit-writing with a few like-minded friends, or even alone, solely for their private interest, be it by writing poetry, like the eminent writer You Tong in his youth, or by seeking divine help in inner alchemy, such as Lu Xixing.[89] There

87. Goossaert, *Taoists of Peking*, 319.

88. Tang Yun, "Shenpan yu guansi."

89. Zeitlin, "Spirit-Writing and Performance"; see also Goyama Kiwamu, *Min Shin jidai no josei to bungaku*, 324–64; and Lin Xiaohan, "Zhenhuan zhijian," on the case of Huang Zhouxing 黃周星 (1611–80).

were also temples that offered spirit-writing as part of their ritual services. But when we focus on the question of published revealed texts, these types of practice appear secondary, and the institutionalized *jitan* group practice takes center stage. How can we account for the multiplication of these groups? For that, we must place them in the larger context of groups of gentry who were religious activists, people with education and money and in search of a useful social role as well as their own spiritual elevation.

Naturally such groups have a long history in China, but the conditions of the late Ming caused them to proliferate. During the Wanli period, a general increase in literacy and the monetarization of the economy produced similar effects to those of the first modernity of the Song. Members of educated classes formed all kinds of groups to pursue their religious and cultural interests. Among them, some focused particularly on self-cultivation and divinization. To that end, they engaged in the work of the gods, professed to seek the good of the population in general, and provided it with services. The political and social atmosphere of the late Ming made such endeavors more acceptable than they had been in the early Ming.

This world of activist gentry groups was extremely varied, and I can think of no neat typology. Some groups focused on one aspect, such as revealing and printing the teachings of the gods, practicing charity, or campaigning for moral reform; but a good number engaged in all of them at the same time. In most cases, the evidence we have is far from comprehensive; a record of a given group doing charity does not preclude they were also practicing spirit-writing, and the converse. Beyond their considerable variety, their shared ideology is the articulation between "work for oneself," *neigong* 内功, and "work for others," *waigong* 外功: members practice self-cultivation (including inner alchemy) and are initiated disciples of the gods on the one hand, and they preach, print books, give charity, and distribute medicine in public view on the other.

The second aspect, charity, is better documented, because it was more visible and socially important and has therefore attracted more scholarly attention. Impressive work has been done on the rise of the charitable halls, *shantang* 善堂, from the late Ming onward.[90] This research, however, tends to pay little attention to the internal aspect (*neigong*), that is, the spiritual practice (such as spirit-writing) and aspirations of their members.[91] Many *shantang*—not all, of course—were organized around a core *jitan*. The charitable activities they conducted were a real-life application of the teachings in the morality books that they printed and, in some cases, produced. Late Qing evidence shows that *shantang* required the beneficiaries of their charity to take vows to the gods to respect moral rules.[92]

Moreover, there was a clampdown on many types of local elite associations after the Manchu takeover, but crucially not of charities, which were encouraged by the new regime. While repression of sectarian groups increased, the elite spirit-writing groups, although technically illegal, were openly tolerated. Thus, groups devoted to charity and moral education (often based on spirit-writing) became a major if not the major locus for elite sociality, first in the late Ming and more extensively so from the 1660s onwards.

Naturally, not all groups of gentry religious activists took up spirit-writing. Many groups were Buddhist-oriented and favored scripture chanting, meditation, releasing life, *fangsheng* 放生, and other merit-making activities. Because many people joined several groups and the milieu was quite fluid, we cannot isolate spirit-writing groups from others. But we can point out two important characteristics of the *jitan* within the larger world of the gentry activist groups: their focus on printing and their provision of ritual services.

90. Handlin Smith, *Art of Doing Good*; Fuma Susumu, *Chūgoku zenkai zendōshi kenkyū*; Liang Qizi, *Shishan yu jiaohua*.

91. The major exception is Yau Chi-on, *Shan yu ren tong*.

92. Notably, see charities' rules collected in the *Deyilu*. Goossaert, "Guérison, révélation et société locale," discusses the case of a charity, the Pujitang 普濟堂 in Gaochun 高淳 (south of Nanjing), that published in 1900 a very large gazetteer (*Gaochun Pujitang zhi*) detailing their activities. It is almost entirely devoted to their intense spirit-writing communications (70 percent of the almost 700 pages are devoted to revelations); the gods dictated every single aspect of their activities.

First, printing: The *jitan* are to a significant extent a result of the evolution of print culture. Just as the Song period was the first stage of the rapid development of printed books and literacy, as well as the flourishing of spirit-writing, the Wanli period saw the proliferation of commercial printing, including large amounts of religious literature. This is the period when one begins to see spirit-written texts included in commercial books. I would, however, prefer to view that as a favorable context rather than a direct cause. It is conceivable that the demand for divine texts from publishers spurred their production through spirit-writing. But, many *jitan* did not publish with commercial presses but on their own, for merit; they published both earlier revelations (hence, for instance, the staggering number of editions of the *Ganyingpian*) and their own.

Books explicitly presented as the collective revelations in the name of one *jitan* start to appear in the eighteenth century at the latest; we have already seen the example of the Jade Altar, Yutan. They usually did not carve the blocks and print books themselves, although some very large *jitan* eventually did that, but paid print shops to print for them while they took charge of the distribution; during the nineteenth century, a specific type of press, the morality book press, *shanshuju* 善書局, specialized in printing religious material, much of it from the *jitan*.[93] Printing revelations was their preferred way of saving the world (and themselves in the process), and this created a friendly competition between groups to publish more authoritative, newer moral tracts, thus fueling revelation. The active engagement of so many groups in preaching moral reform certainly explains the rise of the genre of morality books and tracts. As seen above, the notion of secrecy had practically vanished from the post-Wanli revelations, which were now diffused outside controlled networks.[94]

Ambitious, long-term printing projects were based on the stability of the *jitan* groups, which often maintained their activities for decades

93. Wang Chien-ch'uan, "Morality Book Publishing and Popular Religion in Modern China."

94. Goossaert, "Divine Codes."

and published continuous records of their revelations over the years, something that we do not see in earlier periods, with the exception of the Xu brothers cult in Yuan times. As a result, the *jitan* publications are thus characterized not only by scriptures and tracts but also by detailed institutional histories, accounts of miracles performed by the gods, and regulations. A detailed set of regulations for a *jitan*, the earliest I have seen, included in a 1805 collection from a spirit-writing group in Hankou, shows how the gods actually attempted to restrain the members' drive to summon them all the time and for any reason.[95]

Second, ritual services: Some spirit-writing groups were more outward-looking than others, developing a reputed full-fledged *shantang* in contrast to more self-cultivation-oriented ones; yet, the idea of service to the population at large is so omnipresent in all the modern spirit-written revelations that the *jitan* simply could not have entirely dispensed with it. Besides teaching through preaching and printing books, *jitan* also often provided ritual services, using either existing liturgies or ones they produced, notably the litanies discussed above; we also find in *jitan* publications many liturgical documents to be sent to the gods during a ritual (such as *shuwen* 疏文) and orders from the gods to their living adepts to perform certain rituals. An essential part of the services they offered was healing. This they did by a combination of various means; many members of the *jitan* were trained doctors and offered consultations, whereas others could perform healing rituals (exorcism, talismans, incantations). Gods also revealed medical prescriptions, *jifang* 乩方, through spirit-writing to both individuals and on a large scale during epidemics; indeed, epidemics (such as the 1894 bubonic plague in the Cantonese world) played a major role in the development of very large spirit-writing charities.[96] Some *jitan* even published full-fledged, spirit-written medical treatises.[97] The range of medical competence among the *jitan* was considerable, from full-

95. "Li yingqing guitiao 立迎請規條," *Xixin yulu*, zhongji 中集, 48a–50b.

96. Yau Chi-on, "Boji xianfang"; Shiga Ichiko, "Difang daojiao zhi xingcheng."

97. Luk Crystal Tsing-Tsing, "Fuji xinyang dui Qingdai daojiao yixue."

fledged medical centers to groups that merely printed a few simple prescriptions. The same was true for inner alchemy, with some groups producing detailed manuals and training advanced practitioners, whereas others (including groups focused on Patriarch Lü, such as the Qiyunshe 齊雲社, see below), based on the extent evidence, only mentioned it in very general terms.

Beyond healing, some *jitan* offered a large array of rituals, mostly Daoist. Here again, the range of liturgical competence among late imperial and contemporary spirit-writing groups is very large, precluding any generalization; in some groups, members could not perform anything beyond chanting, whereas others had priests among them, like the early modern altar (*tan*). Some groups combined spirit-writing with a specific local Daoist ritual tradition, with some members choosing to specialize in one or the other.[98] Since early modern times, China has had a long and uninterrupted tradition of scholars finding social prestige and personal fulfillment in performing Daoist rituals for free, as a service, in contrast to paid professionals.[99] We have seen that many Song era scholars and officials were trained in and practiced *daofa*, including spirit-writing. In so doing, they adopted a Daoist identity, which in no way contradicted their Confucian one as scholars and officials. This tradition continued uninterrupted in later centuries. For instance, the high officials who ran the Jueyuantan 覺源壇 spirit-writing altar in Beijing around 1800 (that published the *Daozang jiyao* canon) produced among many other texts a set of precepts, *Tianxian dajie* 天仙大戒 (Great precepts of heavenly immortals), which they used as their own ordination precepts as Daoists. They also produced their own morning and evening chant book. There is substantial evidence, especially for the Jiangnan region, about how members of the gentry who were affiliated with spirit-writing groups

98. Two well-documented late Qing cases are the Jin'gaishan network in Jiangnan, combining Patriarch Lü spirit-writing and Quanzhen ritual, and the Zixiatan 紫霞壇 network in Hunan and Jiangxi, which practiced Jingming liturgy; see Goossaert, "Jin'gaishan Network"; Zhu Mingchuan, "Qingmo yilai de Guandi shengge."

99. On the tension between professional and amateur ritualists, see Goossaert, "A Question of Control."

were trained in and practiced Daoist rituals, and I will explore this in detail in a separate book.[100]

The most significant evolution I see is that scholar-Daoists of the Song-Yuan in particular engaged in exorcistic rites, but they often do not do so in the modern period, preferring to perform dignified scripture chanting, litanies, and prayers to the Dipper. However, there are important exceptions; the Yutan members practiced alchemical salvation of the dead (*liandu*, the most prestigious *daofa* rites).[101] Leaders of the eighteenth-century Jin'gaishan 金蓋山 group (discussed in chapter 7), for instance, practiced thunder rites and exorcism and revealed a new liturgy for *liandu* that was widely used by other *jitan*. Such liturgies (meant only for the eyes of ordained priests) were often not included in the *jitan* publications but circulated among their members nonetheless.[102] In other words, some Qing-period *jitan* were in direct continuity with the complex ritual practices of their early modern predecessors, whereas others only learned simpler, but nonetheless prestigious, liturgies.

Possibly because many *jitan* did not have among their core members a Daoist priest with advanced training in ritual techniques, they did not practice visualizations and, in contrast to the early modern altars that practiced spirit-writing along with other types of rituals for creating divine presence, the late imperial *jitan* tended to practice *fuji* only. Spirit-writing, which was originally closely linked to the exorcistic *daofa*, had now become a standard tool for all sorts of Daoist rituals. From the late nineteenth century onward, a tradition of altars claiming a more focused Confucian identity developed, performing Confucian rituals (they are an important part of the active groups in contemporary Taiwan), whereas others had a Buddhist orientation; we can see them as further variations and expansions of a model that in the seventeenth and eighteenth centuries seems to have privileged Daoist liturgy.

100. Goossaert, *Spirit-writing and Elite Religiosity in Modern Jiangnan.*
101. "Yutan qijiu zhuan 玉壇耆舊傳," *Yixing juji*, 7.1a–11b.
102. Xu Wei, "Wenben liuchuan yu keyi pinjie."

Because of their open nature and their mission to help all humans, some of the *jitan* became halls within public temples, or even temples, such as the Hansangong 涵三宮 founded in 1702 in today's Wuhan, which played a central role in the first Patriarch Lü canon. Such halls and temples certainly provided ritual and other services to the local population; the line distinguishing them from temples of local gods that offered spirit-writing among other services (we have seen late Ming examples above) is very blurred indeed, except for the *jitan*'s distinctive mission to publish. How ancient is the phenomenon of spirit-writing halls open to the public within temples? Early evidence is inconclusive. We have seen Song laws against public spirit-writing shrines, which were certainly divination oriented. There was spirit-writing going on at Wenchang temples during the Song. However, most of the early evidence suggests private settings. It is likely that there always were both private and public settings, but the late Ming turn saw the development of relatively open spirit-writing *tan* within temples, where people could visit, and some of them were run by *fashi* priests and others by groups such as the *jitan*—again, the distinction being a question of degree.

6.5.3. The *Jitan*'s Acceptability

The growing public profile of the *jitan* needs to be examined in the context of the political and social acceptability of spirit-writing. It was illegal in Ming and Qing China, and it still is in the People's Republic of China. Continuing Song and Yuan bans, in a famed 1370 edict against a broad range of religious practices, the first Ming emperor prohibited "all techniques including mediums, *fuluan*, praying to the saints, writing talismans, and incanted water" 巫覡、扶鸞、禱聖、書符、咒水諸術.[103] This was enshrined in the Ming code, in the article *Jinzhi shiwu xieshu* 禁止師巫邪術 (Banning *shiwu* [spirit-mediums or *fashi*] and devious techniques), and continued in the Qing code. The fact was regularly restated by local prohibitions in late Qing Jiangnan.[104]

103. *Jin yinci zhi* 禁淫祠制, *Ming Taizu shilu*, 53.1037.

104. For instance, see the 1890 ban on spirit-writing by the magistrate of Yinxian (Ningbo) in "Chuxie chongzheng shi" 黜邪崇正示, *Shenbao*, GX16/10/21.

What justified this ban, to what extent was it implemented, and how did spirit-writing's illicit nature influence the practice and its textual production? Fear of political prophecies certainly played an important role, even though they were even more directly addressed by another law in the code (on "demonic talk and books," *yaoyan yaoshu* 妖言妖書); the very proregime and antirebellion eschatological messages produced by the *jitan* were an implicit but clear response to that fear. The fact that the huge majority of revealed texts upheld the imperial regime and the existing social order and that many officials (including some of the most famous and powerful) engaged in it gave tacit approval to spirit-writing. The prohibition was seldom enforced in the case of elite spirit-writing, and the Wenchang, Guandi, and Patriarch Lü temples where this spirit-writing took place derived legitimacy from elite participation and official sacrifices. The status of these cults was highly ambivalent—they were sites of elite patronage, official sacrifices, and illegal spirit-writing. This complicates the conventional picture of orthodox, official elite religiosity in opposition to (mostly) illegal popular religion. The religious groups targeted for repression by the Ming and Qing produced revelation not by spirit-writing (until the mid-nineteenth century) but by other means.

Indeed, we have little evidence of the state repressing spirit-writing groups for no other reason. In Qing state documents, mentions of the practice come up when a person or a group was arrested for another reason (often circulating seditious tracts) and the investigation reveals that spirit-writing was involved.[105] But the legal ban was not entirely ignored either. A remarkable case is the Qiyunshe (or Qiyunge 齊雲閣), a gentry spirit-writing group active in Hankou between 1793 and 1805, which published in that year a very large compilation of the revelations received during these twelve years, primarily from Lüzu along with other gods, and titled *Xixin yulu* 洗心語錄 (Recorded sayings on washing

105. Jordan and Overmyer, *Flying Phoenix*, 44, mention two cases, dated 1792 and 1815, of spirit-written rebellious tracts leading to arrests. There is no evidence that these cases led to a larger repression of spirit-writing groups.

one's heart).[106] On the occasion of this publication, the group received several revelations to the effect that it should cease asking questions to the gods and instead practice the instructions it had just edited; the gods added that the group should respect the law banning spirit-writing and as a result closed the spirit-writing altar, *fengtan* 封壇.[107] This is an exceptional case, but it shows that spirit-writing could be a contentious activity.

In between spirit-writing group members who advocated for it and clerics and lawmakers who opposed it, the majority of the population was probably in a gray zone, usually ready to admit the reality that gods reveal texts but also prompt to doubt the authenticity of such a text or such a medium; the same person could consult a spirit-writing altar at a given moment and be critical of the practice at another.[108]

Buddhist (and a few Daoist) clerics discouraged the practice, as it offered unverified and suspect instructions and teaching; they found it very difficult to convince their lay followers to eschew it, however, and often had to devise compromises.[109] Confucians could also be critical, although more often of specific mediums and texts rather than on principle—blanket denunciations only developed with the antisuperstition movements of the 1910s and later.

One of the correlates of acceptability is the public nature of spirit-writing. In contemporary times, in places such as Taiwan or Hong Kong,

106. The group was apparently renowned as it is listed among the important interventions of Lüzu in Li Xiyue's 李西月 (1806–56) *Haishan qiyu*, 7.22b-23a, which mentions the *Xixin yulu*; however, the latter is rare.

107. Various prefaces in *Xixin yulu*. This collection also includes critical discussions of the spirit-writing practice, claiming that many altars were just frauds, and others, where the mediums did not cultivate themselves, merely received occasional, trivial information from the gods; "Luanshou zhenwei bian 鸞手真僞辯," *Xixin yulu*, xiaji 下集.43a–b.

108. See also my discussion of Yu Yue's 俞樾 (1821–1906) records of elite spirit-writing in Goossaert, "Yu Yue (1821–1906) Explores the Other World"; and Lackner, "Between Belief and Disbelief."

109. Fan Chun-wu, "Jinxiandai Zhongguo fojiao yu fuji." However, not all Buddhist clerics were so standoffish; for a case study of a seventeenth-century spirit-writing cult patronized by Buddhist monks, see Russell, "Chen Tuan at Mount Huangbo."

certain spirit-writing temples are entirely open to the public and anyone can join séances; we know very little about historical antecedents of such openness. We do know that in late imperial times, spirit-writing was conducted both in entirely private spaces (homes) and in temples, but we still know too little about where, when, how, and who. One artist, Bao Tianxiao 包天笑 (1879–1973), tells in his memoirs how two types of spirit-writing altars (the vast majority of them devoted to Patriarch Lü and/or Jigong 濟公) were extremely common in late Qing Suzhou: public ones in the charitable halls and private ones in homes, both training the sons of literati families to be mediums and decipher the god-prescribed drugs, *jifang*.[110]

Access for women was a major issue in terms of acceptability and respectability, and some upper-class spirit groups made a point of excluding them.[111] Yet, whereas women and female concerns seem very marginal in the early modern revelations (the *daofa* milieu of priests being very male oriented, in spite of a few rare mentions of female priests and of the importance of female deities producing revelations), the new atmosphere of the *jitan* was more conducive of female participation, including as mediums. In the 1740s, one of the altars that contributed to the first Wenchang canon was led by a female medium, Lin Ying 林瑩, who was Liu Qiao's concubine: in 1743 it produced (through the *bilu* technique) the *Kunningjing* 坤寧經 (Scripture on female stillness), a text on female self-cultivation.[112] The development of female inner alchemy, *nüdan* 女丹, from the late Ming onward was closely linked to spirit-writing, as most of its core manuals were revealed this way in the eighteenth and nineteenth centuries.[113] Female mediums were much sought after and took male disciples, such as in the case of Wang Duan

110. *Chuanyinglou huiyilu*, 84–90.
111. On a late Qing case, see Liang Qizi, "Daotang hu? Shantang hu?"
112. Hu Jiechen, "*Lüzu quanshu* yu *Wendi quanshu* bianzuanzhe Liu Qiao xiaokao."
113. Valussi, "Female Alchemy," esp. 204.

汪端 (1793–1839).[114] From the turn of the twentieth century, some large spirit-writing groups became numerically dominated by women.[115]

6.5.4. The Missing Link

Our scenario for explaining the rise of the *jitan* and their revelations from the late sixteenth century onward is that they are one particular form of the variegated groups of gentry who were religious activists seeking to ensure their self-divinization and save humanity. They were doing the work of the gods and becoming gods themselves; the method to that end was communicating regularly with their divine masters through spirit-writing. The model they were using was created during the Song by the *daofa* spirit-writing altars, and they developed it with simpler ritual methods, a more open recruitment, and a focus on publishing revelations and morality books.

The most credible venue for continuity between the early spirit-writing altars and the late Ming *jitan* is the Jingming tradition. We know that Jingming groups practiced spirit-writing during the Yuan, and the tradition is continuously documented through the Ming, when successive versions of the Jingming canon, the large majority of which was spirit written, were published by Jingming groups. Also, the Yuan-period Jingming material provides the only early modern case I know of an altar practicing spirit-writing that is described as a large-scale institution with hundreds of disciples, as became common in modern times.[116] Typically, early altars seem to have been made of small groups.

One element of the Jingming lore that was particularly popular was the Dragon Sand prophecy, discussed above; by the late Ming a good number of Jingming adepts thought the time of fulfilling the prophecy

114. Liu Xun, "Of Poems, Gods, and Spirit-writing Altars."
115. Goossaert, "Jin'gaishan Network."
116. *Jingming zhongxiao quanshu*, 1.36–39.

had come and they would become immortals in Transcendent Lord Xu's heavenly realm. This belief is clearly mentioned in a preface to the 1589 Patriarch Lü scripture discussed above.[117] Lai Chi Tim has shown that Jingming adepts adopted Patriarch Lü in their pantheon during the mid-seventeenth century. At that time, Patriarch Lü and Lord Xu both revealed important scriptures that present inner alchemy as the way to save humanity. One of these revelations from Patriarch Lü is a rather esoteric *neidan* manual, *Taiyi Jinhua zongzhi* 太乙金華宗旨 (The secret of the golden flower), revealed in several stages from 1668 onward to a Jingming group in Piling (modern Changzhou in Jiangsu).[118] This text would be immensely popular during the Qing and later refashioned as a Quanzhen text, but it originated in Jingming spirit-writing groups. The recipients of the *Taiyi Jinhua zongzhi* were told by Patriarch Lü that thanks to this text and its alchemical teaching, they would join the immortals announced by the Dragon Sand prophecy. Another alchemical scripture revealed in the late Ming by Patriarch Lü and Lord Xu, the *Qiaoyangjing* 樵陽經 (Scripture of Master Qiaoyang), carried the same message.

It thus seems likely that the model of a spirit-writing altar producing Patriarch Lü revelations originated in Jingming altars, which had maintained this form of organization since the Song, and later groups grew apart from the Jingming tradition and focused on Patriarch Lü only, developing distinct ordination procedures and ritual practices in the process. These procedures and practices were simpler (not just the new *fuji* spirit-writing techniques but the whole array of early modern Jingming liturgy is quite demanding and seems to have declined in modern times); groups that sought to attract more members needed simpler rituals. They never ceased to be Daoist, but they invented a simplified form of Daoism. This simplification ushered in the golden age of spirit-writing.

117. *Bapinjing*, *Lüzu quanshu* (33-*juan* edition), preface.
118. Esposito, *Creative Daoism*, 274–84; Lai Chi Tim, "*Revisiting the Jingming Origin.*"

CHAPTER SEVEN

Canonizations

This chapter focuses on the period between approximately 1700 and 1858. This period is characterized by processes of canonization, as evidenced by two interrelated phenomena: the compilation of canons, literally "complete books," *quanshu* 全書, for major savior gods (textual canonization), and the granting of very high-ranking titles by the imperial state (state canonization) to these gods.[1] Events of a comparable nature (especially state canonization) had occurred before, but I contend that this stage between 1700 and 1858 was marked by their systematic development, spurred by the activism of elite groups, the *jitan*, which promoted their values through their chosen divine saviors and their scriptural canons.

I use the notions of canon and canonization in a very wide sense, based on Western (Christian) concepts that might be helpful as etic tools to tease out processes that are not usually identified within Chinese scholarship: canonization thus refers to processes of establishing sacred texts and divine persona as authoritative and conducive to salvation. At

1. This chapter is a revised version of Goossaert, "Spirit-writing, Canonization and the Rise of Divine Saviors."

the same time, for the purpose at hand, I define a specific type of textual canon, "the *quanshu* canon," as an authoritative compendium of revealed texts ascribed to one god or group of gods. Canons in general, and *quanshu* canons in particular, are not meant to be all-encompassing but rather to separate orthodoxy from heterodoxy; indeed, all the *quanshu* canons were the result of a careful examination of all available revealed scriptures, with some rejected as spurious. Monica Esposito has shown the way by discussing the status of the *Daozang jiyao* as a canon; I would like here to expand that discussion to other textual collections.[2]

The canonization process involves compiling textual canons for certain gods, but also granting authority to them by promoting them to higher status, in both the heavenly bureaucracy and this-worldly pantheons. It is a multifaceted process that involves textual production and diffusion, doctrinal innovation, the building of social networks dedicated to these gods, and political legitimization. The dynamics on these various levels were, as I hope to show, closely interrelated.

This chapter begins with a survey of several Qing spirit-writing groups, all of which produced a *quanshu* canon. It should be kept in mind that they constitute only a small part of the documented scripture-producing spirit-writing altars of that period, themselves the mere tip of the iceberg of all spirit-writing altars. It then proceeds to analyze the canonization processes that the surveyed groups engaged in according to three different but interrelated dynamics: social, doctrinal, and political. I will focus my attention on three gods, Patriarch Lü, Wenchang (or Wendi), and Guandi, and look at different types of groups promoting their cult. By the mid-nineteenth century, each of these three gods had over a dozen different editions of their *quanshu* canon, usually massive multivolume editions.

2. Esposito, "Invention of a Quanzhen Canon."

7.1. The Gradual Canonization of Scriptural Productions during the Qing

Textual canonization of spirit-written revelations can occur at several levels and had begun long before our time period. Inclusion of such revelations (notably by Wenchang, Transcendent Lord Xu, and Zhenwu) in the Daoist canon was a first, major step. Indeed, later canons discussed below would often claim to be the quintessence of the Daoist canon.[3] As for post-Daozang canonization projects, there were anthologies, notably of morality books (*shanshu*), gathering the main revelations of major gods in handy collections that were widely distributed, and they certainly played a very significant role in the process of establishing certain gods and texts as the most authoritative. An unprecedented number of such anthologies were published during the eighteenth century, as discussed in chapter 6. All of these anthologies prominently feature scriptures revealed by Wenchang, Patriarch Lü, and Guandi, along with other gods (notably Doumu and Zhenwu).

Another type of canonization is the creation of specific canons for each of these gods. There existed various works collecting data (mostly hagiography and historical material) about a given god; for instance, we have the *Lüzuzhi* 呂祖志 (Treatise on Patriarch Lü; compiled around 1600 in the Ming Daoist canon), and the *Lüzu wenji* 呂祖文集 (Prose texts from Patriarch Lü; several Ming editions), or the *Guansheng dijun shengji tuzhi quanji* 關聖帝君聖跡圖誌全集 (Complete and illustrated collection of the saintly traces of Imperial Lord Saint Guan; compiled around 1692) devoted to Patriarch Lü and Guandi respectively. The *quanshu* canons of the mid-Qing period were different, though, because they were the result of active spirit-writing groups that added very substantial content, especially in the form of doctrinal scriptures

3. As early as the first Patriarch Lü canon in 1744, the compilers clearly express the idea that their work represents the essence of the Daoist canon; Lai Chi Tim, "Qingdai sizhong *Lüzu quanshu*," 186.

(*jing*) that did not exist for these gods previously (except in the case of Wenchang). In so doing, these groups raised their gods to a higher theological level and promoted them as universal saviors. Any revelation, as a rule, promotes its revealing god to a high status; in the present case, however, the spirit-writing-driven promotion of Patriarch Lü, Wenchang, and Guandi did have a major impact on Chinese religious hierarchies as a whole. I certainly do not aim to account for all of the richness, variety, and complexity of the canons under discussion; rather, I hope to show that all the groups compiling these canons were to a significant degree engaged in the same larger historical trend that constituted a key stage in the longer history of Chinese spirit-writing and doctrinal production.

Let us now turn to some of the most prominent of these spirit-writing groups in order to suggest some of their general features and to outline the gradual canonization of their textual production as *quanshu* during the eighteenth and early nineteenth centuries.

7.1.1. Wuhan, 1670s–1744: Patriarch Lü

We have seen how *jitan* dedicated to Patriarch Lü multiplied from the late sixteenth century onward. One particular group systematized and amplified the corpus of texts revealed by Lü. It formed in Wuchang (today Wuhan, Hubei Province), first at the residence of a local scholar, Song Shinan 宋式南, then in a temple that the group founded around 1702, the Hansangong; this group was in direct continuity with an earlier one that had already produced a scripture, the *Wupinjing*, in 1679.[4] Thanks to this temple, the group acquired an institutional structure and became permanent. A later adept, Liu Qiao 劉樵 (fl. 1727–49), compiled all the texts attributed to Patriarch Lü and considered authentic, including scriptures apparently revealed in various parts of China between 1589 (the date given for the revelation of the *Bapinjing*) and the 1730s, as well as a significant number revealed at the Hansangong

4. Lai Chi Tim, "Qingdai sizhong *Lüzu quanshu*," 187–96; Li Jiajun, "*Lüzu quanshu* yanjiu"; see also Yin Zhihua, "*Lüzu quanshu* de bianzuan he zengji."

itself. Liu Qiao (*daoming* Tishu 體恕), a native of Yiling (Hunan), was an official who rose to the rank of prefect before being dismissed for corruption in 1749.[5] The compilation was published in 1744 and titled *Lüzu quanshu*. Texts revealed at earlier altars and at the Hansangong between 1700 and 1740 were in large part scriptures that were longer and doctrinally more complex than the earlier revelations circulating during the Ming in the abovementioned *Lüzuzhi* and *Lüzu wenji*. The group around Song Shinan and Liu Qiao thus significantly altered the content of the Patriarch's teachings and his image. The canon looks very different from previous collections of Patriarch Lü's texts; not only is it several times longer, but a good half of it is composed of long scriptures instead of mostly poetry.

Arguably, the most important innovation in the texts produced at Wuhan was to present Patriarch Lü as a universal savior, sent by the Jade Emperor on a special mission to save humanity. In the last scripture composed by this group to be included in the *Lüzu quanshu*, the *Sanpinjing*, whose full title is *Qingwei sanpin zhidao jixuan cantong miaodian dasheng dujie zhenjing* 清微三品至道極玄參同妙典大乘度劫真經 (True scripture to cross the turning of the kalpa, of the Great Vehicle of marvelous records and unified correspondence, [exposing] the ultimate Dao, most mysterious, in three chapters, of the Qingwei tradition; note the eschatological element in the title), revealed at the Hansangong in 1740, Patriarch Lü is very clearly designated as the one god in charge of "presiding over disasters," *zhuchi jiehui* 主持劫會, "saving humans from the brink of the change of kalpa," *wanhui jieyun* 挽回劫運, and "expanding his compassion to save humans from the apocalypse," *guangtui jiujie zhi ren* 廣推救劫之仁.[6]

The *Lüzu quanshu* rapidly proved extremely influential; during the following decades, it was modified, supplemented, and reprinted several times by other spirit-writing groups in other regions, showing that traveling elites spread these texts rapidly. Equally remarkable is that this

5. Hu Jiechen, "*Lüzu quanshu* yu *Wendi quanshu* bianzuanzhe Liu Qiao xiaokao."
6. *Lüzu quanshu* (33-*juan* edition), j. 13–15.

milestone in the process of scripture formation and canonization was not limited to Patriarch Lü: the same Liu Qiao also compiled the comprehensive corpus of revelations from Wenchang.

7.1.2. Wuhan, 1740s: Wenchang

The *Wendi quanshu* edited by Liu Qiao in thirty-two *juan* (the same number as the *Lüzu quanshu*) was published in 1743 (date of the only dated original preface) or slightly later, that is, at the same time as the *Lüzu quanshu*.[7] The original edition seems lost, but in the 1775 edition (discussed below), we have both Liu's original prefaces and abundant additional information on the canon's editorial history. Apparently, a certain Yu Wenyao 俞文耀 (*zi* Xiyuan 憩園) reprinted it in 1746, with the help of Liu Qiao's nephew.[8] In 1767 Zhu Gui 朱珪 (1731–1807; more on him below) published a shorter edition in fourteen *juan*, *Wendi shuchao* 文帝書鈔 (Manuscript copy of the Emperor Wen[chang's canon]).[9]

In his 1743 preface, Liu says that whereas many literati have an imperfect knowledge of Buddhism and Daoism, all revere Wenchang on the same level as Confucius; and his own teacher, though a strict and exclusive Cheng-Zhu Confucian, taught him to worship Wenchang.[10] Liu thus had long harbored the idea of compiling a Wenchang collection but then was fully absorbed by his Patriarch Lü project. After the latter was completed, he reflected that Patriarch Lü is the ancestor of Daoism, *xianjiao dazong* 仙教大宗, and Wenchang is the ancestor of Confucianism,

7. *Wendi quanshu*, preface by Guan Huai; "fanli 凡例." The best study of the various editions of the *Wendi quanshu* is Hu Jiechen, "Qingdai liuzhong Wendi lei quanshu"; I am not quoting it systematically here, but the factual data I present are a simplified version of his in-depth analysis.

8. *Wendi quanshu*, preface by Wu Yingfang 吳穎芳; preface by Yu Wenyao ("Jiuxu 舊序," 20a–21a).

9. Undated Zhu Gui preface in *Wendi quanshu*, "Jiuxu," 22b–23a, where he explains that he expurgated all the talismans and registers from his edition to keep only the key scriptures. He also claims that his stellar career was entirely due to Wenchang's protection.

10. "Dexintang yuanxu 德馨堂原序," *Wendi quanshu*.

rujiao zhengzong 儒教正宗, and there cannot be the one without the other.[11] Taken together, they sum up the whole of the Three Teachings (*sanjiao* 三教)—note how Buddhism is finessed here, a question to which we will have to return. Liu then recounts extraordinary coincidences that pushed him to edit all Wenchang texts in his possession and add a hagiography he wrote himself. He does not allude to any Wenchang scripture he received through spirit-writing but notes elsewhere that he received revelations from "both divine Lords" (Patriarch Lü and Wenchang) that were instrumental in persuading a devotee to pay for printing the *Wendi quanshu*.[12] One of the coincidences is that a certain Jin Bencun 金本存 (*hao* Fuyang 復陽) was also at the same time compiling Wenchang materials and looking for funds to get them published. This is followed by another preface from Liu's brother (Liu Wucheng 劉悟誠) who provides more details about his family's devotion to Wenchang, both in a family setting and by funding and patronizing the public Wenchang temple. Next, a preface by Chen Derong 陳悳榮 explains that Wenchang is the "before creation" (*xiantian* 先天, that is, divine, transcendent) face of Confucianism, and Confucius is its "after creation" (*houtian* 後天, that is, human, this-worldly) face.

This canon gathered all Song-period Wenchang texts together with new ones that were revealed during the seventeenth century (the most widely circulated one being the *Yinzhiwen*). The role of Wenchang as universal savior was already clearly expressed in Song scriptures and further reinforced in later revelations such as the *Jiujie baozhang*.[13]

A closer look at the contents of the *Wendi quanshu* shows that an important part of the new content was actually revealed at Jin Bencun's

11. All the Liu Qiao prefaces very explicitly claim that the *Wendi quanshu* was published after the *Lüzu quanshu*. Yet the latter work generally is considered to have been published in 1744, even though the work was completed and prefaces written in 1743; the *Wendi quanshu* prefaces are also dated 1743.

12. Some Wenchang texts were revealed at Hansangong, though; see *Wendi quanshu*, j. 31.

13. On the *Jiujie baozhang*, which was revealed before the *Yinzhiwen*, see Hu Jiechen, "*Wenchang dijun yinzhiwen* qiyuan xinyan."

altar (named Zhantan 鱣壇). It would seem that Liu Qiao (as the organizer of the compilation project) downplayed the role of Jin's altar, and as a result we know very little about this Zhantan; but Jin is nonetheless listed (below Liu) as a coeditor throughout the canon. Shorter revelations (such as tracts, *xunwen*) were revealed at this altar, as well as techniques for self-cultivation and a ledger of merits and demerits.[14] Most importantly, a new text was produced there: the *Dongjing shidu* 洞經示讀 (Revealed meaning of the [Great] Cavern scripture). This is a revised edition of the *Dadong xianjing* (revealed in 1168), with a detailed commentary by Kuixing 魁星, one of Wenchang's divine underlings. The *Dongjing shidu* preface tells us how Jin Bencun (an initiated disciple of Wenchang, with the title of Instructor in Charge of Talismans and Charts, *futu sijiao* 符圖司教) felt frustrated at not having a reliable edition of the *Dadong xianjing* with which to practice and petitioned Wenchang to be granted an authoritative version. This Wenchang provided in 1727 (though by way of a medium other than Jin), and then in 1736 the commentary was revealed. It was considered, then and later, as a major scripture, as it provided the definitive cosmology, theology, and theory of self-cultivation for Wenchang adepts.[15] Furthermore, a number of new divine prefaces for older scriptures were revealed in 1734, and I suspect these were also the product of the Zhantan.[16]

In short, then, the compilation of the first Wenchang canon was spurred by new revelations (in particular the *Dongjing shidu*) during 1727–36 at the Zhantan, which were to be enshrined in a complete canon. This is very similar to the story of the *Lüzu quanshu*—with a twist, since the canon was taken over and published by another group. Not only are the first canons of the two gods very similar in their history,

14. *Zhantan xunwen* 鱣壇訓文, *Wendi quanshu*, 14.24a–31a; *Zhantan yulu* 鱣壇語錄, *Wendi quanshu*, 15.25b–34b, and j. 41–42. The *Kunningjing* (*Wendi quanshu*, j. 44–45, a scripture on female self-cultivation with a commentary added by Liu Qiao) was revealed to Jin Bencun's group in 1743 (Liu Qiao's concubine was the medium).

15. On the *Dongjing shidu* and its place in the long textual tradition of the *Dadong zhenjing*, see Kim Jihyun, "Invention of Traditions."

16. *Benyuanjing* (*Wendi quanshu*, j. 10); *Yansijing* (*Wendi quanshu*, j. 12).

but the two stories also are actually very intimately intertwined, so much so that we might speak of twin canons.

7.1.3. Jiangnan, 1770s: *Wendi quanshu* (1775)

One generation after Liu Qiao and his affiliates had published their Patriarch Lü and Wenchang canons, a group of Jiangnan literati did the same. Contrary to what happened in Wuhan and Guizhou (where the Wenchang canon was first printed) in the 1740s, the Jiangnan literati worked on Wenchang first and then Patriarch Lü immediately after. But, in the prefaces, they hold the same discourse: Patriarch Lü represents Daoism and Wenchang represents Confucianism, but the two deities expound basically the same teaching and should be worshiped together and on a par with each other.

The 1775 *Wendi quanshu* was compiled under the supervision of Guan Huai 關槐 (1749–1806; *jinshi* 1780), a Hangzhou scholar and official who was mostly known as a painter. The other name to appear on the cover page is Wang Shibi 王世陛, a rich merchant who was the main donor for the project. This edition has fifty *juan*: it is based on the 1744 edition, with substantial additions. The editorial rules, *fanli* 凡例, show that the 1744 edition was the basis, and corrections were made through comparisons with other editions of individual scriptures; a few texts were expurgated because of their dubious "authenticity"—a procedure common to many if not all canons. An undated preface by Peng Qifeng 彭啟豐 (1701–84; father of Peng Shaosheng and a top-ranking official) explains that Guan Huai sent him his *Wendi quanshu* and wanted to print it together with Peng Shaosheng's *Zhishenlu* (published in 1773), and indeed, the *Zhishenlu* makes up *juans* 46–47 of the fifty-*juan Wendi quanshu*.

7.1.4. *Lüzu quanshu* (1775)

The 1775 enlarged edition of the *Lüzu quanshu* was edited by Shao Zhilin 邵志琳 (or Zhikun 志錕; 1748–1810).[17] Lai Chi Tim has shown that one

17. I explore Shao Zhilin's life in detail in Goossaert, *Spirit-Writing and Elite Religiosity in Modern Jiangnan*; see also Lai Chi Tim, "Qingdai sizhong *Lüzu quanshu*"; and Yin

major purpose of this compilation, beyond claims that the original had become rare, was to include newly revealed texts and recenter it on the Jiangnan region: he counts twenty-seven new texts revealed at seventeen different spirit-writing shrines in Jiangnan, notably at Jin'gaishan—a very active Patriarch Lü spirit-writing center just south of Huzhou 湖州, which at this stage had yet to print most of their own texts, not to mention their own canon.[18] Shao was a regular visitor to Jin'gaishan and personally received an initiation from Patriarch Lü there, as well as a divine order to print his scriptures.

Shao Zhilin and his master Cai Laihe 蔡來鶴 actually operated a spirit-writing shrine dedicated to both Wenchang and Patriarch Lü, named Guixiangji 桂香集, and a temple to both gods, Tianxiangge 天香閣 (the former was presumably located within the latter). This was located just outside Jingci Monastery 淨慈寺, on the southern shores of the West Lake in Hangzhou.[19] Shao's family also ran a hall for performing Buddhist rituals in the Jingci monastery. All the major participants in the editorial work of both *Wendi quanshu* and *Lüzu quanshu* were members of this shrine, including the major donor, Wang Shibi. Cai Laihe was a scion of a Suzhou scholarly family who dedicated his life to running religious projects, including cherishing the written word, *xizi* 惜字, running temples, and teaching rituals and self-cultivation. Other people worked on both projects, or wrote prefaces for both canons, notably Wang Shibi and Peng Qifeng. The support offered by the rich and powerful Peng clan certainly contributed significantly to the publication of the two canons; in his writings, Peng Shaosheng repeatedly mentions Wang Shibi as a friend and their meetings in Buddhist temples.[20]

Zhihua, "*Lüzu quanshu* de bianzuan he zengji," which provide a very convenient list of the scriptures added to the 1775 edition when compared to the 1744 edition.

18. Lai Chi Tim, "Qingdai sizhong *Lüzu quanshu*," 196–202. The editors of the 1775 *Lüzu quanshu* note that they obtained most of the Jin'gaishan texts as manuscripts (prefaces to j. 43, 44).

19. Zhao Jinjian 趙金簡 preface, *Lüzu quanshu* (1775).

20. *Yixing juji*, 5.27b–28a, 2.17a–18a, 5.13b–17b; Burton-Rose, "Mid-Qing Spirit-Altars."

Shao Zhilin's biography portrays him as a man who was not only extremely active setting up charities of all kinds but also a superb ritualist famed for his salvation rituals for the dead, *shishi keyi* 施食科儀.[21] The biography describes him as performing rites so efficacious that the audience could see the myriad saved souls ascending to Heaven. And all this was sustained by a very intense devotion focused on reciting the *Dabeizhou* 大悲咒 (Dharani of Great Compassion). Shao recited the incantation continuously all his adult life, until he could recite it several tens of thousands of times a day, a score few eminent monks ever attained. He could do this because of a very elaborate visualization technique, which he learned from his master Cai Laihe. Biographies of elites seldom deal so precisely with the technical aspects of spirituality and self-cultivation. We should note here that Buddhist spirituality was seen as entirely compatible with a self-proclaimed Confucian identity and the performance of Daoist ritual. This potent *sanjiao* religiosity is the essence of the Patriarch Lü, Wenchang, and other canons discussed here.

The 1775 *Wendi quanshu* and *Lüzu quanshu* have a lot in common: they were compiled almost simultaneously by two overlapping groups of people with the same aims; they are different, however, inasmuch as the history of the *Lüzu quanshu* is largely about successive spirit-writing groups adding the scriptures they had themselves produced to the canon; this is much less the case with the 1775 *Wendi quanshu*. All compilers are extremely clear about the fact that all the texts in the *Wendi quanshu* were revealed by spirit-writing at different times and places, and we have seen that the Liu Qiao network included a large number of texts revealed at Jin Bencun's successive shrines (and a few revealed at Hansangong). However, the Guan Huai group did not produce any of the Wenchang texts included in the canon; those rather few texts added in the 1775 *Wendi quanshu* do not come with enough detailed explanation to ascertain their precise origin. One was revealed

21. *Jin'gai xindeng*, 7.50a–52a.

in 1769; another one bears a preface by a Hangzhou man, but it is unclear if either was connected to the Guan Huai group.[22] More generally, there is much less data on the spirit-writing groups themselves in the *Wendi quanshu* than in the *Lüzu quanshu*. Why this is so is, of course, extremely difficult to determine. What we can say is that the absence of a self-written history by the group suggests a dynamic of canonization partially different from that of the Patriarch Lü cult.

To sum up, the situation in mid-1770s Jiangnan closely resembles the one in Wuhan a generation before: a spirit-writing shrine with elite members and many connections pooling resources to compile canons for both Patriarch Lü and Wenchang, with the two collections intricately connected by numerous cross-references (Patriarch Lü commenting on and prefacing Wenchang texts by way of spirit-writing and vice versa).

7.1.5. Jin'gaishan, 1760s–Today

Shao's biography appears in the famous *Jin'gai xindeng* 金蓋心燈 ([Record of the transmission of the] Mind-lamp at Mount Jin'gai; the large collection of biographies of Daoists connected with Jin'gaishan and its Patriarch Lü spirit-writing cult), because he and Cai visited there regularly. Included in the *Lüzu quanshu* are an important number of scriptures and other texts revealed at this altar and another closely related and nearby one, Yunyi caotang 雲怡草堂, established by Zhu Xuan 朱烜 (1733–93), a prolific spirit-writer and famed performer of Daoist rituals.[23] Starting in the mid-eighteenth century, the Patriarch Lü spirit-writing cult at Jin'gaishan was a rather modest operation patronized by local gentry families that produced several texts but had not printed any. One of the scions of these families, Min Yide 閔一得 (1749–1836), became an official but resigned, and around 1796 he devoted his considerable energy and resources to building Jin'gaishan into the center of a vibrant Daoist network covering most of the Jiangnan region.

22. *Wendi quanshu*, j. 40 and 32 respectively.
23. *Jin'gai xindeng*, 7.50a–52a.

Because he was healed as a youth by a Quanzhen Daoist, Min reoriented the altar by merging it with the local Quanzhen Daoist tradition. The adepts were accepted as disciples by Patriarch Lü through spirit-writing and given a name in the Longmen 龍門 lineage but were allowed to marry; later in the twentieth century, massive genealogies of this lineage were published with thousands of names of these "lay Daoists." The previous shrine became a very large, still active, Patriarch Lü temple, Chunyanggong 純陽宮, which attracted many pilgrims. Min published two successive canons (not of the *quanshu* type): *Daozang xubian* 道藏續編 (Sequel to the Daoist canon; twenty-three texts) and *Gushu yinlou cangshu* 古書隱樓藏書 (Texts from the library of old hidden volumes; thirty-seven texts, including all twenty-three texts from *Daozang xubian* and fourteen others, but none of the texts revealed at Jin'gaishan before Min Yide took charge). Both canons were first published by the Chunyanggong in 1834, shortly before Min Yide's death.[24] Their contents mostly deal with inner alchemy as a tool offered by Patriarch Lü to heal and save humanity. Most of these texts were obtained by Min from his masters and through encounters; however, he also received a scripture and a litany from his own deceased and apotheosized master, Shen Yibing 沈一炳 (1708–86), through spirit-writing.[25]

Although it suffered heavily during the Taiping War, the temple at Jin'gaishan was soon restored, the spirit-writing activities continued, and members created branch *jitan* all over the region, eventually creating a formal network with over seventy shrines in Shanghai and all major cities of the region. This powerful network, counting many politicians, intellectuals, and doctors among its thousands of members, actively produced and disseminated its revelations and trained its members in Daoist rituals until 1949. It has now been partially restored, even though spirit-writing activities are perforce conducted underground.[26] It is a particular, but not abnormal, case of a Daoist identity for a spirit-writing

24. Esposito, "La Porte du Dragon"; Mori Yuria, "Ryo Dōhin to Zenshinkyō."
25. Maruyama Hiroshi, "Qingchao Daoguang nianjian."
26. Goossaert, "Jin'gaishan Network."

group; what is most remarkable is its expansion as a hierarchical network and its institutional resilience over two centuries.

7.1.6. Beijing, 1790–1806

Around 1790 one of the groups that appropriated the Patriarch Lü corpus to reshape and further expand it formed in the capital around high-ranking officials and a Buddhist monk named Mingxin 明心 (lay name Wang Shuxun 王樹勳).[27] Jiang Yupu 蔣予蒲 (*zi* Yuanting 元庭; 1755–1819), whose career culminated as head of several ministries between 1806 and 1814, led this group. Their spirit-writing altar, Jueyuantan, was active during the last years of the eighteenth and the first decade of the nineteenth century.[28] It first published a new version of the *Lüzu quanshu*, *Quanshu zhengzong* 全書正宗 (Authentic tradition of the [*Lüzu*] *quanshu*; 1803), then embarked on a much more ambitious project, achieved around 1806 with the publication of the *Daozang jiyao*. This collection includes over 300 texts, two-thirds of which come from the Ming Daoist canon, and about 100 texts that were produced (mostly spirit-written) during the seventeenth and eighteenth centuries. Although some of these new texts were produced by earlier spirit-writing altars (including the scriptures revealed at the Hansangong and in 1770s Jiangnan), an important number were produced at the Jueyuantan itself. The *Daozang jiyao* thus constitutes a culmination of a canonization process featuring a wide selection of the scriptures revealed by various gods. It is a particularly important collection because it encapsulates the state of doctrinal production by the turn of the nineteenth century.

The *Daozang jiyao* project, initiated by Monica Esposito and completed by Lai Chi Tim, has compiled a comprehensive description

27. "Wang Shuxun," *Xiaoting zalu*, 8:236; Esposito, "Discovery of Jiang Yuanting's *Daozang Jiyao*," 100–1; and Esposito, "Invention of a Quanzhen Canon."

28. On Jiang Yupu and the *Daozang jiyao*, see notably Esposito, "Discovery of Jiang Yuanting's *Daozang Jiyao*"; and "Invention of a Quanzhen Canon"; and Mori Yuria, "*Dōzō shūyō* to Shō Yoho"; "Identity and Lineage"; and "Shō Yoho no Ryoso fukei shinkō."

and analysis of the canon.[29] I am thus not discussing its history here but merely inserting it into my larger argument. From this perspective, the *Daozang jiyao* is a higher-order canon, as it spotlights different gods who feature through: 1) a hagiography, 2) main scripture(s), and 3) in a few cases, a specific litany.[30] Among these canonized gods, Patriarch Lü takes pride of place, along with his divine associates such as Liu Shouyuan 柳守元 who, a generation later, in 1833, came to have his own canon, the *Liuzi cangshu* 柳子藏書 (Stored book of Master Liu). Wenchang comes in a clear second, with all his major scriptures included.[31] Guandi is represented with just one scripture,[32] which clearly shows that in 1806, he was still a rather minor god in the world of spirit-writing groups. The other gods who have their own scriptures (revealed through spirit-writing during the late Ming and Qing) in the *Daozang jiyao* are Doumu,[33] Wei Huacun,[34] and Sun Buer 孫不二:[35] the latter two do not seem to have acquired the status of salvational gods nor to have had their own *quanshu* canon; the former, by contrast, certainly was at the center of a universal cult in late imperial China but was above the business of managing human society and rather sent other gods (such as Wenchang or Patriarch Lü) to save humanity. The 1906 Sichuan edition of the *Daozang jiyao* (the 1906 Chongkan 重刊 edition) added the canon of Zhang Sanfeng 張三丰 (on whom see more below). A notable absence from this list is Zhenwu, who was prominent in earlier periods and has several spirit-written scriptures in the *Daozang*, but he gradually receded to a less prominent position in the pantheon of elite spirit-writing cults during the mid- and late Qing.

29. Lai Chi Tim, ed., *Daozang jiyao tiyao*; hereafter *Daozang jiyao* texts are referred to by their number *JY* in this catalog.

30. I am focusing here on the 100-odd "extracanonical" texts in the *Daozang jiyao* (those not copied from the Daozang).

31. *JY* 7, 257, 258, 259, and 260.

32. *JY* 261.

33. *JY* 100, 101.

34. *JY* 6, 8.

35. *JY* 204.

7.1.7. Toward a Guandi Canon: 1791–1858

Guandi had long been the subject of a major cult by the early eighteenth century, but the process of his textual canonization developed later than in the cases of Wenchang and Patriarch Lü.[36] Probably the first canon devoted to Guandi was the *Guansheng dijun shengji tuzhi* (around 1692) that focused on hagiography but also included one revealed scripture, the *Zhongyijing*.[37] Another short scripture, a morality book (*Guansheng dijun jueshi zhenjing*, likely revealed around 1660–90), had also entered circulation by the turn of the eighteenth century. A very impressive number of anthologies devoted to Guandi continued to be produced. Two late Qianlong scholars, Zhou Guangye 周廣業 (1730–98) and Cui Yingliu 崔應榴 (dates unknown), listed fifty-five anthologies that they could consult, four of which were called *quanshu*.[38] But most of them were apparently not (or at least primarily not) collections of revealed scriptures. Zhou and Cui themselves were not much interested in these scriptures, which they did not include in their work.

At least one of these Qianlong-period Guandi *quanshu* is still extant: the *Guansheng dijun quanshu* 關聖帝君全書, compiled by Peng Shaosheng and prefaced in 1772 by his eminent father, Peng Qifeng. As stated in the preface and the *fanli* of this work, it was largely based on Lu Zhan's 盧湛 *Guansheng dijun shengji tuzhi* (with numerous additions and corrections); it thus carried over the *Zhongyijing* (which Peng Shaosheng explicitly describes as a spirit-written morality book) and adds shorter spirit-written "sermons," *fayu* 法語,[39] which he describes as mostly concerned with Buddhist and Daoist self-cultivation. These sermons are reprints of the revelations by Guandi at four altars in the Suzhou area, including two closely related to the Peng family. Peng Shaosheng had also separately published some of the same revelations as part of the

36. This section summarizes Goossaert, "Textual Canonization of Guandi." See also Yau Chi-on, "Fuhua yunei"; ter Haar, *Guan Yu*, chap. 8.

37. For details on the *Zhongyijing* (which went by numerous alternative titles), see my entry on *JY* 261 in Lai Chi Tim, ed., *Daozang jiyao tiyao*, 1452–56.

38. "Shulüe 書略," *Guandi shiji zhengxinbian*, j. 30.

39. *Guansheng dijun quanshu*, 2.11a–24b.

anthology of the Yutan altar, *Yuquan*.[40] We have here one more instance of an extremely common process: a scholar reprints a divine *quanshu* canon while adding new revelations that he or his immediate circle has produced through spirit-writing.

Production of Guandi scriptures must have begun to accelerate during the mid-eighteenth century, and the idea of a *quanshu* canon proper (with revealed texts forming the bulk of the material and hagiographical-historical material being secondary) followed. One early attempt was the 1791 *Wudi huibian* 武帝彙編.[41] This edition does not appear to be extant, but a much later edition (1876) is likely to be mostly a reprint of the original (it consists of only four *juan*, but it includes at least one later addition, a tract clearly written during the Taiping War).[42] Besides hagiographical material and oracles (*lingqian*), it contains the two scriptures mentioned above (*Jueshijing* and *Zhongyijing*) and short instructions. This edition has very little in the way of paratexts. A short preface by a certain Wu Hui 吳惠 (*zi* Liuqing 柳卿) explains that he tried to compile a Guandi canon on the model of the *Wendi quanshu* that his family had already reprinted (because the two, civil and martial, emperors should be treated with equal devotion) but could find but few texts, and thus he put together what he had found under the more modest title of *Wudi huibian*. One should note, then, that Wu was apparently not involved in producing new revelations.

Guandi's spectacular rise to prominence as the universal savior of end-times would only come in the following decades, with the revelation (undated but likely 1805 or shortly before) of the *Taoyuan mingshengjing* 桃園明聖經 (Scripture on illuminating sainthood at peach

40. *Guansheng dijun quanshu*, 2.16b–22a, corresponds mostly with *Yuquan*, 44a–48b. The *Yuquan* contains revelations by a large number of deities, among whom Guandi features rather prominently.

41. This preface is dated to the *xinhai* year in accordance with the stems and branches system. The first *xinhai* year after the publication of the *Wendi quanshu* is 1791, and this definitely seems to be the right dating for this text.

42. I am extremely grateful to Paul R. Katz and Wu Cheng-che for obtaining a partial copy of this work for me.

garden).[43] We have no clue as to the precise context of its appearance, but it clearly was an instant success and was eventually put in first place as the highest-ranking among the Guandi texts in some later canons; it was also later republished in countless editions throughout the nineteenth and twentieth centuries. The scripture presents itself as having been originally revealed in dream to a Buddhist monk of the Yuquansi 玉泉寺 (the temple in Hubei Province at the spot where Guandi was executed and where he was supposedly first worshiped), and later retransmitted (for a larger dissemination) through spirit-writing; but this story is clearly a myth and not an actual account of the scripture's production. The text is much longer than earlier Guandi scriptures. It is mostly in parallel sentences, with some rhymed passages and with brusque shifts of subject matter, in a style very common among spirit-written texts. Indeed, in an 1840 revealed preface to a commentary (see below), Guandi acknowledges that it is poor literature but nonetheless provides very frank and clear admonitions.

In the *Taoyuan mingshengjing*, Guandi recounts his life story, taking it as representative of the virtues he preaches. He then discusses how the Jade Emperor promoted him to ever higher celestial positions, until he reached the supreme position below the Jade Emperor, where he was in charge of the retribution of humans. In one fascinating passage, he mentions how he took under his command the immortal Zhang (Zhang *xian* 張仙), who was without a proper position: this clearly refers to Wenchang and thus represents an attempt to co-opt and subsume the Wenchang cult, even though the latter clearly served as a model for the Guandi spirit-writing cult. Guandi goes on to explain that he came down to Earth repeatedly throughout history, each time the world was on the brink of chaos, in order to restore order (a theme likely borrowed from Wenchang lore).

43. The most detailed study of this text's origins is Wang Chien-ch'uan's introduction to *Jindai Guandi, Yuhuang jingjuan yu Xuanmen zhenzong wenxian*. This text, like so many revealed scriptures, also went by several alternative titles, including *Yingyan (mingsheng) jing* 應驗(明聖)經. See also Ter Haar, *Guan Yu*, chap. 8.

Some elements in the *Mingshengjing* are very typical of Daoist scriptures composed for various deities: it promises this-worldly blessings of all kinds to those who will copy and recite the scripture; and, in direct continuation with earlier texts such as the *Jueshi zhenjing*, it discusses the heavenly bureaucracy at work monitoring humans and noting every single good or bad action, and accordingly granting rewards or punishments. Other elements appear as innovations. First, Guandi's divine status has been raised, as he presents himself as the overall supervisor of rewards and punishments to humans. In listing virtues that humans need to cultivate, Guandi subsumes them under eight categories: filial piety, *xiao* 孝; brotherliness, *ti* 悌; loyalty, *zhong* 忠; trustworthiness, *xin* 信; propriety, *yi* 義; justice, *li* 禮; honesty, *lian* 廉; and decency, *chi* 恥. This is probably one of the earliest mentions of the "eight virtues," *bade* 八德, that would during the course of the nineteenth century become a major, well-identified discourse on morality in subsequent texts revealed by both Guandi and other deities (including Wenchang).[44] Much of the scripture is devoted to describing the current moral decadence of humanity, beginning with, and putting much emphasis on, officials—this focus also characterizes many later, shorter Guandi tracts. The end of the text mentions twenty-four calamities, *ershisi jie* 二十四劫, that will come, but overall (and similar to the earlier *Zhongyijing* and *Jueshi zhenjing*), the eschatological element is not prominent in the scripture as a whole.

The next Guandi canon was published in 1828, when Gan Yushi 甘雨施, a scholar from Rongchang County (near Chongqing), compiled a *Guandi quanshu*. This appears as a rather "conservative" canon; it does not include the *Jueshi zhenjing* nor the already-circulating *Taoyuan mingshengjing*. As far as revealed scriptures are concerned, and very much like earlier canons, it features one scripture (the *Zhongyijing*) and a limited set of shorter tracts, in this case twenty-one, including the *Jieshizi wen*, which was already circulating in the eighteenth century.

44. On the "eight virtues," see Wang Chien-ch'uan, "Spirit Writing Groups in Modern China"; Fan Chun-wu, "Bade."

One important feature of this canon is that it was compiled in the same effort and published together with a *Wendi quanshu*, and several prefaces closely relate the two deities. The Gan family in eastern Sichuan was actually a well-known propagator of the Wenchang cult.[45]

A slightly earlier collection of Guandi texts, the *Qiankun zhengqilu* 乾坤正氣錄 (Record of correcting the energies of the universe; which is mentioned as a recent source by Gan Yushi), was somewhat more inclusive—if we can judge by an 1880 edition that has later additions.[46] It features the *Zhongyijing* plus, in a separate section in the last chapter (suggesting that these revelations were still considered less important than the *Zhongyijing*), the *Taoyuan mingshengjing*, the *Jueshi zhenjing*, and a set of shorter tracts, none of which (except one added in 1859) has a strong eschatological element.

A still later, but yet rather "conservative," collection is the *Guandi jingchan* 關帝經懺 (Scriptures and litanies of Emperor Guan), compiled and published in 1857 by the major Guandi temple in Quanzhou, Fujian. This rather short book, clearly geared toward liturgical use, includes *Zhongyijing* and *Jueshi zhenjing* (but not the *Taoyuan mingshengjing*), along with two very short *jing* (actually, tracts), and a long litany (different from those included in the 1858 canon). It is unclear why these collections did not include all existing texts (such as the Gan Yushi canon and the *Guandi jingchan*, not including the *Taoyuan mingshengjing*): it is possible (but quite unlikely) that the compilers were not aware of the text's existence; it seems more likely that they chose to exclude it, whether because they were doubtful of its authenticity or because they did not approve of its contents.

These Guandi canons thus contained less scriptures than the contemporary Patriarch Lü and Wenchang canons, even though compilers such as Wu Hui or Gan Yushi had wished to put them on the same level. In these texts, Guandi assumes a soteriological role, but, again in

45. Hu Jiechen, "*Wendi quanshu* yanjiu," 93–95; Hu Jiechen, "Qingdai liuzhong Wendi lei quanshu."

46. The 1880 edition has one text explicitly revealed in 1859.

contrast to Patriarch Lü and Wenchang, it is not deployed in an eschatological context. His spectacular rise to prominence as the universal savior of end-times would only come in the following decades. The textual canonization process reached full maturity with the 1858 *Guandi quanshu* that, for the first time in documented Guandi *quanshu* canons, identified the *Mingshengjing* as its most prominent scripture and thus placed a full-fledged scripture rather than a morality book at the forefront. This canon was produced in the context of the Taiping War, and I discuss it further when covering the war's impact on Chinese revelations in chapter 8. Guandi thus had to wait a full century more than Wenchang and Patriarch Lü before having his own full-fledged *quanshu* canon honoring him as a supreme deity in charge of the salvation of humanity.

7.1.8. The Zhang Sanfeng Canon in Sichuan, 1844

Many spirit-writing groups were active in Sichuan; some of them had as their main revealing god Zhang Sanfeng, a legendary alchemist, who reputedly lived during the early Ming.[47] The reason why I insert a brief discussion of Zhang Sanfeng here is that even though his cult cannot really compare with those of Wenchang, Patriarch Lü, and Guandi, it was nonetheless engaged in a canonization process very similar to that of these three major gods. Zhang's revelations, from the early Ming onward, had long focused on inner-alchemical self-cultivation. A collection of Zhang Sanfeng's spirit-written instructions was assembled by a certain Wang Xiling 汪錫齡 (1664–1724) during the Kangxi period but not published. It was inherited by a nonmonastic Daoist practitioner, Li Xiyue 李西月 (1806–56), who established a lineage (called Yinxianpai 隱仙派 or Youlongpai 猶龍派) of self-cultivators of inner alchemy. Li (who also edited Patriarch Lü's revealed texts) collected earlier Zhang Sanfeng material, but added a considerable amount, most of which he

47. Seidel, "Taoist Immortal of the Ming Dynasty"; Wong Shiu Hon, *Mingdai daoshi Zhang Sanfeng kao*. On spirit-writing in Sichuan, see Valussi, "Printing and Religion in the Life of Fu Jinquan."

produced from spirit-writing.[48] This resulted in a major collection, the *Zhang Sanfeng quanji* 張三丰全集 (Canon of Zhang Sanfeng), edited and published by Li in 1844. In this canon, one indeed finds numerous poems, didactic essays, and commentaries pertaining to inner alchemy. But at the time of compilation, the editor also added several scriptures: one of them, *Xiantian shenhou Doumu yuanzun dadao jiuhuang zhenjing* 先天神后斗姆元尊大道九皇真經 (True scripture of the Great Way of the Nine Emperors, preached by Anterior Heaven Divine Empress Mother of the Dipper Primal Worthy), is devoted to the worship of Doumu and her sons the Nine Emperors (the stars of the Big Dipper). This scripture explains how Doumu sent Zhang Sanfeng to Earth and subsequently made him her messenger to transmit her teachings in order to save humanity.[49] The compilation of the Zhang Sanfeng canon was thus marked by the production of a scripture that gave Zhang Sanfeng a soteriological role in the history of humanity.

Now that I have introduced my case studies of spirit-writing groups engaged in processes of canonization, let us consider commonalities and larger patterns at three distinct but interrelated levels: social, doctrinal, and political.

7.2. The Social Dynamics of Canonization: Elite Religious Networks

At the social level, the canonization processes were based on an intense circulation of people, texts, ideas, and resources. Texts produced at one shrine were very quickly read, commented upon, adapted, and republished by other groups. The people discussed above often concurrently participated in several spirit-writing groups at multiple shrines. To take

48. Wong Shiu Hon, "Cong daoshu de xingcheng kan Qingdai wenren de zongjiao shenghuo."

49. In *Zhang Sanfeng quanji*, j. 7. Another scripture, *Jiuhuang xinjing zhujie*, devoted to the Nine Emperors and revealed by Patriarch Lü is found in the *Daozang jiyao*.

one example, the Jin'gaishan shrine to Patriarch Lü counted as members people like Shao Zhilin and Zhu Gui, who published and/or actively participated in the compilation of canons in other spirit-writing shrines. This circulation was part and parcel of literati networks. Spirit-writing groups thus engaged in both active cooperation and competition with each other; they cooperated in promoting their gods and competed in producing and publishing "better" scriptures and canons. This social dynamic certainly accounted for the sheer number of publications, many of which were massive, costly projects.

These groups were built from diverse social building blocks. Family and lineage were of course very important, and we repeatedly see extended family ties at work when reading prefaces. To take one example, the Liu family, who was instrumental in publishing the 1743–44 Patriarch Lü and Wenchang canons, was clearly a deeply devout family with a sustained, corporate devotion to Wenchang. At least three members (Liu Qiao, his brother Liu Wucheng, and a relative, Liu Zhanjue 劉占爵) wax eloquent in their prefaces and other paratexts on their family tradition, including a miraculous Wenchang statue long present in the family home, daily worship, solemn vows to Wenchang, etc.[50] Spirit-writing cults could also allow the alliance of local lineages, such as the Patriarch Lü shrine at Jin'gaishan, which developed under the tutelage of the two dominant local lineages, the Min and the Shen 沈.

Localism also played an important role, with several prefaces mentioning solidarity between literati from the same locale vowing to work together in publishing divine revelations. This makes perfect sense when we realize that the spirit-writing shrine often served as the elite club in villages and neighborhoods, and sometimes concurrently with the local academy (where the Wenchang cult was often housed). Spirit-writing shrines were important venues for elite sociability. Institutions like the Wenchang Pavilions 文昌閣 (which, unlike the Confucius temple-schools, were not official and thus less subject to scrutiny and

50. Liu Qiao and Liu Wucheng prefaces, Liu Zhanjue postface in *Wendi quanshu*.

legal constraints) developed into key places for the cultivation of elite moral values and cultural production.[51] Third, professional networks also helped. Monica Esposito has noted how Jiang Yupu recruited fellow adepts from among his professional network of men involved in water conservancy.[52]

But there was at the same time a strong associational, voluntary dimension to the spirit-writing groups. Common moral and religious values allowed for the bonding of people of different origins and different social statuses, for we find among the key activists discussed above very high-ranking officials (Zhu Gui, Peng Qifeng, and Jiang Yupu), low- to mid-ranking officials (Liu Qiao and Guan Huai), and exam failures who turned into local scholars and activists (Liu Wucheng and Shao Zhilin). Certainly, some groups are much better documented than others, all have their specificities, and it is risky to generalize too much. Yet, in these groups, it seems that values other than official careers played an important role, and religious merit could trump/mitigate official rank. Activism in spirit-writing was certainly a pathway to prestige and honor that was just as valid as (and certainly not exclusive of) official careers and cultural achievements (poetry, calligraphy, painting, and scholarship) for the lower gentry. Consider Min Yide: Min resigned from an official post as county magistrate to become a healer and spiritual master at Jin'gaishan, most sought after by other Jiangnan elites.[53] His large collection of biographies of people active at Jin'gaishan (the *Jin'gai xindeng*) provides an excellent window into the values and social dynamics of a Patriarch Lü spirit-writing shrine in Qianlong- and Jiaqing-period Jiangnan.[54] It shows how local elite families were closely associated with the operation of the shrine and the production of its texts, but outsiders were also welcome. The primary criterion of prestige

51. Burton-Rose, "Establishing a Literati Spirit-Writing Altar."

52. Esposito, "Invention of a Quanzhen Canon," 58.

53. See in particular the famed poet Chen Wenshu's 陳文述 (1775–1845) discussion of his being a disciple of Min, see Liu Xun, "Intoning Immortal"; and Liu Xun, "Of Poems, Gods, and Spirit-Writing Altars."

54. Goossaert, "Jin'gaishan Network."

was the level of recognition granted by Patriarch Lü to the individual, as well as the amount of merit produced in service to the shrine.

These spirit-writing shrines attracted people with different motivations—some more text-oriented, some more focused on social work and charity. Intellectually they were very inclusive, as they fully embraced the union of the Three Teachings (*sanjiao*). Confucian and Daoist gods featured prominently (we have seen how the canons present Wenchang and Guandi as Confucian and Patriarch Lü as Daoist, while maintaining that all of them represent the Three Teachings), and the liturgical texts included in the *quanshu* canons were predominantly Daoist in inspiration and structure, yet we should not neglect the Buddhist element in the groups we have discussed. Many key actors in the canonization processes were committed Buddhists (Huang Chengshu 黃誠恕, one of Liu Qiao's closest associates, Peng Shaosheng, and Shao Zhilin), and the groups also socialized in Buddhist settings.

The Buddhist clergy rarely approved of the practice of spirit-writing, and some monks actively discouraged believers from engaging in it. Yet, there were exceptions, such as the mid-seventeenth-century Fujianese monk Yinyuan Longqi 隱元隆琦 (1592–1673), who settled in Japan, where he founded the Ōbaku school of Zen, and who actively engaged in spirit-writing exchanges with immortals.[55] Mingxin (Jiang Yupu's master) is another notable exception. And, notwithstanding clerical misgivings, numerous lay Buddhists like Peng Shaosheng enthusiastically combined monastic-led Buddhism with communications with gods who taught their own doctrine (occasionally eschatological). Clerics and lay Buddhists generally approved of the contents of spirit-written morality books but drew the line at spirit-written texts addressing core doctrinal issues (such as producing sutras or even commentaries on existing sutras).[56] And yet, some spirit-written commentaries on the

55. Russell, "Chen Tuan at Mount Huangbo."

56. A notable example is Zhou Mengyan 周夢顏 (1656–1739), a "lay" (*jushi*) Buddhist whose *Anshi quanshu* 安士全書 (Canon of [layman] Anshi), a bestseller in modern times, includes commentaries on Wenchang's *Yinzhiwen*.

sutras even made it into a Qing Buddhist canon.[57] On the other hand, the *quanshu* canons do not contain that much Buddhist material. A text on Buddhist doctrine was revealed at the Hansangong, the *Chanzong zhizheng* 禪宗正指 (Correct meaning of the Chan lineage), but it was considered controversial by some and removed from most subsequent Patriarch Lü canons.[58] Indeed, no major specifically Buddhist god emerged in the world of spirit-writing groups before the Guanyin revelations (mostly in sectarian contexts) from the mid-nineteenth century and the spectacular rise of the Jigong spirit-writing cult from the 1880s onwards.[59]

Intellectual inclusiveness can explain why so many elites joined spirit-writing groups and supported their publication projects. But we also need to explain why during the eighteenth century they increasingly relied on three gods (Wenchang, Patriarch Lü, Guandi) to embody their religious values and canonized them textually and theologically. One possible answer is that these gods came to stand as the best bulwarks of an open Three Teachings orthodoxy in response to the stiffening of state orthodoxy during the Qianlong reign. Indeed, state-sponsored projects to establish textual and intellectual orthodoxy also figured as part of the context for the accelerated process of scripture production and their *quanshu* canonization in the last decades of the eighteenth century. These projects included, first, the Buddhist canon (the Longzang 龍藏, 1734–38) and then the gigantic imperial canon, the *Siku quanshu* project that lasted from 1773 to 1782—and which also had its inquisitorial aspects.[60] Daoism and Buddhism appeared in the *Siku quanshu* imperial canon, but in a very marginal way. The impression one gets from the *Siku quanshu* is that official culture had lost most of its earlier variety and spiritual richness. Yet, some of those who worked on

57. Fan Chun-wu, "Jinxiandai Zhongguo fojiao yu fuji"; Wang Chien-ch'uan, "Jindai Zhongguo de fuji"; Fan Chun-wu, ed., *Fuluan wenhua yu minzhong zongjiao.*

58. Lai Chi Tim, "Qingdai sizhong *Lüzu quanshu*," 194.

59. Wang Chien-ch'uan, "Qingmo Minchu Zhongguo de Jigong xinyang yu fuji tuanti."

60. Guy, *Emperor's Four Treasuries.*

the *Siku quanshu* project (Zhu Gui, for instance) were simultaneously involved in canonizing Patriarch Lü and Wenchang scriptures.[61] There certainly was compartmentalization at work, with different canons (the official *Siku quanshu* and the private spirit-written canons) reflecting different realms of thought and practice. One does not (and should not expect to) find comments to the effect that the Patriarch Lü and Wenchang canons were complements to the "incomplete" *Siku quanshu*. It is nonetheless extremely tempting to consider that the incomplete coverage of the *Siku quanshu* and the attendant ossification of official culture was one motive that drove people like Zhu Gui and Jiang Yupu to compile their own canons, even though these canons built on textual productions that long predated the Qianlong period. Indeed, earlier spirit-writing productions, possibly as early as the Song, might be explained as responses to earlier stages in the ossification of official culture. Another element of the eighteenth-century context for the dissemination of *quanshu* canons (as well as the state canonizations projects) is the expansion of private libraries and publication activities by wealthy merchants and scholarly families. These families brought their resources (including books) and networks, as well as their devotion and money, to spirit-written canons.

Indeed, intense devotion to divine saviors, the hope for self-divinization, pessimism toward the collective fate of humanity, and a project of universal salvation through moral reform were very meaningful parts of the worldview of numerous Qing-period intellectuals. Such ideas and beliefs, which could not be expressed in official genres (essays and commentaries on the classics) canonized in the *Siku quanshu*, found an outlet in revealed scriptures. The latter themselves betray numerous signs of a conscious, collective, and sustained effort at synthesis with Confucian orthodoxy. A good way to understand how people could take part simultaneously in the two types of networks and canonization processes (the state-managed *Siku quanshu* project and the private

61. See also Esposito, *Creative Daoism*, 207.

Patriarch Lü and Wenchang *quanshu* canons) is to look at one example, that of Zhu Gui. Best known to historiography as a top-ranking official and the preceptor of the future emperor Jiaqing, Zhu was also a devoted adept of self-cultivation and spirit-writing cults to Wenchang and Patriarch Lü.[62]

Zhu's father, Zhu Wenbing 朱文炳 (1696–1764), was a local official whose own father had moved from Xiaoshan 蕭山 (near Hangzhou, Zhejiang) to the capital. He was the youngest of four brothers, all of whom had an official career, the two most prominent being himself and Zhu Yun 朱筠 (1729–81).[63] Zhu Yun was at the origin and apex of the *Siku quanshu* project and took an active part in the compilation process between 1772 and 1779, a project in which Zhu Gui also participated. Zhu Gui was something of a child prodigy; he obtained his *jinshi* degree in 1748, when only seventeen years of age, and started his career in the capital. Beginning in 1759, he had a series of postings in the provinces, in Fujian, Hubei, and Shanxi, before being called back to Beijing in 1775 to become, among other functions, the preceptor to Prince Yongyan 顒琰 (1760–1820), who had been secretly designated heir to the throne in 1773 and who was to become the Jiaqing emperor in 1796. The bond between teacher and pupil was apparently very strong: they shared intense epistolary exchanges, and after 1796, the emperor continuously bestowed marks of favor on Zhu Gui. In subsequent years, Zhu Gui again alternated between high-ranking postings in the provinces as a governor and in the capital as president of various boards. In 1799, after the death of the Qianlong emperor and the full assumption of power by Jiaqing, Zhu settled in the capital, where the emperor granted him a mansion just outside the Forbidden City. He died while holding high office in 1807, was buried in the Western Hills, and was granted exceptional posthumous honors (including the prestigious posthumous title of Wenzhenggong 文正公).

62. For standard accounts of his career, see *Qing shigao*, j. 127; and Hummel, ed., *Eminent Chinese*, 185–86.

63. On Zhu Yun and Zhu Wenbing, see Hummel, ed., *Eminent Chinese*, 198–99.

Not much is known of the Zhu family's religious practices; one of his brothers, Zhu Yuan 朱垣 (1723–73), devoted the latter part of his life to studying Buddhism. In a preface he wrote in 1798 for a reprint (by one of his nephews) of Hui Dong's 惠棟 (1697–1758) edition of the *Taishang ganyingpian* (1749, with commentary), Zhu also wrote that his father would recite the *Ganyingpian* every day and taught his sons with it.[64] Whereas many if not most Qing elites would have been familiar with this text, this story points to the Zhu family's more intense than average devotion. Zhu Gui himself wrote a number of prefaces and presumably supported the publication of a number of morality books.[65]

As for Zhu Gui, most of his known religious activities date from the latter part of his life in the capital, between 1799 and 1807. His devotion to Wenchang seems especially evident. As early as 1767, he published an abridged version of the Wenchang canon, the *Wendi shuchao*. Although certainly not atypical among his milieu, his devotion had an exceptional result: Wenchang's entry into the state pantheon in 1801 (see below).

During this period, Zhu Gui not only played an instrumental role in supporting an imperial cult to Wenchang but was also involved in spirit-writing cults among circles of Beijing-based literati. He participated actively in the spirit-writing altar (primarily devoted to Patriarch Lü, but also where Wenchang was worshiped) organized by Jiang Yupu, who was his colleague in the *Siku quanshu* compilation office. Later anecdotes mention Zhu along with Jiang Yupu as one of the disciples of Mingxin. He wrote in 1803 a postface to the *Quanshu zhengzong* (Jiang's own edition of the Patriarch Lü's complete book), where he discussed spirit-writing as well as *neidan* self-cultivation and signed as a disciple (*dizi*).[66] In another postface to this work, Dai Junyuan 戴均元 (1746–1840), another member of Jiang's group, explains that Zhu Gui's practice of self-cultivation and involvement in the spirit-writing cult to Patriarch Lü

64. Preface in Hui Dong, *Taishang ganyingpian zhu*.

65. See his 1798 preface to the *Quanren juhuo*; also discussed in Sakai Tadao, *Zōho Chūgoku zensho*, 194–95.

66. Zhu Gui, "*Quanshu zhengzong* houxu 全書正宗後序," in *Quanshu zhengzong*.

predated his late Beijing years, as both already practiced together in Guangzhou when they were posted there in 1797.[67] The following year, in 1798, when posted in Zhejiang, he met with Min Yide, another leading Patriarch Lü devotee and spirit-writing shrine leader, and patronized the Jin'gaishan shrine.[68]

As a result of this long-term involvement, Jiang Yupu included in the *Daozang jiyao* five texts edited by Zhu Gui (probably taken from Zhu's *Wendi shuchao*), all connected to Wenchang: *Dongjing shidu*; *Wendi xiaojing*; *Yuanhuang dadao zhenjun jiujie baojing* 元皇大道真君救劫寶經 (a new title for the *Jiujie baozhang*); *Wenchang yansijing* 文昌延嗣經 (Scripture on obtaining children by Wenchang); and *Yinzhiwen zhu* 陰騭文注 (Commentary on the *Yinzhiwen*). Only the last text is really authored, rather than merely edited, by Zhu, who wrote glosses to the famous morality book and selected citations to comment it. Interestingly, Zhu thereby endorsed not only the scriptures associated with Wenchang that extolled "mainstream" morality, such as the *Yinzhiwen*, but also revealed scriptures that carried a more pronounced eschatological discourse, such as the *Jiujie baozhang*.

In short, then, Zhu appears as one among a large number of eighteenth- and nineteenth-century Chinese elites who combined a successful career and perfectly orthodox writings in their official capacity with a more diverse religious life in the private sphere and the semiprivate spaces of spirit-writing groups, including cults to gods such as Patriarch Lü, Wenchang, and Guandi, self-cultivation in the Daoist inner-alchemical tradition, and the editing of morality books.[69] These individuals certainly saw no basic contradiction between these different aspects of their lives, yet their personal religious life is often invisible in the historical records, except for glimpses in the published spirit-writing revelations

67. Dai Junyuan, "Quanshu zhengzong houxu," in *Quanshu zhengzong*.

68. Esposito, "La Porte du Dragon," 249 n.210; Zhu Gui biography in *Jin'gai xindeng*, 7.10a–b.

69. See also the case of the Wanyan 完顏 family in Liu Xun, "Immortals and Patriarchs."

and morality books (genres which tend to be read only by scholars specializing in religion—thus compounding the problem of the invisibility of religious life in scholarship), or when exceptionally successful individuals, such as Zhu Gui, managed to translate their devotion into official policy, as attested by the Wenchang canonization of 1801. I can only hint here at this issue; hopefully future research based on a thorough analysis of the private writings of prominent officials and scholars like Zhu Gui will shed light on how exactly these men articulated the various aspects of their lives (private devotion, collective engagement with spirit-writing, public cultural life, and political career).

7.3. The Doctrinal Dynamics among Spirit-Writing Groups

Social dynamics can account for people joining spirit-writing groups to promote their values and the gods who embodied these values. But once they joined, they also became part of the internal collective dynamics that led these groups to develop more complex soteriological doctrines. I argue that we can see these groups' doctrinal innovations at work by the kinds of texts they were producing; they tended to first produce shorter texts on morality and self-cultivation, and when they reached maturity, they eventually produced full-fledged scriptures and liturgies and, in the same movement, enshrined them in *quanshu* canons.

As already said, not all spirit-writing groups (past or present) engage in the production of scriptures; indeed, most do not, and some stop producing scriptures at some point. Several fieldwork-based studies of spirit-writing groups have shown that many (if not most) such groups are primarily devoted to providing divine responses to individual needs and are not interested in (or not equipped for) the production of normative texts.[70]

70. Katz, "Spirit-Writing Halls and the Development of Local Communities."

We have seen in chapter 6 that the *jitan* mostly produced four types of revelation: morality books and short instructions (*xunwen*) that provide a guide for action for living members as they enjoin readers to consider the consequences of all their actions; recorded sayings and self-cultivation instructions often in poetic form, which instruct adepts in the physiopsychological practices, notably inner alchemy, leading to transcendence; scriptures that develop a full-fledged doctrine of salvation integrating self-cultivation and the moral retribution of actions; and litanies, which stage the moral self-transformation of the *jitan* members and the salvational intervention of their gods. *Quanshu* canons all comprise—and perhaps they *must* comprise—all these types of texts, and in this order: scriptures, morality and/or self-cultivation books, and litanies. The fact that scriptures were placed first shows how crucial their production was to the *jitan*.

As I focus here on spirit-written scriptures, my aim is not to grant more value and importance to the doctrinal contents rather than to moral, liturgical, and self-cultivational aspects of the productions of spirit-writing groups. Indeed, on the one hand, one should distinguish the use-value of revealed scriptures for the groups that produce them, and on the other, their interest for us as scholars who study these texts in view of the religious, cultural, and intellectual history of China. In other words: some groups have produced scriptures that may appear to the historian as quite obscure and as representing playing with an esoteric lexicon rather than a coherent doctrinal exposition, yet these scriptures are to their adepts (including very literate ones) precious divine words that legitimize the group's existence and actions. Fieldwork observations suggest that members of spirit-writing groups are typically proud of having their own *jing*, even when they do not easily grasp its meaning, and even when other types of revealed texts are actually more important in shaping their practices. That said, there also are numerous *jing* that do develop an original doctrinal construction. A close reading of the content and structure of revealed scriptures shows that in some cases, spirit-writing groups use them to legitimate themselves by inserting an orthodox (according to one or several of the Three Teachings) discourse within a specific devotional framework. The case of one contemporary scripture, studied by Philip Clart, provides an analytical model that can be applied to earlier texts.[71] Clart skillfully shows how spirit-writing allows for the elaboration of a new doctrinal text through the recycling of preexisting elements in a new ritual and devotional framework.

Another major element motivating the production of revealed scriptures is the ritual use of such texts. A *jing* (by contrast with most other revealed texts) can be chanted during the meetings of the group that has received it (this is mentioned in sources and observed nowadays) and learned by rote by the most engaged adepts—in some cases, the scripture can be used in the liturgy of other groups, sometimes quite broadly and far afield, as in the case of the *Yuhuangjing* (spirit-written in Sichuan around 1220). The *jing* thereby becomes the symbol of the religious identity of the group independently of the originality of its doctrinal contents. In some cases, revealed texts that originally were circulated as instructions are repackaged as *jing* by adding a prologue and hymns, and in this new form they can be integrated in the liturgy.[72]

The whole point is thus to understand first the dynamic that leads some spirit-writing groups (but by no means all of them) to produce revealed scriptures on top of other types of texts and thus engage in doctrinal innovation, and second how this dynamic fueled processes of canonization. By using the term dynamic I would like to draw attention to the inner logic of the ideas and texts circulated by the spirit-writing groups that push them to develop in certain directions and produce specific types of texts (especially scriptures) independently of the social and political context. For instance, the development of an eschatological discourse in spirit-writing groups is not necessarily a response to actual disasters and social anxiety, even though such a discourse was

71. Clart, "Anchoring Guanyin."

72. See the example of the *Wudangshan Xuantian shangdi chuixunwen* for which we find early editions with the revealed text only, and modern editions where it is retitled "scripture" and formatted for ritual performance with introductory and closing hymns.

activated in times of disaster. Emulation among the numerous spirit-writing groups as well as intense circulation of texts and persons between them reinforced such dynamics.

Whereas there was (and is) a large range of types and developmental paths for spirit-writing groups, I think we can identify one particular path that was followed by many of the groups discussed above to produce doctrinal scriptures and *quanshu* canons. In such cases, the once small group of self-cultivation practitioners (interested in inner-alchemical manuals and morality books, and thus in **their own** salvation) moves, in accordance with an internal dynamic, toward a quest for **universal** salvation. This is certainly not an inevitable or irreversible path, but for some of the elites involved in the spirit-writing groups discussed above, it certainly provided an exalted sense of mission and meaning.

Adepts, while keeping their own self-divinization at heart, develop a desire for integrating their individual practices with a coherent doctrine, and thus they begin to employ a broader, more universal discourse. They then (to some degree) shift their priority from individual salvation to the salvation of humanity. In many (although by no means all) cases, this entails developing the rhetoric of moral decline, divine punishment, impending apocalypse, and the intervention of the divine savior. This dynamic is most certainly linked with the actual extension of the group's activities from self-cultivation of only the registered disciples to charity and ritual services provided to the whole local community (including nonmembers)—a process observed in many well-documented contemporary groups. It is also linked to the promotion of the revealing god from individual master to universal savior—these gods climb up the divine bureaucracy *because* of the merits produced by their having revealed scriptures for the salvation of humanity.

In conjunction with the production of scriptures, the production of litanies also played a very significant role in the development of a doctrinal system, as it places the god in the supreme position where he can erase the sins of its devotees and offer them salvation. It is noteworthy that, as pointed out in chapter 6, litanies appear rather late in the history of our gods (only after major scriptures already existed).

Arguably, a spirit-writing group requires a certain experience and stability, as well as a critical mass, before it can transform spirit-given instructions into a mature doctrinal system expressed in a scripture (*jing*), and even more so before it can engage in canonizing scriptures and other texts (its own as well as preexisting ones). Of course, spirit-writing groups printed and disseminated individual scriptures. But the production of a scripture also offered the opportunity to enshrine it in a canon as its central piece. This happened with the *Sanpinjing*, which was immediately included in the 1744 *Lüzu quanshu*; again with the *Chaojiejing* 超劫經, immediately included in the 1775 *Lüzu quanshu*; and with numerous texts revealed between 1798 and 1803, included in the *Daozang jiyao*.

Wenchang and Transcendent Lord Xu offer the earliest documented examples of a gradual process of building a doctrinal system, already mature by the late twelfth century. This likely worked as a template for later spirit-writing cults. The case of Patriarch Lü illustrates the gradual process of doctrinal construction during the late Ming and Qing. Revelations (not spirit-written) by Patriarch Lü are attested as early as the twelfth century, but the corpus was for several centuries made up of poetry and short essays, dealing essentially with technical instructions for the adepts of inner alchemy. The first major doctrinal texts seem to appear during the late Ming, and they become more numerous from the 1670s onward. The revelation of the *Sanpinjing* in 1740 triggered the compilation of the first *Lüzu quanshu*. Even though the *Sanpinjing* did not in the long term prove particularly successful, it nonetheless constitutes a turning point as it integrates, as many other later texts revealed by the patriarch will also do, a discourse on alchemical self-cultivation with the question of the collective fate of humanity, applying the alchemical vocabulary to the situation of universal moral decline, and presenting Patriarch Lü as the universal savior.

One can, in a similar vein, follow the process that led to the building of a corpus revealed by Guandi. His first revelations seem to be morality books entirely in line with preexisting *shanshu*, notably the *Guansheng dijun jueshi zhenjing*, which is similar in inspiration to the *Taishang ganyingpian* and the *Wenchang dijun yinzhiwen*. Then, at the turn of the nineteenth century, a longer and more complex scripture is produced (the *Taoyuan mingshengjing*), which delineates an original doctrinal system. Some scholars consider this system as more "Confucian"—alchemical self-cultivation is much less prominent than in the corpus revealed by Patriarch Lü and family-based morality more central even than in Wenchang's scriptures, even though the three corpuses are themselves internally varied. Eschatological texts appear from the 1840s onward and soon become prominent in the Guandi corpus: they feature prominently in the 1858 canon, the *Guandi quanshu*. I thus suggest that there is, in Guandi's case, a direct causal connection between the later (when compared to Wenchang and Patriarch Lü) formation of scriptures and the later *quanshu* canonization.

Among the thousands of *jitan* spirit-writing groups that were active throughout the Chinese world from the twelfth century onward, and particularly under the Qing, a dynamic of doctrinal production was at work and inscribed in the very logic of the development of these groups. When expanding their activities, they produced a theory of salvation and moral reform, buttressed by doctrinal scriptures that extol the cosmological role of their divine savior. When such scriptures and accompanying litanies came to elaborate on and (attempted to) supersede earlier ones, the structure of a *quanshu* canon was in place. One of the aspects of doctrinal innovation that clerical authorities found most objectionable was the eschatological element, linked to the salvational dimension of the revealing gods.

Some scholars have described the new revelations of the seventeenth and eighteenth centuries and the resulting canons, especially Wenchang and Guandi, as a Confucianization of spirit-writing groups and cults. It is true that a Confucian identity was explicitly claimed, and the ritual dimension downplayed in favor of morality books in many of these texts and collections, but I do not think the notion of Confucianization, implying a transformation into something different, is helpful. As Hu Jiechen notes, it is more a question of broadening the scope of the revealed discourses and practices to accommodate even more of the gentry class, without ever discarding the Daoist liturgy and theology that remains foundational in the practice and texts of the *jitan*.[73]

7.4. The Political Dimension: State Canonization of the Spirit-Writing Gods

As is by now obvious, the progressive canonization of corpora of revelation is intimately linked to the promotion of cults that gradually rose, between the twelfth century and the late Qing, from relatively obscure local gods to universal and official cults with state-supported networks of temples throughout the empire: Wenchang, Guandi, Patriarch Lü, and, to a lesser extent, Zhenwu and Transcendent Lord Xu. Spirit-written scriptures contributed to their promotion in official, Daoist, and popular pantheons, while singling them out as saviors (in the eschatological sense) who maintain an intense individual relationship with each of their devotees and provide templates for a good life to their elite disciples.

By the 1800s, the scriptures of Patriarch Lü, Wenchang, and (to a lesser extent) Guandi had been *quanshu* canonized. At this time another crucial aspect of the larger process I call canonization occurred: the granting of official titles. The *quanshu* canons of each of the three gods presented them as not only orthodox but also as chief enforcers of the cosmic moral order. Yet their status in the Qing official religion was less than rock-solid. Guandi was firmly supported by the state, but Patriarch Lü, and even more so Wenchang, were objects of debates among officials

73. Hu Jiechen, "Qingdai liuzhong Wendi lei quanshu." One may also think of it in terms of the connection of what John Lagerwey calls the double orthodoxy of the early Ming state (Neoconfucianism and thunder-rites Daoism); Lagerwey, "Ming Dynasty Double Orthodoxy."

and between devotees and opponents. Things changed dramatically during the Jiaqing reign with the granting of titles to all major spirit-writing gods: Wenchang in 1801, Transcendent Lord Xu in 1803, Patriarch Lü in 1804, and a further canonization for Guandi in 1814 (Wenchang and Patriarch Lü were being honored with an Imperial Lord *dijun* Daoist title, which Guandi had already obtained in the early seventeenth century).[74] I shall not discuss Transcendent Lord Xu here, as I am not aware of new spirit-written revelations from him that entered his canon, but it remains significant that this earlier canon continued to be reprinted in modern times and was included in the *Daozang jiyao*.[75]

This string of canonizations of spirit-writing gods by the Qing state between 1801 and 1814 seems highly singular and cannot be a coincidence. The Qing state regularly worked with the Daoist establishment to canonize local gods: the Jiaqing canonizations are atypical, however, because of their number and high profile, especially considering the fact that spirit-writing remained illegal. Even though spirit-writing gods were given pride of place in the state pantheon in the early nineteenth century, the Qing government never legalized the practice of spirit-writing—an apparent ambiguity typical of the dynasty's religious policy. We cannot help notice that Jiang Yupu had to resign from office in 1815 (i.e., after Zhu Gui's death) for his association with Mingxin, who was condemned and banished for his involvement with high officials.[76] Causal relationships between the canonization of texts and the inclusion in the sacrificial canon (*sidian*) are in most cases impossible to prove with clear evidence. In order to establish a connection, we need to focus on individual cases and extrapolate their wider meaning.

74. *Da Qing huidian shili*, 438:978, 981, 983; 445:35. Xu Xun's title was Linggan puji zhi shen 靈感普濟之神 (the state did not endorse his Daoist title of *zhenjun*); it came after a memorial from the Jiangxi provincial government following Xu's help in averting a drought.

75. *Jingming zongjiao lu*. This canon opens with four scriptures, all revealed during the Song and already included in the *Daozang*.

76. Esposito, "Invention of a Quanzhen Canon," 56.

7.4.1. WENCHANG

The 1801 canonization of Wenchang appears as an achievement of one of the most prestigious officials of the time, and also of an ardent Wenchang devotee, Zhu Gui. More archival work needs to be done before we can fully understand how this canonization came about, but in any case, in 1801 an imperial edict decreed that Wenchang (titled Wenchang dijun), was the equal of Guandi and that he should be honored and receive state sacrifices (modeled on those offered to Guandi) in a temple in Beijing and in all administrative seats throughout the empire.[77] Wenchang would further be elevated to the rank of secondary sacrifice, *zhongsi* 中祀, in 1856.

The imperial edict makes no mention of Zhu's role in this canonization of Wenchang, but it was apparently widely understood by contemporaries that he was the one who persuaded the Jiaqing emperor to make this move. According to a later chronicler (who had scathing comments for Zhu Gui's "excessive" dabbling in Daoism), Zhu Gui had presented a copy of the *Zitong dijun huashu* to the emperor, which persuaded him to grant this canonization.[78] Zhu Gui wrote the stele inscription that commemorated the rebuilding of the Wenchang temple, Wenchang dijun miao 文昌帝君廟, in Beijing, just outside Di'anmen 地安門, immediately after the canonization in spring 1801; he credits himself with drawing the emperor's attention to the Di'anmen temple after Wenchang had performed a miracle in favor of the imperial armies in the course of the 1796–1804 war against the so-called White Lotus insurgents in 1800. He also expounds his own understanding of Wenchang that reconciles the classical definition of Wenchang as a stellar god with the Song-period revelations of Wenchang's own human history.[79]

77. *Da Qing huidian shili*, 438:981, 983; Wang Chien-ch'uan, "Qingdai huangdi dui Wenchang dijun de fengci," 463–67.

78. "Zhang Ezi wei Wenchang dijun 張惡子為文昌帝君," *Langqian jiwen*, Sibi, j. 8.

79. *Chijian Wenchang dijun miao bei* 敕建文昌帝君廟碑, in *Zhizuzhai wenji*, 2:23–24.

7.4.2. Patriarch Lü

The 1804 imperial canonization of Patriarch Lü with the lofty title of Xieyuan zanyun chunyang yanzheng jinghua fuyou dijun 爕元贊運純陽演正警化孚佑帝君 (Imperial lord of dependable succor, who harmonized origins, promotes destinies, is of pure yang, teaches what is correct, and warns people about transformations) was the first such canonization of him since 1310, and it was all the more remarkable since the title was not only awarded with reference to a single temple where worship was mandated, as was usually the case with imperial canonizations. Instead, the imperial mandate required that one temple in each county throughout the empire be renovated and receive official sacrifices.[80] This canonization was granted on the request of Jiang Sheng 姜晟 (1730–1810), a Suzhou native and long-time minister, who memorialized Patriarch Lü's many miracles linked to water conservancy and flood control, for which Jiang had official responsibility.[81] I am not aware of any connection between Jiang and the Patriarch Lü spirit-writing cult, but Wu Jing 吳璥 (?–1822), a noted member of the Jueyuantan, was in charge of the water conservancy work that led to Patriarch Lü's canonization, and afterwards he immediately wrote a stele inscription for a Patriarch Lü temple, stating that he had contributed to asking for the immortal's canonization.[82] Thus, as in the case of Wenchang, Patriarch Lü's entry in the register of sacrifices was a direct effect of the elite spirit-writing devotees.

80. *Da Qing huidian shili*, 445:35, does not actually prescribe official sacrifices in these Patriarch Lü temples in all counties, but this is made clear in other sources (notably local gazetteers) that also add that these sacrifices were to be vegetarian. See also Wang Chien-ch'uan, "Qingdai de Lüzu xinyang yu fuji," 31–35, who quotes the memorials requesting the canonization. Wang also discusses alternative unofficial canonization titles that also circulated at the same time.

81. *Chongxiu Fujiguan Lü zushi dadian ji* 重修福濟觀呂祖師大殿記, in Wu Yakui, comp., *Jiangnan daojiao beiji ziliaoji*, #93. This text, as well as several local gazetteers, lists Jiaqing 10 (1805) instead of 1804, as the date of the canonization. See also Yin Zhihua, "Qingchao Jiaqing nianjian chifeng Lüzu jiqi yingxiang."

82. *Zhejiang Pinghuxian xinjian Fuyou dijun dongnan diyiguan beiji* 浙江平湖縣新建孚佑帝君東南第一觀碑記, in *Quanshu zhengzong*, j. *shou*.

As in Wenchang's case, the 1804 canonization did not spread the cult, which was already firmly entrenched, but it certainly contributed to making it even more acceptable as a locus for elite activism and organization. Local officials had to select one Patriarch Lü temple in each jurisdiction for official sacrifices, in cooperation with Daoists and local elites, a choice that may or may not have corresponded to the most active local Patriarch Lü temples.[83] The effect on spirit-writing activities may have been complex and multifaceted: the canonization seems to have implicitly endorsed the practice, but it may also have brought more official scrutiny. We have also seen the case of a Lüzu spirit-writing group in Hankou, the Qiyunshe, which published their revelations in 1805 (*Xixin yulu*), opening with the canonization edict and going on to spirit-written prefaces where the immortals remind humans of the legal ban on spirit-writing, and close the altar as a result.

7.4.3. Guandi

The 1814 canonization of Guandi was less remarkable than the imperial recognition accorded to Wenchang and Patriarch Lü, because Guandi had already been promoted by the Qing state, first as early as 1652 as Zhongyi shenwu Guansheng dadi 忠義神武關聖大帝 (Great emperor Saint Guan, loyal and just, of divine martial [virtue]), and with the addition of further words to his title in 1768. In 1814 the words *renyong* 仁勇 (humane and brave) were added, and further additions would occur in 1828, 1852, 1853, 1857, 1858, 1870, and 1879.

7.4.4. Larger Significance

How can we interpret these canonizations? A major element was that devout officials very active in spirit-writing (Zhu Gui is but the most prominent example) had reached the apex of the state and found in Jiaqing an emperor more open to their views than Qianlong had been.

83. One detailed description of how a Patriarch Lü temple in the Hangzhou area was enlarged just after the canonization can be found in (*Jiaqing*) *Yuhang xianzhi*, 6.4a–b.

But there was certainly more to this than just court politics. The canonizations came in the wake of the 1796–1804 White Lotus Rebellion in the uplands of Sichuan-Hubei-Shanxi, which was the first large-scale rebellion that the Qing had faced since the Three Feudatories Rebellion (1673–81). Major wars in late imperial China often concluded with renewed alliances with the gods that had sided with the regime—this would again be the case during and after the Taiping War, when the dynasty canonized large numbers of gods, including Guandi (1853; 1855), Wenchang (1856), and Patriarch Lü (1857; 1865). The 1814 Guandi canonization is also linked to the 1813 Eight Trigrams Uprising (a sectarian attempt to enter the Forbidden City), when he appeared on the walls of the Forbidden City to defend it. Faced with rebellion, the imperial state strengthened its alliance with elite, loyalist gods—even though these deities were at this time also revealing fiery eschatological teachings.

A second element is that these gods were promoted almost simultaneously and were thus seen as a group by the state as well as by their elite promoters. The early nineteenth century saw the emergence and development of the idea that the Jade Emperor had entrusted Wenchang, Patriarch Lü, and Guandi with a last-ditch mission to save humanity and that the three spirit-writing gods were thus working as a group. When did they become a trio? By the twentieth century, these three deities were known in Taiwan as the San enzhugong 三恩主公 (Three Lords of Benevolence; there are other lists for this divine trio). In nineteenth-century revelations, they are described as the three ministers, *sanxiang* 三相, sent by the Jade Emperor to attempt to save as many humans as possible before the impending apocalypse. I have not found any reference to this notion in eighteenth-century texts, and it is likely that it developed with the rise of the Guandi spirit-writing cult in the first decades of the nineteenth-century. But by the eighteenth century we already see Wenchang and Patriarch Lü working as a pair. This period also saw the emergence of joint shrines for Wenchang and Guandi (the Wenwu temples 文武廟) and Two Emperors shrines (Erdimiao 二帝廟; often Wenchang and Patriarch Lü).

7.5. Conclusion

This brief survey shows that understanding the production and compilation of spirit-written texts during the Qing requires us to look at various *quanshu* canons as part of a single general process. The cults of Patriarch Lü, Wenchang, and Guandi, to consider the three most prominent examples, must be analyzed together. The very same people were instrumental in compiling their various canons, and they built shrines for one or several of these spirit-writing saviors. These people were elites who found a place to express their religious and moral values in spirit-writing altars devoted to these divine saviors, and where they could play an active role in saving society from moral decline. This fueled the production of ever more complex scriptures, and eventually of *quanshu* canons.

As a result of this canonization process, the religious landscape around spirit-writing changed to a very remarkable extent between around 1700, when Wenchang, Patriarch Lü, and Guandi were among a large pool of gods revealing moral tracts and self-cultivation instructions to spirit-writing groups, and only one (Guandi) was recognized by the state, and the eve of the Taiping War in 1850, when these gods, often considered to form a heavenly triumvirate, were honored by the state, had their textual canons widely circulating, and were recognized as chief enforcers of morality and embodiment of elite values in a world facing apocalyptic times. One of the effects of this process was that printed new revelations that circulated in the nineteenth century were dominated by spirit-writing. Other modes of revelation (such as dreams and incarnations) continued to be actively practiced, but spirit-writing attracted most of the social and financial resources.

Spirit-writing practices and scriptures continued to evolve during the second half of the nineteenth century into a new stage, as we will see in the next chapter: social, intellectual, and political dynamics changed (with the end of state canonization around 1904). By this time, new *quanshu* canons almost ceased to be compiled. Still, all of the new developments after 1850 were built on the foundations laid out during the early and mid-Qing "canonization stage," notably the idea that a few major deities, aligned with elite values, were in charge of saving humanity from impending apocalypse, based on a reformulation of traditional moral norms enshrined in massive scriptural productions.

CHAPTER EIGHT

The Taiping War and the Sectarian Turn

Seen in the longue durée, the historical development of spirit-writing went through four major turning points: the first was its emergence and codification during the Song; the second, its simplification in the late Ming. A third major turning point, the topic of this chapter, was its nineteenth-century adoption first by Xiantiandao 先天道 and then by other "sectarian" traditions.[1] The last one was its relative marginalization since the mid-twentieth century.

Xiantiandao emerged in the eighteenth century from the background of earlier sectarian groups. In the twentieth century it would in turn become the matrix of the redemptive societies (such as Tongshanshe 同善社, Daoyuan 道院, and Yiguandao 一貫道), the most important religious groups of the Republican period—most redemptive societies intensely practiced spirit-writing.[2] Xiantiandao teachings combine inner-alchemical self-cultivation with Eternal Mother 無生老母 devotion and soteriology. Early Xiantiandao and other sectarian

1. This chapter is in part based on Goossaert, "Competing Eschatological Scenarios." An earlier, much shorter version of this chapter was published in French as Goossaert, "Guerre, violence et eschatologie."

2. Ownby, "Redemptive Societies."

sources reveal no trace of spirit-writing.[3] Indeed, one of the facts that elite spirit-writing groups criticized about sectarian traditions is that the latter did not respect and practice spirit-writing.[4]

This situation of a clear distinction between the modes of revelation of elite state-supported groups (spirit-writing) and sectarian ones (living patriarchs as incarnations of Maitreya) dramatically changed during the mid-nineteenth century wars as a result of transformations in both types of groups. For this reason, the present chapter will not only focus on the sectarians but also explore all wartime revelations, beginning with the elite type, and look at their hybridizations. Anti-Taiping groups engaged in spirit-writing with abandon, all the way from Zeng Guofan 曾國藩 (1811–72) to villagers, and a huge number of revelations were published during the war. Groups such as Xiantiandao, who were on the same side of the battle as the loyalist armies, joined the movement. As a result, sectarian groups interacted, or sometimes merged with, elite spirit-writing groups. This new common ground ushered in long-running consequences. On the doctrinal level, elite and sectarian soteriology and morality cross-fertilized. Texts revealed during the 1860s and later show the proliferation of hybrid eschatological scenarios, combining the elite, bureaucratic type with the sectarian, messianic type.

On the social level, merging with elite spirit-writing groups opened a way for sectarian groups to exist more openly. By the Republican period, this merging had coalesced into redemptive societies that had a largely elite and self-declared Confucian following and, at the same time, had developed the Three Ages, *sanqi* 三期, type of apocalyptic teachings; it also, even more largely, resulted in the wide acceptance of such teachings in all sorts of elite groups.

3. Wang Chien-ch'uan, "Spirit Writing Groups in Modern China," 658–59.

4. See two tracts in the 1858 Guandi canon (but possibly earlier) where Guandi attacks the "sects" (*jiaofei* 教匪 and *xiejiao* 邪教) explicitly described as vegetarian (with several mentions of the 1796–1804 White Lotus Rebellion), which he believed deluded people and rejected spirit-writing; "Chu yiduan wen" 黜異端文 and "Bianduan wuji wen" 辨端誣乩文, *Guandi quanshu*, 22:402–5 and 23:546–50.

8.1. Eschatological Revelations in the Context of the Taiping War

To understand the convergence of *jitan* and sectarian groups, we must first look at the former's activities during the wars and their production of eschatological revelations. The eschatological inspiration of spirit-written revelation was in evidence ever since the Song-period scriptures revealed by Wenchang, Zhenwu, and other gods; a massive number of scriptures developing this spirit-writing eschatological scenario were produced from the thirteenth century onward, with a marked acceleration starting in the late seventeenth century that has not abated since. In these scriptures, anxiety about terminal decline is expressed in various metaphors, one of the most common being black vapors, *heiqi* 黑氣, produced by human sins that fill up Heaven and Earth. When these black vapors reach them, the higher gods may at any given moment unleash billions of demons on Earth to kill most humans, cleanse the universe, and start afresh.

The multiplication of apocalyptic spirit-written scriptures during the Qing period cannot be solely explained by the social, political, and environmental context. In some instances, a major disaster can be related to the production of certain eschatological scriptures: Yamada Masaru in particular has documented the rise of "eschatological morality books," *jiujie shanshu* 救劫善書, in response to actual disasters, beginning with a revelation by Wenchang explaining disastrous flooding in 1801 as a warning of the coming apocalypse, *dajie* 大劫.[5] However, this discourse developed during the eighteenth century at a time when disasters were local and hardly threatening to the Chinese world as a whole; any explanation based solely on the immediate context would be weak and unconvincing. I propose that it is the internal dynamics of the spirit-writing groups, competition between them (and their texts), and the unique capacity of an eschatological threat to mobilize adepts toward moral

5. Yamada Masaru, "Sekai no hametsu to sono kyūsai."

reform that best account for doctrinal innovation and rising concerns about the end of times. Nonetheless, the widely accepted eschatological discourse did provide a ready framework to understand disasters when they happened, culminating with the Taiping War (1851–64).

It is well known that the Taiping rebels were moved by a messianic vision of annihilating the Manchu demons in order to establish their Heavenly Kingdom, but historiography has so far underestimated the extent to which loyalist forces, and the vast majority of people who just wanted to save their own lives, also understood the events in eschatological terms. Many loyalist elites understood the apocalyptic events and the descent of Demon-kings (*mowang* 魔王, i.e., the Taiping generals) to Earth as a heavenly reaction to humanity's moral decadence. Trying to make sense of the chaos around them, they expressed their eschatological ideas in essays, diaries, poetry, and, most articulately, in divine spirit-writing revelations.

The Taiping War, which nobody saw coming, did seem like the end of the world, spreading utter chaos, famine, and massacres on an unprecedented scale across large parts of the empire.[6] It remains the bloodiest civil war in human history, with casualties estimated to number between 20 and 50 million people. Moreover, if the conflict between the Qing state and the Taiping Heavenly Kingdom dominated the scene during the period, many other bloody conflicts developed in various parts of the empire, each claiming staggering death tolls: the Nian 捻 organized banditry in northern China (1851–68), the Miao uprisings (1854–73) in Guizhou, the Red Turbans Rebellion in Guangdong (1854–56), the Panthay Rebellion in Yunnan (1856–73), and the Dungan Revolt in northwestern China (1862–77), among others. Very few parts of the empire remained untouched. I call this period the Taiping War period (in some places continuing beyond 1864), while keeping in mind that it is for our purposes defined by generalized warfare rather than the specific challenge posed by the Taiping regime.

6. For a general history of the Taiping War, see Platt, *Autumn in the Heavenly Kingdom*.

These traumatic events were perceived by many actors as an apocalypse, with gods widely considered to be playing an active role in the battles. Each conflict was specific, but the eschatological revelations and interpretations that they spurred were highly homogeneous: chaos is unleashed by the gods as a consequence of human sins, and the enemies are demons sent down to Earth to punish humans, but they will be called back and order will be restored if humans repent and reform themselves. As a consequence, in these discourses we find remarkably little information on the enemy and usually no explicit mention of their identity: Taiping and other rebels are treated alike as bandits, *zei* 賊 and *kou* 寇, and demons, *mo* 魔; their specificities were probably not ignored by the authors of the eschatological texts, but within such texts they were irrelevant. This may be explained by the fact that in elite eschatologies, demonology and ritual means of warding off demons play a much less important role than in medieval and "sectarian" texts. Demons act on the orders of the heavenly bureaucracy, so it does not matter much whether one knows their names or the formulas for repelling them; the key thing is to convince the bureaucrats above to call them back. This is clearly elite bureaucratic procedure-driven religiosity at work. Even so, ritual means are not entirely absent from elite spirit-written eschatological texts.

Rather than describing the demonic enemy, these texts talk about the war experience from the authors' own personal viewpoints, not about the larger confrontation between two camps: often the war is just the worst among a larger set of calamities marking the end of our world. On the other hand, the war experience is unmistakable in many such texts: descriptions of large-scale massacres and mountains of corpses, death by sword or firearm, the omnipresence of countless "bandits," and the evocation of the destruction of temples and icons (referring to Taiping iconoclasm).

Let us begin our exploration of these texts with one of the most famous revelations: the *Jiujiepian* 救劫篇 (Verses on saving humanity from the apocalypse; also called the *Jiujie baoxun* 救劫寶訓, Precious instructions), revealed by Guandi at Jingzhou 荊州 (southernmost Hubei) in 1855.[7] The place of the revelation is not incidental: Guandi died in Jingzhou in 220, and this was the place where his cult first flourished in medieval times.[8]

Translating the first lines of this short text (ca. 780 characters) provides a sense of the language used:

> Bandits come and go, without any pause
> And the human corpses and bones pile up like mountains.
> Yet, if you acted according to true morality
> The black registers (of the condemned) would be erased, and you would ascend the white jade tower.
> Alas! The great apocalypse has come.
> The nobles are all receiving punishment on your behalf
> And yet you remain tranquil and leisurely!
> The (Jade) Emperor's heart is benevolent and loving,
> How can he inflict murder and cataclysm on the people?
>
> 賊去賊來何日休，人間尸骨擁如邱，爾曹但自行真善，黑籍潛消白玉樓。嗚呼。大劫臨矣。五等皆為爾曹受罰，爾等猶優游自如耶。恭維帝心仁愛，何忍以大劫荼毒斯民?

Guandi then goes on to describe the mountains of corpses left by the war and explains that this is a result of the apocalypse ordered by the Jade Emperor after the failure of Guandi's attempts (through spirit-writing) to bring humanity back to virtue. After 200 years of peace and prosperity, says Guandi, Qing officials have fallen into utter corruption. He then compares these disasters with other wars in Chinese history, from the Yellow Turbans of the late Han to the Zhang Xianzhong 張獻忠 (1607–47) Rebellion in Sichuan, and he adds that these earlier disasters were minor when compared with the current situation. Heaven has sent Demon-kings down to Earth (the Taiping are not mentioned explicitly, but this obviously refers to the Taiping generals) to wage war, spread

7. *Guandi quanshu*, 24.662–65.
8. Ter Haar, *Guan Yu*, chap. 2.

terror, and destroy temples. In spite of all this, Guandi promises that those who repent and engage in good actions in earnest will be saved.

This short text proved remarkably successful; it was reprinted many times during the war in various parts of the Chinese world, and even more times afterwards.[9] In order to understand its appeal, I will first elucidate the role of Guandi in the war before taking a larger look at other spirit-written revelations.

8.1.1. Guandi and the Hunan Army

It was during the Taiping War that Guandi emerged as the dominant savior god of the elite tradition: indeed, the evidence is marked by an overwhelming number of eschatological texts featuring Guandi that were produced in the immediate war context. One of the most spectacular results of this process is the 1858 *Guandi quanshu*, a massive collection of forty *juan* almost entirely consisting of spirit-written revelations. There were several earlier canons of Guandi revelations, from the mid-eighteenth century onward; the 1858 one is several times larger than any that came before it. The main reason for this massive increase in the size of the Guandi canon is its incorporation of the many spirit-writing revelations produced in the 1850s.

The people behind the revelations and the compilation of the canon are not well documented: the *Guandi quanshu* merely states that its compiler, Huang Qishu 黃啟曙 (dates unknown), hailed from Xiangtan 湘潭 in central Hunan. However, evidence throughout the canon shows that it was the product of a group of central Hunan elites with a well-established Guandi cult.[10] Hunan was both a major battlefield during the first phase of the war and the cradle of the army that eventually defeated the Taiping; after 1853, large sections of the province were mobilized in the loyalist Hunan army (Xiangjun 湘軍; with its leaders being mostly

9. Besides the 1858 *Guandi quanshu*, 24.662–65, discussed below, other printings include *Jiujie zhenjing* in 1860; *Jiujie yuwen huike* in 1861; and *Wudi huibian*, 3.43a–45a, in 1876.

10. Ter Haar, "Divine Violence to Uphold Moral Values."

Xiangtan elites). The Hunan army was created by Xiangtan native Zeng Guofan. I have yet to find detailed evidence that the Hunan army had spirit-writing altars traveling with it, but it is extremely likely; the cult of Guandi was ever present, and the army was a prime mover behind the state canonizations of Guandi as a top-level official cult in 1853 and 1855. Zeng Guofan's personal involvement with spirit-writing is also well documented.[11] Being the result of a well-established Guandi spirit-writing cult in central Hunan, the canon's compilation was given increased significance due to the war, which several of its texts clearly allude to as an apocalyptic disaster sent by the gods.

Of particular interest in the 1858 canon is the section of short tracts (*xunwen*, j. 22–24, with 144 texts covering some 400 pages of the modern reprint), of which the 1855 *Jiujiepian* discussed above is but one. Most of those that carry a place name are from the central Hunan area. Many of these tracts are eschatological, and some clearly hint at the war context. In the most common scenario, the Jade Emperor or Lord of Heaven decides that humanity is too sinful to be redeemed and must be annihilated by demons bringing disasters (wars, floods, famines, epidemics, etc.), from which only a few virtuous people will be saved. Guandi then leads a group of gods to plead with the Jade Emperor and obtain a reprieve, while attempting to convert and save as many humans as possible though spirit-writing revelations. The *Jiujiepian* and many other Guandi tracts reflect a two-pronged effort on the part of these militarized loyalist elites: fight the rebels/demons on the ground and fight moral corruption within to convince the gods to tilt the balance in their favor. The core of the anti-Taiping forces was deeply eschatological.

8.1.2. Guandi Revelations during the Taiping War

The Guandi spirit-writing groups in Hunan that produced the 1858 canon while fighting the war were not an isolated and atypical case. Between 1851 and 1864, considerable numbers of elite loyalist activists

11. Wang Chien-ch'uan, "Qingmo de guanshen yu fuji."

produced scriptures and tracts through spirit-writing, presenting the war as an apocalyptic punishment of sinful humanity and promising salvation to those who would repent and embrace strict moral ways. Spirit-writing was intensively used during the war for all kinds of purposes, from providing immediate information and protection during battles to salvational and doctrinal formulations. These texts have not been systematically collected to date, and many (usually in later, late Qing or Republican, editions) keep appearing in collections of reprints; I am merely skimming the surface of a huge corpus. One must also keep in mind that large numbers of texts, including many morality books, were produced during the war period, and not all of them had explicit or prominent eschatological messages—which does not mean their authors ignored or refuted such messages. This chapter focuses on those texts that were stridently apocalyptic.

A simple typology of the wartime spirit-written texts I have read so far would distinguish between three types: first, texts that discuss specific war events and promise military protection; second, texts that detail programs of moral reform as the solution to the eschatological crisis; and third, texts that systematically describe the rationale for the eschatological events.

8.1.2.1. Divine Interventions in the War

The first type of divine revelations in the war context, and possibly the most common, were comments, predictions, and interpretations about the war events directly at hand. Educated people were frequently asking the gods about the immediate future and the outcome of the war. To give but one example, the diary of a Jiangnan literatus engulfed in the 1860 invasion of the Suzhou area by Taiping armies reports that texts circulating around him talked about demons, saying that "those who are in the list (of those who will perish) will not be able to escape" 在數難逃, and he immediately goes on to describe his questioning of Guandi through spirit-writing:

Imperial Lord Saint Guan manifested his presence on the altar and revealed this poem: Heaven is sending disasters to kill all inhumane beings, inhumane beings kill other inhumane beings. When will this killing of inhumane beings be complete? When the humane beings will have killed (all the) inhumane beings.

關聖帝君降乩，詩曰：天降災殃殺不仁，不仁人殺不仁人。不仁人殺何時了？自有仁人殺不仁。[12]

At the same time as they commented on battles just past or about to unfold, the gods often explained the events as part of a larger eschatological plan. I will give two examples of such texts. The first is a preface to a morality book devoted to female virtues, *Xinggui bian* 醒閨編 (Treatise to awaken [women] in the private apartments). The preface was revealed in 1861 by the Golden Mother of the Jasper Pond, Yaochi jinmu 瑤池金母 (more on her below) in Kaihua 開化府, Yunnan, a region that was at the time engulfed in the Panthay Rebellion.

The litanies of repentance to cancel the apocalypse have been revealed to you at this spirit-writing altar [. . .] You have been protected by August Heaven in person, and He has eliminated the apocalyptic disasters (planned for you). The barbarous savages have rebelled, but the whole southeastern half of Kaihua Prefecture has been preserved. Even though victories were won thanks to human fighting, it was actually possible entirely thanks to the gods' efforts. I have descended into a medium and exterminated Ma Lang; in a single day I have vanquished eleven rebel fortresses.

壇中所降消劫懺 [. . .] 乃蒙皇天眷顧，劫難潛消。狪夷之亂，而開邑之獲保東南一半者。雖借人力，實賴神功。降神童，勦馬狼，一日破連營十一寨。[13]

In this text, the goddess switches easily from describing battles and claiming merit for military success to explaining how all of this is part of

12. *Gengshen binan riji*, 200. Note the strong resemblance between this poem and one spirit-written in the context of the late Yuan wars and discussed in chapter 5.

13. Preface to *Xinggui bian*.

a larger moral scenario. A comparable example is found in a text revealed by Guandi in 1858 in Jiaying (present-day Meixian, northeast Guangdong, and the Hakka heartland). This time the immediate context is the the Red Turbans Rebellion linked to the Tiandihui 天地會 society, who are taking advantage of the general chaos and the mobilization of all imperial armies around the Taiping capital in Nanjing to besiege and capture the barely defended cities in the south.[14] The local gentry hold a spirit-writing séance at the prefectural Guandi temple, and the god reveals a tract that begins as follows:

> I enjoin you good people not to follow the orders of the rebels! The apocalypse is coming and the people must be pitied. When I was a human, I studied the *Annals of the Springs and Autumns*, and I understood its core meaning.[15] Therefore I have since supported the country and protected the saintly emperor. I cannot stand to see the brains and livers of the people being spilled on the ground.
>
> 戒良民勿從賊諭。大劫將降，下民可憐。吾生前讀春秋，明大義，故至今扶社稷護聖君。不忍蒼生之肝腦塗地。[16]

After having described the unfolding apocalyptic battle pitting himself, the imperial government, and the good people (the gentry he is addressing) against the rebels, Guandi describes the latter as demons, *yao* 妖, and promises that he will exterminate them with his armies of divine soldiers, *shenbing* 神兵.

The role of divine soldiers in the battles is omnipresent in the texts of this period.[17] Some loyalist leaders held an openly messianic discourse based on their command of otherworldly forces: Bao Lisheng 包立生

14. Kim Jaeyoon, "Heaven and Earth Society." The Tiandihui, now called "Triads," themselves had a highly developed eschatological and messianic discourse, see ter Haar, *Ritual and Mythology of the Chinese Triads*.

15. In their revelations, gods frequently remind readers of their own deeds when alive to buttress their claims to moral superiority.

16. Untitled text in *Jindai Guandi, Yuhuang jingjuan yu Xuanmen zhenzong wenxian*, 1.11–16.

17. On this question, see Meulenbeld, *Demonic Warfare*.

(?–1862), a peasant who had received divine encounter-type revelations and set up a militia in Zhuji (Zhejiang) that successfully held up against the Taiping armies for a year, claimed to be able to defeat Taiping demons with the help of divine soldiers.[18]

8.1.2.2. Programs of Moral Reform

Many loyalist elites understood the apocalyptic events and the descent of Demon-kings (the Taiping generals) to Earth as a heavenly reaction to humanity's moral decadence. When explaining precisely which sins had convinced the Jade Emperor to unleash the demons of apocalypse, these groups called upon classical themes from morality books. Radical moral reform, however, offered a way out of annihilation, both individually (the virtuous will be saved) and collectively (Heaven can still be persuaded to call off or postpone—*huijie* 回劫, *wanjie* 挽劫—the apocalypse). Last-minute redemption remains a possibility, on the condition of a radical change of mind (sometimes formalized by oaths). Texts developing such a program can be further divided into four subtypes: litanies of repentance, self-cultivation manuals, tracts on morality in general, and treatises on specific moral issues. Such a typology is necessarily imperfect, as many texts straddle the boundaries, but it provides a sense of the main trends within the revealed literature.

8.1.2.3. Litanies of Repentance

Litanies explicitly aimed at postponing or averting the apocalypse have existed since the eighteenth century and do not constitute a peculiarity of the Taiping War period. However, one can only attest to the numbers of newly revealed eschatological litanies during the 1850s. The 1858 Guandi canon contains five different litanies (j. 33–37), with the first (and presumably most recent and honored) being the *Jiujie jingchan* 救劫經懺 (Litany and scripture to avert the apocalypse).[19] After the psalmody of a few classical short Guandi scriptures, the litany invokes a

18. Cole, *People Versus the Taipings*, esp. 33–35.
19. *Guandi quanshu*, j. 33.

series of Daoist gods and lists all sorts of sins in twenty-three categories. It is introduced by a narrative that tells how humans have been engulfed in disasters caused by demons since the year *dingmao* (1807) and that, upon inspecting the world in the year *xinsi* (1821) and witnessing how it is filled with black vapors, the Jade Emperor decided to proceed with executions, *zhu* 誅, but allowed Guandi to reveal tracts through spirit-writing. The latter reported that he did so starting in the year *bingzi* (1816), but with little result, so he asks now to try a litany of repentance; he claims that all those who take part in the recitation and repent will not perish in the upcoming disasters.[20] The text is undated, and it is possible that it predates the war, but it is equally likely that it is a product of the war period.

8.1.2.4. Self-Cultivation Manuals

Different in sensibility from litanies, in which the force for averting the apocalypse is primarily the gods' power to open the way to redemption, self-cultivation manuals propose to change the individual based on sustained, continuous spiritual exercises; one can thereby first save oneself and then, through example and admonition, the whole of humanity. A remarkable example of such a revealed eschatological self-cultivation manual is the *Fengsheng huijie xianhualu* 奉聖回劫顯化錄 (Records of the revelations aimed at calling off the apocalypse and expounding the veneration of the Saint [Confucius]), prefaced in 1860. The editor, Xu Qian 徐謙 (1776–1864), was a scholar and academy teacher who practiced spirit-writing and published morality books throughout his life; as noted by Hu Jiechen, his writings became distinctly more eschatological during the Taiping War.[21]

Xu Qian's manual is devoted to the practice of *fengsheng*, venerating the Saint (Confucius), which combines moral self-cultivation, meditation, and an intense personal devotion to Confucius, whom one must visualize constantly. Xu Qian learned this self-cultivation technique

20. *Guandi quanshu*, 33.13b–15b.
21. Hu Jiechen, "Xu Qian xiaokao."

from his own master, Deng Fengguang 鄧逢光 (dates unknown), when he was young and had been propagating it for decades. Now, in the war context, he received a long series of spirit-written revelations from various Confucian saints (including Confucius's disciples), as well as Guanyin and Daoist deities, who developed the method and explained that it was the only hope to postpone the apocalypse: "If you want to save (yourselves/humanity) during this great apocalypse, besides worshiping the Ultimate Saint (Confucius), there is no other method" 若欲解救此大劫，非虔奉至聖，斷無別法.[22] Espousing the "black vapors" (*heiqi*) theory, it describes how unvirtuous humans create vapors that rise up and anger Heaven, who then declares the apocalypse (*haojie*).[23] Only proper spiritual practice can cleanse the universe of these vapors. In this scenario, Confucius is described in messianic terms as the transformation body of Heaven descended to Earth to save humanity, 夫子之身即上帝之化身也, and to preside over a paradise (Confucius Hall, Fuzi zhitang 夫子之堂), where the virtuous ones are welcomed.[24] He is described as sending many gods to teach humans to reform themselves.

Another example is the *Dijun jiujie baoyu* 帝君救劫寶諭 (Precious edict to save humans from the apocalypse, [revealed by] the Imperial Lord [Guan]), a slim booklet revealed and made public in Hebei in 1860. In it, Guandi explains the cause of the upcoming apocalypse and then details a program of reform in the shape of a ledger of merits and demerits in fourteen points. One of them is the daily psalmody of the most sacred morality book, the *Taishang ganyingpian*, and the text of the *Ganyingpian* is appended to the revelation.

The contents of the spiritual exercises proposed as part of venerating the Saint (*fengsheng*) or the practice of the ledgers are typical of late imperial elite religiosity, with its central role for moral self-cultivation. That the authors argued that a new age of moral reform could reverse the process of human decline, postpone the apocalypse, and return

22. *Fengsheng huijie xianhualu*, 2.65b.
23. *Fengsheng huijie xianhualu*, 1.7a–b.
24. *Fengsheng huijie xianhualu*, 1.4a.

humanity closer to the pristine conditions of antiquity presumably made the discourse broadly acceptable, even though the talk of hordes of demons unleashed onto the sinning masses still colored these scriptures in a way that was not entirely palatable to everyone.

8.1.2.5. Morality Tracts

Certainly the most common type of texts revealed during the war were the short tracts called "instructions" (*xunwen*) or "edicts," *yu* 諭, that outlined the eschatological scenario and listed the vices and sins that caused it. The people who received and disseminated morality tracts believed that humans were caught in apocalyptic disasters and murdered by demons because they lacked filial piety, loyalty to their lord, honesty in their trade, compassion toward the weak and the poor, sexual morality, and respect for life; additional sins highlighted in some tracts include gambling and consuming opium.[25] Some texts were especially targeted at officials and decried their role in the coming of the apocalypse, which was attributed to their corruption, cruelty, and lack of care for the destitute. The *Jiujiepian* revealed in 1855 by Guandi is a typical example of this genre, and the 1858 *Guandi quanshu* contains dozens of others.

Many of these texts circulated independently, as manuscripts or printed on single sheets of paper. They were also often anthologized in short volumes. One such anthology is the *Jiujie yuwen huike* 救劫諭文彙刻 (Anthology of [divine] edicts to save humanity from the apocalypse)—a collection of eight short texts revealed by various gods between 1855 and 1860 (mostly in the Hunan-Hubei region) and published in early 1861.

8.1.2.6. Saving Lives

Of all the moral themes listed above, respect for life acquired unique relevance. The idea that killing animals was one of the direct causes of the

25. "Ci yi chiyu wen 慈邑敕諭文," *Guandi quanshu*, 23.522–26. On sexual morality in late imperial spirit-writing texts, see Zhang Wanrong, "Qingdai jieyinshu bianzhuan kaolüe"; and Goossaert, "La sexualité dans les livres de morale chinois."

Taiping War seems to have been very widespread.[26] Numerous texts revealed by the gods, or written and compiled during the Taiping War, posit an explicit and direct link between the number of animal lives taken by humans and the advent of a savage war that was taking human lives on an unprecedented scale. For instance, it informs a large compilation of spirit-written revelations by one group in Sichuan that spans most of the war's duration—the *Jiushengchuan* 救生船 (A boat to save lives; the four *juan* have prefaces ranging from 1860 to 1863).[27] The title of this compilation primarily refers to saving the lives of people destined for an apocalyptic death, but it also includes discussions on saving animal lives, containing tracts on various taboos (concerning bovines and dogs in particular).[28] Guandi's revelations (as included in the *xunwen* tracts) also consistently argue against killing animals and strongly promote the beef and dog taboos.[29] They claim that when people eat beef or dog meat and poison the rivers, the killing *qi* rises up to Heaven and Shangdi becomes so angry that he wants to destroy humanity.[30]

In *Jiushengchuan*, death by war is explained as a direct consequence of killing animals. Patriarch Lü says, "If you want to understand the disasters of war and killing at the present, just listen to the sounds coming out of butchers' shops at night" 欲知世上刀兵劫，但聽屠門夜半聲.[31] This is actually a quotation from a poem by the Song-dynasty Buddhist monk Yuanyun 願雲 (dates unknown), but the verse took on a new meaning from this reuse in a war context.[32] In the divine law code discussed below and revealed in 1856–59, we also read:

26. This topic has been previously covered in Goossaert, "Animals and Eschatology in the Nineteenth-century Discourse."

27. On this text, see Wang Chien-ch'uan, "Spirit Writing Groups in Modern China," 661–63. There are markedly different editions of this text, and I am only using one particular edition here.

28. *Jiushengchuan*, 3.54b–55a.

29. *Guandi quanshu*, 23.514–18.

30. "Ci yi chiyu wen," *Guandi quanshu*, 23.522–26.

31. *Jiushengchuan*, 2.4b–5a.

32. *Lianxiu qixinlu*, 6 ("Jiesha shi" 戒殺詩); see also www.sutrapearls.org/hushen/hs04.htm#sthash.pXnDLzXe.dpuf (accessed on January 19, 2016).

In the world, when wars or famines occur, this is caused by the fact that humans are unable to refrain from killing (animals). The *qi* produced by such crimes naturally causes such disasters.

世之有兵荒劫運，以世人不能劫殺。戾惡之氣，成召而然。[33]

This idea was the driving theme of the *Haosheng jiujie bian* 好生救劫編 (An anthology of loving life and being saved from the apocalypse). Compiled in 1854 by the education commissioner for the province of Guizhou, Bao Yuanshen 鮑源深, the book is entirely devoted to respect for animal life.[34] The five-*juan* work is a compilation of quotes from earlier morality books, essays, and anecdotes. One text broaches the eschatological discourse: a tract spirit-written by Patriarch Lü in the eighteenth century that equated human warfare with killing animals.[35] In a later addition to the 1901 reprint of Bao's anthology, one text explains that previous bloody revolts and massacres in Chinese history, such as the fall of Chang'an and Luoyang during the Tang and Hangzhou during the Song, were all caused by the decadence of urbanites indulging in meat.[36] But the explicit connection to the Taiping War is made in Bao's own introduction, where he graphically describes the massacres that were taking place at the time he was writing, explaining them as punishments from the gods for killing animals. So here we have an official, steeped in the long-standing literati discourse of compassion for living beings and utmost moderation in eating meat, recasting this tradition in the light of the immediate context of savage war.

Bao was not alone in seeing the link between meat-eating, the war, and the end of the world. Xu Qian, discussed above, published a book on the topic in 1856, *Wuyou ruci* 物猶如此 (Animals are also like [us]). Another well-distributed text further documents how widespread the

33. *Yuding jinke jiyao*, 542.

34. I have seen three different versions of this work, and only one (the 1892 edition) gives the author's identity as Education Commissioner Bao.

35. *Haosheng jiujie bian*, 1.8a–9a.

36. *Jieshashuo* 戒殺說 in *Haosheng jiujie bian*, 6.9a.

idea was: the *Pangong mianzai baojuan* 潘公免災寶卷 (Precious volume on avoiding disasters, revealed by Mr. Pan), which was published in 1853 and met with instant success, with dozens of reprints in subsequent years and decades. This *baojuan* (here not revealed but written by a human) was most certainly written by Yu Zhi 余治 (1809–74), a Jiangnan scholar famous for his activist philanthropism. Yu's brother committed suicide when their city of Wuxi 無錫 was conquered by the Taiping in 1860, after which Yu Zhi lived as a refugee, collecting funds for the loyalist armies and militia, organizing anti-Taiping propaganda, and relentlessly preaching in public that people must repent and engage in moral reform so that the gods would be appeased and peace could return to China.[37]

The protagonist of *Pangong mianzai baojuan* is Pan Zengyi 潘曾沂 (a well-known lay Buddhist and philanthropist and the son of a high official and member of a powerful lineage who died shortly before the Taiping invaded Nanjing in 1853). He is described as a saint and a vegetarian beloved by the gods, who was promoted to general comptroller of the register of the living and the dead in the administration of the Eastern Peak immediately after his death.[38] Pan then appears in a dream to his relatives (the favorite Buddhist mode of revelation), telling them that the Jade Emperor, furious at humanity's moral decadence, had sent down an apocalyptic disaster in the form of the Taiping and planned the death of all Nanjing's inhabitants. But thanks to Pan's negotiations, 30 percent of them would be saved, on the condition that they swore a twelve-point oath of repentance. These twelve points included not killing baby girls (no. five), the familiar prohibition on killing animals (no. nine), and not eating beef or dog meat (no. twelve). Indeed, a substantial section of the *Pangong mianzai baojuan* narrative recounts how the gods helped those who swore to abstain from meat and stop killing animals to escape Nanjing as it fell to the Taiping army, whereas those

37. Meyer-Fong, *What Remains*, chap. 2; Alexander, "Virtues of the Vernacular," chap. 3.

38. On Pan Zengyi, see Shao Jiade, "Pan Zengyi de xinyang."

who did not were massacred by the rebels. Each of these twelve points was discussed in great detail in *Pangong mianzai baojuan*, but they were also disseminated separately as part of a different scripture—the *Xinchu xianchuan liyuan baojuan* 新出仙傳立願寶卷 (Precious volume on making a vow, newly revealed by the immortals)—which continued to circulate after the war and expanded this oath to contain fourteen points, including the same three discussed above.[39]

In all these texts, animal life is not considered separately from human life, but both are understood as part of a continuum of life ranging from the most exalted to the lowest forms. The question of female infanticide, also omnipresent in wartime eschatological discourse, is part and parcel of the question of respect for life and linked to care for animals.[40] This continuum is often apprehended through a quantification of the relative value of various forms of life.

8.1.2.7. The Divine Code

One of the most remarkable texts produced by spirit-writing during the war is the *Yuding jinke jiyao* 玉定金科輯要 (Compilation of the golden rules on order of the Jade Emperor), a huge divine law code that lists in excruciating detail the punishments for every imaginable sin (expressed in years taken off one's lifespan or, frequently, death in the form of specific disasters, themselves called *jie*; e.g., some sinners are slated to perish in war action, *bingjie* 兵劫), as well as rewards for do-gooders.[41] It is organized around the eight virtues (*bade*)—filial piety (*xiao*), brotherliness (*ti*), loyalty (*zhong*), trustworthiness (*xin*), propriety (*yi*), justice

39. Alexander, "Virtues of the Vernacular," 159, 179–80, argues that *Xinchu xianchuan liyuan baojuan* is also probably from Yu Zhi's hand.

40. Alexander, "Virtues of the Vernacular," 207–16; King, *Between Birth and Death*.

41. Along with several sequels revealed in subsequent decades, this code was adopted and widely diffused during the Republican period by a redemptive society, the Tongshanshe 同善社. On the *Jinke jiyao*, see Wang Chien-ch'uan, "Qingdai huangdi dui Wenchang dijun de fengci." There seems to be no extant copy of the original edition; all available copies date from 1922 and later. See Wang Chien-Ch'uan's comments in the introduction to *Ming Qing yilai shanshu congbian*.

(*li*), honesty (*lian*), and decency (*chi*)—comprising a framework for theorizing morality that had emerged during the first half of the nineteenth century and remained prevalent until the mid-twentieth century.[42]

The thousand-odd pages of this penal code were revealed in Liling 醴陵 (eastern Hunan) between 1856 and 1859 by Wenchang, who was given authorization to reveal it to humans from the Jade Emperor. An introduction explains that the Jade Emperor had decided to trigger an apocalypse as early as 1816, then proceeded to ask the gods to compile a precise code so as to decide rationally who should die, when, and how. This code was eventually promulgated in Heaven in 1848, but it took several supplications from Wenchang before the Jade Emperor allowed the information to be made available to humanity so that at least some people could repent and save themselves. Numerous texts from this period (including the *Pangong mianzai baojuan*) asserted that gods did not cause human deaths in the war randomly or arbitrarily, but in fact, they were strictly enforcing a celestial law code, *tianlü* 天律. The revelation of the *Yuding jinke jiyao* is the most developed expression of this idea. The very existence of this code, which binds gods as well as humans, provides a solution to the conundrum created by the idea that the war was a response to humanity's disrespect for life. It was a Chinese version of the theodicy problem: how can the gods, who are supposed to "love life," *haosheng* 好生, engage in such mass slaughter? In a preface to the aforementioned *Jiushengchuan*, revealed in 1863, Zhang Fei 張飛 explains that, as a god in the ministry of thunder, he loves life and loathes having to kill humans, but he is bound by the code to punish sinners and dutifully does so.[43]

42. Fan Chun-wu, "Bade."
43. *Jiushengchuan*, 3.1a–b ("Huanhou dadi xu" 桓侯大帝序).

8.2. The Non-Elite Revelations

Thus far we have been exploring wartime spirit-written revelations and cognate texts that express various versions of the elite scenario of the unfolding apocalypse. I call this the **threat scenario**: the supreme god (the Jade Emperor) **threatens** apocalypse, and savior gods, notably Guandi, (and their human followers) try to recall or mitigate it through preaching and moral reform. However, this was not the only eschatological discourse circulating at the time; indeed, a major characteristic of the Taiping War period is the extent to which different eschatological scenarios intersected and in some cases intermingled. We must now look at these other scenarios.

8.2.1. The Taiping Revelations

Another scenario, widely circulated at the time, of course, was the Taiping discourse. To what extent the loyalist elites were aware of the contents of the enemy propaganda and its religious significance probably varied considerably depending on the personal experiences of each.[44] But whether or not they were conscious of the fact, the Taiping eschatology, although reinforced and inflected by Christian eschatology, shared considerable ground with discourses found on the other side of the battle lines. It was fed by an intense flow of mediumistic revelations to Hong Xiuquan 洪秀全 (1812–64) and his inner circle, although not through spirit-writing. Hong and his generals were possessed by Jesus, the Holy Spirit, and other members of the holy family, and they made oral pronouncements that were later printed in booklets that widely circulated among the Taiping; some were used to produce the Taiping version of the Bible, also massively printed.

Barend ter Haar has analyzed this brand of eschatology, which is a variant of the entropy scenario discussed below, as the "demonological

44. On loyalist efforts to understand the Taiping, see Meyer-Fong, "To Know the Enemy."

messianic paradigm" and shown that it had a long history before the Taiping.[45] It can be summarized thus: The world is at regular intervals invaded by demons who come from the underworld to spread chaos and death; the ensuing war is thus not waged so much between humans as between humans and demons. The elect will be saved by a savior-king, a youthful messianic figure of light, who will raise an army of the faithful supported by spirits. They will find their way to a safe haven (a fortress or walled city; ter Haar shows that the Taiping capital of Nanjing was understood to be such a haven), where they will see the millennial kingdom of Great Peace (Taiping). The Taiping discourse followed this tradition when labeling the Qing emperor and the imperial officials and soldiers as demons.

8.2.2. Sectarian Eschatology

An entropy scenario, which builds on elements of medieval Daoist and Buddhist eschatology, was developed in the scriptures (often called *baojuan*) of many "sectarian" groups from the thirteenth century onward. The groups and their scriptures were outlawed by the imperial state but have remained active to the present day; one of their most important proponents today is the Yiguandao. In this scenario, the world will naturally come to an end, no matter what humans do. This moment can be predicted (calculated) in accordance with complex cosmological models, notably within the theory of the Three Ages (*sanqi*), the first two of which end with a smaller apocalypse, and the last, in which we now live, ends with a great apocalypse. In the meantime, loving deities (notably the Unborn Eternal Mother) try to bring back to them as many humans as possible; she regularly sends Buddhas, bodhisattvas, and gods (notably Maitreya) to incarnate and preach to humans (thus making incarnate revelations). In many traditions there is a set quota of souls to be saved. Once all these souls have reunited with her at the

45. Ter Haar, "China's Inner Demons." On Taiping eschatology, see also Wagner, *Reenacting the Heavenly Vision.*

Dragon-Flower Meeting (Longhuahui 龍華會), the world will be destroyed.

During the war, many sectarian groups in various parts of the empire were busy producing new scriptures that explained the events within their own soteriological scenario. One example from northern China is the 1858 *Wanbao baojuan* 萬寶寶卷 (Precious volume of the myriad treasures) that has been studied by Thomas Jansen.[46] Besides describing how the unfolding war was the final phase before the Dragon-Flower Meeting, in its scenario this *baojuan* also gave an eschatological role to the brutal irruption of Europeans in China; here, foreigners are signs of the end-times but are not demonic themselves—by contrast, in many eschatological scriptures of the early twentieth century, Westerners are the demons of the apocalypse.

8.2.3. The Xiantiandao Revelations

The Taiping and the sectarian revelations were produced and circulated in a space largely separate from that of the elite spirit-written texts. However, a momentous turn in Chinese modern religious history is that sectarian groups began to practice spirit-writing in the mid-nineteenth century and, as a result, to interact or sometimes merge with elite spirit-writing groups.[47] The practice was probably not unknown in the sectarian traditions before that period—given how common it was in society, this would have been surprising—but it was not used to produce scriptures or take important decisions. Indeed, as said above, one of the criticisms of sectarian traditions by elite spirit-writing groups is that they did not respect and practice spirit-writing.

Scholars of the sectarian traditions have noticed how quickly it happened that around the mid-nineteenth century, sectarian *baojuan* were replaced with spirit-written scriptures.[48] To be sure, the *baojuan* continued to be revered and performed, and a few new ones were

46. Jansen, "Sectarian Religions and Globalization in Nineteenth-Century China."
47. Wang Chien-ch'uan, "Spirit-Writing Groups in Modern China," 658–59.
48. Jordan and Overmyer, *Flying Phoenix*, chap. 3.

composed, but the mainstream textual production in these milieus shifted. When and why did sectarian traditions begin using spirit-writing as their main mode of textual production? The answer seems, at least in good part, to lie with one particular tradition that was soon imitated by many (but not all) others: the Xiantiandao 先天道. One of the most important sectarian traditions in southern China and first known to the state as Qinglianjiao 青蓮教, it emerged in the eighteenth century from the background of earlier sectarian groups (but did not produce *baojuan*). It would in turn become in the twentieth century the matrix of the redemptive societies, the most important religious groups of the Republican period.[49] Xiantiandao teachings combine inner-alchemical self-cultivation with Eternal Mother devotion and soteriology.

Takeuchi Fusaji has dated the earliest instance of spirit-writing in a Xiantiandao context to the 1820s.[50] It becomes well documented in 1843, when the leaders of various branches met in Hanyang (Hubei) to coordinate and ask the deceased twelfth patriarch Yuan Zhiqian 袁志謙 (1761–1834) to give them spirit-written instructions. We have (in later editions) a manual of rules and procedures that seems to be a result of this effort titled *Yuncheng baolu* 雲城寶錄 (Precious records of Cloud Fortress).[51] State documents produced during a repression in 1845, when several of the leaders were arrested and executed, confirm the new importance of spirit-writing. Apparently, in the context of a succession crisis, the movement shifted from the charismatic authority of a patriarch (seen as an incarnated Buddha) to collective management through spirit-writing, a model that is extremely common in all kinds of groups, sectarian or not, in modern and contemporary times.

49. Wang Chien-ch'uan, "Qinglianjiao daomai yuanliu xinlun"; Takeuchi Fusaji, "Shindai Seirenkyō kyūsai shisō."

50. Public lecture at EPHE, May 2018. Mozina, "Living Redactions," traces the fascinating history of an early Qing inner alchemy manual that was both used as Xiantiandao instructional manual and taken up by spirit-writing groups (that added revealed prefaces and reprinted it), but does not document Xiantiandao direct involvement in spirit-writing.

51. Wei Dingming, *Shumin de yongheng*, 55, 90–91.

Within Xiantiandao circles, spirit-writing was used not only for making decisions and enacting rules but also for producing eschatological scriptures. Textual evidence becomes abundant during the Taiping War, with the production of Xiantiandao texts, such as the *Yuncheng baolu*, *Zhilu baofa* 指路寶筏 (Precious raft to show the way), and the *Yulu jinpan* 玉露金盤 (Golden plate to collect jade dew).[52] These texts explaining the war events in apocalyptic terms were revealed by standard *jitan* gods such as Guandi, Wenchang, Patriarch Lü, and Zhenwu, but they also introduced Guanyin to this group of savior gods, an innovation that changed the parameters for placing Buddhism within the practice of spirit-writing. These savior gods were now under the orders of the benevolent Mother Goddess. The latter was now named Yaochi jinmu: this was an early title for the Daoist goddess Xiwangmu 西王母 (and as such appears in earlier *jitan* revelations), but she was now equated with the Unborn Eternal Mother, Wusheng laomu 無生老姆, of the sectarian tradition. We have already met her spirit-writing to protect her devotees in the middle of war action in 1861 Yunnan.

All the branches and offshoots of Xiantiandao that developed after the 1860s used spirit-writing; for instance, the Yiguandao founder, Wang Jueyi 王覺一 (1821?–84?), claimed to be a manifestation of Maitreya, in good sectarian form, but was confirmed by spirit-writing in 1877. Kenneth Dean also noted that spirit-writing became prominent in the activities of the Sanyijiao 三一教, established in Fujian in the late sixteenth century by Lin Zhaoen (whose own practice of revelations we have seen in chapter 6) from the last years of the nineteenth century onward.[53]

52. On this last title, see Jordan and Overmyer, *Flying Phoenix*, 57.

53. Dean, *Lord of the Three in One*, 176, 252.

8.3. Hybrid Eschatologies

Given the continuity between the entropy scenario, as propounded notably by Xiantiandao groups, and the Taiping scenario, one might expect that the former would be entirely condemned by loyalist literati. In fact, the opposite happened. A crucial feature of the eschatological texts produced in the context of the war is the rise of hybrid scenarios that combine the themes and styles of the sectarian entropy and elite threat scenarios.

Hybridity took two main forms: juxtaposition and complete merger. In the first case, texts resorting to different scenarios were combined into one publication, showing how authors found them at least compatible. I would like to present one fascinating case of this configuration here: the *Jiujie zhenjing* 救劫真經 (True scripture to save humanity from the apocalypse), a slim volume of thirty pages published in Tianjin in 1860 by a retired local official, Ye Yizhuang 葉以莊, with a preface from a prominent member of the Kong lineage in Qufu. The volume contains three main scriptures: the first, *Foshuo dasheng mojie zhenjing* 佛說大聖末劫真經 (True scripture on the end of the kalpa and [the role] of the great saint, spoken by the Buddha) was revealed by Guanyin, not by spirit-writing but on an inscribed stone that landed on Earth—a modern version of the cave encounter.[54] It fits squarely within the sectarian scenario and is couched in popular language; it focuses on enumerating various disasters that will kill 90 percent of humanity and provides cyclical years for them. A short extract will give a sense of the language:

> If evil people do not have faith in (this revelation), they will just have to wait for the *shen*, *you*, *xu*, and *hai* years[55] when there will be food, but no human to eat it, clothes, but no human to wear them, roads, but no human to walk them, houses, but no human to dwell in them, and fields, but no human to plant them. By the fifth and sixth months, poisonous snakes will

54. *Jiujie zhenjing*, 229–33.

55. These are four consecutive "branches" and thus years.

cover the earth. By the eighth and ninth months, all evil people will die; their corpses will pile up and cover the earth.

若有惡人不信者,但看申、酉、戌、亥年有飯無人吃,有衣無人穿,有路無人走,有屋無人住,有田無人種。至五六月間惡蛇滿地,八月九月惡人盡死,屍堆滿地。

This is, to my knowledge, the earliest version of a family of Guanyin apocalyptic texts that circulated in large numbers from the last years of the nineteenth century on.[56]

The second is an untitled spirit-written revelation by Guanyin. It is closer to an elite scenario: Guanyin explains how she convinced the Jade Emperor to separate the good from the bad instead of killing everyone and to "unleash war only at selected places" 刀兵擇地.[57] The third is the Guandi *Jiujiepian* introduced at the beginning of this chapter. We thus have a juxtaposition of both scenarios and writing styles, from crude and graphic descriptions of disasters to the more reasoned admonition for moral self-cultivation—even though within the Guandi and other elite revelations, the style also varies considerably from the more literate to the vernacular and oral.

Just as interesting as the juxtaposition of these various scenarios is a four-page personal account by the author explaining his motivations for publishing such a book.[58] Ye Yizhuang starts by claiming that many different apocalyptic books are circulating 近年印送末劫真經不少, but that he was moved by this one when he saw it at a friend's house. He hand copied it and sent it to his eldest son, then a student, who promised to make ten copies but only made a few. The younger son and a daughter soon died; the eldest son fell gravely ill and saw hellish soldiers who accused him of reneging on his vow. Ye Yizhuang then confronted the hellish soldiers and successfully bargained to print a hundred copies

56. Li Shiwei, "Jindai Guanyin jiujie shanshu de xingzhi yu neihan"; Li Shiwei, "Mojie jiejiu."

57. *Jiujie zhenjing*, 234–40.

58. *Jiujie zhenjing*, 249–53.

on his son's behalf so as to redeem his sin. On a friend's advice, Ye added the Guandi text (which was not part of the original book that was therefore more "sectarian"). He then commented that officials' lives such as his tend to be very sinful, and he understood his two children's deaths, as well as his eldest child's close encounter with death, only saved from the brink by Guandi, as retribution. Now that the apocalypse (*dajie*) is at hand, he writes, everyone must follow his example, repent from their sins, and live according to the scriptures found in the book. This poignant testimony shows how for literati and officials like Ye, the eschatological discourse made full sense at the levels of both their personal and collective experience.

We do not know how close to war events Ye ever came, but the war context is obvious in the book: the next text after his testimony is an "invocation to avoid being killed in battle," *bibing zhou* 避兵咒.[59] More generally, some of the texts discussed in this chapter were written or edited by people with direct experience of battles, and others by people who lived outside the war zones and only heard or read about the reality of the massacres. It is very difficult, however, to know exactly from the sources and to discern how intimate experience shaped the production of revealed scriptures and moral tracts.

The second configuration of hybridity concerns narratives where elements of both scenarios are combined within one text. This phenomenon is not entirely new, as there already existed elite texts with elements of the sectarian scenario: for instance, some eighteenth-century elite spirit-written texts allude to the Three Ages (*sanqi*) theory.[60] However, during the war we witness an unprecedented effort to combine the two scenarios. How this came to be is still unclear; the fact that sectarian traditions, most importantly the Xiantiandao, began to use spirit-writing around that time is a major part of the story. It is also possible that in the

59. *Jiujie zhenjing*, 254.

60. Hsieh Ts'ung-hui, *Xin tiandi zhi ming*, 214–18. It should be noted that the Three Ages (*sanqi*) discourse was prevalent in medieval Daoist texts and is therefore not a sure marker of "sectarian" influence.

war context, where the sectarian groups were usually not on the enemy side, many elites began to view their discourse as more credible. Starting in the mid-nineteenth century, the convergence of "sectarian traditions," notably Xiantiandao, which carry a millenarian, messianic message, and elite spirit-writing cults, which typically had a nonmessianic form of eschatology, indeed represents a turning point in the history of the production of revealed scriptures and eschatological ideas.

The proliferation of such hybrid scenarios shows how porous the boundaries were between the realms of "Buddhism," "Daoism," "Confucianism," "redemptive societies," and "sectarian religions" (however we or the late imperial Chinese define these categories). Wang Chien-ch'uan has made the important point that during the same period (the second half of the nineteenth century), morality book presses (*shanshuju*) started to distribute "sectarian" texts and thereby contributed to rendering them mainstream and acceptable.[61] By the Republican period, this merging had coalesced into redemptive societies that had a largely elite and self-declared Confucian following and, at the same time, developed the Three Ages (*sanqi*) type of apocalyptic teachings; it also, even more so, resulted in the wide acceptance of such teachings across all sorts of elite groups. This background is necessary to understand why the hybrid eschatological teachings that formed during the Taiping War have continued to be so prevalent among all classes of society throughout the twentieth century and down to the present day.

Two main elements of the entropy scenarios enter the threat narratives: predictions of the date of the apocalypse and set numbers of the elect who will survive.

8.3.1. The Date of the Last Judgment

A consequence of the negotiations between the Jade Emperor and savior gods that underline the threat scenario is that no calculation is made for

61. Wang Chien-ch'uan, "Morality Book Publishing and Popular Religion in Modern China."

the duration of the kalpa and no date is set for the apocalypse. The moment when the cataclysmic disasters strike depends, up to the last minute, on what humans do and on the heavenly bureaucracy's decision. This stands in contrast to frequent mentions of a *renshen* 壬申 or *jiazi* 甲子 year as the preordained date for the end-times in, for instance, medieval or *baojuan* entropy scenario eschatologies. The kalpa ends not by necessity (the exhaustion of the old *qi*) but by decree, itself based on due process.[62]

By contrast, wartime eschatological threat scenario texts introduce a calendar in their narratives and make more or less precise predictions of upcoming disasters. Leading scholars, notably Takeuchi Fusaji and Wang Chien-ch'uan, have argued that this turn originated with new revelations starting in 1840 (a *gengzi* 庚子 year in the sixty-year cycle) at a temple near Chongqing (Sichuan) called Longnüsi 龍女寺. According to them, these revelations explain that the Jade Emperor has decided to annihilate humanity, which he considers irredeemably sinful; only after pleas by Guandi is one last reprieve given, during which time he and other gods will multiply spirit-writing revelations in order to save as many humans as possible.[63] This hybrid scenario dates the ultimatum but not the apocalypse itself (nor the date of the beginning of the third and last age, *moqi* 末期, even though later texts will equate the two); after the ultimatum, there is still a short but unspecified period during which repentance is possible. It nonetheless insists on the turning point represented by certain cyclical dates.

Wang Chien-ch'uan has traced the origins and rapid diffusion of this discourse from the mid-1850s onward, with numerous revelations

62. The naturalistic description of the apocalypse being caused by an accumulation of black vapor, itself a byproduct of sin, which is quite common in elite eschatology from the eighteenth century, is a bridge between the "entropy" (apocalypse is a natural, unavoidable phenomenon) and "bureaucratic" models.

63. Takeuchi Fusaji, "Shinmatsu Shisen no shūkyō undo"; Wang Chien-ch'uan, "Taiwan 'Guandi dang Yuhuang' chuanshuo de youlai"; see also Yau Chi-on, "Fuhua yunei," 225–28. The Longnüsi revelations are explicitly mentioned in numerous later texts; curiously, no extant original text seems to survive (only later, revised versions).

referring to the *gengzi* ultimatum and a few explicitly mentioning the Longnüsi texts. However, I have not seen any text reliably dated to 1840 that proposes this scenario; what we have from the 1840 Longnüsi spirit-writing altar is a commentary on the *Taoyuan mingshengjing*, which is not apocalyptic.[64] I would thus propose a modification of the Takeuchi-Wang narrative: this *gengzi* scenario around Guandi emerged *during* the Taiping War, and it was then (in the 1850s) said that the ultimatum was declared in 1840 and attributed to the Longnüsi group. Indeed, during the war, variants of this dated ultimatum multiply; according to the *Yuding jinke jiyao*, it was initiated in 1814 and declared in 1848, while other tracts found in the 1858 Guandi canon date it from 1816.[65] Also, the Longnüsi revelations were claimed as foundational by Xiantiandao spirit-writing groups, but the original Longnüsi adepts very likely had no connection to Xiantiandao.

8.3.2. The Quotas of the Elect

Another key difference between threat and entropy scenarios in prewar times is the definition of who will be saved. In the threat scenario, there is no preset number of humans who will be saved and survive the kalpa: each person will be judged according to her or his merits. In contrast, the entropy scenario is based on the idea that there is a predetermined number of souls (originally from Heaven) who must find their way back to the Eternal Mother when the time approaches. The number of these souls (which varies according to the traditions) is a marker of sectarian eschatology. Hybrid scenarios of the war period introduce a number, although usually in terms of a percentage rather than an absolute number, in spirit-written and other elite texts. Such percentages, most commonly 10 percent ("nine out of ten will perish"), are found in many elite texts: for instance in *Pangong mianzai baojuan*, Pan Zengyi pleads

64. *Mingshengjing zhujie*; we have two later reprints, with different prefaces and other paratexts. I discuss this text in detail in Goossaert, "Textual Canonization," 517–19; see also ter Haar, *Guan Yu*, 229–31.

65. Wang Chien-ch'uan, "Spirit Writing Groups in Modern China," 655–59.

with the gods and is informed that 30 percent will be saved. The number is negotiated between savior gods and the Jade Emperor, rather than (in the sectarian scenario) corresponding to an original number of wayward divine souls.

One of the most common characteristics of the hybrid scenario texts is that they are revealed by elite savior gods (Guandi, Patriarch Lü, and Wenchang, of threat scenario origin, and Guanyin, whose role comes largely from the entropy scenario) and take on many elements of the classical elite eschatology, notably the role of the Jade Emperor, while calling for a return to the sectarian goddesses and gathering all her children at the Dragon-Flower Meeting. In these hybrid versions, we have both a bureaucratization of the "sectarian" movements (with messianic elements being toned down) and a "sectarianization" of elite spirit-writing cults (with the acceptance of the Mother Goddess and her paradise). As discussed by Wang Chien-ch'uan, one early Xiantiandao text that includes threat scenario elements, the *Zhilu baofa*, may date from the war period, even though we only have later editions.[66] Yet another "sectarian" element that becomes current in hybrid scenarios is the importance of possessing the eschatological scripture itself, as well as protective talismans, in order to be saved.

8.4. The Diffusion of the Eschatological Scenarios

To what extent was the eschatological discourse widespread beyond the groups that produced it? This is obviously impossible to measure. Very likely, it was largely understood, at least passively. Spirit-writing was by the nineteenth century a mainstream practice widely observed in public and private spaces, even though the imperial code banned it. The notion of moral retribution for actions and divine punishment was nearly universal among all strata of society; the fact that eschatological texts

66. Wang Chien-ch'uan, "Spirit Writing Groups in Modern China," 659.

had been widely circulating for centuries made the scenarios a part of common culture that could be easily mobilized in times of crisis. As the examples discussed above suggest, literati and officials at various levels and in different regions fully subscribed to it.

Brief allusions to the apocalyptic vocabulary (which were certainly clear enough to the readers) can be found in the writings of wartime officials and were certainly made possible by the many meanings of the words, some of which referred to retribution but not to apocalypse.[67] Such allusions are also extremely common in anecdotes, *biji* 筆記, and other private writings discussing the events, even though these were most often written after the end of the war. For instance, Liang Gongchen 梁恭辰 (b. 1814)—a scholar from Fuzhou who published moral anecdotes throughout his life, between 1842 and 1882, which were reprinted in many editions in the late Qing—wrote stories about the massacres of Hangzhou and Suzhou (in 1860), as well as of Nanjing. These were preordained by the gods, who had established a register of those who would die in the war apocalypse, *bingjiebu* 兵劫簿, and some humans had the revelation of these lists beforehand.[68]

At the same time, the official imperial narrative of the events was decidedly not eschatological, and this made it difficult for officials to use eschatological language in their official proclamations. Whether they saw any cognitive dissonance between the two discourses is uncertain; officials had been trained for centuries to use different language in their official and private capacities and to reconcile them as different facets of their worldview. In other words, I propose that many if not most wartime officials were sincere in thinking that they were at the same time (1) facing a rebellion by uncivilized southerners and (2) engaging in an end-times eschatological battle, both outside and within themselves, with gods helping them through revelations and with divine armies.

67. See, for example, Cole, *People Versus the Taipings*, 25.

68. "Zhe Su dajie 浙蘇大劫," "Jinling dajie 金陵大劫," *Quanjielu leibian pingzhu*, 8.801–2.

This is not to say that apocalyptic scenarios fitted seamlessly in the larger cultural world of wartime loyalists. Distinguishing different eschatological scenarios and the status of the social groups that entertained them helps us address the issue of the varying acceptability of eschatological discourses.[69] Nonetheless, even in the most elite, nonmessianic threat scenario versions, the reception of the eschatological explanation of the war in the writings of officials and gentry activists raises some difficult questions, of which I will mention three.

First, who was to blame? Was the collapse of the imperial moral order the responsibility of officials and the emperor himself? Implicating the emperor was of course impossible, unless one was willing to run the risk of being branded a traitor and pro-Taiping convert. It was somewhat safer, although not entirely logical and credible, to claim that the emperor was good but was duped by corrupt officials; some Guandi revelations say so in no uncertain terms.[70] But it must have been on the minds of many that the apocalypse had some connection to moral failure from top to bottom, hence there were some strenuous efforts to claim the contrary. Yu Zhi writes in the *Pangong mianzai baojuan*,

> This apocalypse has nothing to do with the cycle (of rise and decline) of our dynasty; it is due to the extreme amount of sin committed by ordinary people that caused the Demon-kings to rise in arms and spread havoc in our world.
>
> 此番大劫，不關國運，實為下民作孽太重，所以混世魔王大起刀兵。[71]

This constitutes the most important difference between the Taiping eschatological scenario (in which a change of regime is central to salvation) and that of the loyalist elites.

69. Goossaert, "Modern Daoist Eschatology," 238–40, shows that already during the 1796–1804 millenarian White Lotus Rebellion (whose leaders propounded an entropy scenario), elite officials were themselves publishing threat scenario books.

70. For example, "Quanshi wen 勸世文," *Guandi quanshu*, 24.609–12.

71. *Pangong mianzai baojuan*, 2.20a.

A second and equally difficult question is the nature of the war victims: were they sinners duly punished ("people whose names were on the list of the doomed" 在劫數) or martyrs to be commemorated? As we have seen, texts like the *Yuding jinke jiyao* code and the *Pangong mianzai baojuan* assured readers that contrary to their impression of utter chaos, nothing happened by chance, and those who died in the war had deserved it. This certainly served the purpose of providing the hope that if one was virtuous, one would not die, but it also ran contrary to the dominant discourse of the imperial state, during and especially after the war, which set up a massive system of commemoration of the war dead (on the loyalist side) as martyrs.[72]

If civil victims were humans punished for their sins, what about Taiping recruits? Were they all demons toward whom pity held no sense? To what extent can the reciprocal demonization of the enemy explain the extreme violence that characterized the whole war? Of course, any war entails dehumanization of the enemy; but what we read in the wartime eschatological discourses, of any scenario, is a systematic theological justification of complete annihilation of the opponents. I suspect this may help us understand why loyalist generals, especially in the Hunan army, who were fighting in the name of Confucian values such as humanity, *ren* 仁, gave explicit orders to execute entire civil populations (women and children included) within cities recaptured from the Taiping, such as Anqing in 1861.[73] I hasten to add that such thinking was by no means hegemonic; such people as Yu Zhi, deeply convinced of the eschatological threat scenario, pleaded openly for saving the lives of ordinary Taiping soldiers who had been conscripted by force.[74]

The third difficult question was whether the war, understood as an apocalyptic disaster through war, *bingjie* 兵劫, was merely a warning or the final apocalypse. Reading from the texts published during the war, the issue seems to have been undecided: the gods were watching developments

72. Meyer-Fong, *What Remains*, chap. 5.
73. Platt, *Autumn in the Heavenly Kingdom*, 215.
74. Meyer-Fong, *What Remains*, 47–48.

during the period of the ultimatum. These texts opened the possibility of redemption but did not guarantee it. It is only later that the Taiping War could be described as a warning. Interpretations could vary between different people and also over the years: Katherine Alexander has drawn attention to how Yu Zhi's three essays (with the shared title *Jiehai huilan shuo* 劫海迴瀾說, Great waves in the apocalyptic ocean) on the eschatological understanding of the war, written in 1853, 1858, and 1864, evolve toward a pessimistic reading.[75]

One might think that apocalyptic texts produced in the context of the Taiping War would have been put aside when the war was over, some order was restored, and everybody could see that the demons sent out by the gods had not annihilated humanity after all—but merely killed several tens of millions of people. This proved not to be the case. These texts continued to be regularly reprinted, distributed, anthologized, and developed—after all, understanding what the Taiping War meant in the larger scheme of things mattered a lot to twentieth-century revolutionaries and conservatives alike.[76] Most of the Taiping-period texts we now read are actually Guangxu-period (1875–1909) reprints or Republican-period editions. As Shiga Ichiko has shown, postwar activists trying to rebuild imperial society were still largely thinking in terms of impending apocalypses, and further flows of revelations were triggered by new disasters, such as flooding and famines (especially in north China), as well as plague epidemics (especially on the southern coast).[77] The Taiping War had now become one among several historical "smaller apocalypses" that forewarned of the final one to come, variously understood as the Boxers, World War 1, the Sino-Japanese War, and more recent events.

75. Alexander, "Virtues of the Vernacular," 154–56.

76. See the chapter "Morality Books" in Katz and Goossaert, *Fifty Years that Changed Chinese Religion*; and Goossaert, "1919, shijie de mori."

77. Edgerton-Tarpley, *Tears from Iron*, chap. 3; Shiga Ichiko, "Qingmo Minchu de jiujiejing suo fanying de weiji."

8.5. The Postwar World of Revelations

The period from 1864 to the 1940s was marked by a production of revelations at a level of intensity probably never seen before. Spirit-writing continued to be a dominant mode of revelation because of its association with the upper classes and its omnipresence. It also spread over the borders, with active Guandi spirit-writing altars sponsored by the Korean kings and others mushrooming in Vietnam and elsewhere in Southeast Asia.[78] It was now practiced by an unprecedented variety of groups. In addition to the established *jitan* organized around Daoist salvation and rituals, we see from the 1880s onward the rapid rise, especially in the Jiangnan region, of altars dedicated to the cult of the Song-period mythical antinomian monk Jigong.[79] These groups ordained their members as lay Buddhists, promised them Buddhahood, and practiced Buddhist liturgy; they engaged in large-scale charity and produced large numbers of revealed morality books and Buddhist doctrinal texts. The two types easily cooperated or even merged; many Jiangnan altars worshiped both Jigong and Patriarch Lü, gave their members Daoist and Buddhist ordination names, and practiced both liturgies.[80]

Equally important, groups, most remarkably in Western China (Sichuan and Yunnan), claimed a Confucian identity, with names such as "Confucian altar," *rutan* 儒壇; such altars were omnipresent in Sichuan cities from the 1890s to the 1940s and were major providers of ritual services (including healing, funerals, and exorcism).[81] Self-identified Confucian spirit-writing groups are still an important part of the scene in contemporary Taiwan. Last but not least, Xiantiandao and its many

78. Kim Jihyun, "Enlightenment on the Spirit-Altar."

79. Wang Chien-ch'uan, "Qingmo Minchu Zhongguo de Jigong xinyang yu fuji tuanti."

80. Goossaert, "Jin'gaishan Network."

81. Wang Chien-ch'uan, "Popular Groups Promoting 'The Religion of Confucius' "; Zhu Mingchuan, "Rutan jingdian."

offshoots also built large networks of spirit-writing shrines and publishing houses to disseminate their revelations, not only in China but throughout Southeast Asia (and to a lesser extent the West), where they are still a notable presence. This naturally is a list of ideal types, with many groups creating their own synthesis, or evolving from one to another (and as a result producing revelations with equally evolving contents) following both internal dynamics and external political and social conditions.

This period is probably the best studied in the history of spirit-writing, and the sheer amount of material makes it very difficult to draw any synthesis.[82] I am therefore stopping at the threshold of the twentieth century, hoping to have provided a compelling historical explanation of how modern and contemporary Chinese society came to be flooded with spirit-written texts.

In lieu of a conclusion, I would like to point out two key developments during the Republican period. First, spirit-writing ceased to be illegal under the new regime (even though the Qing ban was never a hindrance to its development) and was a fact of social life. Routine publication of spirit-written revelations in the press showed their public acceptability. The redemptive societies, many of which practiced it intensively, turned the practice into a mass activity.[83] They also continued to create new techniques, such as producing spirit-photography along with texts.[84] At the same time, the rising antisuperstition discourse started to target spirit-writing in ways not seen before. These discourses, as well as the close association of spirit-writing with redemptive societies, which were targeted as their number one enemy by the Chinese Community Party, led to the first strict and effective ban in Chinese history. The practice has continued in Taiwan, Hong Kong, and other parts of the Chinese world, but this political turn radically changed the

82. Among the best studies, see Fan Chun-wu, *Qingmo minjian cishan shiye yu luantang yundong*; Valussi and Schumann, *Spirit-Writing in Chinese History*.

83. Schumann, "Protecting the Dao and Transmitting the Classics."

84. Wu Shengqing, "In Search of Soul."

place of revelations in general, and spirit-writing in particular, in Chinese culture. This, after the emergence and codification in the early modern period, its simplification in the late Ming, and the sectarian turn of the mid-nineteenth century proved to be the fourth and so far last major stage in a thousand-year long history of making Chinese gods write.

Conclusion

This book has shown that the continuous flow of revelations in Chinese history since the Han period cannot be considered independently of the ordinary experiences of divine presence as staged, in the vast majority of cases, by religious specialists according to set ritual techniques. These specialists, either working in temples, from home, at clients' homes, or in any public space, create and manage divine presence for healing, divination, exorcism, and prayers to obtain blessings. As gods are at hand and may be asked questions, the possibility of revelation is ever present and thus culturally accepted; we have seen that many debates raged about the authenticity or desirability of specific revelations, but the principle of revelation was, until contemporary times, a mainstream cultural postulate. In most such cases of divine presence, revelations did not happen; the gods "only" addressed the immediate needs of the devotees. But when revelations occurred, they emerged from such a context of ritual production of divine presence, with particularly gifted ritual specialists and particularly interested audiences who produced discourses placing the immediate religious requests at hand (disease, suffering, anguish, and hopes of salvation) in a larger theological framework, typically eschatological. The case of the modern *jitan* that narrowly specialized in producing revelations is atypical; most such groups routinely provided ritual services to individuals and communities before they produced scriptures and other revelations.

From this perspective, then, the production of revelations is not practically different from routine rituals. The fundamental ritual tool kit for creating divine presence—possession, summoning, and visualization—had been in place since early medieval times, but new combinations and innovations appeared frequently; I have argued that the rise of presence-type rites of controlled possession in the early modern period, and spirit-writing in particular, was an especially important turning point in the history of Chinese revelations, as it widely expanded the field of possibilities, especially in terms of group participation. As varied as the ritual techniques, the identity of specialists involved in revelations covers a large spectrum: I have highlighted the crucial role of Daoists, but they were never alone; Buddhists were constantly involved, even though for theological reasons, they were ever wary of revelations that would challenge the authority of the received sutras. By contrast, with the affirmation of the continuous active presence in our world of the Dao and its emanations (Taishang laojun and other lords) that is at its core, Daoist theology fully justified and encouraged revelation. Sectarian leaders in the modern period further developed the theological foundations and the practical modes of revelations, adopting and enriching the spirit-writing traditions.

Mediums and shamans have always been key actors of revelations, either on their own or under the control of priests. The dividing line between these categories is blurry; literati often used the same word, *wu* 巫, to qualify mediums and *fashi* priests. Just as importantly, the distinction between "lay" people and clerics is often a blunt etic tool that obscures the fact that a man or woman initiated and ordained in a Buddhist or Daoist tradition can perform rites even though he or she is married and has a profession. It is the ritual tradition that enables the creation of divine presence and revelation, not the status as professional cleric.

A Panorama of Revelations

The variety of ritual traditions that provide divine presence has created over time a rich repertoire of techniques, genres, and scenarios for revelations, with niches for every taste and expectation. Some of them have disappeared over time, such as some of the *daofa* techniques described in early modern manuals, but most have been transmitted to the present. In modern and contemporary times, Daoist priests still practice complex visualizations for themselves or during communal rituals, even though they do not seem to be often used for producing revelations anymore. Charismatic teachers still claim to have had encounters with immortals, Buddhas, or other entities who have given them revelations, or to be themselves incarnations of such entities and thus living gods constantly producing divine speech.[1] But the most common contexts for producing revelations in modern and contemporary times are possession and spirit-writing. There is no denying that the success of these two modes of divine presence is linked to the agency and active participation they provide to participants individually and as groups, even though there is always the need for a ritual specialist who masters the required techniques.

As a result, revelations of all types amount to a considerable mass of texts and are found throughout society. When we look at the catalogs of the major religious presses of the Republican period, such as the Tongshanshe-affiliated Mingshan shuju 明善書局 or Tianhuaguan 天華館, or the Buddhist presses, beginning with the Foxue shuju 佛學書局, we find thousands of revealed books, including scriptures, morality books, liturgies, self-cultivation manuals, and more.[2] Among them, sutra-type texts account for the earliest and, usually, the most prestigious titles, but there are few recent ones. We also find encounter-type and visualiza-

1. See Ownby, Ji, and Goossaert, eds., *Making Saints*, for cases of twentieth-century charismatic leaders and their negotiation of divine status in antisuperstitious contexts.

2. See the chapters by Katz and Wang Chien-ch'uan in Clart and Scott, eds., *Religious Publishing and Print Culture in Modern China.*

tion-type titles; again, mostly for earlier periods, even though these traditions were never discontinued. And then, among the modern titles, the overwhelming majority is the product of spirit-writing.

A look at the contents of a modern, very inclusive canon, the *Fushou baozang* 福壽寶藏 (Precious canon on blessings and longevity) edited and funded by Wang Yiting 王一亭 (1867–1938), a prominent industrialist-cum-philanthropist, provides an entirely similar picture. Wang included Buddhist sutras in his canon, but the vast majority of the 140 individual titles were spirit-written, many during and after the Taiping War.[3] Other collections of the Republican period confirm this impression; respect and devotion for the ancient revelations that form the foundation of Chinese religious culture did not in any way preclude a keen interest in new divine discourse, especially as the latter directly addressed the realities and challenges of living in the specific here-and-now of their readers.

The Modern Ecology of Revelations

Zhu Mingchuan has shown that after 1840 there emerged a common discourse identifying four legitimate modes of producing revelations: *ji* 乩, spirit-writing; *luan* 鸞, automatic spirit-writing, without a medium; *ming* 冥, shamanism, and more specifically spirit travels to the underworld to ask about the fate of the dead; and *xiang* 相 or 象 or 像, spirit possession. Certain groups trained their members in these four different techniques, and various revelations clearly advocate for their joint practice, showing how the spirit-writing-focused *jitan* of the high Qing literati had evolved through the turmoil of the nineteenth century to become more inclusive, including in terms of ritual techniques.[4] Yet

3. The contents of this canon are discussed in Katz and Goossaert, *Fifty Years that Changed Chinese Religion*, chap. 4.

4. Zhu Mingchuan, "Gengzi Chuandong shenjiao chu."

another technique became significant in the modern period: *kanguang* 看光, whereby practitioners gaze at a hanging piece of cloth and see characters appearing, which they note down. It was used to compose the scripture of a redemptive society in the 1940s and is also attested in modern south Vietnam, where Chinese and Vietnamese revelation practices intensively cross-hybridized; I have not found yet earlier mentions.[5]

In these nineteenth- and twentieth-century sources, automatic spirit-writing techniques are usually termed *feiluan*, even though *feiluan* was also often used in the much larger generic sense of spirit-writing. We have seen this ritual technique in various early modern sources, and it is attested again from the eighteenth century onward, even though we cannot ascertain whether this was a continuous tradition transmitted since the Song period.[6] It was practiced in a specific storied building, usually called the Phoenix Pavilion 鸞樓, some of which still stand. Zhu Mingchuan quotes a 1935 ethnographic survey from Fengdu, Sichuan, describing large-scale, several-day communal Daoist rituals during which participants each place sheets of paper with their questions to the gods in the Phoenix Pavilion, and when the ritual is concluded, the pavilion is opened and papers are covered with divine responses.[7]

This shows how the thirst for revelations continued to fuel their production in an ecology with various types where each had its own contribution. But the various ritual techniques did not all have the same prestige. In February 1919, three months before the famed events of May 4, a twelve-year old girl in Manchuria was possessed by Guanyin. The girl revealed a scripture explaining that accumulated human sins had provoked the outbreak of the final apocalypse, but thanks to Guanyin's relentless pleading with the Jade Emperor, a limited number of virtuous

5. Ownby, "Text and Context."

6. Hu Jiechen, "Terminology and Typology," translates and discusses a description in the 1744 *Lüzu quanshu* and another dated 1904 that is found in the *Qingbai leichao* 清稗類鈔. Wang Chien-ch'uan, "Qingdai de Lüzu xinyang yu fuji," 35 adds another description from the early Qing *Chuanjiabao* 傳家寶.

7. Zhu Mingchuan, "Gengzi Chuandong shenjiao chu," 59–61.

people would be saved. She composed a scripture, published under the title *Cihang baoxun* 慈航寶訓 (Precious instructions of the boat of compassion), to exhort people to do good so as to be included among the elect.[8] This was one of many eschatological revelations that read the events of the 1910s not as geopolitics or as the difficult but hopeful birth of a modern China but as the end of the world.[9] Yet, unlike many spirit-written eschatological revelations of that period, it was not included in the collections and the catalogs of respected publishing houses such as those mentioned above.

This illustrates a pattern we have seen at work throughout this book; various types of revelations exist in an ecology where every element is tagged with a value judgment; elite traditions of interiorized visualization or writing with refined calligraphy have higher cultural value than coarse oral pronouncements. And yet, all these revelations are deeply interdependent, as ideas, visions, and ritual techniques circulate ceaselessly between all niches and ever-inventive specialists of divine presence recombine them for their own purposes.

Comparative Overtures

I would finally like to comment briefly on what the findings in this book may bring to the larger field of comparative religions. I have tried here to account for the extraordinarily rich and diverse Chinese evidence without imposing on it any preexistent theory or analytical framework. This seems justified by the sheer pervasiveness of revelation in Chinese society over the last two millennia, in apparent contrast with European and Middle Eastern societies shaped by monotheistic traditions that tend to (try to) close revelation—even though experiences of divine presence

8. This text was disseminated by a sectarian group, the Huangtianjiao 黄天教; see Li Shiyu, *Xiandai Huabei mimi zongjiao*, 20.

9. Goossaert, "1919, shijie de mori."

are certainly pervasive in these contexts as well. Comparison seems more immediately fruitful with societies where possession is widely performed and therefore instructions from spirits are more common, and commonly accepted. Yet, many if not most of these societies have neither a cultural valuation of writing comparable to that of the Chinese nor the elaborate forms of producing revealed texts that the latter have honed over time. A thick comparison would include ritualistically plural societies, such as the Indian world or the antique Mediterranean world, where diverse systems of relating to the gods coexist. As is often the case, the most obvious comparisons are with neighboring countries, such as Korea, Japan, and Vietnam, which also have a rich and living revelatory tradition including possession, dreams, spirit-writing, and more. In these cases, however, comparison will need to be disentangled from the study of historical transfer and influence, since the revelatory practices in these countries often have direct Chinese sources. In the same spirit, I have also mentioned the Tibetan traditions such as the *ter-ma* treasure texts, which certainly have some historical connections with the Chinese techniques.

Beyond the study of the circulation of revelatory techniques in East Asia and other countries, the comparative potential of the data I have presented may reside in the typology introduced in chapter 1, which hopefully can be adopted, modified, and improved by scholars working in other cultural contexts. I hypothesize that most of the monotheistic revelations can be ascribed to my type 2, encounter, even though I expect this proposition to come as a surprise to the scholars of these texts. Obviously, certain types will be more marginal or even absent in some cultures, which does not invalidate the model per se. More intriguingly, I hope future discussions will bring up new types not covered here and show than even the remarkably diverse Chinese culture did not exhaust the spectrum of possibilities for making the gods speak and write.

APPENDIX

Timeline of Revelations in Chinese History

		0	
Buddhism introduced	Han		Laozi revelations
Tianshidao		200	
			Shangqing
		400	Lingbao
		600	
	Tang		
		800	
Block printing technology			
	Song	1000	*daofa* develop spirit-written texts
		1200	
	Yuan		
	Ming	1400	
		1600	*jitan* multiply
economic, demographic growth			
literacy develops	Qing	1800	
			Xiantiandao adopts spirit-writing
Taiping War			
		2000	

Bibliography

Abbreviations

DZ: *Daozang* 道藏, numbers following Schipper and Verellen, eds., *The Taoist Canon*.

JY: *Daozang jiyao* 道藏輯要, numbers following Lai Chi Tim, ed., *Daozang jiyao tiyao*.

T: *Taishō shinshū daizōkyō* 大正新修大藏經. 100 vols. Tokyo: Daizō shuppan kabushiki kaisha 大蔵出版株式會社, 1988 edition.

X: *Manji shinsan Dai Nippon zokuzōkyō* 卍字新纂大日本續藏經. Kyoto: Zōkyōshoin 藏經書院, 1905–12.

Primary Sources

Baopuzi neipian 抱朴子内篇. Edited by Wang Ming 王明. Beijing: Zhonghua shuju, 1985.

Ba-Shu daojiao beiwen jicheng 巴蜀道教碑文集成. Compiled by Long Xianzhao 龍顯昭, Huang Haide 黄海德 et al. Chengdu: Sichuan daxue chubanshe, 1997.

Bianweilu 辯偽錄. Xiangmai 祥邁. T 2116.

Bichuan Zhengyang zhenren lingbao bifa 祕傳正陽真人靈寶畢法. DZ 1191.

Chanfa daguan 懺法大觀. JY 247.

Chaojiejing 超劫經 (*Guanghui xiuxin baoming chaojie jing* 廣慧修心保命超劫經). *Lüzu quanshu*, *j*. 18.

Chao shi Baowentang shumu 晁氏寶文堂書目. Chao Li 晁瑮 (*jinshi* 1541). Ming manuscript on ctext.org.

Chenzhonglu 晨鐘錄. 1886 edition in *Sandong shiyi*, vol. 6.

Chongxu tongmiao shichen Wang xiansheng jiahua 冲虛通妙侍宸王先生家話. Compiled by Yuan Tingzhi 袁庭植 (fl. 1153). DZ 1250.

Chu Sanzang jiji 出三藏記集. Sengyou 僧祐 (445–518). T 2145.

Chuanyinglou huiyilu 釧影樓回憶錄. Bao Tianxiao 包天笑. In *Minguo biji xiaoshuo daguan* 民国笔记小说大观, vol. 4. Taiyuan: Shanxi guji chubanshe, 1999.

Chunyang dijun shenhua miaotongji 純陽帝君神化妙通紀. Miao Shanshi 苗善時 (fl. 1324). DZ 305.

Cihang baoxun 慈航寶訓. No date. In *Zhongguo yuyan jiujie shu*, vol. 10.

Da Ming Renxiao huanghou menggan Fo shuo diyi xiyou dagongde jing 大明仁孝皇后夢感佛說第一希有大功德經. X 010.
Da Ming Renxiao huanghou quanshanshu 大明仁孝皇后勸善書. 1407 edition in *Siku quanshu cunmu congshu*.
Da Qing huidian shili 大清會典事例. 1908 edition. Reprint Beijing: Zhonghua shuju, 1991.
Danguiji 丹桂籍. Undated edition at Bibliothèque nationale de France. See https://gallica.bnf.fr/ark:/12148/btv1b9006564t.image.
Daode zhenjing jiyi dazhi 道德真經集義大旨. DZ 723.
Daofa huiyuan 道法會元. Early 14th c. DZ 1220.
Daojia jinshilüe 道家金石略. Compiled by Chen Yuan 陳垣. Edited by Chen Zhichao 陳智超 and Zeng Qingying 曾慶瑛. Beijing: Wenwu chubanshe, 1988.
Daojiao lingyanji 道教靈驗記. Du Guangting 杜光庭 (850–933). DZ 590.
Daomen dingzhi 道門定制. DZ 1244.
Daomen kefan daquanji 道門科範大全集. DZ 1225.
Daomen shigui 道門十規. DZ 1232.
Daoxuan lüshi gantonglu 道宣律師感通錄. T 2107.
Deng tianjun xuanling bamen baoying neizhi 鄧天君玄靈八門報應內旨. DZ 1266.
Deyilu 得一錄. 1869. Yu Zhi 余治 (1809–74).
Dianshizhai huabao 點石齋畫報. Shanghai: Shenbaoguan, every ten days, 1882–98. Rpt. Guangzhou: Guangdong renmin chubanshe, 1983.
Dijun jiujie baoyu 帝君救劫寶諭. 1860 edition at IHEC Library, Collège de France.
Dongjing shidu 洞經示讀. JY 7.
Dongpo quanji 東坡全集. *Siku quanshu* edition.
Dongpo zhilin 東坡志林. *Siku quanshu* edition.
Dongyuan shenzhou jing 洞淵神咒經. DZ 335.
Duren shangpin miaojing tongyi 度人上品妙經通義. DZ 89.
Fahai yizhu 法海遺珠. Late Yuan? DZ 1166.
Fayuan zhulin 法苑珠林. T 2122.
Fengsheng huijie xianhualu 奉聖回劫顯化錄. 1894 edition in *Ming Qing minjian zongjiao jingjuan wenxian*, vol. 11.
Fozu lidai tongzai 佛祖歷代通載. T 2036.
Fujian zongjiao beiming huibian. Quanzhoufu fence 福建宗教碑銘彙編. 泉州府分. Compiled by Zheng Zhenman 鄭振滿 and Kenneth Dean 丁荷生. Fuzhou: Fujian renmin chubanshe, 2003.
Fushou baozang 福壽寶藏. Compiled by Wang Yiting et al., 92 vols. Shanghai: Leshanshe, 1936.
Gaochun Pujitang zhi 高淳普濟堂志. Compiled by Dai Fengjun 戴鳳筠 et al. 1900, in *Jiangsu jinxiandai shehui jiuji yu cishan wenxian congkan* 江蘇近現代社會救濟與慈善文獻叢刊. Nanjing: Fenghuang chubanshe, 2015.
Gaoshang dadong Wenchang silu ziyang baolu 高上大洞文昌司祿紫陽寶籙. DZ 1214.
Gaoshang shenxiao yuqing zhenwang zishu dafa 高上神霄玉清真王紫書大法. DZ 1219.
Gaoshang shenxiao zongshi shoujing shi 高上神霄宗師受經式. DZ 1282.
Gaoshang yuegong taiyin yuanjun xiaodao xianwang Lingbao jingming huangsu shu 高上月宮太陰元君孝道仙王靈寶淨明黃素書. DZ 555.

Gaoshang Yuhuang benxing jijing 高上玉皇本行集經. DZ 10. Same text with commentary by Zhang Liang: DZ 11.
Gaoshang Yuhuang benxing jingsui 高上玉皇本行經髓. DZ 12.
Gengshen binan riji 庚申避難日記. In *Taiping tianguo shiliao zhuanji* 太平天國史料專輯. Shanghai: Shanghai guji chubanshe, 1979.
Guandi jingchan 關帝經懺. 1857 edition from the Quanzhou Guanhuai temple in *Ming Qing minjian zongjiao jingjuan wenxian*, vol. 10.
Guandi quanshu 關帝全書. 1858, 1889 edition in *Guandi wenxian huibian* 關帝文獻匯編. Compiled by Huang Qishu 黃啟曙. Beijing: Guoji wenhua chuban gongsi, 1995.
Guandi shiji zhengxinbian 關帝事蹟徵信編. Compiled by Zhou Guangye 周廣業 (1730–98) and Cui Yingliu 崔應榴. 1882 edition in *Guandi wenxian huibian* 關帝文獻匯編. Beijing: Guoji wenhua chuban gongsi, 1995.
Guansheng dijun quanshu 關聖帝君全書. Compiled by Peng Shaosheng 彭紹升 (1740–96). 1772 edition at Guojia tushuguan.
Guansheng dijun shengji tuzhi quanji 關聖帝君聖跡圖誌全集. Compiled by Lu Zhan 盧湛 (fl. 1692–93). 1849 edition in *Zhongguo daoguan zhi congkan xubian* 中國道觀志叢刊續編. Yangzhou: Guangling chubanshe, 2004, vols. 1–2.
Guierji 貴耳集. Zhang Duanyi 張端義 (1179–ca. 1235). *Siku quanshu* edition.
Guixin zashi xuji 癸辛雜識續集. Zhou Mi 周密 (1232–1308). *Siku quanshu* edition.
Haiqiong Bai zhenren yulu 海瓊白真人語録. DZ 1307.
Haishan qiyu 海山奇遇. Undated edition in *Zhonghua xu daozang*, vol. 19.
Hanshu 漢書. Beijing: Zhonghua shuju, 1962.
Haosheng jiujie bian 好生救劫編. Youfu dushu tang congke 有福讀書堂叢刻. Yangzhou, 1901.
Houhanshu 後漢書. Beijing: Zhonghua shuju, 1973.
Huadangge congtan 花當閣叢談. Xu Fuzuo 徐復祚 (1560–?). *Xuxiu siku quanshu*, vol. 1175.
Huagaishan Fuqiu Wang Guo san zhenjun shishi 華蓋山浮丘王郭三真君事實. DZ 778.
Huangdi Yinfujing shu 黃帝陰符經疏. DZ 110.
Huangjing jizhu 皇經集註. DZ 1440.
(*Wanli*) *Huangyan xianzhi* (萬曆)黃巖縣志. Wanli era edition.
Hunyuan shengji 混元聖紀. DZ 770.
Jiangnan daojiao beiji ziliaoji 江南道教碑記資料集. Compiled by Wu Yakui 吳亞魁. Shanghai: Shanghai cishu chubanshe, 2007.
Jindai Guandi, Yuhuang jingjuan yu Xuanmen zhenzong wenxian 近代關帝、玉皇經卷與玄門真宗文獻. Edited by Wang Chien-ch'uan. 6 vols. Taipei: Boyang, 2012.
Jin'gai xindeng 金蓋心燈. Compiled in 1821 by Min Yide 閔一得 (1749–1836). 1876 edition in *Daojiao wenxian* 道教文獻, vol. 10. Taipei: Danqing tushu, 1983.
Jingming zhongxiao quanshu 淨明忠孝全書 (DZ 1110). Critical edition by Xu Wei 許蔚. Beijing: Zhonghua shuju, 2018.
Jingming zongjiao lu 淨明宗教錄. JY 152.
Jinshi cuibian 金石萃編. Wang Chang 王昶 (early nineteenth century). 1921 edition. Reprint: Beijing: Zhongguo shudian, 1985.
Jishenlu 稽神錄. Xu Xuan 徐鉉 (916–91). *Siku quanshu* edition.
Jiuhuang xinjing zhujie 九皇新經註解. JY 109.
Jiujie yuwen huike 救劫諭文彙刻. 1861 edition at IHEC Library, Collège de France.

Jiujie zhenjing 救劫真經. 1860 edition in vol. 9 of *Shanshu baojuan yanjiu congshu* 善書寶卷研究叢書, compiled by Li Zhengzhong 李正中. Taipei: Lantai chubanshe, 2014.

Jiushengchuan 救生船. 1905 edition in *Ming Qing minjian zongjiao jingjuan wenxian xubian*, vol. 9.

Jiutian yingyuan leisheng puhua tianzun yushu baojing jizhu 九天應元雷聲普化天尊玉樞寶經集註. DZ 99.

Kezuo xinwen 客座新聞. Shen Zhou 沈周 (1427–1509). Manuscript edition in *Xuxiu siku quanshu*, vol. 1167.

Kuitanlu 愧郯録. Yue Ke 岳珂 (1183–1234). *Sibu congkan* edition.

Langqian jiwen 郎潛紀聞. Chen Kangqi 陳康祺 (1840–90). Beijing: Zhonghua shuju, 1984.

Laojun yinsong jiejing 老君音誦誡經. DZ 785.

Laozi bianhuajing 老子變化經. Dunhuang manuscript S. 2295 in *Zhonghua daozang*, vol. 8.

Leshanlu 樂善錄. *Xuxiu siku quanshu*, vol. 1266.

Lianxiu qixinlu 蓮修起信錄. X 1204.

Lidai shenxian tongji 歷代神仙通紀. Early Qing copy reprinted in *Siku weishoushu jikan* 四庫未收書輯刊, series 8, vol. 11–14.

Lingbao jingming huangsu shu shiyi bijue 靈寶淨明黃素書釋義秘訣. DZ 556.

Lingbao jingming xinxiu Jiulao shenyin fumo mifa 靈寶淨明新修九老神印伏魔秘法. Preface 1131. DZ 562.

Lingbao jingmingyuan jiaoshi Zhou zhengong qiqing huayi 靈寶淨明院教師周真公起請畫一. DZ 554.

Lingbao lingjiao jidu jinshu 靈寶領教濟度金書. DZ 466.

Lingbao tianzun shuo Hong'en lingji zhenjun miaojing 靈寶天尊說洪恩靈濟真君妙經. DZ 317.

Lingbao wuliang duren shangqing dafa 靈寶無量度人上經大法. DZ 219.

Lingbao yujian 靈寶玉鑑. DZ 547.

Linzi benxing shilu 林子本行實錄. 1939 edition in *Ming Qing minjian zongjiao jingjuan wenxian*, vol. 11.

Lishi zhenxian tidao tongjian 歷世真仙體道通鑑. Compiled by Zhao Daoyi 趙道一. DZ 296.

Lishi zhenxian tidao tongjian houji 歷世真仙體道通鑑後集. Compiled by Zhao Daoyi 趙道一. DZ 298.

Lishi zhenxian tidao tongjian xubian 歷世真仙體道通鑑續編. Compiled by Zhao Daoyi 趙道一. DZ 297.

Liuzi cangshu 柳子藏書. 1833 original edition from the Yunyi caotang 雲怡草堂.

Lushan Taiping xingguogong Caifang zhenjun shishi 廬山太平興國宮採訪真君事實. DZ 1286.

Lüzu quanshu 呂祖全書. 33-*juan* edition. Shanghai: Qianqingtang, 1917.

Lüzu quanshu 呂祖全書. 1775. *Zhonghua xu Daozang*, vol. 20.

Lüzu xingxin zhenjing 呂祖醒心真經. In *Lüzu quanshu* (33-*juan* edition), j. 21.

Lüzuzhi 呂祖志. DZ 1484.

Maoshanzhi 茅山誌. Liu Dabin 劉大彬 (fl. 1317–28). Critical edition by Richard Wang 王崗. Shanghai: Shanghai guji chubanshe, 2016.

Mengxi bitan 夢溪筆談. Shen Kua 沈括 (1031–95). *Sibu congkan* edition.
Ming Qing minjian zongjiao jingjuan wenxian 明清民間宗教經卷文獻. Compiled by Wang Chien-Chuan 王見川 and Lin Wanchuan 林萬傳. 12 vols. Taipei: Xinwenfeng, 1999.
Ming Qing minjian zongjiao jingjuan wenxian xubian 明清民間宗教經卷文獻續編. Compiled by Wang Chien-ch'uan. Taipei: Xinwenfeng, 2006.
Ming Qing yilai shanshu congbian 明清以來善書叢編. Edited by Wang Chien-ch'uan 王見川, Philip Clart 柯若樸, Hou Chong 侯沖, and Fan Chun-wu 范純武. 18 vols. Taipei: Xinwenfeng, 2018.
Ming Taizu shilu 明太祖實錄. Taipei: Academia Sinica, 1962.
Minghe yuyin 鳴鶴餘音. DZ 1100.
Mingshengjing zhujie 明聖經註解. 1873 edition in *Jindai Guandi, Yuhuang jingjuan yu Xuanmen zhenzong wenxian*, vol. 1.
Mingshengjing zhujie 明聖經註解. Undated edition from the Yongxingtang 永興堂 (Gaoxiong) in *Ming Qing minjian zongjiao jingjuan wenxian*, vol. 10.
Mingxin baojian 明心寶鑑. 1855 Lingyunge 凌雲閣 edition in *Ming Qing yilai shanshu congbian*, vol. 6.
Moyulu 墨餘錄. Mao Xianglin 毛祥麟 (1812–?). Shanghai: Shanghai guji chubanshe, 1985.
Nancun chuogenglu 南村輟耕錄. Tao Zongyi 陶宗儀 (fl. 1360–68). Beijing: Zhonghua shuju, 1959.
Nansha wenji 南沙文集. Hong Ruogao 洪若皋 (*jinshi* 1655). *Qingdai shiwenji huibian* 清代詩文集彙編, vol. 91.
Nenggaizhai manlu 能改齋漫錄. Wu Zeng 吳曾 (fl. 1127–60). *Siku quanshu* edition.
Ningyang Dong zhenren yuxian ji 凝陽董真人遇仙記. DZ 308.
Pangong mianzai baojuan 潘公免災寶卷. 1883 edition at Waseda University Library (Sawada Mizuho collection), accessible online.
Qiantang yishi 錢塘遺事. Liu Yiqing 劉一清 (Yuan). *Siku quanshu* edition.
Qiaoyangjing 樵陽經. In Fu Jinquan 傅金銓 (fl. 1800), *Jiyizi daoshu shiqizhong* 濟一子道書十七種, *Zangwai daoshu*, vol. 11.
Qidong yeyu 齊東野語. Zhou Mi 周密 (1232–1308). *Siku quanshu* edition.
Qing shigao 清史稿. Beijing: Zhonghua shuju, 1976.
Qinghe neizhuan 清河內傳. DZ 169.
Qingwei yuanjiang dafa 清微元降大法. DZ 223.
Qionglongshan zhi 穹窿山志. Wu Weiye 吳偉業 (1609–72), Xiang Qiu 向球, and Li Biao 李標. 1673. Reprinted in *Zhongguo daoguan zhi congkan* 中國道觀志叢刊. Nanjing: Jiangsu guji chubanshe, 2000, vols. 14–15.
Qiuzu yulu 邱祖語錄. *Zangwai daoshu*, vol. 11.
Quan Songwen 全宋文. Shanghai: Shanghai cishu chubanshe, Anhui jiaoyu chubanshe, 2006.
Quan Yuanwen 全元文. Nanjing: Jiangsu guji chubanshe, 1998–2004.
Quanjielu leibian pingzhu 勸戒錄類編評註. Liang Gongchen 梁恭辰. *Fushou baozang* edition.
Quanren juhuo 全人矩矱. 1843 edition in *Zangwai daoshu*, vol. 28.
Quanshu zhengzong 全書正宗. Compiled by Jiang Yupu 蔣予蒲 (1755–1819). 1805 edition (stored at Ōtani University, Kyoto, Japan).

Quyi shuo 祛疑說. Chu Yong 儲泳 (Song). *Siku quanshu* edition.
Sanguozhi 三國志. Beijing: Zhonghua shuju, 1962.
Sanzang zhenquan 三藏真詮. In *Fanghu waishi. Daojiao dongpai Lu Xixing neidan xiulian dianji* 方壶外史.道教东派陆西星内丹修炼典籍. Beijing: Zongjiao wenhua chubanshe, 2010.
Shanfang suibi 山房隨筆. Jiang Zhengzi 蔣正子 (fl. 1279). *Siku quanshu* edition.
Shangqing Lingbao dafa 上清靈寶大法. Transmitted by Ning Benli 寧本立 (*hao* Quanzhen 全真, 1101–81). DZ 1221.
Shangqing shi dichen Tongbo zhenren zhen tuzan 上清侍帝晨桐柏真人真圖讚. DZ 612.
Shanju xinhua 山居新話. Yang Yu 楊瑀 (1285–1361). *Siku quanshu* edition.
Shenbao 申報. Shanghai: Shenbaoguan, daily, 1872–1949.
Shengjing huizuan 聖經彙纂. 1806 edition at Bibliothèque nationale de France. See https://gallica.bnf.fr/ark:/12148/btv1b9006545g.r=sheng%20jing%20hui%20zuan?rk=21459;2.
Shenxian ganyuzhuan 神仙感遇傳. Du Guangting 杜光庭 (850–933). DZ 592.
Shuijinglu 水鏡錄. DZ 1479.
Shuzhong guangji 蜀中廣記. Cao Xuequan 曹學佺 (1574–1647). *Siku quanshu* edition.
Sisheng zhenjun lingqian 四聖真君靈籤. DZ 1298.
Songchao shishi 宋朝事實. Li You 李攸 (early Song). Beijing: Zhonghua shuju, 1955.
Song huiyao jigao 宋會要輯稿. Beijing: Zhonghua shuju, 1957.
Suishu 隋書. Beijing: Zhonghua shuju, 1973.
Taiping guangji 太平廣記. Beijing: Zhonghua shuju, 1961.
Taipingjing hejiao 太平經合校. Wang Ming 王明, ed. Beijing: Zhonghua shuju, 1960.
Taishang ganyingpian 太上感應篇. DZ 1167.
Taishang ganyingpian zhu 太上感應篇注. Hui Dong 惠棟 (1697–1758), 1749. *Congshu jicheng* edition.
Taishang shilu 太上實錄. Manuscript with 1357 colophon, *Zhonghua xu Daozang*, vol. 1.
Taishang shuo Chaotian xielei zhenjing 太上說朝天謝雷真經. DZ 17.
Taishang shuo Xuantian dasheng zhenwu benzhuan shenzhou miaojing 太上說玄天大聖真武本傳神呪妙經 (commentary by Chen Zhong 陳伀). DZ 754.
Taishang taiqing huanglao dijun yunlei tiantong yinfan xianjing 太上泰清皇老帝君運雷天童隱梵仙經. DZ 633.
Taishang wuji zongzhen Wenchang dadong xianjing 太上無極總真文昌大洞仙經. DZ 5.
Taishang xiuzhen tiyuan miaodaojing 太上修真體元妙道經. Postface 1261. DZ 41.
Taishang xuanling beidou benming changsheng miaojing 太上玄靈北斗本命長生妙經. DZ 623.
Taishang xuanling beidou benming yansheng zhenjing zhu 太上玄靈北斗本命延生真經註. DZ 750.
Taishang yuanshi tianzun shuo Beidi fumo shenzhou miaojing 太上元始天尊說北帝伏魔神咒妙經. DZ 1412.
Taishang yuhua dongzhang bawang dushi shengxian miaojing 太上玉華洞章拔亡度世昇仙妙經. DZ 77.
Taishang zhuguo jiumin zongzhen biyao 太上助國救民總真秘要. DZ 1227.
Taiwei xianjun gongguoge 太微仙君功過格. DZ 186.

Tianhuang zhidao taiqing yuce 天皇至道太清玉冊. Zhu Quan 朱權 (1378–1448). DZ 1483.
Weishan yinzhi 為善陰隲. 1419 edition in *Siku quanshu cunmu congshu.*
Weishu 魏書. Beijing: Zhonghua shuju, 1974.
Wenchang Dadong xianjing 文昌大洞仙經. 1840. *Zangwai daoshu*, vol. 4.
Wenchang yansijing 文昌延嗣經. JY 259.
Wendi quanshu 文帝全書. 1775 edition at Waseda University Library. Available at: https://waseda.primo.exlibrisgroup.com/discovery/.
Wendi shuchao 文帝書鈔. Compiled by Zhu Gui 朱珪 (1731–1807). 1882 reprint held by Waseda University Library.
Wendi xiaojing 文帝孝經. JY 257.
Wenshi zhenjing zhu 文始真經註. Niu Daochun 牛道淳 (fl. 1296). DZ 727.
Wuche bajin 五車拔錦. 1597 edition at Österreichische Nationalbibliothek, available online.
Wudangshan Xuantian shangdi chuixunwen 武當山玄天上帝垂訓文. Ming edition (date illegible), in *Zangwai daoshu*, vol. 22, 416–18.
Wudi huibian 武帝彙編. 1876 edition at Taiwan National Library.
Wushang xuanyuan santian yutang dafa 無上玄元三天玉堂大法. DZ 220.
Xianguo suilu 現果隨錄. X 1642.
Xianjulu 閑居録. Wu Yan 吾衍 (1272–1311). *Siku quanshu* edition.
Xiaoting zalu 嘯亭雜録. Zhaolian 昭槤 (1776–1830). Beijing: Zhonghua shuju, 1980.
Xinbian lianxiang Soushen guangji 新編連相搜神廣記. Qin Zijin 秦子晉. Late Yuan. In Wang Qiugui 王秋桂 and Li Fengmao 李豐楙, eds., *Zhongguo minjian xinyang ziliao huibian* 中國民間信仰資料彙編. 30 vols, vol. 2. Taipei: Taiwan xuesheng shuju, 1989.
Xinchu xianchuan liyuan baojuan 新出仙傳立願寶卷. 1897 edition in *Ming Qing minjian zongjiao jingjuan wenxian*, vol. 11.
Xinggui bian 醒閨編. 1861. *Fushou baozang* edition.
Xinke huiji Wanzhen miaodi jiejing 新刊彙集完真妙諦捷徑. Tianqi era (1621–27) edition at Taiwan National Library.
Xishan Xu zhenjun bashiwu hua lu 西山許真君八十五化錄. DZ 448.
(*Wanli*) *Xiushui xianzhi* (萬曆)秀水縣志. 1596, 1925 reprint.
Xiuzhen shishu 修真十書. DZ 263.
Xiuzhen xianchan 修真仙懺. In *Lüzu quanshu* (33-*juan* edition), j. 23.
Xixin yulu 洗心語錄. 1824 edition kept at the University of Chicago Library.
Xu Yijianzhi 續夷堅志. Yuan Haowen 元好問 (1190–1257). Beijing: Zhonghua shuju, 2006.
Xuantian shangdi qishenglu 玄天上帝啟聖錄. DZ 958.
Xuanzhen lingying baoqian 玄真靈應寶籤. DZ 1299.
Xuxian hanzao 徐仙翰藻. DZ 1468.
Xuxian zhenlu 徐仙真錄. DZ 1470.
Yijianzhi 夷堅志. Hong Mai 洪邁 (1123–1202). Beijing: Zhonghua shuju, 1981.
Yinju tongyi 隱居通議. Liu Xun 劉壎 (1240–1319). *Siku quanshu* edition.
Yinzhiwen zhu 陰騭文注. JY 260.
Yisheng baode zhuan 翊聖保德傳. 1016. DZ 1285.

Yixing juji 一行居集. Peng Shaosheng 彭紹升 (1740–96). 1825. Unpaginated facsimile reproduction, Taipei: Xinwenfeng, 1973.
Youhuan jiwen 游宦紀聞. Zhang Shinan 張世南 (13th c.). *Siku quanshu* edition.
Yuan dianzhang 元典章. Tianjin: Zhonghua shuju and Tianjin guji chubanshe, 2011.
Yuanhuang dadao zhenjun jiujie baojing 元皇大道真君救劫寶經. JY 258.
Yuanshi tianzun shuo Zitong dijun benyuanjing 元始天尊說梓潼帝君本願經. DZ 29.
Yuanshi tianzun shuo Zitong dijun yingyanjing 元始天尊說梓潼帝君應驗經. DZ 28.
Yuanshi wuliang duren shangpin miaojing zhujie 元始無量度人上品妙經註解. Xue Jizhao 薛季昭 (fl. 1303). DZ 92.
Yuchu xinzhi 虞初新志. Compiled by Zhang Chao 張潮. *Qingdai biji xiaoshuo daguan* 清代筆記小說大觀. Shanghai: Shanghai guji chubanshe, 2007.
Yudi jisheng 輿地紀勝. Wang Xiangzhi 王象之 (*jinshi* 1196). *Xuxiu Siku quanshu*, vol. 585.
Yuding jinke jiyao 玉定金科輯要. In vol. 12 of *Sandong shiyi* 三洞拾遺. Hefei: Huangshan shushe, 2005.
(*Jiaqing*) *Yuhang xianzhi* (嘉慶)餘杭縣志. Edited by Zhang Ji'an 張吉安 et al. *Zhongguo difangzhi jicheng – Zhejiang fuxian zhi ji*, vol. 5.
Yuju xinchan 玉局心懺. In *Wendi quanshu*, j. 38.
Yulu daguan 語錄大觀. JY 168.
Yulu jinpan 玉露金盤. In *Ming Qing minjian zongjiao jingjuan wenxian xubian*, vol. 5.
Yuncheng baolu 雲城寶錄. In *Minjian sizang: Zhongguo minjian xinyang minjian wenhua ziliao huibian* 民間私藏：中國民間信仰民間文化資料彙編, series 1. Compiled by Wang Chien-ch'uan 王見川 et al. Taipei: Boyang, 2011.
Yunji qiqian 雲笈七籤. DZ 1032.
Yunyangji 雲陽集. Li Qi 李祁 (*jinshi* 1333). *Siku quanshu* edition.
Yuquan 玉詮. JY 244.
Yuxiaji 玉匣記. Ming. DZ 1480.
Yulü baojuan 玉律寶卷. *Ming Qing minjian zongjiao jingjuan wenxian xubian*, vol. 7.
Zangwai daoshu 藏外道書. Chengdu: Bashu shushe, 1992–94, 36 vols.
Zengding Jingxinlu 增訂敬信錄. 1797 edition at Bibliothèque nationale de France. See https://gallica.bnf.fr/ark:/12148/btv1b90065479.image.
Zhang Sanfeng quanji 張三丰全集. JY 237.
Zhengao 真誥. DZ 1016.
Zhengyi fawen tianshi jiao jieke jing 正一法文天師教戒科經. DZ 789.
Zhilu baofa 指路寶筏. Undated edition in vol. 11 of *Ming Qing minjian zongjiao jingjuan wenxian*.
Zhishenlu 質神錄. Edited by Peng Shaosheng 彭紹升 (1740–96). in *Wendi quanshu*, j. 46–47.
Zhizuzhai wenji 知足齋文集. Zhu Gui 朱珪 (1731–1807). *Congshu jicheng* edition.
Zhongguo yuyan jiujie shu 中國預言救劫書彙編. Compiled by Wang Chien-ch'uan 王見川, Song Jun 宋軍, and Fan Chun-wu 范純武, 10 vols. Taipei: Xinwenfeng, 2010.
Zhonghua xu Daozang 中華續道藏. 20 vols. Taipei: Xinwenfeng, 1999.
Zhoushi mingtongji 周氏冥通記. DZ 302.
Zitong dijun huashu 梓潼帝君化書. DZ 170.

Secondary Sources

Akizuki Kan'ei 秋月觀暎. *Chūgoku kinsei dōkyō no keisei: Jōmyōdō no kisoteki kenkyū* 中國近世道教の形成：淨明道の基礎的研究. Tokyo: Sōbunsha, 1978.

Alexander, Catherine Laura Bos. "Virtues of the Vernacular: Moral Reconstruction in Late Qing Jiangnan and the Revitalization of *baojuan*." Ph.D. diss., University of Chicago, 2016.

Andersen, Poul. *The Paradox of Being: Truth, Identity, and Images in Daoism*. Cambridge: Harvard University Asia Center, 2019.

———. "Talking to the Gods: Visionary Divination in Early Taoism (the Sanhuang Tradition)." *Taoist Resources* 5, no. 1 (1994): 1–24.

———. "Tan Zixiao." In Fabrizio Pregadio, ed., *The Encyclopedia of Taoism*, 963–64. London: Routledge, 2013.

Ang, Isabelle. "Le culte de Lü Dongbin des origines jusqu'au début du XIVe siècle: Caractéristiques et transformations d'un Saint Immortel dans la Chine pré-moderne." Ph.D. diss., Université Paris VII, 1993.

———. "Le culte de Lü Dongbin sous les Song du Sud." *Journal Asiatique* 285.2 (1997): 473–507.

Baptandier, Brigitte. "Entrer en montagne pour y rêver. Le mont des Pierres et des Bambous." *Terrains*, 26 (1996): 83–98.

———. "Façonner la divinité en soi: À la recherche d'un lieu d'énonciation." (Special issue *Negotiating Transcendence / Négocier la transcendence.*) *Ethnologies* 25.1 (2003): 109–53.

Bikir, Radu. "Divination et destinée sous la dynastie Song (960–1279): Étude de la mise en scène des méthodes mantiques dans le *Yijian zhi* de Hong Mai." Ph.D. diss., Université de Paris, 2019.

Birnbaum, Raoul. "The Manifestation of a Monastery: Shen-Ying's Experiences on Mount Wu-t'ai in T'ang Context." *Journal of the American Oriental Society* 106.1 (1986): 119–37.

Bokenkamp, Stephen R. *Early Daoist Scriptures*. Berkeley: University of California Press, 1997.

———. *A Fourth-Century Daoist Family: The Zhen'gao, or Declarations of the Perfected*. Vol. 1. Berkeley: University of California Press, 2020.

———. "The Peach Flower Font and the Grotto Passage." *Journal of the American Oriental Society* 106.1 (1986): 65–77.

Boltz, Judith Magee. "On the Legacy of Zigu and a Manual on Spirit-Writing in Her Name." In Philip Clart and Paul Crowe, eds., *The People and the Dao: New Studies in Chinese Religions in Honour of Daniel L. Overmyer*, 349–88. Sankt Augustin: Monumenta Serica, 2009.

———. "Not by the Seal of Office Alone. New Weapons in Battles with the Supernatural." In Patricia Buckley Ebrey and Peter N. Gregory, eds., *Religion and Society in T'ang and Sung China*, 241–305. Honolulu: University of Hawai'i Press, 1993.

Brokaw, Cynthia J. *The Ledgers of Merit and Demerit: Social Change and Moral Order in Late Imperial China*. Princeton: Princeton University Press, 1991.

Bujard, Marianne. "Le culte de Wangzi Qiao ou la longue carrière d'un immortel." *Etudes chinoises* 19.1–2 (2000): 115–58.

Burton-Rose, Daniel. "Establishing a Literati Spirit-Writing Altar in Early Qing Suzhou: The *Optimus* Prophecy of Peng Dingqiu (1645–1719)." *T'oung Pao* 106.3–4 (2020): 358–400.

———. "Mid-Qing Spirit-Altars, Officialdom, and Patrilineal Power: Peng Qifeng's Prefaces to the Complete Works of Thearch Guan, Patriarch Lü, and Wenchang (1772–1775)," *Daojiao xuekan* 道教學刊, 3 (2019): 130–56.

———. "A Prolific Spirit: Peng Dingqiu's Posthumous Career on the Spirit Altar, 1720–1906," *Daoism: Religion, History and Society* 道教研究學報, 7 (2015): 7–63.

———. "Terrestrial Reward as Divine Recompense: The Self-Fashioned Piety of the Peng Lineage of Suzhou, 1650s–1870s." Ph.D. diss., Princeton University, 2016.

Bussio, Jennifer J. "Neither Dust nor Gold: A Comprehensive Study of the Dadao School from 1115–1398." Ph.D. diss., Arizona State University, 2017.

Cahill, Suzanne E. "Taoism at the Sung Court: The Heavenly Text Affair of 1008." *Bulletin of Sung-Yüan Studies*, 16 (1980): 23–44.

Campany, Robert F. "Buddhist Revelation and Taoist Translation in Early Medieval China." *Taoist Resources* 4.1 (1993): 1–29.

———. *The Chinese Dreamscape, 300 BCE–800 CE*. Cambridge: Harvard University Asia Center, 2020.

———. "Return-from-death Narratives in Early Medieval China," *Journal of Chinese Religions* 18.1 (1990): 91–125.

———. *Signs From the Unseen Realm: Buddhist Miracle Tales from Early Medieval China*. Honolulu: University of Hawai'i Press, 2012.

———. *To Live as Long as Heaven and Earth: A Translation and Study of Ge Hong's Traditions of Divine Transcendents*. Berkeley: University of California Press, 2002.

Capitanio, Joshua. "Ritual and Self-Cultivation in the Daoist Practice of 'Oblatory Refinement.'" *Numen* 67.1 (2019): 29–72.

Chao Shin-yi. *Daoist Ritual, State Religion, and Popular Practices: Zhenwu Worship from Song to Ming (960–1644)*. London: Routledge, 2011.

Chao Wei-pang. "The Origin and Growth of the Fu Chi," *Folklore Studies*, 1 (1942): 9–27.

Chen Yuan 陳垣. *Nan Song chu Hebei xin daojiao kao* 南宋初河北新道教考. Beijing: Zhonghua shuju, 1962 [1941].

Clart, Philip. "Anchoring Guanyin: Appropriative Strategies in a New Phoenix Hall Scripture." *Min-su chü-i* 民俗曲藝, 173 (2011): 101–28.

———. "Confucius and the Mediums: Is there a 'Popular Confucianism'?" *T'oung Pao*, 89 (2003): 1–38.

———. "The *Mingxin baojuan* (Precious Mirror for Enlightening the Mind) and Its Transmission in the West." In *Ming Qing yilai shanshu congbian*, 1: 13–29.

———. "Moral Mediums: Spirit-Writing and the Cultural Construction of Chinese Spirit-Mediumship" *Ethnologies* 25.1 (2003): 153–89.

———. "Text and Context in the Study of Spirit-Writing Cults: A Methodological Reflection on the Relationship of Ethnography and Philology." In Philip Clart, David Ownby, and Wang Chien-chuan, eds., *Text and Context in the Modern History of Chinese Religions. Redemptive Societies and their Sacred Texts*, 309–22. Leiden: Brill, 2020.

———, and Vincent Goossaert. "Spirit Writing." In Stephan Kory, ed., *IKGF Handbook of Chinese Divination Techniques*. Forthcoming.

———, and Gregory Adam Scott, eds. *Religious Publishing and Print Culture in Modern China, 1800–2012*. Boston: de Gruyter, 2015.

Cole, James H. *The People Versus the Taipings: Bao Lisheng's "Righteous Army of Dongan."* Berkeley: Institute of East Asian Studies, 1981.

Csikszentmihalyi, Mark. "Traditional Taxonomies and Revealed Texts in the Han." In Livia Kohn and Harold D. Roth, eds., *Daoist Identity: History, Lineage and Ritual*, 81–101. Honolulu: University of Hawai'i Press, 2002.

Davis, Edward L. "Arms and the Tao, 1: Hero Cult and Empire in Traditional China." In *Sōdai no shakai to shūkyō* 宋代の社会と宗教, 1–56. Tokyo: Kyūko shoin, 1985.

———. "Arms and the Tao, 2: The Xu Brothers in Tea Country." In Livia Kohn and Harold D. Roth, eds., *Daoist Identity: History, Lineage and Ritual*, 149–64. Honolulu: University of Hawai'i Press, 2002.

———. *Society and the Supernatural in Song China*. Honolulu: University of Hawai'i Press, 2001.

De Bruyn, Pierre-Henry. *Le Wudang shan: Histoire des récits fondateurs*. Paris: Les Indes savantes, 2010.

Dean, Kenneth. *Lord of the Three in One: The Spread of a Cult in Southeast China*. Princeton: Princeton University Press, 1998.

———. *Taoist Ritual and Popular Cults of Southeast China*. Princeton: Princeton University Press, 1993.

Drewes, David. "Dharmabhāṇakas in Early Mahāyāna." *Indo-Iranian Journal* 54.4 (2011): 331–72.

Edgerton-Tarpley, Kathryn. *Tears from Iron: Cultural Responses to Famine in Nineteenth-Century China*. Berkeley: University of California Press, 2008.

Espesset, Grégoire. "Cosmologie et tri fonctionnalité dans l'idéologie du *Livre de la Grande paix* (*Taiping jing*)." Ph.D. diss., Université Paris VII, 2002.

———. "Latter Han Religious Mass Movements and the Early Daoist Church." In John Lagerwey and Marc Kalinowski, eds., *Early Chinese Religion. Part One: Shang through Han (1250 BC–220 AD)*, 1061–1102. Leiden: Brill, 2009.

———. "La religiosité de l'Autre. Essai sur les représentations religieuses en Chine au haut Moyen-Âge et leur interprétation sinologique," mémoire inédit présenté pour une soutenance de HDR, EPHE, 2019.

Esposito, Monica. *Creative Daoism*. Wil / Paris: UniversityMedia, 2013.

———. "The Discovery of Jiang Yuanting's *Daozang Jiyao* in Jiangnan. A Presentation of the Taoist Canon of the Qing Dynasty." In Mugitani Kunio 麥谷邦夫, ed., *Kōnan dōkyō no kenkyū* 江南道教の研究, 79–110. Kyoto: Jinbun kagaku kenkyūjo, 2007.

———. "The Invention of a Quanzhen Canon: The Wondrous Fate of the *Daozang jiyao*." In Liu Xun and Vincent Goossaert, eds., *Quanzhen Daoists in Chinese Society and Culture, 1500–2010*, 44–77. Berkeley: Institute of East Asian Studies, 2013.

———. "La Porte du dragon: L'école Longmen du mont Jin'gai et ses pratiques alchimiques d'après le *Daozang xubian* (Suite au canon taoïste)." Ph.D. diss., Université Paris VII, 1993.

Fan Chun-wu 范純武. "Bade: Jindai Zhongguo jiushi tuanti de daode leimu yu shijian 八德:近代中國救世團體的道德類目與實踐." In Paul R. Katz and Vincent Goossaert, eds., *Gaibian Zhongguo zongjiao de wushinian* 改變中國宗教的五十年, 1898–1948, 225–59. Taipei: Academia Sinica, Institute of Modern History, 2015.

———, ed. *Fuluan wenhua yu minzhong zongjiao guoji xueshu yantaohui lunwenji* 扶鸞文化與民眾宗教國際學術研討會論文集. Taipei: Boyang, 2020.

———. "Jinxiandai Zhongguo fojiao yu fuji 近現代中國佛教與扶乩." *Yuanguang foxue xuebao* 圓光佛學學報, 3, 1999, 261–91.

———. *Qingmo minjian cishan shiye yu luantang yundong* 清末民間慈善事業與鸞堂運動. Taipei: Boyang, 2015.

Fuma Susumu 夫馬進. *Chūgoku zenkai zendōshi kenkyū* 中国善会善堂史研究. Kyoto: Dohosha shuppan, 1997.

Ganany, Noga. "Origin Narratives: Reading and Reverence in Late-Ming China." Ph.D. diss., Columbia University, 2018.

Gao Zhenhong 高振宏. "Chaofeng, daofeng yu minfeng: cong sange lizi tan fengchi dui shenqi xinyang de xingsu yingxiang 朝封、道封與民封：從三個例子談封敕對神祇信仰的形塑與影響." *Huaren zongjiao yanjiu* 華人宗教研究, 9 (2017): 45–77.

Goossaert, Vincent. "1919, shijie de mori. Wusi shiqi de jiujie lunshu 1919 世界的末日.五四時期的救劫論述." In Lü Miaofen 呂妙芬 and Paul Katz 康豹, eds., *Wusi yundong yu Zhongguo zongjiao de diaoshi yu fazhan* 五四運動與中國宗教的調適與發展, 315–36. Taipei: Academia Sinica, 2020.

———. "Animals and Eschatology in the Nineteenth-Century Discourse." In Roel Sterckx, Martina Siebert, and Dagmar Schäfer, eds., *Animals through Chinese History*, 181–98. Cambridge: Cambridge University Press, 2019.

———. *Bureaucratie et salut. Devenir un dieu en Chine*. Genève: Labor & Fides, 2017.

———. "Competing Eschatological Scenarios during the Taiping War, 1851–1864." In Hans-Christian Lehner, ed., *The End(s) of Time(s): Apocalypticism, Messianism, and Utopianism*, 269–306. Leiden: Brill, 2021.

———. "Daoism and Local Cults in Modern Suzhou: A Case Study of Qionglongshan." In Philip Clart, ed., *Chinese and European Perspectives on the Study of Chinese Popular Religion(s)* 中國民間宗教民間信仰研究之中歐視角, 199–228. Taipei: Boyang, 2012.

———. "*Daojiao yuanliu*, the History and Uses of a Late Imperial Daoist Primer." *Harvard Journal of Asiatic Studies*, forthcoming.

———. "Divine Codes, Spirit-Writing, and the Ritual Foundations of Morality Books." *Asia Major*, 3rd series 33.1 (2020): 1–31.

———. "Guérison, révélation et société locale: Gaochun en 1900," *Etudes Chinoises*, forthcoming.

———. "Guerre, violence et eschatologie. Interprétations religieuses de la guerre des Taiping (1851–1864)." In Jean Baechler, ed., *Guerre et Religion*, 81–94. Paris: Hermann, 2016.

———. "The Heavenly Master, Canonization, and the Daoist Construction of Local Religion in Late Imperial Jiangnan." *Cahiers d'Extrême-Asie*, 20 (2011): 229–45.

———. *Heavenly Masters: Two Thousand Years of the Daoist State*. Honolulu: University of Hawai'i Press and Hong Kong: Chinese University Press, 2021.

———. "Inner Alchemy and Eschatology." Forthcoming.

———. *L'Interdit du boeuf en Chine: Agriculture, éthique et sacrifice*. Paris: Collège de France, Institut des hautes études chinoises, 2005.

———. "The Jin'gaishan Network." In Vincent Goossaert and Liu Xun, eds., *Daoism in*

Modern China: Clerics and Temples in Urban Transformations, 1860–Present, 83–119. London: Routledge, 2021.

———. "Late Imperial Chinese Piety Books," *Studies in Chinese Religions* 5.1 (2019): 38–54.

———, ed. and trans. *Livres de morale révélés par les dieux*. Paris: Les Belles Lettres, 2012.

———. "Modern Daoist Eschatology. Spirit-Writing and Elite Soteriology in Late Imperial China." *Daoism: Religion, History and Society* 道教研究學報, 6 (2014): 219–46.

———. "A Question of Control: Licensing Local Ritual Specialists in Jiangnan, 1850–1950." In Paul R. Katz and Liu Shufen 劉淑分, eds., *Xinyang, shijian yu wenhua tiaoshi. Papers from the Religion Section of the Fourth International Conference on Sinology* 信仰、實踐與文化調適. 第四屆國際漢學會議論文集, 569–604. Taipei: Academia Sinica, 2013.

———. "Ritual Techniques for Creating a Divine Persona in Late Imperial China: The Case of Daoist Law Enforcer Lord Wang," *Journal of Chinese Religions*, forthcoming.

———. "Scorched Head Daoists. Exorcist Priests and Divine Generals in Jiangnan Lore," forthcoming.

———. "La sexualité dans les livres de morale chinois." In Florence Rochefort and Maria Eleonora Sanna, eds., *Normes religieuses et genre : Mutations, résistances et reconfiguration, xixe–xxie siècle*, 37–46. Paris: Armand Colin, 2013.

———. *Spirit-Writing and Elite Religiosity in Modern Jiangnan*. Work in progress.

———. "Spirit-Writing, Canonization and the Rise of Divine Saviors: Wenchang, Lüzu, and Guandi, 1700–1858." *Late Imperial China* 36.2 (2015): 82–125.

———. *The Taoists of Peking, 1800–1949: A Social History of Urban Clerics*. Cambridge: Harvard University Asia Center, 2007.

———. "The Textual Canonization of Guandi." In Barbara Hoster, Dirk Kuhlmann, and Zbigniew Wesołowski, eds., *Rooted in Hope / In der Hoffnung verwurzelt: Festschrift in Honor of Roman Malek S.V.D. on the Occasion of His 65th Birthday*, 509–26. Sankt Augustin: Monumenta Serica, 2017.

———. *Vies des saints exorcistes : Hagiographies taoïstes, 11e–16e siècles*. Paris: Les Belles Lettres, 2021.

———. "Yu Yue (1821–1906) Explores the Other World: Religious Culture of the Chinese Elites on the Eve of the Revolutions." In Hsun Chang and Benjamin Penny, eds., *Religion in Taiwan and China: Locality and Transmission*, 59–107. Taipei: Academia Sinica, Institute of Ethnology, 2017.

Goyama Kiwamu 合山究. *Min Shin jidai no josei to bungaku* 明清時代の女性と文学. Tokyo: Kyūko Shoin, 2006.

Greene, Eric M. *Chan Before Chan: Meditation, Repentance, and Visionary Experience in Chinese Buddhism*. Honolulu: University of Hawai'i Press, 2021.

———. "Meditation, Repentance, and Visionary Experience in Early Medieval Chinese Buddhism." Ph.D. diss., University of California Berkeley, 2012.

Gummer, Natalie D. "Listening to the Dharmabhāṇaka: The Buddhist Preacher in and of the *Sūtra of Utmost Golden Radiance*." *Journal of the American Academy of Religion* 80.1 (2012): 137–60.

Guy, R. Kent. *The Emperor's Four Treasuries: Scholars and the State in the Late Ch'ien-lung Era*. Harvard East Asian Monographs 129. Cambridge: The Council on East Asian Studies, 1987.

Handlin Smith, Joanna F. *The Art of Doing Good: Charity in Late Ming China*. Berkeley: University of California Press, 2009.

He Lei 何蕾. "Songdai 'jixian' shi kaolun 宋代"箕仙"诗考论." *Zongjiaoxue yanjiu* 宗教学研究, 2 (2017): 259–67.

Hendrischke, Barbara. *The Scripture on Great Peace: The Taiping Jing and the Beginnings of Daoism*. Berkeley: University of California Press, 2007.

Hsieh Shu-wei. "Writing from Heaven: Celestial Writing in Six Dynasties Daoism." Ph.D. diss., Indiana University, 2005.

Hsieh Ts'ung-hui 謝聰輝. "Ming Qing *Yuhuang benxing jijing* zhong Lüzu jianggao yanjiu 明清玉皇本行集經呂祖降誥研究." *Daoism: Religion, History and Society* 道教研究學報, 6 (2015): 201–21.

———. *Xin tiandi zhi ming: Yuhuang, Zitong yu feiluan* 新天帝之命：玉皇、梓潼與飛鸞. Taipei: Shangwu yinshuguan, 2013.

———. "*Yuhuang benxing jijing* chushi de beijing yu yinyuan yanjiu《玉皇本行集經》出世的背景與因緣研究." *Daoism: History, Religion and Society* 道教研究學報, 1 (2009): 155–99.

Hu Jiechen 胡劼辰. "'Bilu' gouchen: Qingdai Wenchang xinyang lei fuji shijian yanjiu「筆籙」鉤沉—清代文昌信仰類扶乩實踐研究." Paper delivered at 2016 Inaugural Joint Renmin-Rutgers International Daoist Studies Conference. Pingjiang, Hunan, China, July 29–August 1, 2016.

———. "*Lüzu quanshu* yu *Wendi quanshu* bianzuanzhe Liu Qiao xiaokao《吕祖全书》与《文帝全书》编纂者刘樵小考." *Daojiao xuekan* 道教学刊, 5 (2020): 66–80.

———. "Qingdai liuzhong Wendi lei quanshu de chubanshi yanjiu 清代六種文帝類全書的出版史研究." *Bulletin of the Institute of History and Philology Academia Sinica*, 91 (2020): 227–92.

———. "Terminology and Typology of Spirit-Writing in Early Modern China: A Preliminary Study." In Valussi and Schumann, eds., *Spirit-Writing in Chinese History*, forthcoming.

———. "*Wenchang dijun yinzhiwen* qiyuan xinyan: yi *Weishan yinzhi*, *Quanxing yinzhiwen* yiji *Zitong dijun jiujie baozhang* wei zhongxin《文昌帝君陰騭文》起源新研：以《為善陰騭》、《勸行陰騭文》以及《梓潼帝君救劫寶章》為中心." *Lishi, yishu yu Taiwan renwen luncong* 歷史、藝術與台灣人文論叢, 11 (2017): 133–69.

———. "*Wendi quanshu* yanjiu: Qingdai Wenchang dijun xinyang de wenxianshi《文帝全書》研究：清代文昌帝君信仰的文獻史." Ph.D. diss., Chinese University of Hong Kong, 2017.

———. "Xu Qian (1776–1864) xiaokao: Fuji, jiangxue yu shanshu chuangzhi 徐謙 (1776–1864) 小考：扶乩、講學與善書創製." In Fan Chun-wu, ed., *Fuluan wenhua yu minzhong zongjiao guoji xueshu yantaohui lunwenji*, 89–143.

———. "Zailun fuji de fangfa yu leixing: zhaji erze 再論扶乩的方法與類型：劄記二則." *Shanshu, jingjuan yu wenxian* 善書、經卷與文獻, 3 (2020) : 131–52.

Hughes, April D. "Re-examining the *Zhengming Jing*: The Social and Political Life of an Apocryphal Maitreya Scripture." *Journal of Chinese Religions* 45.1 (2017): 1–18.

Hummel, Arthur W. *Eminent Chinese of the Ch'ing Period*. Washington DC: US Government Printing Office, 1943.

Hureau, Sylvie. "Translations, Apocrypha, and the Emergence of the Buddhist Canon." In John Lagerwey and Lü Pengzhi, eds., *Early Chinese Religion. Part Two: The Period of Division (220–589 AD)*, 741–74. Leiden: Brill, 2010.

Hymes, Robert. *Way and Byway: Taoism, Local Religion, and Models of Divinity in Sung and Modern China*. Berkeley: University of California Press, 2002.

Idema, Wilt. *Personal Salvation and Filial Piety: Two Precious Scroll Narratives of Guanyin and Her Acolytes*. Honolulu: University of Hawai'i Press, 2008.

Jansen, Thomas. "Sectarian Religions and Globalization in Nineteenth-Century China: The *Wanbao baojuan* 萬寶寶卷 (1858) and Other Examples." In Thomas Jansen, Thoralf Klein, and Christian Meyer, eds., *Globalization and the Making of Religious Modernity in China*. 115–35. Leiden, Boston: Brill, 2014.

Jordan, David K., and Daniel Overmyer. *The Flying Phoenix: Aspects of Chinese Sectarianism in Taiwan*. Princeton: Princeton University Press, 1986.

Kalinowski, Marc. "La littérature divinatoire dans le Daozang." *Cahiers d'Extrême-Asie*, 5 (1989) : 85–114.

Katz, Paul R. *Images of the Immortal: The Cult of Lü Dongbin at the Palace of Eternal Joy*. Honolulu: University of Hawai'i Press, 1999.

———. "Spirit-Writing Halls and the Development of Local Communities: A Case Study of Puli (Nantou County)." *Min-su chü-i* 民俗曲藝, 174 (2011): 103–84.

———, and Vincent Goossaert. *The Fifty Years That Changed Chinese Religion*, 1898–1948. Ann Arbor: AAS, 2021.

Kim Jaeyoon. "The Heaven and Earth Society and the Red Turban Rebellion in late Qing China." *Journal of Humanities and Social Sciences* 3.1 (2009): 1–35.

Kim Jihyun. "Enlightenment on the Spirit-Altar: Eschatology and Restoration of Morality at the King Kwan Shrine in *Fin de siècle* Seoul." *Religions*, 11 (2020): no page numbers.

———. "The Invention of Traditions: With a Focus on Innovations in the *Scripture of the Great Cavern* in Ming-Qing Daoism." *Daoism: Religion, History and Society* 道教研究學報, 7 (2015): 63–115.

King, Michelle T. *Between Birth and Death: Female Infanticide in Nineteenth-Century China*. Stanford: Stanford University Press, 2014.

Kleeman, Terry F. *Celestial Masters. History and Ritual in Early Daoist Communities*. Cambridge: Harvard University Asia Center, 2016.

———. "The Expansion of the Wen-ch'ang Cult." In Patricia Buckley Ebrey and Peter N. Gregory, eds., *Religion and Society in T'ang and Sung China*, 45–73. Honolulu: University of Hawai'i Press, 1993.

———. *A God's Own Tale: The Book of Transformations of Wenchang, the Divine Lord of Zitong*. Albany: State University of New York Press, 1994.

Kohn, Livia. *God of the Dao: Lord Lao in History and Myth*. Ann Arbor: Center for the Chinese Studies, University of Michigan, 1998.

Lackner, Michael. "Between Belief and Disbelief: Ji Yun 紀昀 on Spirit-Writing and the Mantic Practices." In Valussi and Schumann, eds., *Spirit-Writing in Chinese History*, forthcoming.

———, and Zhao Lu, eds. *Handbook of Prognostication and Prediction in China*. Leiden: Brill, forthcoming.

Lagerwey, John. "Introduction." In John Lagerwey and Lü Pengzhi, eds., *Early Chinese Religion: Part Two: The Period of Division (220–589 AD)*, 1–50. Leiden: Brill, 2010.

———. "Introduction: Special Issue on the Emergence of a Temple-Centric Society," *Min-su chü-i* 民俗曲藝, 205 (2019): 1–27.

———. "The Ming Dynasty Double Orthodoxy: Daoxue and Daojiao." *Cahiers d'Extrême-Asie*, 25 (2016): 113–29.

Lai Chi Tim 黎志添. "The Cult of Spirit-Writing in the Qing: The Daoist Dimension." *Journal of Daoist Studies*, 8 (2015): 112–33.

———, ed. *Daozang jiyao tiyao* 道藏輯要·提要. Hong Kong: Chinese University Press, 2021.

———. "*Lüzu quanshu zhengzong*: Qingdai Beijing Jueyuantan de lishi jiqi Lüzu Tianxianpai xinyang 《呂祖全書正宗》- 清代北京覺源壇的歷史及其呂祖天仙派信仰." *Zhongguo wenzhe yanjiu jikan* 中國文哲研究集刊, 46 (2015): 101–49.

———. "Ming Qing daojiao Lüzu jiangji xinyang de fazhan ji xiangguan wenren jitan yanjiu 明清道教呂祖降乩信仰的發展及相關文人乩壇研究." *Journal of Chinese Studies* 中國文化研究所學報, 65 (2017): 139–79.

———. "Qingdai sizhong *Lüzu quanshu* yu Lüzu fuji daotan de guanxi 清代四種《呂祖全書》與呂祖扶乩道壇的關係." *Zhongguo wenzhe yanjiu jikan* 中國文哲研究集刊, 42 (2013): 183–230.

———. "Revisiting the Jingming Origin of the *Taiyi jinhua zongzhi*: Pan Jingguan and His Spirit-Writing Community in Changzhou during the Early Qing." *Cahiers d'Extrême-Asie*, 25 (2016): 45–75.

Lamouroux, Christian. "Rites, espaces et finances : la recomposition de la souveraineté dans la Chine du 11e siècle." *Annales. Histoire, Sciences Sociales* 51.2 (1996): 275–305.

Li Jiajun 李家駿. "*Lüzu quanshu* yanjiu: cong Liu Tishu *Lüzu quanshu* de bianji he yingxiang tantao Qingdai Lüzu daotan de xinyang tese 《呂祖全書》研究：從劉體恕《呂祖全書》的編集和影響探討清代呂祖道壇的信仰特色." Ph.D. diss., Chinese University of Hong Kong, 2012.

Li Shiwei 李世偉. "Jindai Guanyin jiujie shanshu de xingzhi yu neihan 近代觀音救劫善書的形制與內涵." In Wang Chien-ch'uan 王見川, ed., *Lishi, yishu yu Taiwan renwen luncong* 歷史、藝術與台灣人文論叢, 9:295–324. Taipei: Boyang, 2016.

———. "Mojie jiejiu—cong Guanyin jiujie shanshu tantao Guanyin xinyang zhi minjianhua 末劫解救—從觀音救劫善書探討觀音信仰之民間化." *Xin shiji zongjiao yanjiu* 新世紀宗教研究 16.2 (2017): 197–230.

Li Shiyu 李世瑜. *Xiandai Huabei mimi zongjiao* 現代華北秘密宗教. Taipei: Guting shuwu, 1975.

Li, Thomas Shiyu, and Susan Naquin. "The Baoming Temple: Religion and the Throne in Ming and Qing China." *Harvard Journal of Asiatic Studies* 48.1 (1988): 131–88.

Li Yi 李冀. "*Taishang ganyingpian* wenben laiyuan jiqi chengshu shijian kaoxi《太上感应篇》文本来源及其成书时间考析." *Zongjiaoxue yanjiu* 宗教学研究, 1 (2017): 111–19.

Li Yongping 李永平. "Shenshou tianshu yu daisheng liyan: baojuan laiyuan de renleixue jiedu, yi *Xiangshan baojuan* wei zhongxin de kaocha 神授天书与代圣立言：宝卷来源的人类学解读—以《香山宝卷》为中心的考察." *Minsu yanjiu* 民俗研究, 6 (2012): 63–74.

Li Zhihong 李志鸿. *Daojiao Tianxin zhengfa yanjiu* 道教天心正法研究. Beijing: Shehui kexue wenxian chubanshe, 2011.

Liang Qizi (Angela Leung) 梁其姿. "Daotang hu? Shantang hu? Qingmo Minchu Guangzhou chengnei Xingong caotang de dute moshi 道堂乎?善堂乎?清末民初廣州城內省躬草堂的獨特模式." In Chen Yung-fa 陳永發, ed., *Ming-Qing diguoji qi jinxiandai zhuanxing* 明清帝國及其近現代轉型, 395–434. Taipei: Yunchen congkan, 2011.

———. *Shishan yu jiaohua. Ming Qing de cishan zuzhi* 施善與教化. 明清的慈善組織. Zhangjiakou: Hebei jiaoyu chubanshe, 2001 [1997].

Lin Fu-shih. "Shamans and Politics." In John Lagerwey and Lü Pengzhi, eds., *Early Chinese Religion. Part Two: The Period of Division (220–589 AD)*. Leiden: Brill, 2010, 275–318.

Lin Xiaohan 林小涵. "Zhenhuan zhijian—Huang Zhouxing de zongjiao shuxie yu yimin yishi 真幻之間–黃周星的宗教書寫與遺民意識." *Hanxue yanjiu* 漢學研究 34.2 (2016): 73–106.

Liu Shufen. "The Return of the State: On the Significance of Buddhist Epigraphy and Its Geographic Distribution." In John Lagerwey and Lü Pengzhi, eds., *Early Chinese Religion. Part Two: The Period of Division (220–589 AD)*, 319–42. Leiden: Brill, 2010.

Liu Xun. "Immortals and Patriarchs: The Daoist World of a Manchu Official and His Family in Nineteenth Century China." *Asia Major*, 3rd series 17.2 (2004): 161–218.

———. "An Intoning Immortal at the West Lake: Chen Wenshu and his Daoist Pursuits in Late Qing Jiangnan." *Cahiers d'Extrême-Asie*, 25 (2016): 77–111.

———. "Of Poems, Gods, and Spirit-Writing Altars: The Daoist Beliefs and Practice of Wang Duan (1793–1839)." *Late Imperial China* 36.2 (2015): 23–81.

Liu Yi 劉屹. "Myth and History: The Contribution of Six Dynasties Daoism to the Formation of the Image of the Heavenly Master Zhang Daoling." In Florian C. Reiter, ed., *Purposes, Means, and Convictions in Daoism: A Berlin Symposium*, 57–82. Wiesbaden: Harrassowitz Verlag, 2007.

Luk Crystal Tsing-Tsing 陸晶晶. "Fuji xinyang dui Qingdai daojiao yixue de tuidong yu yingxiang – yi *Yidao huanyuan* wei zhongxin de yanjiu 扶乩信仰對清代道教醫學的推動與影響—以《醫道還元》為中心的研究." *Daoism: Religion, History and Society* 道教研究學報, 10 (2018): 177–220.

Marsone, Pierre. *Wang Chongyang (1113–1170) et la fondation du Quanzhen: ascètes taoïstes et alchimie intérieure*. Paris: Collège de France, 2010.

Maruyama Hiroshi 丸山宏. "Qingchao Daoguang nianjian Jin'gaishan Lüzu daotan suo chuangzao zhi jingdian chutan: yi *Yuqing zanhua jiutian yanzheng xinyin jijing*, *Yuqing zanhua jiutian yanzheng xinyin baochan* wei zhongxin zhi tantao 清朝道光年間金蓋山呂祖道壇所創造之經典初探：以《玉清贊化九天演政心印集經》、《玉清贊化九天演政心印寶懺》為中心之探討." *Daoism: Religion, History and Society* 道教研究學報, 7 (2015): 171–200.

Mayer, Robert. "Rethinking Treasure (Part One)," *Revue d'Études Tibétaines*, 52 (2019): 119–84.

Meinert, Carmen. "Embodying the Divine in Tantric Ritual Practice: Examples from the Chinese Karakhoto Manuscripts from the Tangut Empire (ca. 1038–1227)." *Revue d'Etudes Tibétaines*, 50 (2019): 56–72.

Meulenbeld, Mark R. E. *Demonic Warfare: Daoism, Territorial Networks, and the History of a Ming Novel*. Honolulu: University of Hawai'i Press, 2015.

Meyer, Christian, ed. *The Concept of Ling: Between Efficacy and Spirituality*. Work in progress.

Meyer-Fong, Tobie. "To Know the Enemy: The *Zei qing huizuan*, Military Intelligence, and the Taiping War." *T'oung Pao*, 104 (2018): 384–423.

———. *What Remains: Coming to Terms with Civil War in 19th Century China*. Stanford: Stanford University Press, 2013.

Mollier, Christine. *Une apocalypse taoïste du Vè siècle* (*le livre des incantations divines des grottes abyssales*). Paris: Institut des hautes études chinoises, 1990.

———. "La méthode de l'empereur du nord du mont Fengdu: Une tradition exorciste du Taoïsme médiéval." *T'oung Pao*, 83 (1997): 329–85.

Mori Yuria 森由利亜. "*Dōzō shūyō* to Shō Yoho no Ryoso fukei shinkō 道蔵輯要と蔣予蒲の呂祖扶乩信仰." *Tōhō shūkyō* 東方宗教, 98 (2001): 33–52.

———. "Identity and Lineage: The *Taiyi jinhua zongzhi* and the Spirit-Writing Cult to Patriarch Lü in Qing China." In Livia Kohn and Harold D. Roth, eds., *Daoist Identity: History, Lineage, and Ritual*, 165–84. Honolulu: University of Hawai'i Press, 2002.

———. "Ryo Dōhin to Zenshinkyō: Shinchō koshū Kingaisan no jirei o chūshin ni 呂洞賓と全真教—清朝湖州金蓋山の事例を中心に." In Sunayama Minoru 砂山稔 et al., eds., *Kōza Dōkyō daiichikan: Dōkyō no kamigami to kyōten* 講座道教第一巻:道教の神々と経典, 242–64. Tokyo: Yūzan kaku, 1999.

———. "Shō Yoho no Ryoso fukei shinkō to Zenshinkyō 蔣予蒲の呂祖扶乩信仰と全真教." In Horiike Nobuo 堀池信夫 and Sunayama Minoru 砂山稔, eds., *Dōkyō kenkyū no saisentan* 道教研究の最先端, 82–108. Tokyo: Taiga shobō, 2006.

Mozias, Ilia. "Immortals and Alchemists: Spirit-Writing and Self-Cultivation in Ming Daoism." *Journal of Daoist Studies*, 11 (2018): 83–107.

———. *The Literati Path to Immortality: The Alchemical Teachings of Lu Xixing*. St. Petersburg, FL: Three Pines Press, 2020.

Mozina, David. *Knotting the Banner: Ritual and Relationship in Daoist Practice*. Honolulu: University of Hawai'i Press, 2021.

———. "Living Redactions: The Salvationist Roots of Daoist Practice in Central Hunan." *Daoism: Religion, History and Society* 道教研究學報, 11 (2019): 1–61.

———. "Oaths and Curses in Divine Empyrean Practice." *Journal of Chinese Religions* 48.1 (2020): 31–58.

Orzech, Charles, Henrik Sørensen, and Richard Payne, eds. *Esoteric Buddhism and the Tantras in East Asia*. Leiden: Brill, 2010.

Overmyer, Daniel L. *Precious Volumes: An Introduction to Chinese Sectarian Scriptures from the Sixteenth and Seventeenth Centuries*. Cambridge: Harvard University Asia Center, 1999.

Ownby, David. "Redemptive Societies in China's Twentieth Century." In John Lagerwey, Jan Kiely, and Vincent Goossaert, eds., *Modern Chinese Religion, 1850–2015*, 685–728. Leiden: Brill, 2015.

———. "Text and Context: A Tale of Two Masters," in Philip Clart, David Ownby, and Wang Chien-chuan, eds., *Text and Context in the Modern History of Chinese Religions: Redemptive Societies and their Sacred Texts*, 173–216. Leiden: Brill, 2020.

———, Ji Zhe, and Vincent Goossaert, eds. *Making Saints in Modern China: Profiles in Religious Leadership*. New York: Oxford University Press, 2017.

Pan Junliang. "A la recherche de l'unité. Religion, société et politique du haut moyen-âge chinois (IIIe-VIe siècles de notre ère) au prisme du phénomène de la possession." Ph.D. diss., EPHE, 2013.

Pettit, J. E. E., and Matthew Wells. "Revelation in Early Daoist Hagiography: A Study of The Traditions of Lord Pei." *Asia Major*, 3rd series 33.2 (2020): 1–24.

Platt, Stephen R. *Autumn in the Heavenly Kingdom: China, the West, and the Epic Story of the Taiping Civil War*. New York: Knopf, 2012.

Pregadio, Fabrizio, ed. *The Encyclopedia of Taoism*. London: Routledge, 2013.

———. *Great Clarity: Daoism and Alchemy in Early Medieval China*. Stanford: Stanford University Press, 2006.

———. "The Man-Bird Mountain. Writing, Prophecy, and Revelation in Early China." *International Journal of Divination and Prognostication*, 2 (2021): 29–82.

———. *The Way of the Golden Elixir: An Introduction to Taoist Alchemy*. Mountain View: Golden Elixir Press, 2014.

Puett, Michael J. "Becoming Laozi: Cultivating and Vizualizing Spirits in Early-Medieval China," *Asia Major*, 3rd series 23.1 (2010): 223–52.

———. "Humans, Spirits, and Sages in Chinese Late Antiquity: Ge Hong's Master Who Embraces Simplicity (*Baopuzi*)." *Extrême-Orient, Extrême-Occident*, 29 (2007): 95–119.

Robinet, Isabelle. *La révélation du Shangqing dans l'histoire du taoïsme*. Paris: Ecole française d'Extrême-Orient, 1984.

Robson, James. "Signs of Power: Talismanic Writing in Chinese Buddhism" *History of Religions* 48.2 (2008): 130–69.

Rols, Johan. "Les interdits de destruction de la faune et de la flore de l'Antiquité tardive au haut Moyen-Âge chinois." Ph.D. diss., EPHE, 2020.

Russell, Terence C. "Chen Tuan at Mount Huangbo: A Spirit-Writing Cult in Late Ming China." *Asiatische Studien* 44.1 (1990): 107–40.

Sakai Norifumi 酒井規史. "Sōdai dōkyō ni okeru dōhō no kenkyū 宋代道教における道法の研究." Ph.D. diss., Waseda University, 2011.

Sakai Tadao 酒井忠夫. *Zōho Chūgoku zensho no kenkyū 增補中國善書の研究*. Tokyo: Kokusho kankōkai, 1999.

Schachter, Bony Braga. "Nanji Chongxu Miaodao Zhenjun: The *Tianhuang zhidao taiqing yuce* and Zhu Quan's (1378–1448) Apotheosis as a Daoist God." Ph.D. diss., Chinese University of Hong Kong, 2018.

———. "Printing the Dao: Master Zhou Xuanzhen, The Editorial History of the *Jade Slips of Great Clarity* and Ming Quanzhen Identity." *Daoism: History, Religion, and Society* 道教研究學報, 10 (2018): 1–86.

Schafer, Edward H. "The Jade Woman of Greatest Mystery." *History of Religions* 17.3/4 (1978): 387–98.

Schipper, Kristofer. "Taoist Ritual and Local Cults of the T'ang Dynasty." In Michel Strickmann, ed., *Tantric and Taoist Studies in Honour of R. A. Stein*, 3:812–34. Brussels: Institut Belge des Hautes Etudes Chinoises, 1985.

———, and Franciscus Verellen, eds. *The Taoist Canon: A Historical Companion to the Daozang* (*Daozang Tongkao* 道藏通考). 3 vols. Chicago: University of Chicago Press, 2004.

Schumann, Matthias. "'Protecting the Dao and Transmitting the Classics': The Confucian Dimension of Spirit-Writing in Republican China." In Valussi and Schumann, eds., *Spirit-Writing in Chinese History*, forthcoming.

Seaman, Gary. "The Divine Authorship of the *Pei-yu chi* [Journey to the North]." *Journal of Asian Studies* 45.3 (1986): 483–97.

———. *Journey to the North: An Ethnological Analysis and Annotated Translation of the Chinese Folk Novel Pei-yu chi.* Berkeley: University of California Press, 1987.

Seidel, Anna. *La divinisation de Lao tseu dans le taoïsme des Han.* Paris: EFEO, 1969.

———. "Imperial Treasures and Taoist Sacraments: Taoist Roots in the Apocrypha," in Michel Strckmann, ed., *Tantric and Taoist Studies in Honour of RA Stein*, II (*Mélanges Chinois et Bouddhiques*), 291–371. Bruxelles: Institut belge des hautes études chinoises, 1983.

———. "A Taoist Immortal of the Ming Dynasty: Chang San-feng." In Wm. Theodore de Bary and the Conference on Ming Thought, eds., *Self and Society in Ming Thought*, 483–531. New York: Columbia University Press, 1970.

Shao Jiade 邵佳德. "Pan Zengyi de xinyang yu shenghuo shijie—jianlun Qing zhongye Jiangnan de jushi fojiao 潘曾沂的信仰與生活世界—兼論清中葉江南的居士佛教." *Min-su chü-i* 民俗曲藝, 204 (2019): 99–145.

Shiga Ichiko 志賀市子. *Chūgoku no kokkurisan: furan shinkō to kajin shakai* 中国のこっくりさん：扶鸞信仰と華人社会. Tokyo: Taishūkan shoten, 2003.

———. "Difang daojiao zhi xingcheng: Guangdong diqu fuluan jieshe yundong zhi xingqi yu yanbian (1838–1953) 地方道教之形成：廣東地區扶鸞結社運動之興起與演變." *Daoism: Religion, History, and Society* 道教研究學報, 2 (2010): 231–67.

———. *Kindai Chūgoku no shāmanizumu to dōkyō: Honkon no dōtan to fūkei shinkō* 近代中国のシャーマニズムと道教: 香港の道壇と扶乩信仰. Tokyo: Bensei shuppan, 1999.

———. "Qingmo Minchu de jiujiejing suo fanying de weiji—shuyi, jindai Xiyang wenming ji gongchan geming 清末民初的救劫經所反映的危機一鼠疫、近代西洋文明及共產革命." Unpublished conference paper.

Shinohara Koichi. "The Story of the Buddha's Begging Bowl: Imagining a Biography and Sacred Places." In Phyllis Granoff and Shinohara Koichi, eds., *Pilgrims, Patrons, and Place: Localizing Sanctity in Asian Religions*, 68–107. Vancouver: UBC Press, 2003.

Skar, Lowell. "Golden Elixir Alchemy: The Formation of the Southern Lineage and the Transformation of Medieval China." Ph.D. diss., University of Pennsylvania, 2003.

Soymié, Michel. "Histoire et philologie de la Chine médiévale et moderne (résumé de conférence)." *École pratique des hautes études. 4e section, Sciences historiques et philologiques. Annuaire 1974–1975*, 1975, 961–65.

Steavu, Dominic. *The Writ of the Three Sovereigns: From Local Lore to Institutional Daoism.* Hong Kong: The Centre for Studies of Daoist Culture and The Chinese University of Hong Kong: The Chinese University Press; Honolulu: University of Hawai'i Press, 2019.

Strickmann, Michel. *Chinese Magical Medicine.* Edited by Bernard Faure. Stanford: Stanford University Press, 2002.

———. *Chinese Poetry and Prophecy: The Written Oracle in East Asia.* Edited by Bernard Faure. Stanford: Stanford University Press, 2005.

———. *Mantras et mandarins : Le bouddhisme tantrique en Chine.* Paris: Gallimard, 1996.

Takeuchi Fusaji 武内房司. "Shindai Seirenkyō kyūsai shisō—En Mugi no shosetsu o chūshin ni 清代青蓮教の救済思想 - 袁無欺の所説を中心に." *Chugoku, shakai to bunka* 中国,社会と文化, 7 (1992): 53–68.

———. "Shinmatsu Shisen no shūkyō undō 清末四川の宗教運動." *Gakushūin daigaku bungakubu kenkyū nenpō* 学習院大学文学部研究年報, 37 (1994): 59–93.

Tang Yun 汤芸. "Shenpan yu guansi: yige xinan cunzhuang jiangji yishi zhong de songzheng yu jiaoyu 神判与官司：一个西南村庄降乩仪式中的讼争与教谕." *Yunnan minzu daxue xuebao* 云南民族大学学报 29.4 (2012): 13–21.

Tao Jin 陶金. "The City God's New Clothes: A Study of the Articulated Living Image." Presentation at the AAR Conference, 24 Nov. 2019.

———. "Suzhou *Dadong wushang jiuji tianxian chuanjie keyi* chutan: Yi ge Qingdai Beijing yu Jiangnan wenren jitan jiaohu yingxiang de anli 蘇州『大洞無上九極天仙傳戒科儀』初探——一個清代北京與江南文人乩壇交互影響的案例." *Daoism: Religion, History and Society* 道教研究學報, 5 (2013): 111–41.

Ter Haar, Barend. "Book review of Brokaw, *Ledgers of Merit and Demerit*." *T'oung Pao*, 79 (1993): 160–67.

———. "China's Inner Demons: The Political Impact of the Demonological Paradigm." *China Information* 11.2–3 (1996): 54–88.

———. "Divine Violence to Uphold Moral Values: The Casebook of an Emperor Guan Temple in Hunan Province in 1851–1852." In Jeroen Duindam, Jill Harries, Caroline Humfress, and Nimrod Hurvitz, eds., *Law and Empire: Ideas, Practices, Actors*, 314–38. Leiden: Brill, 2013.

———. *Guan Yu: The Religious Afterlife of a Failed Hero*. Oxford: Oxford University Press, 2017.

———. *Practicing Scriptures: A Lay Buddhist Movement in Late Imperial China*. Honolulu: University of Hawai'i Press, 2014.

———. *Religious Culture and Violence in Traditional China*. Cambridge: Cambridge University Press, 2019.

———. *Ritual and Mythology of the Chinese Triads: Creating an Identity*. Leiden: Brill, 1998.

———. "Rumours and Prophecies: The Religious Background of the Late Yuan Rebellions," *Studies in Chinese Religions* 4.4 (2019): 382–418.

———. "Shamans, Mediums, and Chinese Buddhism: A Brief Reconnaissance." *Hualin International Journal of Buddhist Studies* 1.2 (2018): 202–30.

———. "The Sutra of the Five Lords: Manuscript and Oral Tradition." *Studies in Chinese Religions* 1.2 (2015): 172–97.

Valussi, Elena. "Female Alchemy: Transformation of a Gendered Body." In Jia Jinhua, Xiaofei Kang, and Ping Yao, eds., *Gendering Chinese Religion: Subject, Identity, and Body*, 201–24. Albany: SUNY Press, 2014.

———. "Printing and Religion in the Life of Fu Jinquan: Alchemical Writer, Religious Leader and Publisher in Sichuan." *Daoism: Religion, History and Society* 道教研究學報, 4 (2012): 1–52.

———, and Matthias Schumann, eds. *Spirit-Writing in Chinese History*. forthcoming.

Van der Loon, Piet. "Les origines rituelles du théâtre chinois." *Journal Asiatique* 265.1–2 (1977): 141–68.

Verellen, Franciscus. "Encounter as Revelation: a Taoist Hagiographic Theme in Medieval China." *Bulletin de l'École française d'Extrême-Orient*, 85 (1998): 363–84.

von Glahn, Richard. *The Sinister Way: The Divine and the Demonic in Chinese Religious Culture*. Berkeley: University of California Press, 2004.

Wagner, Rudolf G. *Reenacting the Heavenly Vision: The Role of Religion in the Taiping Rebellion*. Berkeley: Institute of East Asian Studies, University of California, 1982.

Waltner, Ann. "T'an-yang-tzu and Wang Shih-chen: Visionary and Bureaucrat in the Late Ming." *Late Imperial China* 8.1 (1987): 105–33.

Wang Chien-ch'uan 王見川. "Jindai fuji tuanti zhong de youming yu wangling duihua: yi Dian, Chuan, Tai wei kaocha zhongxin 近代扶乩團體中的遊冥與亡靈對話：以滇、川、臺為考察中心." In Fan Chun-wu, ed., *Fuluan wenhua yu minzhong zongjiao guoji xueshu yantaohui lunwenji*, 311–43.

———. "Jindai Zhongguo de fuji, cishan yu 'mixin'—Yi Yinguang wenchao wei kaocha xiansuo 近代中國的扶乩、慈善與「迷信」— 以印光文鈔為考查線索." In Paul R. Katz and Liu Shufen 劉淑分, eds., *Belief, Practice and Cultural Adaptation: Papers from the Religion Section of the Fourth International Conference on Sinology* 信仰、實踐與文化調適. 第四屆國際漢學會議論文集, 531–68. Taipei: Academia Sinica Press, 2013.

———. "Morality Book Publishing and Popular Religion in Modern China: A Discussion Centered on Morality Book Publishers in Shanghai." Translated by Gregory Adam Scott, in Clart and Scott, eds., *Religious Publishing and Print Culture in Modern China, 1800–2012*, 233–64.

———. "Popular Groups Promoting 'The Religion of Confucius' in the Chinese Southwest and Their Activities since the Nineteenth Century (1840–2013): An Observation Centered on Yunnan's Eryuan County and Environs." In Sébastien Billioud, ed., *The Varieties of Confucian Experience*, 90–121. Leiden: Brill, 2018.

———. "Qingdai de Lüzu xinyang yu fuji—yi Jiaqing huangdi cifeng wei kaocha zhongxin 清代的呂祖信仰與扶乩—以嘉慶皇帝賜封為考察中心." *Mazu yu minjian xinyang: yanjiu tongxun* 媽祖與民間信仰：研究通訊, 4 (2013): 28–39.

———. "Qingdai huangdi dui Wenchang dijun de fengci—jiantan *Yuding jinke jiyao* zhong de Li Hongzhang zouzhi 清代皇帝對文昌帝君的封賜—兼談玉定金科輯要中的李鴻章奏摺." In *Zhonghua Wenchang wenhua—dierjie haixia liang'an xueshu yanjiu lunwenji* 中華文昌文化 第二屆海峽兩岸學術研究論文集, 462–72. Chengdu: Chengdu shidai chubanshe, 2016.

———. "Qinglianjiao daomai yuanliu xinlun—jiantan Jiuzu Huang Dehui 青莲教道脉源流新论—兼谈九祖"黄德辉." *Qingshi yanjiu* 清史研究, 1 (2010): 20–26.

———. "Qingmo de guanshen yu fuji: Jiantan qishi liuxing de chenyan 清末的官紳與扶乩.兼談其時流行的讖言." *Mazu yu minjian xinyang: yanjiu tongxun* 媽祖與民間信仰：研究通訊, 2 (2012): 34–47.

———. "Qingmo Minchu Zhongguo de Jigong xinyang yu fuji tuanti: Jiantan Zhongguo Jishenghui de youlai 清末民初中國的濟公信仰與扶乩團體-兼談中國濟生會的由來." *Min-su ch'ü-i* 民俗曲藝, 162 (2008): 139–67.

———. "Song-Ming shiqi de fuji, fuluan yu qingxian; jiantan fuji, enzhu deng ci de qiyuan 宋-明時期的扶箕、扶鸞與請仙:兼談扶乩、恩主等詞的起源." In Fan Chun-wu, ed., *Fuluan wenhua yu minzhong zongjiao guoji xueshu yantaohui lunwenji*, 53–88.

———. "Spirit Writing Groups in Modern China (1840–1937): Textual Production, Public Teachings, and Charity." Translated by Vincent Goossaert, in Vincent Goossaert, Jan Kiely, and John Lagerwey, eds., *Modern Chinese Religion: 1850 to the Present*, 651–84. Leiden: Brill, 2016.

———. "Taiwan 'Guandi dang Yuhuang' chuanshuo de youlai 台灣「關帝當玉皇」傳說的由來." In *Hanren zongjiao, minjian xinyang yu yuyanshu de tansuo: Wang*

Jianchuan zixuanji 漢人宗教、民間信仰與預言書的探索：王見川自選集, 412–30. Taipei: Boyang, 2008.

———. "Zhenwu xinyang zai jinshi Zhongguo de chuanbo 真武信仰在近世中國的傳播." *Minsu yanjiu* 民俗研究, 3 (2010): 90–117.

———, and Pi Qingsheng 皮庆生. *Zhongguo jinshi minjian xinyang: Song Yuan Ming Qing* 中国近世民间信仰:宋元明清. Shanghai: Shanghai renmin chubanshe, 2010.

Wang Gang 王崗. "Mingdai Jingmingdao yu Jiangxi difang shehui 明代淨明道與江西地方社會." *Huaren zongjiao yanjiu* 華人宗教研究, 10 (2017): 59–168.

Wang Ya 王亞. "Nansong Jingmingdao de fa, zhi, lu yu Dongshenbu lujie de chedi fuhaohua 南宋淨明道的法、職、籙與洞神部籙階的徹底符號化." *Hongdao* 弘道, 2 (2016): 96–104.

Wei Bing 韦兵. "'Zhang Shouzhen shenjiang' kaoyi: shushi yu Song Taizu, Taizong huangquan gengti "张守真神降"考疑：术士与宋太祖太宗皇权更替." *Huadong shifan daxue xuebao* 华东师范大学学报（哲学社会科学版), 3 (2017): 161–71.

Wei Dingming 危丁明. *Shumin de yongheng* 庶民的永恆. Taipei: Boyang, 2015.

Wong Shiu Hon 黄兆漢. "Cong daoshu de xingcheng kan Qingdai wenren de zongjiao shenghuo 從道書的形成看清代文人的宗教生活." In *Daojiao yanjiu lunwenji* 道教研究論文集, 93–120. Hong Kong: Chinese University Press, 1988.

———. *Mingdai daoshi Zhang Sanfeng kao* 明代道士張三丰考. Taipei: Taiwan xuesheng shuju, 1988.

Wu Shengqing. "In Search of Soul. Psychical Studies and Spirit Photography." In *Photo Poetics: Chinese Lyricism and Modern Media Culture*, 183–212. New York: Columbia University Press, 2020.

Xu Dishan 許地山. *Fuji mixin de yanjiu* 扶箕迷信的研究. Changsha: Shangwu yinshuguan, 1941.

Xu Wei 許蔚. *Duanlie yu jiangou: Jingmingdao de lishi yu wenxian* 断裂与建构：净明道的历史与文献. Shanghai: Shanghai shudian chubanshe, 2014.

———. "Wenben liuchuan yu keyi pinjie—*Taishang Lingbao Jingming daoyuan zhengyinjing* de zai faxian 文本流傳與科儀拼接—《太上靈寶淨明道元正印經》的再發現." *Quanzhendao yanjiu* 全真道研究, 8 (2019): 151–79.

———. "Xin tianjun fa yu Hunyuan daofa de gouzao 辛天君法與混元道法的構造." *Daoism: Religion, History and Society* 道教研究學報, 9 (2017): 141–59.

Yamada Masaru 山田賢. "Sekai no hametsu to sono kyūsai: Shinmatsu no kyūgō no zensho ni tsuite 世界の破滅とその救済: 清末の救劫の善書について." *Shihō* 史朋, 30 (1998): 32–41.

Yau Chi-on 游子安. "Boji xianfang. Qingmo yilai Lingnan diqu xianfang, shanshu yu Lüzu xinyang 博济仙方—清末以来岭南地区仙方、善书与吕祖信仰." *Zhongguo kejishi zazhi* 中国科技史杂志, 32 (2011): 47–63.

———. "Fuhua yunei: Qingdai yilai Guandi shanshu jiqi xinyang de chuanbo 敷化宇內-清代以來關帝善書及其信仰的傳播." *Journal of Chinese Studies* 中國文化研究所學報, 50 (2010): 219–53.

———. *Shan yu ren tong: Ming Qing yilai de cishan yu jiaohua* 善與人同: 明清以來的慈善與教化. Beijing: Zhonghua shuju, 2005.

Yin Zhihua 尹志华. "*Lidai shenxian tongji* chutan《历代神仙通纪》初探." *Shijie zongjiao yanjiu* 世界宗教研究, 2 (2016): 83–92.

———. "*Lüzu quanshu* de bianzuan he zengji《吕祖全书》的编纂和增辑." *Zongjiaoxue yanjiu* 宗教学研究, 1 (2012): 16–21.

———. "Qingchao Jiaqing nianjian chifeng Lüzu jiqi yingxiang 清朝嘉庆年间敕封吕祖及其影响." *Zhongguo daojiao* 中国道教, 141 (2014): 53–57.

Yü Chün-fang. *Kuan-yin: The Chinese Transformation of Avalokiteśvara*. New York: Columbia University Press, 2001.

Zeitlin, Judith. "Spirit Writing and Performance in the Work of You Tong 尤侗 (1618–1704)." *T'oung Pao*, 84 (1998): 102–35.

Zhang Wanrong 張琬容. "Qingdai jieyinshu bianzhuan kaolüe 清代戒淫書編撰考略." *Shanshu, jingjuan yu wenxian* 善書、經卷與文獻, 3 (2020): 109–33.

Zhu Mingchuan 朱明川. "Gengzi Chuandong shenjiao chu: Jindai Zhongguo qishi jingdian shengchan moshi de xingcheng「庚子川東神教出」: 近代中國啟示經典生產模式的形成." *Shanshu, jingjuan yu wenxian* 善書、經卷與文獻, 3 (2020): 53–74.

———. "Qingmo yilai de Guandi shengge yundong—jiantan daojiao Jingmingpai zai jindai de fazhan 清末以來的關帝升格運動—兼談道教淨明派在近代的發展." In Wang Chien-ch'uan 王見川, ed., *Lishi, yishu yu Taiwan renwen luncong* 歷史、藝術與台灣人文論叢, 14:209–27. Taipei: Boyang, 2016.

———. "Rutan jingdian ji qi yingyong: Yi Sichuan jiangyou diqu de 'Zixia tan' wei li 儒壇經典及其應用:以四川江油地區的'紫霞壇'為例." *Shanshu, jingjuan yu wenxian* 善書、經卷與文獻, 1 (2019): 135–61.

Zürcher, Erik. "Prince Moonlight: Messianism and Eschatology in Early Medieval Chinese Buddhism." *T'oung Pao*, 68 (1982): 1–75.

Index

Harvard-Yenching Institute Monograph Series

(most recent titles now in print)

33. *Escape from the Wasteland: Romanticism and Realism in the Fiction of Mishima Yukio and Oe Kenzaburo*, by Susan Jolliffe Napier
34. *Inside a Service Trade: Studies in Contemporary Chinese Prose*, by Rudolf G. Wagner
35. *The Willow in Autumn: Ryutei Tanehiko, 1783–1842*, by Andrew Lawrence Markus
36. *The Confucian Transformation of Korea: A Study of Society and Ideology*, by Martina Deuchler
37. *The Korean Singer of Tales*, by Marshall R. Pihl
38. *Praying for Power: Buddhism and the Formation of Gentry Society in Late-Ming China*, by Timothy Brook
39. *Word, Image, and Deed in the Life of Su Shi*, by Ronald C. Egan
41. *Studies in the Comic Spirit in Modern Japanese Fiction*, by Joel R. Cohn
42. *Wind Against the Mountain: The Crisis of Politics and Culture in Thirteenth-Century China*, by Richard L. Davis
43. *Powerful Relations: Kinship, Status, and the State in Sung China (960–1279)*, by Beverly Bossler
44. *Limited Views: Essays on Ideas and Letters*, by Qian Zhongshu; selected and translated by Ronald Egan
45. *Sugar and Society in China: Peasants, Technology, and the World Market*, by Sucheta Mazumdar
49. *Precious Volumes: An Introduction to Chinese Sectarian Scriptures from the Sixteenth and Seventeenth Centuries*, by Daniel L. Overmyer
50. *Poetry and Painting in Song China: The Subtle Art of Dissent*, by Alfreda Murck
51. *Evil and/or/as the Good: Omnicentrism, Intersubjectivity, and Value Paradox in Tiantai Buddhist Thought*, by Brook Ziporyn
53. *Articulated Ladies: Gender and the Male Community in Early Chinese Texts*, by Paul Rouzer
55. *Allegories of Desire: Esoteric Literary Commentaries of Medieval Japan*, by Susan Blakeley Klein
56. *Printing for Profit: The Commercial Publishers of Jianyang, Fujian (11th–17th Centuries)*, by Lucille Chia

57. *To Become a God: Cosmology, Sacrifice, and Self-Divinization in Early China*, by Michael J. Puett
58. *Writing and Materiality in China: Essays in Honor of Patrick Hanan*, edited by Judith T. Zeitlin and Lydia H. Liu
59. Rulin waishi *and Cultural Transformation in Late Imperial China*, by Shang Wei
60. *Words Well Put: Visions of Poetic Competence in the Chinese Tradition*, by Graham Sanders
61. *Householders: The Reizei Family in Japanese History*, by Steven D. Carter
62. *The Divine Nature of Power: Chinese Ritual Architecture at the Sacred Site of Jinci*, by Tracy Miller
63. *Beacon Fire and Shooting Star: The Literary Culture of the Liang (502–557)*, by Xiaofei Tian
64. *Lost Soul: "Confucianism" in Contemporary Chinese Academic Discourse*, by John Makeham
65. *The Sage Learning of Liu Zhi: Islamic Thought in Confucian Terms*, by Sachiko Murata, William C. Chittick, and Tu Weiming
66. *Through a Forest of Chancellors: Fugitive Histories in Liu Yuan's* Lingyan ge, *an Illustrated Book from Seventeenth-Century Suzhou*, by Anne Burkus-Chasson
67. *Empire of Texts in Motion: Chinese, Korean, and Taiwanese Transculturations of Japanese Literature*, by Karen Laura Thornber
68. *Empire's Twilight: Northeast Asia Under the Mongols*, by David M. Robinson
69. *Ancestors, Virgins, and Friars: Christianity as a Local Religion in Late Imperial China*, by Eugenio Menegon
70. *Manifest in Words, Written on Paper: Producing and Circulating Poetry in Tang Dynasty China*, by Christopher M. B. Nugent
71. *The Poetics of Sovereignty: On Emperor Taizong of the Tang Dynasty*, by Jack W. Chen
72. *Ancestral Memory in Early China*, by K. E. Brashier
73. *'Dividing the Realm in Order to Govern': The Spatial Organization of the Song State*, by Ruth Mostern
74. *The Dynamics of Masters Literature: Early Chinese Thought from Confucius to Han Feizi*, by Wiebke Denecke
75. *Songs of Contentment and Transgression: Discharged Officials and Literati Communities in Sixteenth-Century North China*, by Tian Yuan Tan
76. *Ten Thousand Scrolls: Reading and Writing in the Poetics of Huang Tingjian and the Late Northern Song*, by Yugen Wang
77. *A Northern Alternative: Xue Xuan (1389–1464) and the Hedong School*, by Khee Heong Koh
78. *Visionary Journeys: Travel Writings from Early Medieval and Nineteenth-Century China*, by Xiaofei Tian
79. *Making Personas: Transnational Film Stardom in Modern Japan*, by Hideaki Fujiki
80. *Strange Eventful Histories: Identity, Performance, and Xu Wei's* Four Cries of a Gibbon, by Shiamin Kwa

81. *Critics and Commentators: The* Book of Poems *as Classic and Literature*, by Bruce Rusk
82. *Home and the World: Editing the Glorious Ming in Woodblock-Printed Books of the Sixteenth and Seventeenth Centuries*, by Yuming He
83. *Courtesans, Concubines, and the Cult of Female Fidelity*, by Beverly Bossler
84. *Chinese History: A New Manual, Third Edition*, by Endymion Wilkinson
85. *A Comprehensive Manchu-English Dictionary*, by Jerry Norman
86. *Drifting among Rivers and Lakes: Southern Song Dynasty Poetry and the Problem of Literary History*, by Michael Fuller
87. *Martial Spectacles of the Ming Court*, by David M. Robinson
88. *Modern Archaics: Continuity and Innovation in the Chinese Lyric Tradition, 1900–1937*, by Shengqing Wu
89. *Cherishing Antiquity: The Cultural Construction of an Ancient Chinese Kingdom*, by Olivia Milburn
90. *The Burden of Female Talent: The Poet Li Qingzhao and Her History in China*, by Ronald Egan
91. *Public Memory in Early China*, by K. E. Brashier
92. *Women and National Trauma in Late Imperial Chinese Literature*, by Wai-yee Li
93. *The Destruction of the Medieval Chinese Aristocracy*, by Nicolas Tackett
94. *Savage Exchange: Han Imperialism, Chinese Literary Style, and the Economic Imagination*, by Tamara T. Chin
95. *Shifting Stories: History, Gossip, and Lore in Narratives from Tang Dynasty China*, by Sarah M. Allen
96. *One Who Knows Me: Friendship and Literary Culture in Mid-Tang China*, by Anna Shields
97. *Materializing Magic Power: Chinese Popular Religion in Villages and Cities*, by Wei-Ping Lin
98. *Traces of Grand Peace: Classics and State Activism in Imperial China*, by Jaeyoon Song
99. *Fiction's Family: Zhan Xi, Zhan Kai, and the Business of Women in Late-Qing China*, by Ellen Widmer
100. *Chinese History: A New Manual, Fourth Edition*, by Endymion Wilkinson
101. *After the Prosperous Age: State and Elites in Early Nineteenth-Century Suzhou*, by Seunghyun Han
102. *Celestial Masters: History and Ritual in Early Daoist Communities*, by Terry F. Kleeman
103. *Transgressive Typologies: Constructions of Gender and Power in Early Tang China*, by Rebecca Doran
104. *Li Mengyang, the North-South Divide, and Literati Learning in Ming China*, by Chang Woei Ong
105. *Bannermen Tales (Zidishu): Manchu Storytelling and Cultural Hybridity in the Qing Dynasty*, by Elena Suet-Ying Chiu

106. *Upriver Journeys: Diaspora and Empire in Southern China, 1570–1850*, by Steven B. Miles
107. *Ancestors, Kings, and the Dao*, by Constance A. Cook
108. *The Halberd at Red Cliff: Jian'an and the Three Kingdoms*, by Xiaofei Tian
109. *Speaking of Profit: Bao Shichen and Reform in Nineteenth-Century China*, by William T. Rowe
110. *Building for Oil: Daqing and the Formation of the Chinese Socialist State*, by Hou Li
111. *Reading Philosophy, Writing Poetry: Intertextual Modes of Making Meaning in Early Medieval China*, by Wendy Swartz
112. *Writing for Print: Publishing and the Making of Textual Authority in Late Imperial China*, by Suyoung Son
113. *Shen Gua's Empiricism*, by Ya Zuo
114. *Just a Song: Chinese Lyrics from the Eleventh and Early Twelfth Centuries*, by Stephen Owen
115. *Shrines to Living Men in the Ming Political Cosmos*, by Sarah Schneewind
116. *In the Wake of the Mongols: The Making of a New Social Order in North China, 1200–1600*, by Jinping Wang
117. *Opera, Society, and Politics in Modern China*, by Hsiao-t'i Li
118. *Imperiled Destinies: The Daoist Quest for Deliverance in Medieval China*, by Franciscus Verellen
119. *Ethnic Chrysalis: China's Orochen People and the Legacy of Qing Borderland Administration*, by Loretta Kim
120. *The Paradox of Being: Truth, Identity, and Images in Daoism*, by Poul Andersen
121. *Feeling the Past in Seventeenth-Century China*, by Xiaoqiao Ling
122. *The Chinese Dreamscape, 300 BCE–800 CE*, by Robert *Ford* Campany
123. *Structures of the Earth: Metageographies of Early Medieval China*, by D. Jonathan Felt
124. *Anecdote, Network, Gossip, Performance: Essays on the* Shishuo xinyu, by Jack W. Chen
125. *Testing the Literary: Prose and the Aesthetic in Early Modern China*, by Alexander Des Forges
126. *Du Fu Transforms: Tradition and Ethics amid Societal Collapse*, by Lucas Rambo Bender
127. *Chinese History: A New Manual* (*Enlarged Sixth Edition*), Vol. 1, by Endymion Wilkinson
128. *Chinese History: A New Manual* (*Enlarged Sixth Edition*), Vol. 2, by Endymion Wilkinson
129. *Wang Anshi and Song Poetic Culture*, by Xiaoshan Yang
130. *Localizing Learning: The Literati Enterprise in Wuzhou, 1100–1600*, by Peter K. Bol
131. *Making the Gods Speak: The Ritual Production of Revelation in Chinese Religious History*, by Vincent Goossaert